Impacts of Entrepreneurial Innovation in Economic, Social, and Environmental Sustainability

Reshmy Krishnan
Muscat College, Oman

Araby Madbouly Ahmed Hussain
Muscat College, Oman

Buthaina Yahya Al Kharousi
Muscat College, Oman

Nitha Mary
Muscat College, Oman

IGI Global
Scientific Publishing
Publishing Tomorrow's Research Today

Published in the United States of America by
IGI Global Scientific Publishing
701 East Chocolate Avenue
Hershey, PA, 17033, USA
Tel: 717-533-8845 | Fax: 717-533-7115
Website: https://www.igi-global.com E-mail: cust@igi-global.com

Library of Congress Cataloging-in-Publication Data

Names: Krishnan, Reshmy, 1971- editor
Title: Impacts of entrepreneurial innovation in economic, social, and environmental sustainability / [edited by] Reshmy Krishnan, Araby Madbouly Ahmed Hussain, Buthaina Yahya Al Kharousi, Nitha Mary.
Description: Hershey, PA : IGI Global Scientific Publishing, [2027] | Includes bibliographical references and index. | Summary: "This book explores how entrepreneurship and innovation can drive sustainable and inclusive development amid global challenges. Through multidisciplinary perspectives and practical case studies, it highlights strategies and models that foster resilient economies, equitable growth, and long-term societal impact for a more sustainable future"-- Provided by publisher.
Identifiers: LCCN 2025054425 (print) | LCCN 2025054426 (ebook) | ISBN 9798337373911 hardcover | ISBN 9798337373928 paperback | ISBN 9798337373935 ebook
Subjects: LCSH: Sustainable development--Technological innovations | Technological innovations--Economic aspects | Entrepreneurship
Classification: LCC HC79.E5 I49985 2026 (print) | LCC HC79.E5 (ebook) | DDC 338.9/27--dc23/eng/20260312
LC record available at https://lccn.loc.gov/2025054425
LC ebook record available at https://lccn.loc.gov/2025054426

British Cataloguing in Publication Data
A Cataloguing in Publication record for this book is available from the British Library.

Table of Contents

Detailed Table of Contents

The combination of blockchain, big data, artificial intelligence, and the Internet of Things is experiencing a revolutionary phase of the so-called Fourth Industrial Revolution. In contrast to previous revolutions where the pivotal aspects were mechanization or even mere digitization of processes, 4IR reconstructs whole chains of values by combining digital, physical, or even biological systems. IoT links billions of gadgets that produce actual-time information which is transformed into action intelligence by big data analytics. Machine learning and artificial intelligence are one of the cognitive engines because they recognize patterns, anticipate, and automate decisions, which can result in novel uses of AI, like precision medicine, predictive maintenance and smart manufacturing. This ecosystem is reinforced by blockchain to facilitate transparency, security and trust by means of decentralized, immutable records and smart contracts.

The 21st centurys economic social and environmental problems can be solved through the revolutionary approach of sustainable entrepreneurship. In the Indian context promoting sustainable development requires entrepreneurial innovation that strikes a balance between social justice environmental responsibility and profitability. This chapter looks at how Indian business owners use green and social enterprises—

backed by programs like Startup India and Atmanirbhar Bharat—to incorporate sustainability into their business plans. It also looks at enabling and limiting factors such as social awareness technological advancement financial accessibility and regulatory frameworks. The results highlight innovation as a major force behind resource efficiency responsible production and equitable growth. They also provide theoretical understanding and useful policy suggestions to support Indias path toward sustainable development.

This chapter examines the role of green entrepreneurship in driving sustainable development by integrating environmental, social, and economic objectives. It explores the conceptual foundations, motivations, and strategies underpinning green ventures, highlighting how entrepreneurs innovate through circular economy models, eco-design, sustainable supply chains, and digital technologies. Drawing on case studies such as Tesla, Patagonia, and Grameen Shakti, the chapter illustrates both the opportunities and challenges inherent in pursuing sustainability-oriented business models. It further emphasizes the importance of policy support, institutional frameworks, and systematic impact measurement through ESG and life-cycle assessment. Concluding with emerging trends and future directions, the chapter underscores that green entrepreneurs are pivotal agents of change, shaping resilient, inclusive, and environmentally responsible economic systems.

There is a growing acceptance of green entrepreneurship as a key component of development, although its application in enhancing the realization of the Sustainable Development Goals has not yet been explained systematically. This research paper in this direction establishes and tests the green entrepreneurship approach for Sustainable Development Goal achievement. Maximum effect visualization is brought in through the green entrepreneurship- SDG catalyst model to show how

This chapter investigates the dynamics of green and social entrepreneurship in Tunisia through a multiple case study of four circular initiatives operating in textile recycling, plastic valorization, regenerative agriculture, and organic waste treatment. Using an interpretive qualitative approach supported by methodological triangulation, the analysis identifies shared mechanisms such as frugal innovation, resource circularity, organizational hybridization, and territorial embeddedness. The findings show substantial contributions to SDGs 8, 12, 13, and 15, while highlighting the role of these ventures in compensating for institutional voids in an emerging context. Overall, the chapter demonstrates how small circular enterprises can generate systemic sustainability impacts under conditions of structural constraint

This chapter explores the transformative role of Entrepreneurial Accounting for Sustainable Development (EASD) in aligning financial systems with sustainability transitions through the integration of green innovation, ESG reporting, and SDG impact measurement. Entrepreneurial accounting reconceptualizes conventional financial practices by embedding multi-capital value creation, environmental management accounting (EMA), and impact-weighted approaches into decision-making frameworks. Empirical evidence from Southeast Asia highlights how adaptive governance, green budgeting, and digital trust technologies—including AI and blockchain—enhance transparency, accountability, and scalability in sustainability performance. The study presents a unified framework connecting non-financial

Preface

INTRODUCTION

Entrepreneurial innovation has become one of the defining forces driving sustainable development in an era characterized by rapid technological advancement, environmental uncertainty, and evolving societal expectations. Entrepreneurs today are expected not only to generate economic value but also to address pressing global challenges such as climate change, resource scarcity, social inequality, and responsible governance. Emerging technologies—including artificial intelligence, big data analytics, blockchain, the Internet of Things, and digital platforms—are transforming entrepreneurial ecosystems by enabling innovative business models that integrate economic performance with environmental stewardship and social responsibility. As governments, industries, and communities seek sustainable pathways for growth, entrepreneurial innovation occupies an increasingly central role in shaping resilient economies and inclusive societies.

As editors, we believe that sustainability and entrepreneurship are no longer separate domains but mutually reinforcing dimensions of contemporary development. Modern entrepreneurial ventures are increasingly evaluated not only by financial success but also by their contributions to environmental protection, social inclusion, ethical governance, and long-term societal well-being. Green entrepreneurship, circular economy practices, impact investing, ESG reporting, and sustainable innovation have expanded the traditional understanding of entrepreneurial success, demonstrating that profitability and responsible development can coexist. At the same time, achieving meaningful sustainability requires supportive institutional frameworks, collaborative ecosystems, technological innovation, and policies that encourage responsible entrepreneurship across diverse economic contexts.

This volume brings together an international collection of scholars whose contributions examine entrepreneurial innovation from multidisciplinary perspectives encompassing business management, sustainability, technology, environmental science, accounting, public policy, and economic development. Through conceptual analyses, empirical investigations, comparative case studies, and policy-oriented discussions, the chapters collectively demonstrate how entrepreneurial innovation contributes to achieving sustainable development while responding to contemporary global challenges. Together, they offer valuable insights for researchers, policymakers, educators, entrepreneurs, and industry leaders seeking to build more resilient, inclusive, and environmentally responsible economies.

CHAPTER OVERVIEW

Chapter 1 establishes the technological foundation for the volume by examining how artificial intelligence, big data, blockchain, the Internet of Things, and other emerging technologies are transforming entrepreneurial ecosystems and industrial value chains. The chapter illustrates how Fourth Industrial Revolution technologies enable innovation, operational efficiency, transparency, and sustainable business transformation across multiple sectors.

Chapter 2 explores sustainable entrepreneurship within the Indian context by examining how entrepreneurial innovation simultaneously advances economic prosperity, environmental responsibility, and social equity. Through discussion of national initiatives and institutional frameworks, the chapter highlights the role of entrepreneurship in supporting balanced and inclusive sustainable development.

Chapter 3 investigates the growing influence of green entrepreneurs in addressing environmental challenges through innovative business models. Using international case studies, the chapter demonstrates how eco-design, circular economy principles, sustainable supply chains, and digital technologies contribute to resilient and environmentally responsible enterprises.

Chapter 4 examines green entrepreneurship as a strategic catalyst for achieving the United Nations Sustainable Development Goals. Combining quantitative and qualitative analyses, the chapter develops a conceptual framework illustrating how entrepreneurial ecosystems accelerate sustainability-oriented innovation and contribute to long-term developmental outcomes.

Chapter 5 extends the discussion by exploring conceptual relationships between green entrepreneurship and the Sustainable Development Goals within emerging economies. The authors emphasize the importance of renewable energy, circular production systems, institutional support, sustainability education, and green finance in fostering inclusive economic development.

Chapter 6 focuses on India's evolving landscape of green entrepreneurship and sustainable innovation. Drawing upon policy analysis and sectoral case studies, the chapter examines inclusive business models, institutional support mechanisms, and entrepreneurial ecosystems that promote environmentally sustainable economic growth.

Chapter 7 presents a qualitative investigation of green and social entrepreneurship in Tunisia through the lens of circular economy initiatives. The chapter demonstrates how resource circularity, organizational innovation, and territorial collaboration enable entrepreneurs to generate meaningful environmental, economic, and social impacts despite structural constraints.

Chapter 8 introduces Entrepreneurial Accounting for Sustainable Development as a governance framework integrating financial reporting, environmental management accounting, ESG disclosure, and SDG impact measurement. The chapter illustrates how digital technologies enhance accountability, transparency, and evidence-based sustainability decision-making.

Chapter 9 explores entrepreneurship opportunities in agricultural waste valorization and demonstrates how innovative business ventures convert agricultural residues into valuable products while advancing circular economy principles, environmental protection, rural development, and employment generation.

Chapter 10 examines the contribution of electric vehicles to India's transition toward a circular economy. The chapter discusses policy initiatives, battery recycling, infrastructure development, and sustainability challenges while highlighting the role of entrepreneurial innovation in advancing cleaner transportation systems.

Chapter 11 concludes the volume by presenting a comparative study of jute bags as sustainable alternatives to conventional plastic products. The chapter analyzes environmental, economic, and social benefits while emphasizing how innovation in natural fiber production can support circular economy objectives, rural livelihoods, and environmentally responsible consumer practices.

CONCLUSION

The chapters presented in this volume collectively demonstrate that entrepreneurial innovation has evolved into a fundamental driver of sustainable economic, social, and environmental development. Across diverse industries, geographical contexts, and institutional environments, the contributors illustrate how innovative entrepreneurs are developing solutions that simultaneously generate economic value, protect natural resources, strengthen communities, and contribute to the achievement of global sustainability objectives. The collection reinforces the understanding that entrepreneurship is no longer measured solely by commercial success but increasingly by its capacity to create lasting societal and environmental impact.

A recurring theme throughout the volume is the importance of integrating technological innovation with responsible governance and sustainability-oriented business practices. Emerging technologies such as artificial intelligence, blockchain, big data analytics, and the Internet of Things provide powerful tools for accelerating sustainable transformation, yet their effectiveness depends upon supportive policy environments, collaborative ecosystems, ethical leadership, and robust institutional frameworks. Similarly, green entrepreneurship, circular economy models, ESG reporting, and sustainable accounting demonstrate that innovation flourishes when economic performance is aligned with environmental stewardship and social responsibility.

As editors, we hope that Impacts of Entrepreneurial Innovation in Economic, Social, and Environmental Sustainability serves as a valuable resource for researchers, entrepreneurs, educators, policymakers, and practitioners committed to advancing sustainable development through innovation. We further hope that the interdisciplinary perspectives presented throughout this volume stimulate new research, encourage cross-sector collaboration, and inspire entrepreneurial initiatives that contribute to more resilient economies, healthier societies, and a more sustainable future. Ultimately, the collective insights offered in this book reaffirm that entrepreneurial innovation, when guided by sustainability principles, possesses extraordinary potential to shape a more inclusive, prosperous, and environmentally responsible world.

Reshmy Krishnan
Muscat College, Oman

Araby Madbouly
Muscat College, Oman

Buthaina Al Kharusi
Muscat College, Oman

Nitha Mary Siju
Muscat College, Oman

Acknowledgment

The editors of *Impacts of Entrepreneurial Innovation in Economic, Social, and Environmental Sustainability* would like to acknowledge the support and contributions of everyone involved in this project, and in particular, the authors and reviewers who participated in the review process. Without their dedication and commitment, this volume would not have been possible.

First, the editors express their sincere appreciation to each of the authors for their valuable contributions. We extend our heartfelt gratitude to the chapter authors who generously devoted their time, expertise, and scholarly efforts to enrich this book.

Second, the editors wish to recognize the significant contributions of the reviewers in enhancing the quality, coherence, and overall presentation of the chapters. Many of the authors also served as reviewers, and we deeply appreciate their willingness to undertake this dual responsibility with professionalism and diligence.

The editors would like to express their sincere appreciation to Dr. Krishnan Soundararajan and Dr. Salim Salim Bakhit Al Daraai for their valuable guidance and unwavering support throughout this project. Finally, this book is dedicated to Muscat College, whose wholehearted support and encouragement made this endeavor a reality.

Chapter 1
Impacts of Entrepreneurial Innovation in Economic, Social, and Environmental Sustainability:
How AI, Big Data, IoT, Blockchain, and Other Emerging Technologies Are Transforming Industries

Santhiya Ramu
http://orcid.org/0009-0006-8958-6678
Saveetha School of Management, Saveetha Institute of Medical and Technical Sciences, India

Benita S. Monica
http://orcid.org/0000-0002-0018-7536
Saveetha Institute of Medical and Technical Sciences, India

ABSTRACT

The combination of blockchain, big data, artificial intelligence, and the Internet of Things is experiencing a revolutionary phase of the so-called Fourth Industrial Revolution. In contrast to previous revolutions where the pivotal aspects were mechanization or even mere digitization of processes, 4IR reconstructs whole chains of values by combining digital, physical, or even biological systems. IoT links billions of gadgets that produce actual-time information which is transformed into action

DOI: 10.4018/979-8-3373-7391-1.ch001

intelligence by big data analytics. Machine learning and artificial intelligence are one of the cognitive engines because they recognize patterns, anticipate, and automate decisions, which can result in novel uses of AI, like precision medicine, predictive maintenance and smart manufacturing. This ecosystem is reinforced by blockchain to facilitate transparency, security and trust by means of decentralized, immutable records and smart contracts.

INTRODUCTION

Era of Technological Integration is an era of time where technology is developing at a fast rate and industries are converging. Technological convergence is considered as most significant dimensions of this transformation; it represents the integration and intersection of diverse technologies and business domains. The current study is trying to addressing the question whether convergence is actually taking place or not. The study examines time-series datasets from the 1960s for the United States, Japan, and South Korea to accomplish the stated objective. The study although with minor variations in real-time of data collection resulting from changes in data-gathering methods across the three nations, still provide important insights into long-term industrial trends. However, despite these limitations, the conclusions drawn from the results enable understanding of industrial act in the convergence of technologies and sectors.

As economies have become more complex, technology has grown not only in traditional areas but also in fields that appear unrelated. This greater link can be encapsulated through the term "technology convergence". In the opening address, Convergence split into dual. The first category is technological convergence, which involves the incorporation of fundamental and practical technologies or the combination of numerous applied technologies. The second category is convergence across industries, where adjacent or unrelated industries begin to connect and collaborate more closely.

The automobile industry is one example of technological convergence that can be observed in practice. Electronics has become an essential element of vehicle design with bigger use of microprocessors becoming standard components in modern vehicles. Additional, technological trend which contributes in improving the integration of mechanical and electronic technologies is the advancement of telematics systems, which are used in cars in the integration of telecommunications and information technologies. This is an example of the convergence of technology taking various routes as sectors and technologies become intertwined in the course of time. (Kim & Song, 2024). New technologies such as AI, IoT, blockchain, and big data are converging to reshape industries in the digital era, as shown in Figure 1.

Figure 1. Powered by emerging technologies, digital transformation is underway. Digital transformation is happening with the power of emerging technologies

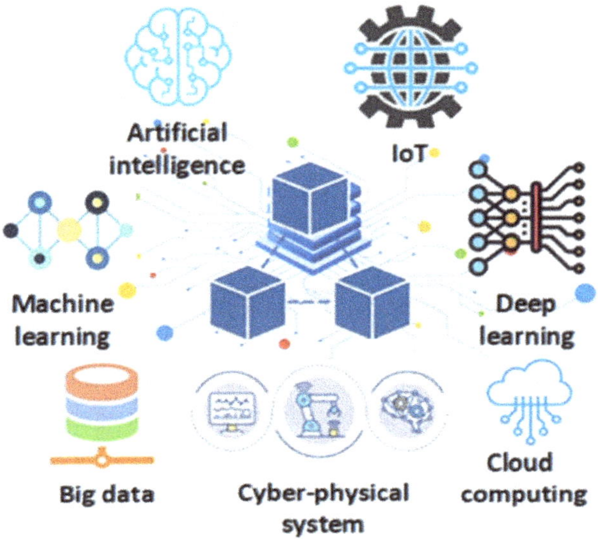

Source: (Ahmed et al., 2022).

BACKGROUND

Throughout the eras, technology has transformed the world of commerce or trade and now, digital transformation is hot. Digital transformation has evolved alongside business development over the years and has now become a central focus. Organisations first started using digital tools in the 60's and 70's, and began to be more widely used in the 90's when the internet became widely available. In 2011, the German government coined the term Industry 4.0, referring to a fourth industrial revolution in which the Internet of Things (IoT), cloud computing and data analytics (DA) are all coming together (Zhong et al., 2017). For long time the scholars had been worried about the impact and change of the existing industries due to technology. So, technological change is not only incremental change, but it is a change of whole economic structures, as (Schumpeter, 1942) observed. This transformation varies considerably across nations, influenced because of distinct regulations, institutional frameworks, and because of distinct regulations of individual countries.

A lot of progress was achieved in every field in the 2010s. The rise of big data, artificial intelligence, and machine learning has facilitated advanced pattern recognition and predictive capabilities. The falling cost of sensors and introduction of the 5G network helped in the adoption of IoT. Though the blockchain started with Bitcoin, it has now grown into a method for a secure and transparent data-recording framework. These introduced a new model of intelligent and data-oriented industry. Today, digital transformation is recognized as a human, strategic, ethical, and organizational culture challenge as well as a technological difficulty. The chapter intersects these technologies and explores what they entail with respect to workforce dynamics, ethics, and regulation.

Artificial Intelligence and Industrial Intelligence

Today, the world is undergoing an era of technological convergence and new technologies are emerging and growing rapidly, such as the Cloud, the Internet (mobile), Artificial Intelligence and the Industrial Internet technologies. Many advanced economies have adopted reindustrialization strategies to promote innovation in manufacturing and create stronger competitive advantages in a rapidly changing environment. For now, several developing nations are working on their own plans to enable them to participate in the emerging global industrial division of labour and to assume a strategic role in the evolving industrial competition. As the industrialization of the world becomes faster, the industrialized countries have urgently begun to develop intelligent manufacturing systems by utilizing their information technology (IT) capabilities. The U.S. National AI Research and Development Strategic Framework (October 2016) for example, highlights how AI can be applied in manufacturing to enhance manufacturing operations, flexibility, product quality, and cost efficiency.

The Artificial Intelligence in American Industry Summit was held at the White House in May 2018. Leaders from the business shared insights on the newest use cases of AI technologies, to drive worker empowerment, company growth and enhance customer engagement. The U.S. National Science Foundation emphasized that AI possesses the capacity to revolutionize all sectors of American industry and generate new opportunities for advanced manufacturing. The Dynamic Systems AI Institute was identified as among eight major focus areas and funding priorities introduced by the NSF in August 2020 through The National Artificial Intelligence Research Institutes. This institute focuses on machine learning research algorithms, fundamental theory of AI, and other engineering applications of AI with special emphasis on simultaneously sensing, learning, decision-making, and predictive capabilities. The primary challenge is to create secure, dependable and efficient AI systems. However, the research and development budgets for FY2020 and FY2021 suggested that the country has to continue to invest in smart manufacturing and digital manufacturing through the Industrial IOT, machine learning and artificial intelligence from time to time to stay abreast of scientific and technological advancements. Since the introduction of their Industry 4.0 initiative, Germany has taken a long step. In September 2017, it facilitated development and implementation of what it calls learning systems to enhance flexibility and operational efficiency in industrial activities.

In November 2018, the German Federal Government released its national AI strategy, in which AI is regarded as a critical component in monitoring, managing, and controlling industrial systems with intelligence and can support the advancement of Industry 4.0. Likewise, in order to be competitive in the era of Industry 4.0 revolution, South Korea has implemented the Manufacturing Innovation 3.0 Strategy, while Japan has adopted the i-Japan Strategy, and the UK is taking the UK Industry 2050 Strategy.

In one of these cases, to jump a technological change, or to go to achieve a higher level of technological development without progressing through every transitional stage, is required to attain the required quick technological advance, especially in process industry. It involves aligning the features and objectives of the process industry with the concepts of intelligent manufacturing. This requires fully utilizing big data and embedding advanced digital technologies, including AI, mobile internet, cloud computing, simulation, control, and optimization, into manufacturing systems and resources. Industries can step towards best as well as optimized processes with the formation of new advanced functions. From this outlook, it is widely recognized that industrial AI and Industrial Internet technologies will be major elements to industrial AI and Industrial Internet technologies. The primary objective is to promote the rapid development of smart, network-enabled, and digital manufacturing systems across China. In this regard, the importance of smart manufacturing in the process industry is explained, important research areas are listed and studies methods are presented for the transition to smart manufacturing (Yang et al., 2021).

As an example, the Gigafactories set by Tesla incorporate Robotic Hands and Computer Vision Systems that are utilized to weld, paint and assemble. The AI is continually learning to produce a car at the Fremont plant, which happens every 45 seconds or so. The wider definition of Industrial AI could include a well-managed space for the purpose of developing, testing, installing and maintaining AI solutions that will work in an industrial environment, and will be long-lived and trusted. Industrial AI should be viewed as an interdisciplinary field rather than simply the adoption of AI in factories, as it integrates multiple technologies to tackle complex industrial problems effectively. In recent years, extensive research has been undertaken to integrate AI solutions into Industry 4.0 manufacturing environments and value networks. By integrating these diverse disciplines, industrial systems can adapt, learn from data, and address operational challenges within predefined parameters while exercising a degree of autonomous decision-making. However, notable distinctions exist between general AI and industrial AI. To process data in real time and meet strict business demands for security, reliability and connectivity, it must have well recognized and sound hardware and software infrastructure.

Second, the volume, speed and high diversity of the data used in the AI Industries are often large, high-speed and highly variable, and are create by machinery, production lines, products, and various operational conditions. Third, AI industry algorithms should rely on the physical understanding of machines and processes, together with digital modelling and practical expertise. Additional challenges arise from the requirement to control, implement, and regulate these sophisticated models. Fourth, there is very little tolerance for errors in decision-making within industrial environments. It is very crucial to be able to conduct large-scale operations effectively and to deal with uncertainty wisely with the potential safety risks, financial losses and lost production time due to error. Last but not least, Industrial AI aims to add value in reality, for instance, through cutting waste, improving product quality, increasing worker productivity while reducing ramp-up production time.

Industrial systems are heterogeneous, multifaceted and, depending on the application, have varying degrees of autonomy in the systems. The degree of autonomous decision making a system can make is explained by a progressively scaled model such as Platform Industrie 4.0's six-level model of autonomy. These are similar to autonomous driving levels used to indicate the autonomous driving capabilities of a system and the autonomous driving capabilities that are planned for the system. To achieve advanced levels of autonomy, additional intelligence must be incorporated into systems, which is enhanced through experience and continuous learning. Therefore, AI industries are currently progressing toward greater autonomy in industrial environments. Nevertheless, currently, it is used to assist and facilitate human workers instead of fully replacing them, and this combination strategy is probably to persist even in the case of more autonoetic systems in the future. (Peres et al., 2020).

Big Data and Analytics-Driven Strategy

Data Analytics is the systematic computation of quantitative information or statistical measures identify trends, patterns and valuable insights the source data, which will be utilized to improve decision-making processes and operational practices in the organization. Data analytics in the business world encompasses analyzing and interpreting structured and unstructured data using analytical software, quantitative models, AI-driven algorithms, and data visualization methods. It is usually broken down into descriptive analytics (what happened), explanatory analytics (why it happened), forecasting analytics (what is likely to happen), and recommendation analytics (what action to take), with each level of organizational strategy supported by each type of analytics. International consulting companies and research institutions have emphasized the significance of data analytics in business, highlighting its impact on strategic coordination, market placement, and institutional learning across multiple sectors, including finance, healthcare, manufacturing, and retail. The United States, Germany, and South Korea, among others, with well-developed digital infrastructure, have shown how the use of analytics enriches the productivity and competitiveness of the nation.

One of its best-studied functions in organizational growth initiatives is the use of data analytics to inform the decision-making framework. Strategic decisions frequently have to navigate high uncertainty and operational complexity, and analytics can help by providing evidence-based findings, predictive simulations and immediate feedback. It reveals that organisations with analytics embedded in their practices have 10% greater precision in financial planning, allocation of resources and performance benchmarking. Furthermore, data analytics enable moving away from intuition-based to evidence-based decisions, thereby improving alignment of strategy with operational goals. Case studies in, for example, the telecommunications and retail industries demonstrate that making use of analytics for segmentation and targeting helped them grow their customer base and retain it. In multinational settings, local and global datasets can be combined to provide a company with insights into local market demand variations, supply chain constraints, and regulatory constraints.

Therefore, analytics is a key element in compiling internal performance data and external market information, and is vital to strategic foresight. Data Analytics integration has proven to be a boon for lean production systems, Six Sigma methodologies, and comprehensive quality management. Process analytics and live analytics have been used to discover inefficiencies in production and supply networks, to take prompt corrective actions. Data analytics is applied to enhance customer service processes, identify anomalies, and predict customer service demands in the service sector, like banking and insurance. Healthcare analytics, healthcare systems to optimize admissions, minimize patient readmissions and manage staffing based on patient movement trends. Likewise, transportation and logistics companies leverage route optimization analysis and demand prediction to streamline delivery schedules and cut down on business expenses. These illustrations demonstrate how data analytics can be used to continuously improve by automated monitoring and performance diagnostics. (Rahman, 2025).

Internet of Things and Smart Infrastructure

The World Wide Web of Things (WW IoT) could revolutionize modern city infrastructure, making cities more sustainable, high-performing individuals or systems to citizens' needs. The conservative practice of "doing something about it" when handling urban management, can be changed to "deciding based on data" with the help of the IoT-powered program. This transformation involves aspects of urban life like traffic management, environmental surveillance, energy management, waste management, water distribution systems and public safety. Cities can also enable interconnected sensors and devices to monitor the urban conditions continually and respond quickly to new issues. However, Although IoT offers considerable opportunities, its large-scale implementation in urban governance faces numerous challenges, particularly in cybersecurity, scalability, data management, and system integration. The urban governance in Singapore is one such example; Singapore is home to one of the world's largest national IoT deployments. More than a million sensors are deployed throughout the city-state to monitor atmospheric quality, dengue mosquito breeding grounds, independently living elderly residents, and so on. Lamppost-as-a-Platform (LaaP) is an stepping up to transforms streetlights into multi-functional sensor nodes collecting real-time insight on the environment, mobility and public safety conditions.

IoT technologies integrate with urban infrastructure is a complex challenge that needs thorough planning and coordination. It entails the implementation of an extensive interconnected network of sensors and intelligent devices across urban areas to gather information on various parameters, including traffic movement, air quality, energy consumption, sewage infrastructure, and crime hotspots. These gadgets can transmit vast amounts of data to central centralized monitoring centers where advanced analytical tools can process and analyze the collected data. This provides municipal authorities and decision-makers with timely information regarding urban performance. The exact and timely insight will help authorities make decisions to increase the complete standard of living in urban regions, resource distribution and public services. As a result, evidence-based governance will make a difference to the efficiency and quality of public services.

To ensure the feature of IoT systems in smart cities, interoperability is essential. Diverse technologies, platforms and communication systems should be able to communicate with each other Perfectly. An comprehensive integrated framework does not only enhance productivity in the operations, but also offers scalability and operational flexibility. The IoT infrastructure is not supposed to be designed strictly as it grows in cities and new future system modifications change of the system without the need of redesigning the whole thing. This flexibility ensures sustainable development in the long term and continued improvement of urban management processes.

Even with these advantages, data privacy and security in the IoT-based environment is a significant problem. As sensitive information is constantly being created and passed around on IoT gadgets, it is vital that it is not reveal to hacking. Individuals are increasingly conscious of risks such as data breaches, unauthorized monitoring, and identity theft. Consequently, robust cybersecurity measures are essential, including encrypted data transmission, secure data storage, restricted access for authorized personnel, and continuous vulnerability assessment. Furthermore, comprehensive regulatory and legal structures should be established to safeguard individual privacy and ensure the responsible use of data. Transparency and fairness in data collection and utilization are critical for maintaining public confidence in smart city initiatives.

There is also a practical aspect to the work of such IoT-enabled systems, which manifests itself, for example, in the field of intelligent traffic optimization, energy utilization, acceleration of waste-management operations and enhancement of public security. Environmental monitoring is more active and is able to respond more effectively and precisely to the pollution or climate-related threats. However, the socio-economic context (economic feasibility and long-term sustainability) has not been part of the focus in the previous literature. They have also not been very interested in potential problems to the society like invasion of privacy, ethical issues in large-scale data acquisition etc.

All in all, the Internet of Things (IoT) in smart urban designs can be seen as a innovative approach to address the issues associated with urbanization. To enable sustainable cities, efficient and comprehensive monitoring schemes can be built by systematic deployment data collection points to cover the widest possible coverage at the minimum overlap and by strategically placing data collection points in relation to the needs of the population (population density), traffic load (traffic density), areas of environmental risk (environmental risk density) and areas of high interaction with the people (human density). (Alshaflut, 2024). Figure 2 illustrates the five key components of a smart city in the context of IoT.

Figure 2. The 5 essential elements of smart cities.

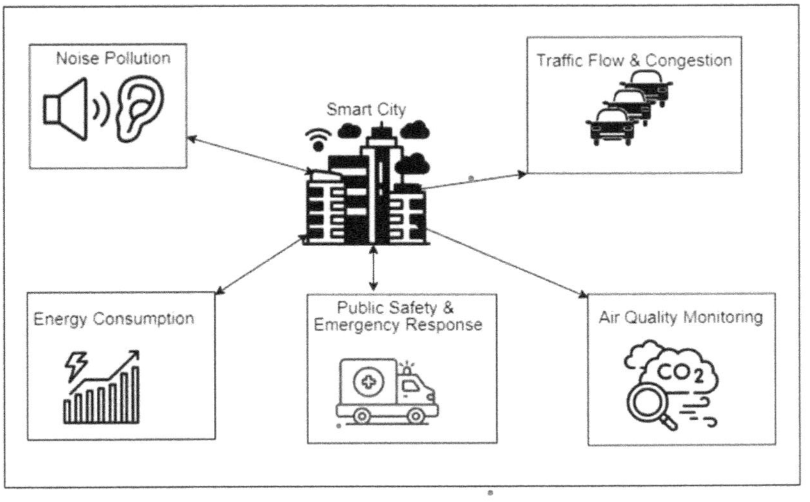

Source: (Alshaflut, 2024)

A smart city is an urban area that leverages the use of information and communication technology (ICT) to enhance the efficiency and quality of the services offered by the city, particularly in the public utilities, transportation and energy sectors. Smart cities aim to improve overall welfare and living standards of their citizens by incorporating the latest technologies into the city's daily life. With smart solutions, cities are looking for ways to become smarter, more Productive, sustainable and more citizens-friendly.

Smart Environment:

smart environment refers to an ecosystem that uses smart devices such as sensing technologies and automated control systems, to monitor and regulate the environment. These technologies can be valuable to control the application of energy, limit pollution, and help achieve better environmental balance through robotic and analytics-driven processes.

Smart Home:

smart home can be defined as equipped with interconnected devices and sensors that allow residents to remotely manage lighting, security systems, household appliances, and other functions. Through automation and internet connectivity, these residences increase comfort, strengthen security, and improve energy performance.

Smart Cars:

Smart cars are conventional vehicles, but with the added benefit of IoT-enabled technology. These vehicles would be smarter because sensors, communication systems and digital tools can be combined to allow them to include enhanced navigation, safety, and connectivity capabilities to make transportation smarter and more efficient.

Smart Technology:

Smart technology refers to digital tools and devices that can improve the life in the city. Such technologies allow citizens to access improved services, support informed decision-making and be integrated as the participants of the city’s connected digital environment.

Smart Transport:

Smart technology encompasses digital devices and tools designed to enhance urban living. These technologies enable citizens to access improved services, make informed decisions, and actively participate in the city's digital ecosystem.

Smart Retail:

Smart retail refers to the use of digital innovations and innovative tools by businesses to enhance customer experiences, improve inventory control, and enhance sales performance.

Smart Security:

Smart security systems utilize advanced monitoring and surveillance technologies to protect smart homes, vehicles, and digital devices from cybersecurity threats and other security risks.

Internet of Things:

The Internet of Things is a network of tangible objects equipped with technologies that make them connect and exchange insight. Smart city infrastructures are systems where these devices are automatically operated by sharing information through networks, and they don't necessarily require a man power to operate the devices. As illustrated in Figure 3, there are numerous technologies in IoT, and a set of enabling technologies can be applied as the base technologies for the IoT systems deployed in a smart environment. (Sharma et al., 2019).

Figure 3. The technologies employed in IoT.

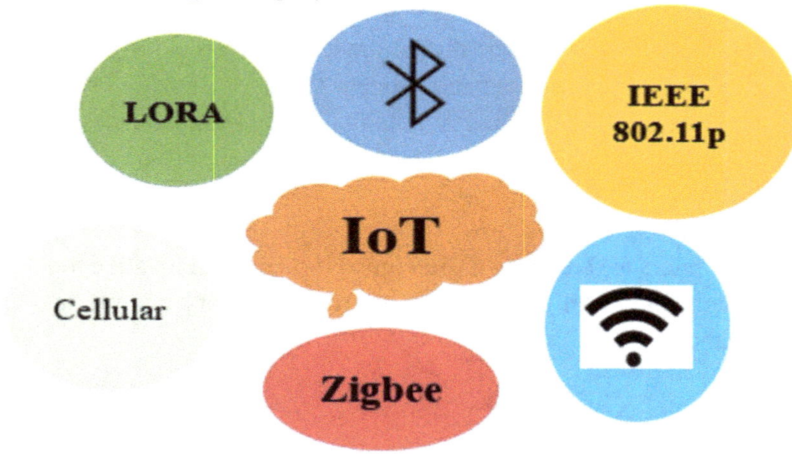

Source: (Sharma et al., 2019).

BLOCKCHAIN AND DECENTRALIZED TRUST SYSTEMS

The term "IoT," first introduced in 1999, has developed significantly into one of the most impactful technological innovations of the modern era. It has been widely used and has a substantial influence on various businesses and research fields, which has generated considerable interest among researchers and industry professionals alike. The Internet of Things (IoT) refers to a network of things that are connected via intelligent technologies and sensor networks and can exchange information and insights with each other. These gadgets, with continuous and widespread connectivity, allow for machine-human interaction. Initially, the IoT application was developed with certain specific and partial goals. However, the expansion rate of wireless communication technology, and the advancement of hardware and software systems, have led to a substantial growth in the number of IoT applications and their accessibility to the masses. The IoT has become the integral component of today's lifestyle and is used extensively in the present world.

The number of interconnected devices is another sign of the rapid growth of IoT. In 2018, it is estimated that more than 8.4 billion devices are connected worldwide. In 2020 this is estimated to exceed more than 20 billion and it is expected to increase in a growing exponential number in following years. IoT solutions are recently used in different businesses. The Internet of the Medical Things provides advanced healthcare systems and distance-based monitoring in the healthcare sector. In order to enhance connectivity and transportation safety, the transportation industry uses the Internet of Vehicles (IoV) and Social Internet of Vehicles. Another field where the IoT is broadly applied is in intelligent agriculture, industrial environments, marine applications, social networking platforms between devices and smart city infrastructure. The applications demonstrate and give the insight into how the Internet of Things facilitate automation, efficiency and intelligent decision-making in various arenas.

While it has its benefits, there are many technical and security issues with IoT. The massive amount of data generated by connected devices, combined with the constrained computational capacity and power resources of many IoT devices, creates significant operational challenges. Secondly, IoT systems are predominantly centralized architecture, which can pose compatibility and scalability challenges. Additionally, numerous vulnerabilities exist, which increases the risk of becoming the target of a cyberattack and thus heightens security and privacy concerns. If full implementation of the cloud-based infrastructure were to take place, time-sensitive IoT applications may not perform well due to the delay, low bandwidth, and absence of security infrastructure that it may encounter.

The success of IoT deployments is largely influenced by strong privacy measures, strategic implementation approaches, and effective communication mechanisms. Traditional Security measures are the conventional ways of securing the systems from external attacks or data leakages such as encryption and access control etc. are called as Hard security solutions. However, such techniques can be inefficient in dealing with internal threats or in the network. Thus, Trust Management (TM) that can be regarded as a software-oriented security approach has added more important. TM systems evaluate device behaviour using earlier communication exchanges and decide on the trustworthiness of a device through direct and indirect observations.

trust within IoT may be described as the predictable trust that a user of the service has in a supplier of the service over time based on trust that the supplier of the service will act in a truthful and reliable manner. Trust management systems collect information on interactions and calculate the trustworthiness of the organisation in the network. It enhances the reliability of the systems and also supports the overall security of the IoT environments with the tracking of communication activities and detection of abnormal behaviour. (Arshad et al., 2023).

The centralized structure of conventional trust systems recommends that they trust on a single authority or agency to monitor, control, and verify transactions. Though these are quite popular and officially endorsed systems, they come with a multiple disadvantage. When the power is concentrated in a solo central unit, there can be concerns regarding power misuse, lack of accountability, risks associated with system failure and data privacy can arise. If the reputation of the authority is affected, uncontrolled and heavy losses can occur in the entire system. The global financial crisis of 2008 exposed the weaknesses of centralized trust systems, particularly in the financial sector, where excessive reliance on central institutions contributed to systemic instability. In response, researchers and technologists began exploring alternative trust models that operate without centralized control. It was then that the search evolved to Bitcoin.

The recognition of Bitcoin in the financial sector inspired the additional research of decentralized technologies. The blockchain technology underpinning Bitcoin drew the interest of a broader audience of applications as a decentralized trust in various businesses in the upcoming future. In 2008, it was popularly called blockchain with Bitcoin, but the concept of the chain of signatures of information goes back to 1993. The earlier model described a digital ledger containing signed records that could be readily verified to detect any unauthorized modifications. Similarly, blockchain functions as a decentralized and distributed ledger maintained collectively by a network of participants. Based on the openness and decentralization of the chain, blockchains can be differentiated into public chain, private chain and consortium chain. Blockchain is made up of various technologies, including peer-to-peer networks, distributed ledgers, asymmetric encryption, consensus algorithms, and digital signatures and smart contracts.

Blockchain technology has progressed through multiple phases of development. Blockchain 1.0 primarily refers to Bitcoin and other decentralized cryptocurrencies. However, Bitcoin's scripting language offers limited functionality and supports only relatively simple transactions. To address these limitations, Blockchain 2.0 emerged, represented by platforms such as Ethereum. During this phase, computer coded self-executing smart contracts entered into the scene. Smart contracts, after being published on the blockchain, cannot be modified and are triggered automatically upon the satisfaction of specified conditions. Even though it was still being used primarily in the financial sector, this innovation expanded blockchain's use to not payment-related transactions only, but programmable financial services. For example, Blockchain-enabled Food Safety in Walmart & IBM Food Trust, to check food distribution networks, Walmart and IBM implemented the Food Trust blockchain on the Hyperledger Fabric platform. The average time used to be 7 days to trace the origin of contaminated products. A mango can be identified in approximately 2.2 seconds from the retail shelf to the source farm using blockchain technology. Blockchain technology enables Walmart to trace a mango from the shop shelf to its origin farm in 2.2 seconds! The technology allows focused product recalls after outbreaks of E. coli contamination in romaine lettuceis detected, which significantly reduces the extent and cost of recalls.

Another technology innovation is the blockchain 3.0, which takes blockchain technology into other areas of life than financial. Platform Hyperledger Fabric and EOS supports decentralized applications (also known by the term D Apps) that are applied to sectors including the healthcare sector, educational sector, the energy sector, supply chain operations and the IoT ecosystem. At this stage, blockchain is considered a universal decentralized platform to provide secure, transparent, and reliable solutions to all kinds of real-world problems. (Deng et al., 2023).

CONVERGENCE: BUILDING INTELLIGENT INDUSTRIAL ECOSYSTEM

Due to the increasing demand for 'individualisation' of products and the rigorous regulations, the world production sector is now more complex. No more standard products being produced in a steady and gradual pace, but complex products that are produced under highly dynamic supply networks. Industrial equipment is becoming increasingly complex and production cycles are becoming shorter. Therefore, there is a risk of losing a critical revenue volume because the machines suddenly and erratically stop functioning. Even a small amount of unplanned downtime can disrupt the entire production process and significantly increase operational costs.

There have been 2 maintenance strategies historically reactive maintenance and preventive maintenance approaches traditionally adopted by manufacturers. One type of upkeep strategy referred to as "reactive maintenance" is the practice of repairing equipment only after it breaks down. While not a servicing method that is being done unnecessarily, it can lead to preventing production, expensive repair, and slow delivery. Although this approach reduces the likelihood of unexpected failures, it may result in the premature replacement of functional components and increased expenditure on workforce and materials resources. Consequently, both maintenance approaches can create operational inefficiencies and elevate overall costs.

To address these issues, many organizations are increasingly adopting Predictive Maintenance (PdM). Predictive maintenance utilizes live operational data and sophisticated analytics to predict equipment malfunctions before they occur. By leveraging the help of the IIoT sensors, the manufacturer can continuously monitor equipment itself, gathering information for the machine vibration patterns, temperature, pressure levels and sound. This allows firms to keep track of unusual developments and take prompt action. But collecting lots of sensor data isn't sufficient. The effectiveness of predictive maintenance lies in its ability to integrate raw data with the broader manufacturing process. For instance, suddenly seeing the vibration of a robotic is valuable only data if it can be correlated with the manufacturing process category that is presently taking place, the specific component recognized from the BOM and the actual component serial number being collected.

It was difficult to achieve this level of integration before because there was no integration between ERP and MES platforms. The Enterprise Resource Planning systems deal with the business information of high level (including the BOMs and production routing), and the MES (Manufacturing Execution Systems) and IoT platforms handle the real-time shop-floor activities. Information in these systems is trapped in different silos because of the detail that they may utilize incompatible data formats and other systems don't share standardized identifiers. This fragmentation limits organizational visibility.

This has been transformed with the introduction of Data Lakehouse architecture. A Data Lakehouse integrates the scalability and adaptability of data lakes with the reliability and structured capabilities of data warehouses. The Manufacturing Data Lakehouse (MDL) consists of technological components, including Delta Lake, to create a combined platform to which both real-time and past data can be processed simultaneously. This is done to provide automatic correlation of sensor data to product and process data at the primary phases.

By integrating IoT sensor data with critical manufacturing elements such as the Bill of Materials (BOM), routing information, and product serialization, organizations can establish a continuous digital thread throughout the production lifecycle. This not only strengthens predictive maintenance capabilities but also enhances product quality, traceability, and regulatory compliance. Last but not least, a single Lakehouse system enables smarter and more efficient and data-driven manufacturing process. (Choudhury, 2018).

The industry 5.0 could revolutionize the industry business through the use of IoT, especially in conjunction with blockchain. These two technologies can be used together to improve productivity, improve the security of data and ensure greater transparency and authenticity of the supply chain management. However, as organizations shift towards research and development of combing IoT with blockchain, it is quite important to choose an appropriate blockchain platform. This may be the reason because the choice of the IoT platform directly affects the performance of IoT applications in Industry 5.0 environments.

Industry 5.0 adopts a human-focused perspective, leveraging advanced technological systems to enhance human involvement rather than eliminate it. IoT plays a key role by linking intelligent devices and equipment, allowing them to gather and exchange information in real time. Rather, blockchain establishes a more solid foundation of trust given the data is immutable, transparent and secure. The two collective, assist in closing the split between the physical and digital world. This integration enables real-time monitoring, automation, secure data sharing, effective supply chain formation and predictive maintenance. Therefore, the industries will be more sustainable, more strong and smarter.

In earlier years, they have observed a huge interest of researchers and businesses in IoT due to its capability in offering novel solutions to many businesses. With the economic, environmental and social issues that are emerging due to quick urbanization, the architecture of the IoT continues to evolve to meet the needs of the present and forthcoming society.

Figure 4. The past, present and future of the Internet of Things (IoT) architecture.

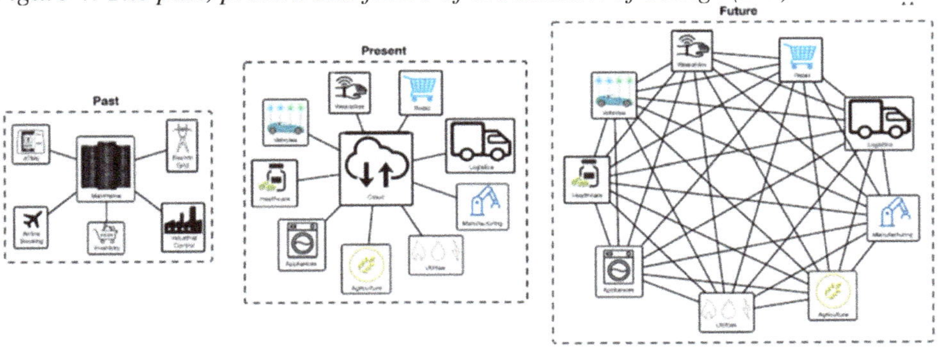

Source: (Sizan et al., 2025).

The Internet of Things is a technology that enables the creation of a network of physical devices that have sensors, software, and other technologies to sense and share data. This permits the monitoring, control and even automated devices and systems. Today, some 29 billion devices can be connected and with the potential of 75 billion more in 2023 and 2050, the IoT is growing at an extremely fast rate. Growth of smart and connected devices across many industries and advancements in connections and sensor technology, which has reduced costs, are largely driving this rapid growth. (Sizan et al, 2025). The growth of IoT architecture from the initial stages (device-centric) to current times (cloud applications) and the future (edge computing, AI and industry connectivity) is illustrated in Figure 4.

ETHICAL, REGULATORY AND WORKFORCE IMPLICATIONS

The Ethics of meaningful work & ethical AI.

Philosophers who explore the purpose of life often question whether our actions and relationships possess genuine value and significance. A common illustration of purposeless work is the story of the mythological figure Sisyphus. In the myth, Sisyphus is condemned to repeatedly roll a boulder uphill, over and over. His work is repetitive, without real meaning, monotonous, doesn't help anybody and isn't freely chosen. Due to this, it represents worthless work. From this example it can be understood that if work is meaningful, it should be of the opposite properties. It needs to be interesting and intriguing and not mundane. It should be a variety of tasks and require a combination of skill and ability. It must have a value to society and others. It should be most importantly, voluntarily undertaken.

Purposeful work is generally understood by researchers in terms of two key dimensions: personal and external meanings. Subjective dimension is how an individual feels about their work, if he or she that their work has significance and enriching. The objective dimensions dwells on whether work is good or socially beneficial or not. Meaningful work can be something that is meaningful both to the person and something that is also valuable from a wider societal perspective. It is a blend of societal contribution and personal fulfillment.

Ethical implications of using AI:

The effect of AI's impact on meaningful work should be looked into as it is an essential component of human dignity and well-being. There have been many scholars and organizations who have already written on the ethical issues of AI. A number of national and international values establish responsible AI use. However, many of these overlook the effects of AI on meaningful work. For example, Amazon recruitment algorithm controversy was a Threatening Story in Amazon, which created trained using a decade of recruitment data, as stated in the chapter. The model an AI-based resume screening tool that was learned to reward the resumes that included the word “women's” (e.g., “women's chess club”) since it would have been more beneficial for the model to accept such resumes since historically, the majority of the recruited candidates were predominantly male, especially in technical positions. In 2018, the tool was blackout. In this case, it has come to symbolize the power of AI to perpetuate and magnify historical bias when trained on non-sampled data at a large scale.

For example, literature ethics for Artificial Intelligence (AI) standards highlight points such as equity, transparency, accountability and safety, but rarely connect to meaningful work. Other debates are about the upcoming of work, namely that AI can replace human labourers. The main suggestion that is offered in these cases is to retrain the employees who have lost their place of work because of automation. This approach, however, does not take into account human-AI association cases or the broader context of changing human work with the help of AI. Other models make a few assumptions that AI will free up people from unenjoyable or repetitive tasks, but don't go into detail about what that means for the overall meaning of what people do.

While many AI ethics don't discuss the meaningful work in the scope of the ethics AI values can still be used to look at the problem. One such framework is known as AI4People framework, which features five foundational principles: beneficence (doing good), individual autonomy (respecting the personal freedom), justice (the creation of equity) and explainability (the creation of openness and accountability). These principles are practical since they aim at protecting human dignity and welfare. The effects on competencies, personal development, independence, social relationships and wellbeing are closely connected to that of meaningful work.

Moreover, the ethical principles are not limited to AI; they have been exported to other digital technologies as well. With the help of such frameworks, it becomes easier to comprehend and analyze the ways AI is designed and deployed to safeguard and encourage meaningful work within the contemporary societies (Bankins & Formosa, 2023).

The role of AI in HRM, is an important aspect that is currently impacting HRM to a great extent. The main driver behind the adoption of AI by businesses is the boost it provides to efficiency, precision, and improved decision-making. AI is talented of automating repetitive administrative tasks, working through substantial quantities of information in a short amount of time, and coming up with actionable insights. This will enable HR professionals to focus more on strategic activities instead of routine tasks. As an illustration, AI-based recruitment systems can evaluate resumes, carry out preliminary online interviews, and even predicting applicant performance potential in the job. This helps to save time and effort which could have been used in the hiring process. Learning and development: AI also assists employees to develop and train according to their preferences, career aspirations, and personal abilities, creating training effective. AI systems can provide feedback, which is more objective, and it is essential to provide feedback to the AI systems.

On an on-going basis, enabling organisations to identify successful performance and identify what needs to be done to improve in performance management. Similarly, AI-powered applications can improve employee engagement by enhancing communication, offering personalized wellness suggestions, and recognizing staff achievements.

However, there are also a number of tasks of AI in HRM, namely, ethical and legal issues. Bias and discrimination are one of the key ethical difficulties. If the AI is based on biased or incomplete data, it may unfairly discriminate against or discriminate other groups of individuals. The most widely known is the Amazon recruiting tool that exhibited a bias in hiring procedures as it was trained on previous data which was gender bias. To prevent these issues, businesses should strive to use diverse and representative datasets to train AI models. The conduct of consistent audits and bias detection processes is required to detect and mitigate the biased results. Another way to reduce the potential for hidden bias is to involve the various teams in the design and development of AI systems.

Other serious issues are privacy and data protection. AI systems must be fed a wealth of data about employees, which poses questions regarding collection, storage, and utilization of such data. The General Data Protection Regulation and other data protection legislation must be adhered to by companies. This suggests that the data should be collected in a responsible manner by finding a clear consent of the employees prior to collection and that the data is not misused. To ensure confidential information is protected, effective security measures are needed, including encryption and anonymization. Regular compliance checks and audits should also be conducted to ensure that AI systems operate within legal frameworks and adhere to ethical standards. With these ethical and legal issues considered, organizations can responsibly use AI in HRM and achieve the maximum benefits (Du, 2024).

This is an era of Generative Artificial Intelligence and its implications in HRM Ethics:

The adoption of Generative Artificial Intelligence, including ChatGPT and similar models, is increasingly being used to streamline and enhance HRM practices, offering improved efficiency and more accurate decision-making. However, like all sophisticated technology, there are a number of ethical issues that it presents that should be addressed by the organization in order to ensure it will be responsible, fair and transparent.

Another primary concern with generative AI is algorithms bias. AI systems are trained on large datasets, and if the data is unfair or created in the earlier or a certain culture, then the AI can either perpetuate the bias, or even amplify it. In HRM, this can lead to discrimination in the hiring process as some clusters of people are favoured or not. Similarly, the introduction of unfair performance appraisals can be linked to other causes, and organizational decisions on talent management can amplify the existing organizational bias. To mitigate such risks, it is crucial to ensure that they have a broad and diverse training set for their AI models, regularly review and test the AI's outputs to detect any errors or biases, and have procedures in place to correct identified biases.

Data Privacy Concerns:

Generative AI is in need of on huge quantities of data, a large share of which in HRM comprises sensitive employee data. Some of the ethical and practical problems are using data in ways that are not appropriate to HR work, accessing information illegally, and not understanding who has access to the data, how long it is kept and what it can be used for. Organizations should implement strict data privacy measures, including encryption, access controls, and compliance with international data protection regulations, to safeguard employee information and build trust.

Making sure employees alter to the changing workplace and giving them training so they may obtain new skills are the main purposes. The main purpose is to ensure that workers adapt to the evolving working context and to train a worker, gaining a new competence.

Incorporating generative AI into HRM also requires the organizations to rethink the training and adaptation of employees. Everyone from the lowest to the highest rank of employees should be trained in the skills and data needed to work with AI systems.

There are different approaches to training effective collaboration of AI and humans:

Skill Augmentation: Employees should be trained to use AI as a supportive tool rather than a replacement. For instance, HR professionals can leverage AI-generated insights to inform decisions, while ensuring that final decision-making remains human-led.

Frequent Updates: Due to the rapid evolution of the technology, consistent training is required to keep the employees updated on changes, devices and best performs in AI-powered HR processes.

Training on Prevention and Identification of Biases: HR should be trained to detect and/or disclose any biases within the AI reports, and to correct them.

Privacy of data Criteria: Workers need training on the importance of good ethical use of information, the close adherence to data protection principles and respect for the privacy of staff in each of the activities that AI tools are helping with.

Figure 5. AI collaboration strategies

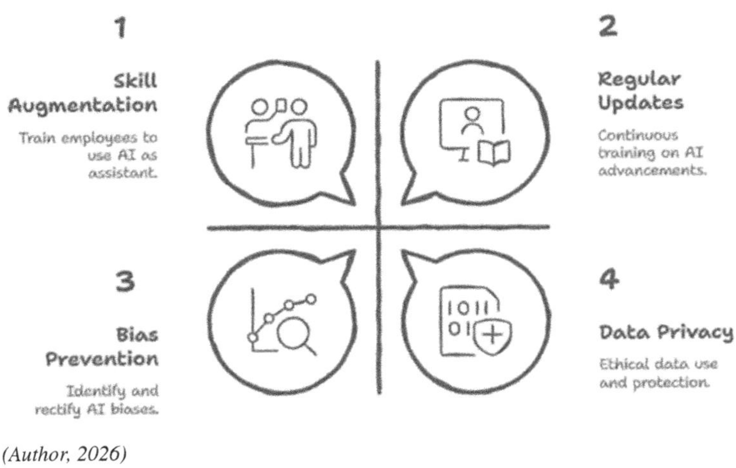

Source: (Author, 2026)

Conclusively, although the generative AI has a transformational potential in HRM, organisations need to take the initiative in dealing with ethical matters surrounding bias and data privacy. At the same time, strengthening training and adaptation among employees will ensure that AI and human intelligence work together to build an effective, ethical, and efficient HR system. Organizations need to employ various strategies to ensure a collaborative effort between humans and AI in HRM, all while upholding ethical standards. To foster an effective and ethical alliance between humans and AI in HRM, organizations must embrace several strategies. (Trivedi et al., 2024).

STRATEGIC ROADMAP FOR SUSTAINABLE DIGITAL TRANSFORMATION

The roadmap aims to offer a approach for small and medium-sized enterprises (SMEs) for sustainable digitalisation. The primary objective is to fill the existing gaps identified within the literature through offering an organization with a structured approach to start and maintain technological revolution. This roadmap further enables ongoing improvement as it assesses the capability of the organisation and its development level, thereby determining the next steps and the development. SDT-SMEs Roadmap has been created following the ISO/IEC TR 33014 guidelines which suggests the three-level approach which contains strategic in addition to operational stages. The framework provides detailed direction on applying process assessments within a holistic continuous improvement framework, emphasizing the development and maintenance of competencies necessary for successful transformation initiatives. The Strategic Roadmap for Sustainable Digital Transformation for SMEs is presented in three levels strategic, tactical, and operational (as represented in Figure 6).

Figure 6. Strategic Roadmap for Sustainable Digital Transformation This is how the strategy will look when it has been finished.

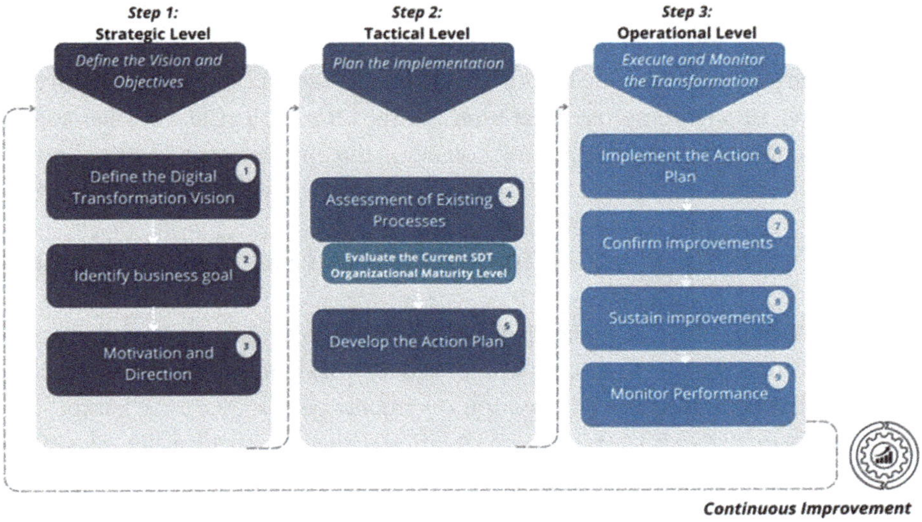

Source:(Mick et al., 2024).

Step 1: Strategic Level- Strategy: Vision and Objectives.

Defining a clear vision for sustainable digital transformation is the primary strategic-level task for an organization. This vision should closely align with the SME's overall strategic objectives, whether focused on improving operational efficiency, enhancing customer experience, or expanding into new markets. After having shaped the vision, measurable, specific goals are identified, such as the need to digitalize processes, rely on new technologies or equip workers with digital skills. In addition, it's the organization that decides on the root cause of the change, whether it's to make the organization more competitive, create new innovations, or increase efficiency, which facilitates decision making and made everyone in the organization move toward the same path.

Step 2: Tactical level: Strategy the Implementation.

The tactical level is concerned with evaluating the existing organizational procedures for the purpose of identifying those that need to be improved. The assessment is based on the maturity model defined by the ISO/IEC 33000 framework. The collected data will be gathered and verified by an assessment team, following the principles of ISO/IEC 33002 on assessing process, by means of guided interviews with process owners along with a review of operational artifacts (records, instruments and communications). once the information is gathered, the team evaluates the information to understand the organization's general level of digital maturity, the strengths and weaknesses, and existing capacities. On the origin of this study, enhancement opportunities are identified and prioritised and a detailed improvement plan is drawn up. The improvement plan outlines the project tasks, roles together with responsibilities, time frames and considers the environment and requirements of the organisation

Step 3: Operational Level, Implement and Review the Change.

The operational level is the level of dedication to implementing the improvement plan and making the changes sustainable. Process evaluations are always met, and results are fed-back to make the next improvements so that every decision is based on real performance indicators and real situation in the organization. This level helps in constant adaptation in the long term so that SMEs are able to report new tasks, and changing digital needs effectively.

Overall, SDT-SMEs Roadmap assists SMEs to head towards sustainable digital transformation by incorporating strategic, tactical and operational processes. It ensures that digitalization transformation is more than a one-time event but a continuous evaluation, improvement and competency building process. The roadmap covers the requirements of ISO/IEC 33000 and a maturity model based on a process reference model, and offers a highly complete and well-structured framework for Digital Transformation for SMEs (Mick et al., 2024).

FUTURE RESEARCH DIRECTIONS

While there are significant advances in the understanding of solo technologies, less is known about the implications of several technologies on the long run. Several issues of significance exist which could be further investigated. Research over time, five to ten years could offer findings regarding competitive benefits that are short term, productivity driven, or long term. which are no procedures for the industrial level of the AI ethics yet. Specific contexts need to be developed and conducted in businesses including similarly manufacturing, logistics and critical infrastructure. The difficulties related to governance are as apparent as the problems with the technology in the case of Trade Lens.

Further research is needed regarding the ways for healthcare stakeholders and logistics and financial services sectors to accomplish blockchain networks. It's not just the job displacement that requires more in-depth study of human-AI collaboration. Different types of workers' collaboration on workers' welfare and competencies, particularly in emerging economies, need to be investigated. With the development of smart cities, the cybersecurity threats increase. The research needs to be directed towards adaptable security frameworks that will protect privacy while maintaining the quality of findings obtained from urban information, through the AI utilization. Finally, there remains a notable gap in studies on digital transformation within small-scale and medium-sized enterprises (SMEs). Upcoming studies should examine the barriers to SME adoption and explore how regulations, industry associations, together with cloud platforms can facilitate greater uptake.

CONCLUSION

Industry 4.0 refers to a German project designed to develop smart factories characterized by extensive digital connectivity. It is an amalgamation of technologies like IoT, cloud-based computing, and cyber-physical technologies, developed to help equipment, sensors and personnel interact immediately to facilitate clever decision-making process and create digital copies of physical assets.

Flexibility and responsiveness are essential for Industry 4.0 in production. It assists major enterprises and small and medium-sized businesses in responding rapidly to changing market conditions while ensuring the continuous availability of data and operational activities across distribution networks.

For intelligent manufacturing, automated systems acquire through experience, familiarize for the varying situation, make independent decisions. In this context, Artificial Intelligence serves as the key, enabling truly robotic and intelligent manufacturing processes. New concepts like cloud-based manufacturing along with the application of IoT applications in manufacturing additional enhance the connectiveness and production adaptability network.

The main technology of the design is: Internet of Things, cyber-physical technologies, cloud-based computing, big data analysis and ICT. The intelligent manufacturing is promoted in the United States, China, Japan and the European Union, and major progresses have been made in relevant areas, enhancing manufacturing systems' efficiency, adaptability and high capability worldwide.

REFERENCES

Ahmed, I., Zhang, Y., Jeon, G., Lin, W., Khosravi, M. R., & Qi, L. (2022). A blockchain-and artificial intelligence-enabled smart IoT framework for sustainable city. *International Journal of Intelligent Systems*, *37*(9), 6493–6507. DOI: 10.1002/int.22852

Alshaflut, A. (2024). Enhancing smart city infrastructure: An iot-integrated system approach for real-time urban management. *Indian Journal of Science and Technology*, *17*(29), 3012–3017. DOI: 10.17485/IJST/v17i29.1070

Arshad, Q. U. A., Khan, W. Z., Azam, F., Khan, M. K., Yu, H., & Zikria, Y. B. (2023). Blockchain-based decentralized trust management in IoT: Systems, requirements and challenges. *Complex & Intelligent Systems*, *9*(6), 6155–6176. DOI: 10.1007/s40747-023-01058-8

Bankins, S., & Formosa, P. (2023). The ethical implications of artificial intelligence (AI) for meaningful work. *Journal of Business Ethics*, *185*(4), 725–740. DOI: 10.1007/s10551-023-05339-7

Choudhury, N. (2018). The influence of IoT and AI convergence on industrial automation ecosystems. https://doi.org/DOI: 10.1080/00207543.2020.1824085

Deng, W., Huang, T., & Wang, H. (2023). A Review of the Key Technology in a Blockchain Building Decentralized Trust Platform. *Mathematics*, *11*(1), 101. DOI: 10.3390/math11010101

Du, J. (2024). Ethical and legal challenges of AI in human resource management. *Journal of Computing and Electronic Information Management*, *13*(2), 71–77. DOI: 10.54097/83j64ub9

Kim, J., & Song, H. G. (2024). Tracing the Convergence of Industrial Sectors: Has the 4th Revolution Arrived Already? Or Are We on the Track?. *Journal of the Korean Society of Industry Convergence, 27*(4_1), 781-795. https://doi.org/DOI: 10.21289/KSIC.2024.27.4.781

Mick, M. M. A. P., Kovaleski, J. L., Mick, R. L., & Chiroli, D. M. D. G. (2024). Developing a sustainable digital transformation roadmap for SMEs: Integrating digital maturity and strategic alignment. *Sustainability (Basel)*, *16*(20), 8745. DOI: 10.3390/su16208745

Peres, R. S., Jia, X., Lee, J., Sun, K., Colombo, A. W., & Barata, J. (2020). Industrial artificial intelligence in industry 4.0-systematic review, challenges and outlook. *IEEE Access : Practical Innovations, Open Solutions, 8*, 220121–220139. DOI: 10.1109/ACCESS.2020.3042874

Rahman, M. M. (2025). Data analytics for strategic business development: A systematic review analyzing its role in informing decisions, optimizing processes, and driving growth. *Journal of Sustainable Development and Policy, 1*(01), 285–314. DOI: 10.63125/he1tfg25

Schumpeter, J. A. (1942). *Capitalism, socialism and democracy.* Harper & Brothers. https://scholar.google.com/scholar_lookup?title=Creative+destruction&publication_year=1942&pages=8285&journal=Capitalism,+Socialism+and+Democracy&author=J.+Schumpeter

Sharma, S., Nanda, M., Goel, R., Jain, A., Bhushan, M., & Kumar, A. (2019). Smart cities using internet of things: Recent trends and techniques. *International Journal of Innovative Technology and Exploring Engineering, 8*(9S), 24–28. DOI: 10.35940/ijitee.I1004.0789S19

Sizan, N. S., Dey, D., Layek, M. A., Uddin, M. A., & Huh, E. N. (2025). Evaluating blockchain platforms for iot applications in industry 5.0: A comprehensive review. *Blockchain: Research and Applications, 100276*(3), 100276. Advance online publication. DOI: 10.1016/j.bcra.2025.100276

Trivedi, A., Juyal, S. A., & Nautiyal, A. (2024). Ethical Implications And Workforce Adaptation In The Era Of Generative AI: A Deep Dive Into HRM Practices. *Migration Letters : An International Journal of Migration Studies, 21*(S3), 1754–1762. https://migrationletters.com/index.php/ml/article/view/9565

Yang, T., Yi, X., Lu, S., Johansson, K. H., & Chai, T. (2021). Intelligent manufacturing for the process industry driven by industrial artificial intelligence. *Engineering (Beijing), 7*(9), 1224–1230. DOI: 10.1016/j.eng.2021.04.023

Zhong, R. Y., Xu, X., Klotz, E., & Newman, S. T. (2017). Intelligent manufacturing in the context of industry 4.0: A review. *Engineering (Beijing), 3*(5), 616–630. DOI: 10.1016/J.ENG.2017.05.015

KEY TERMS AND DEFINITIONS

Artificial Intelligence: The capability of a computer to think, learn, and make decisions in a manner similar to that of humans, such as identifying patterns, comprehending language and performing complicated tasks in business.

Big Data: is the vast amount of rapidly changing, diverse data created every day, which traditional data systems are unable to process. This data can be translated into meaningful and actionable information through the use of analytics tools.

Blockchain: is a decentralized, shared digital ledger. Each transaction is connected to the one that came before it, which makes it very hard to change which helps ensure transparency and trust on all involved parties.

Industry 4.0: is the 4th industrial revolution that combines the automation technologies, Internet of Things (IoT), Artificial Intelligence (AI) and data analytics to make production systems smarter and more connected.

Industrial AI: refers to the application of AI and robotics in solving real-world industrial challenges, like predictive maintenance, quality control, etc.

Internet of Things (IoT): Devices on the Internet or other networks that share information, including sensor enabled devices. The Internet of Things allows people to monitor, control, and manage in real-time in the industrial, urban, healthcare and consumer sectors.

Predictive Maintenance: It is condition monitoring that leverages real-time data from sensors and AI to identify equipment issues before they result in failure. It can track the temperature, vibration, etc., and can alert for repairs when they are needed, which helps to minimize costs and keep things running.

Technological Convergence: It is the process of multiple technologies coming together in a unified system. In the context of this article, AI, big data, IoT, and blockchain are all harnessed together to achieve something that none of these technologies could achieve on its own.

Trust Management: It is a security system that tracks the activity of devices in networks, rates them and alerts to suspicious activity to maintain security and reliability of connected systems.

Chapter 2

Bridging Innovation and the Triple Dimensions of Sustainability:

Sustainable Entrepreneurship From the Indian Perspective

P. C. Libeesh
http://orcid.org/0009-0006-0369-5460
NSB World Business School, India

M. Ashok Kumar
Dr. N.G.P. Arts and Science College, Coimbatore, India

ABSTRACT

The 21st centurys economic social and environmental problems can be solved through the revolutionary approach of sustainable entrepreneurship. In the Indian context promoting sustainable development requires entrepreneurial innovation that strikes a balance between social justice environmental responsibility and profitability. This chapter looks at how Indian business owners use green and social enterprises—backed by programs like Startup India and Atmanirbhar Bharat—to incorporate sustainability into their business plans. It also looks at enabling and limiting factors such as social awareness technological advancement financial accessibility and regulatory frameworks. The results highlight innovation as a major force behind resource efficiency responsible production and equitable growth. They also provide theoretical understanding and useful policy suggestions to support Indias path toward sustainable development.

DOI: 10.4018/979-8-3373-7391-1.ch002

1. INTRODUCTION

Increased awareness of climate change resource scarcity social inequality biodiversity loss and economic volatility have all contributed to the global shift toward sustainable development over the past ten years(Ghimire et al., 2025). The intersection of sustainability and entrepreneurship has emerged as a transformative pathway for inclusive equitable and environmentally responsible growth as countries commit to the Sustainable Development Goals (SDGs) of the United Nations. According to Cohen and Winn (2007) and Shepherd & Patzelt (2011) sustainable entrepreneurship is becoming more widely acknowledged as a key factor in long-term value creation that incorporates social well-being economic development and environmental stewardship. Sustainable entrepreneurship links business operations with social advancement and ecological integrity in contrast to traditional entrepreneurship which frequently prioritizes profit maximization(de Melo & Soares, 2025).

Because of Indias distinct socioeconomic environment sustainable entrepreneurship has become especially important there. India has the largest youth population the fifth-largest economy in the world (World Bank 2023) and one of the fastest-growing startup ecosystems(Sharma et al., 2025). However, it also has to deal with some of the most urgent sustainability issues in the world including waste management crises income inequality water scarcity air pollution and climate vulnerability. With more than 1. 4 billion people and significant differences between rural and urban areas there has never been a greater need for creative and sustainable solutions(Aboflan et al., 2025).

Innovation is essential to connecting sustainability and entrepreneurship. Innovation enables business owners to create models that are consistent with Elkingtons (1997) Triple Bottom Line (TBL) framework: People (social) Planet (environmental) and Profit (economic)(Suryani et al., 2025). This can be achieved through green technologies frugal innovations or social innovations targeted at enhancing community welfare. National initiatives like Startup India Digital India Make in India and the National Action Plan on Climate Change (NAPCC) have all supported innovation-driven sustainable entrepreneurship in India. This chapter looks at how India is combining innovation and sustainability to create a new generation of environmentally conscious socially conscious and financially successful entrepreneurs. It maps theoretical underpinnings examines the Indian environment offers case studies draws attention to sectoral opportunities and suggests a conceptual framework for further study and application.

1.1. Conceptual Background and Theoretical Foundations

According to (Schaltegger & Wagner, 2011) sustainable entrepreneurship is the process of identifying developing and utilizing opportunities to create future products and services while also promoting sustainable development(Tenedero et al., 2025). Through entrepreneurial processes it integrates the creation of economic social and environmental value frequently resolving market failures associated with social inequality and environmental degradation(Kademani et al., 2024).

Different from conventional business model's sustainable entrepreneurship is defined by a unique set of values and practices. Fundamentally it supports long-term orientation in which business owners prioritize long-term value creation over immediate profits to make sure their endeavours continue to be viable and significant for future generations(Kar et al., 2025). A strong focus on resource efficiency underpins this strategy encouraging the best possible use of financial human and natural resources while reducing waste and environmental damage(Farhoud, 2025). Additionally, stakeholder-inclusive value creation is a top priority for sustainable entrepreneurs who make sure that business operations benefit workers communities' clients' suppliers and the environment as a whole(Tombak et al., 2025). Furthermore, all of their operations are guided by ethical decision-making which promotes accountability transparency and responsible behaviour. Finally, their mission is anchored by a strong commitment to the United Nations Sustainable Development Goals (SDGs) which links entrepreneurial endeavours with global priorities like poverty alleviation climate action equality and sustainable economic growth. When combined these traits create a comprehensive basis for business endeavours that promote constructive social economic and environmental change(Supriaddin & Ayu Ningtyas, n.d.).

According to academic's sustainable entrepreneurs spot opportunities that traditional businesses miss especially in fields like waste management healthcare education renewable energy and sustainable agriculture (Dean & McMullen, 2007).

1.2. Triple Bottom Line (TBL): A Framework for Sustainability.

Elkington's (1997) Triple Bottom Line framework emphasizes that organizational success should be assessed on three dimensions that is Economic sustainability, social sustainability, and Environmental sustainability(Rosliani et al., 2025). A balancing act is required for sustainable entrepreneurship to ensure that none of the pillars are compromised. The three pillars are given in *Figure No 1.*

In entrepreneurship the term economic sustainability refers to creating a company that will continue to be profitable and competitive in the long run(Srivani & Prakash, 2024). Its foundation is profitability which guarantees that the business continuously produces enough profits to fund operations and expansion(Anant, 2025). Strong market competitiveness complements this as the company provides distinctive value and adjusts to shifting market conditions(Surbakti et al., 2025). By lowering operating costs and increasing productivity through the best possible use of capital materials and human resources efficient resource utilization enhances economic sustainability(Parrales-Reyes et al., 2025). Lastly innovation-driven growth makes it possible for the company to expand diversify and improve continuously which helps it remain resilient and relevant in changing economic conditions(Budaya et al., 2024). These components work together to provide a strong economic basis for long-term business success(Ismail et al., 2025).

The goal of social sustainability in entrepreneurship is to produce favourable and fair results for those associated with the company. Ensuring safe working conditions fair wages and respect for workers' rights are all part of fair labour practices(Prakash et al., 2023). Additionally sustainable business owners make investments in community development to support local livelihoods and social infrastructure(Sanchis et al., 2025). This strategy places a strong emphasis on promoting equity and well-being since companies want to improve the lives of all stakeholders and lessen inequality. Furthermore, a strong focus on education and empowerment facilitates the development of skills expands opportunities and allows people and communities to actively engage in social and economic advancement(Patrucco et al., 2026). When combined these components guarantee that entrepreneurial endeavours promote development that is people-cantered ethical and inclusive.

The goal of environmental sustainability in entrepreneurship is to reduce the adverse effects that commercial operations have on the environment(Kaetsu et al., 2024). It places a strong emphasis on reducing ecological footprints by cutting emissions conserving water and making responsible use of resources all the way through the value chain. In order to prevent pollution, it is crucial to manage waste responsibly by recycling reusing materials and implementing circular economy practices(Ammar et al., 2024). Additionally sustainable business owners strive to protect biodiversity by making sure that their operations do not negatively impact wildlife ecosystems or natural habitats(Parihar et al., 2025). Furthermore, integrating renewable energy sources—like solar wind or bioenergy—helps lessen reliance on fossil fuels and promotes long-term environmental resilience. When combined these strategies guarantee that corporate expansion takes place in balance with the natural equilibrium of the earth(Said Al-Jahwari et al., n.d.).

Figure 1. Triple Bottom Line

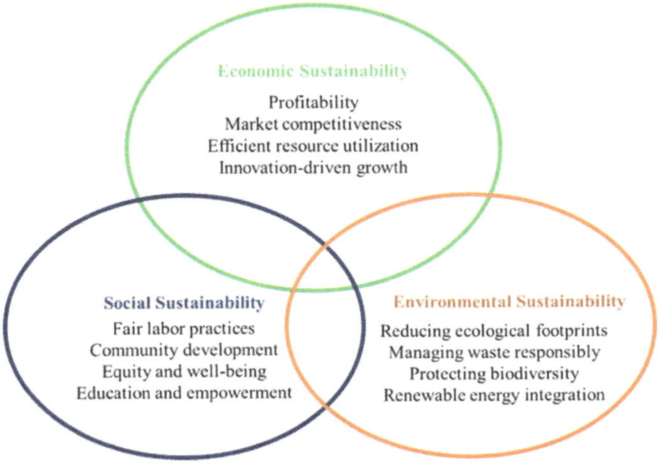

1.3. Key drivers of Sustainable entrepreneurship in India

In India a mix of encouraging legislative frameworks financial incentives technological developments and changing social norms are propelling sustainable entrepreneurship (Juliansyah et al., 2025). Environmentally conscious businesses have been encouraged by government initiatives at the policy level. Green startups can scale effectively thanks to initiatives like Startup India (2016) which offers tax exemptions funding support and incubation facilities(Adebayo, 2025). The Faster Adoption and Manufacturing of Electric Vehicles (FAME) program has expedited the shift to clean mobility while the National Action Plan on Climate Change (NAPCC 2008) has promoted sustainability through initiatives cantered on solar power energy efficiency and water conservation(Prasnowo et al., 2025). The National Green Hydrogen Mission (2023) which aims to promote low-carbon energy solutions and the Smart Cities Mission which prioritizes sustainable urban development complement these initiatives. Furthermore, the Companies Act of 2013s mandatory Corporate Social Responsibility (CSR) provisions have prompted businesses to invest in socially conscious and sustainable business endeavours(Muhammad Rezky et al., 2025).

Economic factors in particular the quick rise in Environmental Social and Governance (ESG) investments and the development of green finance products like green bonds further support this momentum(Ramos-Ruiz et al., 2025). In order to comply with international supply-chain requirements Indian entrepreneurs are increasingly aligning their business models with global sustainability standards particularly in export-oriented sectors(Zeqing et al., n.d.). Technological developments also play a crucial role in facilitating the adoption of new technologies such as artificial intelligence (AI) and the Internet of Things (IoT) thanks to Indias strong digital infrastructure(Jeyarajasekar et al., n.d.). These technologies have enabled startups to create scalable solutions that tackle social and environmental issues particularly in the fields of Agri Tech HealthTech and Clean Tech(Farukh et al., n.d.). This ecosystem is completed by social drivers as a growing number of environmentally conscious consumers and young people who are drawn to businesses with a purpose generate significant demand for sustainable goods and services(Haldar, 2019). Additionally, the foundation of sustainable entrepreneurship in India has been strengthened by entrepreneurs incorporating social equity into their sustainability strategies in response to growing demands for inclusive and accessible solutions(Amutha et al., n.d.).

1.4. Innovation As the Bridge Between Sustainability and Entrepreneurship

According to the Triple Bottom Line (TBL) framework innovation serves as the primary means by which sustainable entrepreneurship combines social justice environmental preservation and economic viability(Dhewa et al., 2025). As evidenced by startups like Selco Solar which uses decentralized solar technologies and flexible financing models to give low-income households access to clean energy entrepreneurs in the Indian context have been able to increase the affordability of sustainable solutions directly contributing to SDG 7 (Affordable and Clean Energy). By increasing production efficiency and incorporating renewable energy innovation also plays a critical role in lowering energy intensity. National initiatives like the Perform Achieve and Trade (PAT) program and the National Action Plan on Climate Change (NAPCC) support these efforts(Anggraini & Hermawan, 2025).

Innovative business models like Phool (Help Us Green) which transforms temple flower waste into biodegradable products and biomaterials in line with SDG 12 (Responsible Consumption and Production) and Indias Circular Economy strategy supported by NITI Aayog have strengthened resource circularity(Sajib et al., 2025). Additionally, thanks to Indias expanding digital infrastructure and programs like Startup India and Digital India digital and platform-based innovations have increased market access by allowing sustainable businesses to reach underserved and rural populations(Bahuriddin et al., 2025). As demonstrated by social enterprises like Jaipur Rugs which integrate rural artisans into global value chains while guaranteeing fair wages and social empowerment innovation has also made it possible for inclusion and social upliftment. This helps achieve SDGs 8 (Decent Work and Economic Growth) and 10 (Reduced Inequalities). When taken as a whole these examples show how innovation in India connects sustainability and entrepreneurship converting global sustainability goals and policy objectives into scalable significant business solutions(Sudario, n.d.).

One of the unique strengths of the Indian entrepreneurial ecosystem is frugal innovation which is defined by the capacity to provide high-value solutions with few resources while meeting the needs of underserved and cost-sensitive populations(Andjelković et al., 2025). Frugal innovation which is based on the idea of doing more with less has arisen in India as a result of structural limitations like poor infrastructure low purchasing power and a variety of socioeconomic circumstances that force business owners to create scalable context-specific and reasonably priced solutions(Wadghane et al., 2025). Frugal innovation has been successfully implemented by Indian businesses in a variety of industries including healthcare energy transportation and education.

Low-cost medical devices reasonably priced diagnostic technologies and decentralized renewable energy solutions that drastically cut costs without sacrificing quality or functionality are notable examples(Kawimbe, 2025). By reducing the amount of materials energy and waste produced this strategy promotes environmental sustainability while also improving accessibility and inclusivity. By facilitating resource efficiency extending product lifecycles and encouraging circular economy practices frugal innovation is closely related to sustainable entrepreneurship(Belgaroui, 2025). Additionally, it gives Indian businesses a competitive edge in local and international markets especially in developing nations with comparable limitations. With the help of policy initiatives like Startup India Atal Innovation Mission and Make in India frugal innovation has developed into a strategic avenue for Indian entrepreneurs to convert regional problems into globally applicable sustainable solutions strengthening Indias standing as a leader in inclusive and sustainability-focused innovation(Gallardo-Vázquez, 2025).

2. REVIEW OF LITERATURE

(Maheshwari & Schrage, 2025) The intersection of social entrepreneurship and sustainability was the subject of this study's thorough systematic review and bibliometric analysis of 442 academic publications published between 2001 and 2023. (Atta & Ali, 2024) The study looked at how social entrepreneurship and sustainability are related highlighting how social business operations act as a mediator. (Aguzman et al., 2024) In terms of the advantages for the environment community and economy this study seeks to explore the important role that social entrepreneurial orientation plays in promoting rural tourism sustainability (also known as the triple bottom line). (Sarlin Venotha & Alex, n.d.) This study examines social and personal factors to determine how sustainable women entrepreneurs are. (Zaza Agustiana

& Pratama, 2025) By conducting a thorough literature review this study examines how cooperative principles contribute to economic sustainability in the digital age.

(Mat et al., 2026) The main objective of this study was to determine the key elements affecting the financial viability of sheep businesses in Turkey. (Thalut & Ghani, 2025) Using panel data from 2010 to 2020 this study examines how economic cooperation affects environmental sustainability in the Organization of Islamic Cooperation (OIC) region. (Margaret Eloyi Atsukwei et al., 2025) This study examines how Nigerian oil and gas companies listed on the Nigerian Exchange Groups economic value added is affected by sustainability reporting. (Grolleau et al., 2025) Using survey data from a large sample of small and medium-sized businesses (SMEs) in Europe we investigate how entrepreneurship experience affects new businesses environmental and social sustainability (ESS). (Kalra et al., 2025) The scope of social entrepreneurship is explored in this research paper by looking at the different strategies employed by social entrepreneurs to build long-lasting businesses. Additionally, the study looks at how social entrepreneurship can be sustained paying particular attention to how these initiatives balance making money with doing good for society.

(Mauraise et al., 2024) This research investigates how green entrepreneurship can improve the sustainability of startups in Nigeria with an emphasis on environmental reporting and disclosure as well as investments in environmentally friendly technologies. (Tekala et al., 2024) Using Green Theory this study investigates how green entrepreneurship (GEN) affects business sustainability (BS) by the moderating effect of environmental dynamism (ED) and the mediating role of green structural capital (GSC). 443 owners and managers of small and medium-sized businesses (SMEs) were studied quantitatively (e. g. 3. Businesses engaged in manufacturing building materials wholesale and retail trade and scientific professional and technical activities) in Istanbul and Izmir Turkey were polled using both electronic and on-site questionnaires. (Alayed et al., 2025) The impact of technological proficiency social sustainability and economic sustainability on organizational values—which in turn impact the financial performance of Saudi manufacturing companies—is examined in this research paper.

2.1. Conceptual Frame work

An increasingly popular strategy for concurrently addressing environmental preservation social inclusion and economic growth is sustainable entrepreneurship. Innovation is a vital facilitator of sustainability-oriented business practices in emerging economies like India where entrepreneurs operate in environments marked by resource limitations social inequalities and environmental challenges. Based on the triple bottom line viewpoint this study offers a conceptual framework that links sustainable entrepreneurship to the economic social and environmental facets of sustainability through innovation. The framework emphasizes how social process and technological innovations help entrepreneurs achieve long-term financial viability social well-being and environmental responsibility all of which support sustainable and comprehensive entrepreneurial outcomes. Conceptual model of the study is given in *Figure 2.*

Figure 2. Conceptual Model

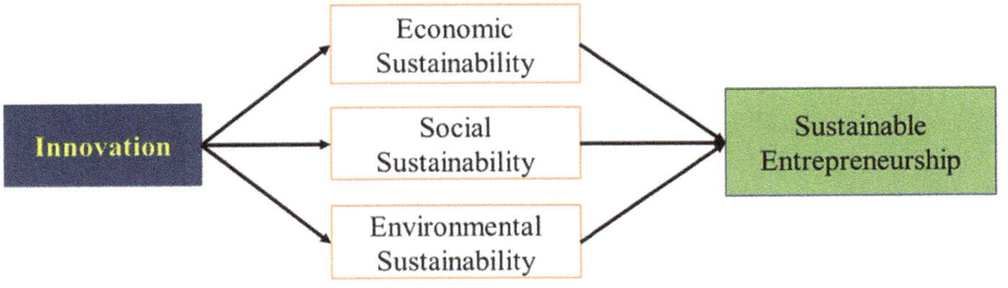

2.1.1. Innovation as the Central Driver

Technology process and social innovation are all included in the multifaceted phenomenon of innovation which forms the frameworks foundational construct. By coordinating business operations with sustainability goals innovation promotes sustainable entrepreneurship. Using digital and green technologies to increase productivity lower resource consumption and improve product quality is known as technological innovation. In India this is demonstrated by developments in agritech fintech for financial inclusion and renewable energy. Process innovation is the term used to describe advancements in supply chain procedures production methods and operational strategies that support long-term viability reduce costs and increase efficiency through strategies like lean production and circular economy practices. By encouraging inclusive business models that incorporate underserved communities into value creation social innovation tackles societal issues like unemployment inequality and restricted access to basic services. When taken as a whole these innovation types serve as strategic facilitators that let business owners accomplish social impact environmental responsibility and economic performance all at once.

2.1.2. Innovation and Economic Sustainability

The ability of a company to sustain long-term financial performance and competitiveness is known as economic sustainability and innovation is essential to bolstering this aspect by increasing productivity cutting expenses and facilitating market differentiation. Sustainable businesses can boost cost effectiveness through resource optimization achieve profitability by providing value-added solutions and secure long-term growth by entering new markets and gaining a competitive edge through innovative products and processes. Because it allows businesses to stay resilient scalable and financially viable while pursuing sustainable business objectives innovation becomes especially important in the fiercely competitive price-sensitive and resource-constrained Indian entrepreneurial ecosystem.

2.1.3. Innovation and Social Sustainability

By empowering entrepreneurs to create goods services and business models that successfully meet societal demands innovation contributes to the social sustainability dimension which places an emphasis on inclusive development job creation and social well-being. Through organizational and social innovation sustainable entrepreneurs can create jobs for marginalized communities encourage social inclusion by expanding access to reasonably priced goods and services and support community development through skill-building healthcare and education programs. Innovation-led social sustainability enables entrepreneurship to serve as a potent catalyst for fair growth and more extensive social change in the Indian context where socioeconomic gaps are still very much present.

2.1.4. Innovation and Environmental Sustainability

Innovation is essential to enabling environmentally responsible practices through the adoption of clean technologies and eco-friendly processes and environmental sustainability focuses on reducing the ecological footprint of entrepreneurial activities. Through the optimization of energy water and raw material use innovative approaches assist businesses in increasing resource efficiency reducing waste through circular economy recycling and reuse practices and promoting eco-friendly operations through the adoption of low-emission technologies and renewable energy. Innovation is crucial for attaining environmental sustainability while preserving economic performance and long-term competitiveness for Indian businesses dealing with tightening environmental regulations and resource scarcity.

2.1.5. Sustainability Dimensions and Sustainable Entrepreneurship

The framework posits that economic, social, and environmental sustainability jointly contribute to sustainable entrepreneurship, which is defined as entrepreneurial activity that creates economic value while simultaneously generating positive social and environmental outcomes. Economic sustainability ensures financial viability and resilience, social sustainability strengthens stakeholder trust and societal legitimacy, and environmental sustainability supports long-term ecological balance. The integration of these three dimensions enables entrepreneurs to develop holistic and resilient business models that align with sustainable development goals (SDGs) and promote long-term sustainable impact.

2.1.6. Bridging Role of Innovation

In order to change sustainability from a limitation into a source of opportunity and competitive advantage innovation serves as a bridging mechanism between sustainability principles and entrepreneurial practice according to the framework's central logic. In India inclusive economic growth long-term environmental preservation and national sustainability initiatives are all aided by innovation-driven sustainable entrepreneurship. As a result, the framework views innovation as a strategic catalyst that can effectively integrate the economic social and environmental aspects of sustainability into entrepreneurial outcomes rather than just as a supporting element.

3. ANALYSIS AND DISCUSSION

The number of DPIIT-recognized startups rose from approximately 500 in 2016 to over 159000 by January 2025 creating over 1. 6 million direct jobs and fostering a broad innovation ecosystem that supports economic and social advancement. Additionally patent activity has increased significantly with total patent filings rising from approximately 26800 in 2014 to over 100000 by 2024 indicating a strong upward trend in R and D and technological innovation capacity. Finally, Indias position in the Global Innovation Index improved significantly to 39th among 133 economies in 2024 reflecting enhanced systemic innovation performance that underpins competitiveness technology development and entrepreneurial dynamism across sectors. These developments quantitatively demonstrate how innovation drives sustainable entrepreneurial outcomes in the Indian context.

In India innovation has been shown to contribute to economic sustainability by accelerating job creation GDP contribution and entrepreneurial growth. As of mid-2025 the country's startup ecosystem had grown to over 11. 8 lakh DPIIT-recognized startups and over 17. 6 lakh direct jobs were created including over 14 lakh jobs in the last five years alone. These innovation-led ventures contributed an estimated USD 140 billion to the Indian economy in FY 2023 or nearly 4 percent of GDP underscoring their significant role in the country's economic performance. Additionally ongoing growth in patent filings with patent applications surpassing 110 000 in FY 2024-2 indicating nearly 20 percent year-over-year growth and the dominance of domestic innovators indicates rising R and D and innovation activity that supports productivity and competitive advantage. Taken together these figures show how innovation boosts productivity encourages entrepreneurial employment and contributes measurably to economic sustainability in India.

Innovation plays a significant role in social sustainability in India by fostering the growth of social enterprises and expanding social impact initiatives that tackle important societal issues. For instance, India is home to an estimated 20 lakh social enterprises that use technology and creative business models to solve problems in industries like healthcare (7537 startups) education (5309) agriculture (3887) and green technology (1844). These companies together account for about 23 percent of all social-impact oriented startups tracked by DPIIT data demonstrating a measurable expansion of innovation-led solutions that improve access inclusion and community welfare. Additionally, the country's social security coverage has increased from 19 percent of the population in 2015 to 64. 3% by 2025 indicating strengthened frameworks for inclusive protection that are supported by innovation-enable platforms and policies through digital services labour market integration and scalable outreach to previously underserved groups.

Through cleantech entrepreneurship and tech-enabled resource management innovation is increasingly driving measurable progress toward environmental sustainability in India. For instance, digital waste-management platforms like Recykal have diverted over 1 million tonnes (1×10^6 MT) of waste into recycling streams preventing 12 billion plastic bottles 100000 MT of metal and 90000 MT of paper and e-waste from landfills by 2023 demonstrating significant reductions in environmental burden through technology-enabled circular economy practices. Additionally Indian cleantech startups like Chakr Innovation have filed more than 15 patents for emission-control technologies and received approval from the Central Pollution Control Board for retrofit devices that reduce particulate emissions from diesel generators demonstrating the direct environmental impact of innovation. Finally broader trends in technology adoption such as the rapid growth of electric vehicle (EV) sales reaching approximately 181000 units with a 14 percent annual growth rate in 2025 reflect innovation-led transitions to lower-emission mobility that support national decarbonization efforts and improved air quality.

Measurable results in economic social and environmental domains are increasingly reflecting sustainable entrepreneurship in India indicating that these sustainability pillars work in tandem to promote entrepreneurial success. According to a study on sustainable ventures they have created over 300000 direct and indirect jobs through activities in waste management renewable energy sustainable agriculture and related sectors highlighting the economic and social impact of sustainability-oriented business models India currently has 4750 environment-tech companies with 1190 funded firms raising over USD 13. 1 billion highlighting the scale of innovation tied to environmental sustainability and economic value creation and a 2024 SAP sustainability survey revealed that 86 percent of Indian businesses perceive a positive relationship between sustainability initiatives and profitability with 77 percent reporting that sustainability strategies contributed moderately or strongly to revenue/profit growth and process efficiency. These findings suggest that incorporating sustainability into business strategy improves economic performance while supporting broader social and ecological outcomes.

3.1. Sectoral Land Scape and Opportunities of Sustainable Entrepreneurship in India.

The country's urgent environmental problems socioeconomic priorities and policy-driven sustainability agenda are reflected in the varied and quickly changing sectoral landscape of sustainable entrepreneurship in India. With initiatives like the National Solar Mission and the Green Hydrogen Mission supporting entrepreneurs driving innovation in solar wind bioenergy and green hydrogen technologies the renewable energy sector has emerged as a cornerstone. Agri Tech solutions cantered on precision farming organic inputs water-efficient irrigation and farm-to-market digital platforms that boost farmer incomes while conserving natural resources are driving sustainable entrepreneurship in agriculture and related fields. Another crucial area is the waste management and circular economy sector where startups are creating scalable models for waste segregation recycling composting and upcycling turning industrial and urban waste into useful resources. Electric cars battery recycling and shared mobility platforms—all supported by the FAME program and stricter emission regulations—are driving the rapid expansion of sustainable mobility.

Green entrepreneurship is encouraging low-carbon production systems eco-friendly materials and energy-efficient processes in the manufacturing sector especially among MSMEs aiming to meet international sustainability standards. Additionally entrepreneurial innovations that combine social inclusion with environmental performance are emerging in industries like affordable housing water management healthcare and sustainable construction. When taken as a whole these sectoral developments show how sustainable entrepreneurship in India encompasses a variety of industries and uses market demand policy support and innovation to build robust business models that promote social well-being economic growth and environmental preservation.

3.1.1. Renewable energy entrepreneurship

Since India is the world's third-largest producer of renewable energy and has set an ambitious goal of reaching 500 GW of non-fossil fuel capacity by 2030 renewable energy entrepreneurship has become an essential part of the country's sustainable development trajectory (IEA 2023). By converting policy goals into market-driven solutions sustainable entrepreneurs are essential to bolstering Indias solar wind and emerging green hydrogen ecosystems. Solar microgrids that facilitate rural electrification solar-powered agricultural pumps that lessen farmers reliance on diesel while reducing carbon emissions and solar rooftop installations for urban and semi-urban households have all emerged as significant opportunity areas. Alongside advancements in energy storage and battery technologies that tackle intermittency issues entrepreneurs are also creating reasonably priced home solar solutions for consumers with low and middle incomes. In line with Indias long-term decarbonization objectives green hydrogen production and supply-chain development are also creating new opportunities for clean energy entrepreneurship.

Declining solar photovoltaic costs government subsidies and incentives from the Ministry of New and Renewable Energy (MNRE) growing ESG-focused investments and growing worries about energy security and reliance on fossil fuels are the main factors driving the expansion of renewable energy businesses. Nonetheless entrepreneurs still have to deal with issues like large-scale project land acquisition constraints high upfront capital requirements and technical issues with grid integration and storage. Despite these obstacles a number of Indian startups - such as *ZunRoof* which uses AI-powered analytics to encourage rooftop solar adoption *Oorjan* which combines solar installation with creative financing models and *ReNew* Power a pioneer in large-scale wind and solar energy generation have emerged as significant players in the renewable energy space. All of these developments highlight how crucial renewable energy entrepreneurship is to furthering Indias transition to clean energy and sustainability.

3.1.2. Agri Tech and Agriculture Entrepreneurship.

With an estimated 18% of the country's GDP coming from agriculture the industry is still a crucial pillar of the Indian economy. However it still faces numerous obstacles including low productivity inefficient water use fragmented landholdings and growing climate change vulnerability. In response sustainable entrepreneurs are using innovation to change conventional agricultural methods in order to produce social and environmental value. The use of IoT devices drones and data analytics to maximize input utilization and boost crop yields as well as soil health monitoring systems that facilitate intelligent nutrient management have created significant opportunity areas in precision farming. Acute water scarcity is being addressed by water-efficient solutions like drip and micro-irrigation technologies while digital farm-to-consumer supply chains are lowering middlemen enhancing farmer price realization and reducing post-harvest losses. Additionally, entrepreneurs are creating ways to lessen food waste throughout the agricultural value chain and promoting organic and regenerative agriculture models. Improved rural connectivity under the Digital India initiative growing domestic and export markets for organic produce and specific government programs like PM-KUSUM for solar-powered agriculture and Pradhan Mantri Fasal Bima Yojana (PMFBY) for crop risk mitigation all contribute to the growth of Agri Tech entrepreneurship. However, issues like low digital literacy in rural areas highly dispersed landholdings that make technology deployment difficult and the sluggish adoption of new farming technologies because of perceptions of risk and cost still exist. Despite these limitations a number of AgriTech startups have become industry leaders such as *DeHaat* which provides an end-to-end farmer support platform *Ninjacart* which simplifies farm-to-retail supply chains *AgroStar* which offers farmers mobile-based advisory services and *Stellapps* which offers IoT-enabled solutions for the dairy ecosystem. When taken as a whole these businesses show how sustainable AgriTech entrepreneurship is transforming Indian agriculture through increased inclusivity resilience and productivity.

3.1.3. Waste Management and Circular Economy

India produces about 62 million tonnes of municipal solid waste a year by 2030 that amount is expected to increase to almost 165 million tonnes posing both a serious environmental problem and a significant opportunity for entrepreneurship driven by the circular economy (MoEFCC 2022). In order to lessen reliance on landfills and increase resource efficiency sustainable entrepreneurs are increasingly creating creative solutions that convert waste into useful resources. E-waste collection and processing which deals with the increasing amounts of discarded electronic devices composting and biofuel conversion programs which turn organic waste into energy and soil enhancers and plastic recycling and upcycling where sophisticated sorting and processing technologies are used to reintroduce recycled plastics into manufacturing supply chains are important opportunity areas.

Additionally, entrepreneurs are innovating in construction and demolition waste management through material recovery and reuse as well as in the repurposing of textile waste by producing sustainable fashion items and recycled textiles. Policies like the *Swachh Bharat Mission* which prioritizes scientific waste management and *Extended Producer Responsibility (EPR)* regulations which hold manufacturers responsible for post-consumer waste are major forces behind the growth of waste management entrepreneurship. Additionally, the market demand for circular solutions has increased due to consumers growing preference for recyclable and sustainable packaging.

However, problems still exist because of disjointed waste supply chains a lack of formal mechanisms for collection and segregation and a significant reliance on the unorganized sector. Despite these obstacles a number of Indian startups have become leaders in the circular economy space such as Banyan Nation which recycles high-quality plastic using AI-powered technologies *Saahas Zero Waste* which offers corporations and institutions end-to-end waste management solutions and *Attero* a pioneer in resource recovery and large-scale e-waste recycling. When taken as a whole these initiatives show how sustainable entrepreneurship is helping to solve Indias waste problem and promote the ideas of the circular economy.

3.1.4. Sustainable Mobility and Electric Vehicles

Since the transportation sector in India contributes almost 13% of all CO2 emissions it is a major area of focus for climate action and sustainable entrepreneurship. With electric two- and three-wheelers battery-swapping systems charging infrastructure fleet electrification and green logistics solutions catered to Indias mobility requirements EV-based businesses are growing quickly. Innovative approaches to sustainable mobility are becoming a vital means of cutting emissions and urban air pollution helped along by FAME-II subsidies more stringent pollution laws and corporate carbon-reduction pledges.

However, there are still issues especially with regard to the cost of batteries the lack of domestic production of cutting-edge battery technologies and deficiencies in the infrastructure for charging particularly outside of large cities. Despite these limitations a number of Indian startups—such as *Ather Energy* which is well-known for its cutting-edge electric scooters *Ola Electric* which is expanding mass-market EV production and *Yulu* which concentrates on electric micro-mobility solutions for short-distance urban travel—have emerged as leaders in the EV ecosystem. When taken as a whole these businesses demonstrate how sustainable mobility entrepreneurship is revolutionizing Indias low-carbon transportation future.

3.1.5. Green Building and Sustainable Construction

In addition to being a significant source of waste carbon emissions and resource consumption the construction industry in India accounts for almost 8% of the countrys GDP offering significant opportunities for sustainable construction entrepreneurship.

Green innovations include energy-efficient and net-zero building designs advanced cooling systems that are appropriate for Indias climate the retrofitting of existing buildings with efficient technologies and environmentally friendly materials like fly ash bricks and bamboo composites. These initiatives which are bolstered by frameworks like IGBC and GRIHA as well as the growing need for sustainable infrastructure demonstrate the expanding role of innovation in advancing ecologically conscious building.

3.1.6. Water and sanitation Innovation

Since almost 600 million Indians lack access to clean water (NITI Aayog 2022) sustainable water and sanitation entrepreneurship is essential for both economic stability and public health. As demonstrated by projects like Sarvajals rural water ATMs and Tata Swachs inexpensive purifiers entrepreneurs are tackling these issues by utilizing smart water management systems rainwater harvesting and recycling technologies in addition to reasonably priced water filters. When combined water-focused innovation and green building models show how Indian sustainable businesses can improve resource efficiency fill in infrastructure gaps and have a positive social and environmental impact.

3.1.7. Social Enterprises and inclusive Innovation

With a thriving network of businesses that place equal emphasis on social impact and financial sustainability India is widely acknowledged as a global leader in social entrepreneurship(Ghosh & Hamid, 2025). In India social enterprises help marginalized and underprivileged groups by providing inclusive and reasonably priced solutions to pressing development issues. Affordable healthcare where cutting-edge delivery strategies and economical technologies increase access to high-quality medical care low-cost educational solutions that use digital platforms and community-based models to enhance learning outcomes and access to financial services through FinTech innovations that support financial inclusion for unbanked and underbanked populations are important areas of opportunity.

A crucial component of inclusive innovation is women-led entrepreneurship which empowers women as change agents and beneficiaries while advancing socio-economic advancement. Indian social entrepreneurs like Akshaya Patra (a massive school meal program) Aravind Eye Care (affordable high-volume healthcare) and SELCO Solar (decentralized clean energy) show how inclusive innovation produces scalable solutions that promote social justice economic empowerment and sustainable development.

3.2. Growth of Sustainable Entrepreneurship in India

With annual growth rates surpassing 50% since 2017 Indias sustainable and eco-driven entrepreneurial ecosystem has grown significantly in recent years due to growing awareness of environmental issues supportive policy frameworks like Startup India and SDG-aligned initiatives and more funding options for climate-focused businesses. With over 6600 cleantech and sustainability startups operating in about 450 districts across nearly 34 states and union territories this dynamic landscape reflects growing sector diversity and geographic dispersion. Over 300000 direct and indirect jobs have been created by these sustainable businesses thus far in sectors like waste management renewable energy and sustainable agriculture. As the shift picks up speed estimates indicate that the green economy could generate up to 500000 jobs by 2025 and over 3 million by 2030.

A key component of this change, the renewable energy sector has been especially revolutionary. Indias installed renewable capacity has grown rapidly surpassing 100 GW in recent years and continuing to rise. By late 2024 it will account for nearly 46. 3% of all installed power capacity. The country added a record ~44. 5 GW of new green energy capacity in 2025 alone bringing the total renewable base to over 250 GW and keeping a strong project pipeline of about 135 GW in development. By 2023 Indias renewable workforce supported more than one million jobs in clean energy with the solar wind hydropower bioenergy and biogas sectors all boosting employment.

As of 2025 there are thousands of environments and climate-tech companies in India with over 1190 funded businesses collectively raising over $13 billion. Even in the face of broader venture capital slowdowns annual funding rounds have increased by 40% year over year. These developments highlight how environmentally driven entrepreneurship is emerging as a key force behind Indias ecological and economic transformation supporting job creation technological innovation and sustainable industrial growth while assisting the nation in achieving its net-zero targets.

This article discusses how state-level policies in Karnataka and Maharashtra are actively promoting sustainable entrepreneurship in India.

In order to decentralize innovation capacity, the state cabinet approved Karnataka's Startup Policy 2025–2030 which will invest 518. 27 crores to support and grow 25000 new startups over a five-year period including 10000 ventures outside Bengaluru in cities like Mysuru Mangaluru Hubballi-Dharwad and Kalaburagi. In addition to infrastructure funding incubation mentorship market access international outreach and simplified regulation the policy highlights emerging technologies such as artificial intelligence (AI) blockchain quantum computing clean energy and biotech. The policy offers incentives such as one-time capital grants up to 50 lakh for private incubators PF/ESI reimbursements for startups (3000 per employee/month capped at 12 lakh per company) cloud storage subsidies and global innovation alliance programs that open markets in more than 30 countries in order to promote equitable and sustainable entrepreneurship.

Almost half of all funded startups and a disproportionate number of unicorns are located in Karnataka which already has over 18000 recognized startups and a strong ecosystem that contributes significantly to Indias innovation activity. The new policy aims to spread this dynamism throughout the state rather than just in Bengaluru. In addition to increasing capital inflow and job creation these policies are anticipated to spur innovation in the climate tech and sustainability sectors where up-and-coming businesses frequently need long-term funding mentorship and access to global value chains(Parvin Banu et al., n.d.).

In a similar vein Maharashtra's Startup Entrepreneurship and Innovation Policy 2025 lays out a five-year strategic framework aimed at recognizing up to 50000 new startups throughout the state and developing 1. 3 lakh entrepreneurs solidifying its standing as one of Indias top innovation ecosystems. The Chief Ministers Maha-Fund which has a 500 crore corpus spread over five years is a key element of this strategy. In order to help startups close the crucial early funding gap this fund will provide mentorship incubation and financial support (through loans between 5 lakh and 10 lakh at subsidized interest rates) to 25000 early-stage entrepreneurs selected from a pool of approximately 5 lakh screened candidates.

Instead of concentrating entrepreneurial activity in a few key urban hubs Karnataka and Maharashtra are increasingly creating startup policies that deliberately decentralise innovation. The state intends to support the establishment of 5000 new startups over five years under Karnataka's Startup Policy 2025–2030. Of these 10000 (roughly 40%) are planned outside Bengaluru in regional centres like Mysuru Hubballi-Dharwad Mangaluru and Kalaburagi indicating a deliberate attempt to foster Tier-II and Tier-III innovation clusters outside the capital city. The policy offers capital grants of up to 50 lakh for incubation centers located outside Bengaluru reimbursement of PF and ESI contributions and the creation of Centres of Excellence and R and D hubs in non-metro districts to bolster local research and innovation capacity in order to further this regionalization agenda. When taken as a whole these actions support a more balanced geographical distribution of entrepreneurial activity job creation and ecosystem development in smaller cities and locally grounded problem-solving startups. This aligns regional economic growth with inclusive and sustainable development goals(Poderytė et al., 2025).

Strategic resources are increasingly being allocated by state policies to deep technology and sustainability-oriented innovation fields that usually require high upfront investment extended R and D cycles and sustained early-stage support. In order to improve market readiness Karnataka's Startup Policy 2025–2030 specifically prioritizes Deep-Tech domains like artificial intelligence blockchain quantum computing semiconductor design climate tech and space technology by combining financial support with structured mentorship industry partnerships and measurable commercialization outcomes. In addition to this strategy previous state-led initiatives such as the Elevate program and Beyond Bengaluru cluster funds have already provided seed funding exceeding 224 crore to hundreds of startups with 25 percent participation from women entrepreneurs and nearly 30 percent of beneficiaries originating from Tier-II and Tier-III cities especially in sectors like clean technology smart cities healthcare agri-tech and biotechnology(Alshibani et al., 2024). These policy measures strengthen innovation capacity in advanced and climate-oriented technologies by enabling early-stage deep tech and sustainable ventures to overcome structural constraints like high R&D costs long gestation periods and limited access to risk capital by integrating research infrastructure institutional funding and sustained mentoring support.

The startup strategies of both Maharashtra and Karnataka prioritize inclusive entrepreneurship specifically women-led and regionally dispersed innovation. Maharashtra's strong institutional commitment to gender-inclusive enterprise development is demonstrated by the fact that nearly 45 percent of registered startups are led by women entrepreneurs which is significantly higher than the national average of roughly 7. 5 percent. Through a 500 crore Maha-Fund that offers seed capital subsidized credit incubation support and reimbursements for infrastructure and intellectual property costs the Maharashtra Startup Entrepreneurship and Innovation Policy aims to empower approximately 1. 25 lakh entrepreneurs and nurture 50000 startups over a five-year period. In a similar vein Karnataka's Startup Policy requires state-sponsored incubators to assign preferential seats for women founders under more general startup missions and includes dedicated training mentorship and financial assistance mechanisms for women-owned enterprises rural entrepreneurs and social-impact ventures. When taken as a whole these policy initiatives support equitable access to entrepreneurial opportunities across gender and geography aid in the democratization of innovation and increase participation in industries that have historically been underrepresented in technology-driven entrepreneurship(Kumar et al., 2025).

4. CONCLUSION

The purpose of this study was to investigate how innovation can bridge the economic social and environmental facets of sustainability in the context of sustainable entrepreneurship in India. Using the triple bottom line framework as a guide the study emphasizes innovation as a key factor that empowers business owners to abandon conventional profit-driven models and embrace strategies that create long-term wealth.

Through increased productivity and competitiveness social sustainability through community development and inclusion and environmental sustainability through resource efficiency and eco-friendly practices the analysis shows that technological process and social innovations are essential to advancing economic sustainability.

Innovation is a key driver that turns sustainability from a limitation into an opportunity in the Indian context where entrepreneurs encounter obstacles like resource scarcity socioeconomic inequality and environmental demands. Sustainable entrepreneurship supports national goals like inclusive growth and sustainable development in addition to firm-level resilience by combining economic viability social responsibility and environmental stewardship. In general, the study supports the idea that sustainable entrepreneurship driven by innovation is crucial to attaining resilient and balanced development in developing nations like India.

Even though this study offers conceptual understanding of the relationship among innovation sustainability aspects and sustainable entrepreneurship there are still a number of areas that need further investigation. While comparative research across economies industries or regions can highlight contextual differences in innovation-led sustainability practices empirical studies employing quantitative techniques like Structural Equation Modelling (SEM) can validate the suggested framework. Future research may also look at how Indias institutional frameworks government policies and innovation support systems function. It may also use longitudinal designs to evaluate how innovation and sustainability practices change over time and affect long-term corporate success and societal well-being.

REFERENCE

Aboflan, Y. E., Kpotchou, K., Kabo, K., & Ionut-Petrisor, A. (2025). Territorial entrepreneurship: A driving force for sustainable innovation. *Journal of Ecohumanism*, *4*(4). Advance online publication. DOI: 10.62754/joe.v4i4.7020

Adebayo, A. A. (2025). Efficacy of digital green supply chain management technologies on triple bottom line performance: Moderating role of mandatory external regulatory pressure. *International Journal of Marketing and Management Sciences*, *6*(1).

Aguzman, G., Pratiwi, C. P., Eni, Y., & Sasongko, A. H. (2024). *The influence of social entrepreneurship orientation on the sustainability of tourism villages through community empowerment*. Indonesian Journal of Business and Entrepreneurship., DOI: 10.17358/ijbe.10.3.488

Alayed, S., Alateeg, S., & Albaz, M. M. (2025). Integrating economic and social sustainability with technological competence: The mediating effect of organizational values on economic performance. *Sustainability (Basel)*, *17*(22), 10404. Advance online publication. DOI: 10.3390/su172210404

Alshibani, S. M., Shabir, S., & Albishri, N. (2024). Women entrepreneur's perspective towards sustainable entrepreneurship in the apparel sector of Saudi Arabia. *Sustainability (Basel)*, *16*(19), 8636. Advance online publication. DOI: 10.3390/su16198636

Ammar, M., Bangsawan, G., & Asriani, A. (2024). Designing the concept of regional innovation sustainability: The triple bottom line concept approach and sustainable evaluation. *Jurnal Bina Praja*, *16*(3), 523–539. DOI: 10.21787/jbp.16.2024.523-539

Amutha, T., Vimala, V., Hemavathy, R., Sathiya, R. D., & Professor, A. (n.d.). The role of women in sustainable entrepreneurship: Addressing challenges and identifying prospects. Library Progress International, 44(3). Retrieved from www.bpasjournals.com

Anant, B. C. (2025). Factors affecting growth and success of green and sustainable entrepreneurship: An empirical study of Indian startups. Journal of Informatics Education and Research, 5. http://jier.org

Andjelković, A., Janković Milić, V., Radosavljević, M., Petković, S., Kule, D., & Debarliev, S. (2025). Sustainable entrepreneurship in the Western Balkan countries: Key constraints. *Sustainability (Basel)*, *17*(21), 9406. Advance online publication. DOI: 10.3390/su17219406

Anggraini, G., & Hermawan, A. (2025). Sustainability awareness in Indonesia's oil and gas sector. *JRAK*, *17*(2), 332–347. DOI: 10.23969/jrak.v17i2.26356

Atsukwei, M. E., Ande, J., & Jim-Suleiman, S. (2025). Effect of Corporate Sustainability Reporting on Economic Value Added of Oil and Gas Companies in Nigeria. Journal of Human Resources and Management Science.

Atta, A., & Ali, L. (2024). Linking social entrepreneurship with sustainability: Mediating role of social business operations. 3, 32–55. https://doi.org/DOI: 10.33282/rr.vx9i4.3

Bahuriddin, N. S., Saman, M. Z. M., Mohamad-Ali, N., Ngadiman, N. H. A., & Maulana, M. I. I. M. (2025). State of sustainability assessments of metal additive manufacturing: Literature review and triple-bottom-line perspectives. *Environmental Science and Pollution Research International*, *32*(35), 20825–20843. DOI: 10.1007/s11356-025-36889-0 PMID: 40866783

Belgaroui, R. (2025). Advancing sustainable entrepreneurship through digital innovation: A systematic review. *Asian Journal of Education and Social Studies*, *51*(12), 229–246. DOI: 10.9734/ajess/2025/v51i122689

Budaya, P., Dan, O., Stakeholder, T., Kemampuan, T., Artisan, B., Madura, E., Ma'arif, T., Hasanah, U., Putu, N., Arnani, R., & Madura, U. T. (2024). The influence of organizational culture and stakeholder pressure on the ability to innovate artisan entrepreneurship Madura. Management Studies and Entrepreneurship Journal, 5(2). https://journal.yrpipku.com/index.php/msej

de Melo, F. L. N. B., & Soares, A. M. J. (2025). Ecofarming: A gamified simulation for teaching sustainable entrepreneurship in Brazilian biomes. Revista de Administração Contemporânea, 29(1). https://doi.org/DOI: 10.1590/1982-7849rac2025240218.en

Dean, T. J., & McMullen, J. S. (2007). Toward a theory of sustainable entrepreneurship: Reducing environmental degradation through entrepreneurial action. *Journal of Business Venturing*, *22*(1), 50–76. DOI: 10.1016/j.jbusvent.2005.09.003

Dhewa, C., Makurumidze, S., & Mukapiku, K. P. (2025). Spearheading sustainable youth entrepreneurship through financial literacy training - A case of one TVET institution in Zimbabwe. *African Journal of Pedagogy and Curriculum*, *7*(1), 95–110. DOI: 10.63569/ajopac/07/01/07

Farhoud, M. (2025). Institutional voids and entrepreneurial generational dynamics in Tunisian corporate sustainability: Multi-method SEM test and comparative analysis (France-Germany-Morocco-UAE), MENA perspective. Arabian Journal of Business and Management Review, 14(4), 125–137. www.j.arabianjbmr.com

Farukh, M. U., Khan, A., & Kumar, A. (n.d.). Entrepreneurship and the environment: A critical examination of the sustainability of entrepreneurship activity. International Journal of Environmental Sciences, 11(24). Retrieved from https://www.theaspd.com/ijes.php

Gallardo-Vázquez, D. (2025). Defining the path to sustainability based on triple bottom line dimensions. *Corporate Social Responsibility and Environmental Management*, *32*(4), 4743–4768. DOI: 10.1002/csr.3216

Ghimire, B., & Dhakal, S. C. Santosh, & Bastakoti, R. C. (2025). Assessing production risks and value chain sustainability in Nepal's lentil (Lens culinaris Medik.) sector: An evidence-based econometric analysis. DOI: 10.21203/rs.3.rs-7043104/v1

Ghosh, D., & Hamid, M. A. (2025). Environment-friendly practices in entrepreneurship for sustainable development: Insights from a qualitative study. *BJBE*, *6*(1), 259–274. DOI: 10.58481/BJBE/2515

Grolleau, G., Mzoughi, N., & Pekovic, S. (2025). Entrepreneurship experience and environmental and social sustainability in new companies. *Business Strategy and the Environment*, *34*(8), 9863–9877. DOI: 10.1002/bse.70109

Haldar, S. (2019). Green entrepreneurship in theory and practice: Insights from India. *International Journal of Green Economics*, *13*(2), 99. DOI: 10.1504/IJGE.2019.103232

Ismail, A., Mohd Nazari, N., & Mohamed Zakaria, H. (2025). Embedding sustainability in cultural events: Insights from the Penang George Town Festival. Journal of Event. *Tourism and Hospitality Studies*, *5*, 94–104. DOI: 10.32890/jeth2025.5.6

Jeyarajasekar, D., Chandran, B. S., & Santhosh, D. S. (n.d.). Sustainability in hospitals: Identifying boosting elements through the triple bottom line framework. International Journal of Environmental Sciences, 11(23). Retrieved from https://theaspd.com/index.php

Juliansyah, E., Agoes, S., & Ahmar, N. (2025, July 19). Development of the pentuple bottom line model in moderating the influence of financial literacy and financial inclusion on the sustainability of MSMEs in West Java. *Global Interdisciplinary Journal of Economics and Administrative Sciences*, *3*(2), 304–315. Advance online publication. DOI: 10.38035/gijea.v3i2.468

Kademani, S., Nain, M. S., Singh, R., Kumar, S., Parsad, R., Sharma, D. K., Roy, S. K., Karjigi, K. D., Prabhakar, I., Mahapatra, A., & Patil, M. (2024). Unveiling challenges and strategizing solutions for sustainable agri-entrepreneurship development. *Frontiers in Sustainable Food Systems*, *8*, 1447371. Advance online publication. DOI: 10.3389/fsufs.2024.1447371

Kaetsu, P. T., Kumasaka, J. M., & Casado, T. (2024). Bioeconomy in Amazonia: Tensions and synergies of corporate sustainability. Revista de Administração Contemporânea, 28(5). https://doi.org/DOI: 10.1590/1982-7849rac2024240072.en

Kalra, D., Dadwal, S., & Arya, P. (2025). Exploring social entrepreneurship: Models, impact, and sustainability. *International Journal of Advanced Research*, *13*(7), 63–69. DOI: 10.21474/IJAR01/21309

Kar, B., Khandai, S., & Zupic, I. (2025). Resolving the "sustainability paradox": A bibliometric and topic modeling analysis of sustainable entrepreneurship and sustainable consumption. Journal of Enterprising Communities. DOI: 10.1108/JEC-11-2024-0235

Kawimbe, S. (2025). Harnessing green entrepreneurship for sustainable growth in Zambia. *Journal of Environment*, *5*(4), 24–35. www.carijournals.org. DOI: 10.47941/je.3215

Kumar, S., Roy, C., Sati, V. P., Pandey, K., Sarkar, T., & Singh, R. (2025). Outmigration from the Indian Himalayan Region (IHR) with drivers, patterns and policy implications for sustainable mountain development. *Discover Sustainability*, *6*(1), 1381. Advance online publication. DOI: 10.1007/s43621-025-02315-1

Maheshwari, G., & Schrage, B. (2025). Emerging trends in social entrepreneurship and sustainability: A Southeast Asia analysis. *The Bottom Line (New York, N.Y.)*. Advance online publication. DOI: 10.1108/BL-06-2024-0064

Mat, B., Çevrimli, M. B., Varalan, A., Barit, B., & Günlü, A. (2026). Determination of economic sustainability factors in sheep enterprises in Türkiye. *Veterinary Medicine and Science*, *12*(1), e70761. Advance online publication. DOI: 10.1002/vms3.70761 PMID: 41508816

Mauraise, J., Amokomoyen, C., Lamino, A., & Bakare, A. (2024). Green entrepreneurship: An empirical investigation of investment in environmental technologies and environmental reporting and disclosure on startup business sustainability in Nigeria. *Journal of Information Systems Engineering & Management*, *2025*(53s). https://www.jisem-journal.com/

Muhammad Rezky, D., Mulyadi, H., Utama, D. H., & Furqon, C. (2025). Fresh to cup coffee business planning and development in West Java using the triple layered business model canvas. Jurnal Riset Bisnis dan Manajemen, 18(2). https://journal.unpas.ac.id/index.php/jrbm/index

Parihar, J. S., Cichon, D., Kharbanda, A., Sala, D., & Sharma, G. D. (2025). Barriers and enablers: Review research on women entrepreneurship and its impact on sustainable tourism development. *Entrepreneurial Business and Economics Review, 13*(4), 185–208. DOI: 10.15678/EBER.2025.130410

Parrales-Reyes, J., Cañarte-Quimis, L. Y., Salazar-Pionce, E., Saltos-Buri, V., Díaz-Romero, Y., Martínez-García, V., Espinoza-Vásquez, G., Rengifo-Lozano, R., Escobar-Molina, D., Delgado, D. R., & Rincón-Guio, C. (2025). Towards sustainability in organic coffee production: A holistic analysis of research trends, challenges, and future prospects. *Logforum, 21*(3), 383–403. DOI: 10.17270/J.LOG.001233

Parvin Banu, I., Sivaramakrishnan, R., Kavithamani, R., & Nanee, M. D. (n.d.). Green entrepreneurship startups. Retrieved from www.ciitresearch.org

Patrucco, A. S., Roath, A. S., Richey, R. G.Jr, Mathiyazhagan, K., & Shankar, R. (2026). From triple-A to AAA+: Recalibrating agility, adaptability, and alignment for digital, responsible, and resilient supply chains. *Journal of Business Logistics, 47*(1), e70049. Advance online publication. DOI: 10.1111/jbl.70049

Poderytė, I., Banaitienė, N., & Banaitis, A. (2025). Life cycle sustainability assessment of buildings: A scientometric analysis. *Buildings (Basel, Switzerland), 15*(3), 381. Advance online publication. DOI: 10.3390/buildings15030381

Prakash, D., Bisla, M., & Arora, T. (2023). Role of environment dimensions to strive sustainable entrepreneurship: A triple bottom line approach. *International Journal of Professional Business Review, 8*(3), e0698. Advance online publication. DOI: 10.26668/businessreview/2023.v8i3.698

Prasnowo, M. A., Aziza, N., & Sulaiman, A. (2025). Entrepreneurship and sustainable development goals: An SCT model analysis. BIMA Journal (Business, Management, & Accounting Journal), 6(1), 11–18. DOI: 10.37638/bima.6.1.11-18

Ramos-Ruiz, J. E., Guzmán-Dorado, L., Ferreira-Gomes, P. C., & Algaba-Navarro, D. (2025). First time in the European Rally Championship: What's next for residents' perceptions of urban sustainability? *Urban Science (Basel, Switzerland), 9*(11), 441. Advance online publication. DOI: 10.3390/urbansci9110441

Rosliani, E., Muhafidin, D., Rusli, B., & Sumaryana, A. (2025). Contextualizing triple bottom line sustainability assessment in secondary education: A rapid appraisal from the Global South. *Sustainability (Basel)*, *17*(14), 6621. Advance online publication. DOI: 10.3390/su17146621

Said Al-Jahwari, N., Bathmanathan, V., & Ahmed, A. (n.d.). Doing good, doing well: The impact of green CSR on manufacturing SME sustainability in Oman. International Journal of Environmental Sciences, 11(8). Retrieved from https://www.theaspd.com/ijes.php

Sajib, T. R., Islam, M. J., & Gowindasamy, M. (2025). Sustainable of HRM system and strategies for corporate sustainability. *International Journal of Advanced Business Studies*, *2*(4), 57–79. DOI: 10.59857/ijabs.1470

Sanchis, J. R., Campos, V., & Ejarque, A. T. (2025). A proposed typology for the validation of corporate sustainability. *Sustainability (Basel)*, *17*(16), 7358. Advance online publication. DOI: 10.3390/su17167358

Sarlin Venotha, A., & Alex, K. (n.d.). Sustainability of women entrepreneurship: Personal and social factors. International Journal of Commerce and Management Research. Retrieved from www.managejournal.com

Schaltegger, S., & Wagner, M. (2011). Sustainable entrepreneurship and sustainability innovation: Categories and interactions. *Business Strategy and the Environment*, *20*(4), 222–237. DOI: 10.1002/bse.682

Sharma, G. D., Kraus, S., Chopra, R., Dev, D., & Ferraris, A. (2025). Strategic innovation for sustainability: A conceptual model linking digitalization, social dynamics, and climate change mitigation. *Business Strategy and the Environment*. Advance online publication. DOI: 10.1002/bse.70471

Srivani, M. G., & Prakash, C. (2024). Green entrepreneurship: A commitment to a sustainable and eco-friendly enterprise and products. International Journal of Multidisciplinary Research, Science. *Engineering and Technology*, *7*(11), 16538. DOI: 10.15680/IJMRSET.2024.0711020

Sudario, M. E. (n.d.). Sustainability struggles: Challenges encountered by small and micro-entrepreneurs in rural Philippines.

Supriaddin, N., & Ayu Ningtyas, S. (n.d.). The role of business performance in mediating relationship between triple bottom line and business survival.

Surbakti, L. P., Sari, R. P., Swatdikun, T., Nugraheni, R., & Wibawaningsih, E. J. (2025). Good corporate governance and corporate sustainability performance in Indonesia. Revista de Administração Mackenzie, 26(5). https://doi.org/DOI: 10.1590/1678-6971/eRAMF250129

Suryani, S., Umar Daihani, D., Gustina Amran, T. G. A., & Septiani, W. (2025). Systematic literature review of sustainable assessment model in vocational higher education. *Spektrum Industri, 23*(2), 240–248. DOI: 10.12928/si.v23i2.459

Tekala, K., Baradarani, S., Alzubi, A., & Berberoğlu, A. (2024). Green entrepreneurship for business sustainability: Do environmental dynamism and green structural capital matter? *Sustainability (Basel), 16*(13), 5291. Advance online publication. DOI: 10.3390/su16135291

Tenedero, E. Q., Sintos, J. R., & Araza, J. B. (2025). Working capital management practices of MSMEs in Samar, Philippines towards triple bottom line sustainability. *Environment and Social Psychology, 10*(2). Advance online publication. DOI: 10.59429/esp.v10i2.3271

Thalut, N., & Ghani, G. M. (2025). Economic cooperation and environmental sustainability in the OIC region: A panel data analysis. Journal of Economic Cooperation and Development, 46.

Tombak, M. L., Aiken, D. M., Toomeoja, E., & Tapaninen, U. P. (2025). Advancing port sustainability in the Baltic Sea region: A comparative analysis using the SMCC framework. *Sustainability (Basel), 17*(15), 6764. Advance online publication. DOI: 10.3390/su17156764

Wadghane, R. H., Madguni, O., & Baisakhi, B. (2025). Unlocking sustainability potential: A SAFA framework analysis of sugarcane agriculture in Marathwada, Maharashtra, India. *Sustainable Futures : An Applied Journal of Technology, Environment and Society, 10*, 101118. Advance online publication. DOI: 10.1016/j.sftr.2025.101118

Zaza Agustiana, U., & Pratama, G. (2025). Evidence from Indonesian cooperatives. 11(2).

Zeqing, L., Alfansi, L., & Usman, B. (n.d.). Greening business for sustainability: The strategic role of green HRM, innovation and employee behavior in coal power plants in Sumatera, Indonesia. International Journal of Science. Retrieved from http://ijstm.inarah.co.id

ADDITIONAL READING

Aayog, N. I. T. I. (2022). India's circular economy: Opportunities in waste-to-wealth. Government of India. https://www.niti.gov.in

Business Standard. (2023). Sustainable entrepreneurship: The way forward for India. https://www.business-standard.com

Business Standard. (2024). India's renewable energy capacity crosses 100 GW mark. https://www.business-standard.com

Business Standard. (2025, November 6). Karnataka cabinet clears 518 crore startup policy to boost emerging tech. https://timesofindia.indiatimes.com/city/bengaluru/karnataka-cabinet-clears-rs-518-crore-startup-policy-to-boost-emerging-tech/articleshow/125138590.cms

Entrepreneur. (2025, November 8). Karnataka Cabinet approves Startup Policy 2025–2030 with INR 518 Cr allocation. https://www.entrepreneur.com/en-in/news-and-trends/karnataka-cabinet-approves-startup-policy-2025-2030-with/499357

Goodreturns. (2025). Maharashtra's new startup policy 2025: Boosting innovation and entrepreneurship. https://www.goodreturns.in/news/maharashtra-startup-entrepreneurship-innovation-policy-2025-011-1447633.html

Government of India, Ministry of New and Renewable Energy. (2024). Physical progress (achievements). https://mnre.gov.in/physical-progress

India Brand Equity Foundation. (2024). Renewable energy industry in India. https://www.ibef.org/industry/renewable-energy

Indian Express. (2025, November 6). Karnataka Cabinet approves Startup Policy 2025–2030 to create 25,000 startups. https://indianexpress.com/article/cities/bangalore/karnatakas-new-startup-policy-setting-up-25000-startups-10350105/

Indian Express. (2025, August 5). 5-year strategy to aid 1.25 lakh entrepreneurs: Startup policy gets Maharashtra Cabinet nod. https://indianexpress.com/article/cities/mumbai/startup-policy-maharashtra-cabinet-10171807/

Magazine India, P. V. (2024). Renewable energy emerging as India's next big jobs engine. https://www.pv-magazine-india.com

Ministry of Environment. Forest and Climate Change. (2023). India's climate action and green entrepreneurship initiatives. Government of India. https://moef.gov.in

Phool.co. (2024). About Phool: Flowercycling and sustainable biomaterials. https://phool.co/pages/about-us

State Bank of India. (2023). SBI partners with Agence Française de Développement to promote green finance in India. https://sbi.co.in/web/press-release

ThePrint. (2023). How sustainable startups are reshaping India's entrepreneurial ecosystem. https://theprint.in

Times of India. (2023). MBA graduate turns waste into sustainable enterprise in Odisha. https://timesofindia.indiatimes.com/city/bhubaneswar/mba-grad-turns-waste-into-art-inspires-sustainable-change/articleshow/123210081.cms

Times of India. (2024). Dharwad emerges as a hub for green entrepreneurship initiatives. https://timesofindia.indiatimes.com/city/hubballi/dharwad-bets-on-green-entrepreneurship/articleshow/125113678.cms

Times of India. (2025, August 5). Startup policy to create 1.3 lakh entrepreneurs in 5 yrs rolled out. https://timesofindia.indiatimes.com/city/mumbai/startup-policy-to-create-1-3-lakh-entrepreneurs-in-5-yrs-rolled-out/articleshow/123724429.cms

Chapter 3

Eco-Innovators:

How Green Entrepreneurs Are Shaping a Sustainable Future

Tahsin Farzana Jisun
http://orcid.org/0009-0005-8653-2669
American International University-Bangladesh, Bangladesh

Md Mahdi Hasan Ahid
http://orcid.org/0009-0008-2304-5283
American International University-Bangladesh, Bangladesh

Zerin Tasnim
http://orcid.org/0000-0002-5705-1648
North South University, Bangladesh

Javed Mahmud
http://orcid.org/0009-0007-8428-6382
Uttara University, Bangladesh

Md. Adnan Rahman
http://orcid.org/0000-0003-3378-0958
Uttara University, Bangladesh

ABSTRACT

This chapter examines the role of green entrepreneurship in driving sustainable development by integrating environmental, social, and economic objectives. It explores the conceptual foundations, motivations, and strategies underpinning green ventures, highlighting how entrepreneurs innovate through circular economy models, eco-design, sustainable supply chains, and digital technologies. Drawing on case studies such as Tesla, Patagonia, and Grameen Shakti, the chapter illustrates both the

DOI: 10.4018/979-8-3373-7391-1.ch003

opportunities and challenges inherent in pursuing sustainability-oriented business models. It further emphasizes the importance of policy support, institutional frameworks, and systematic impact measurement through ESG and life-cycle assessment. Concluding with emerging trends and future directions, the chapter underscores that green entrepreneurs are pivotal agents of change, shaping resilient, inclusive, and environmentally responsible economic systems.

INTRODUCTION

The modern world economic order is in stalemate. Environmental degradation, accelerating climate change, the loss of biodiversity, and the growing socio-economic inequities are becoming major issues of policy, corporate strategy, and social expectations. At the same time, entrepreneurial dynamism has continued to serve as a driver to innovation, job creation, and economic growth in industrialised and developing economies. Green entrepreneurship is a new phenomenon that has been propelled by the urgency of environmental needs and entrepreneurial creativity and is currently experiencing massive expansion. Green entrepreneurs are not only interested in creating economic value, but also in encompassing the environmental preservation and social responsibility in their business model. But, as the eco-innovators started to be seen in greater numbers, conceptual and practical confusions spread like wildfire. The concept of green entrepreneurship has been confused with other concepts like corporate social responsibility and sustainability within existing companies, and it is hard to distinguish the particular rationale behind the latter within the framework of innovative entrepreneurial activities. Additionally, a good story can attract people; however, issues like scarce resources, complex policymaking, uncertainty in the market, and resistance to change hinder the establishment of the green business, which are cited as the barriers that green business owners have to overcome. At the same time, the scholarly field, even though it grows, is likely to disintegrate into specific fields of investigation, including environmental management, innovation, and entrepreneurship studies. Thus, there is a need to have an integrated outlook that links theory with practical realities, motivation with strategy and ambitions with quantifiable results.

The chapter will offer an in-depth examination of how green entrepreneurs are able to grow sustainable futures. The main aim is to explore the viability of green entrepreneurship in the advancement of environmental and social security and economic sustainability. This chapter incorporates a theoretical framework such as the triple bottom line, the stakeholder theory and the institutional theory along with case study analysis and policy discourse analysis. It examines the reasons and drivers behind the creation of environmentally conscious businesses, how they can make their environmental pledges profitable, and the environmental conditions that can either support or cripple their development. The chapter explains the significance of technical, organisational and business model innovation as drivers of transformative change. The critical discourse discusses the issues of green ventures, and it is important to note that a decent legislative environment, availability of green funding, and a proper system to monitor the results must be in place. The green entrepreneurship debate places green entrepreneurship in the global sustainability agenda and emerging changes in the economy and looks at its applicability not only as a corporate trend, but also as a structural sustainable development initiative element. The chapter plays a major role in the discussion among the academic community as it has both conceptual and practical appeal. It offers a scalable framework of understanding eco-innovation to researchers, offers practitioners a platform of strategic thinking in sustainable business practices, and offers policymakers a perspective of creating desired ecosystems. Finally, the chapter highlights the fact that green entrepreneurs are not peripheral players but central participants in the restructuring of markets, institutions, and expectations in the society towards a more sustainable and equitable future.

CONCEPTUALIZING GREEN ENTREPRENEURSHIP

The present situation indicates that the green entrepreneurship has become a more specialized discipline, a sub-discipline of the broader discipline of business entrepreneurship research, because of the increased importance of environmental sustainability and economic equality. Green entrepreneurship simply involves establishing and initiating businesses that simultaneously contribute to the environmental preservation, provide social goodwill and are profitable. As opposed to traditional entrepreneurship, which is founded on the identification of opportunities and profit maximisation, green entrepreneurship is the creation of ecological and social values as the major principle of the venture formation and development (Singh et al., 2025). The new study has highlighted that green ventures are not merely market actors who react to consumer demand of eco-friendly products but rather are transformative agents, which are instigated by institutions to disrupt the paradigms of production and consumption (Al-Mamary, 2025; Tahsina et al., 2024).

There are many conceptual frameworks underlying green entrepreneurship, grounded in various academic traditions. The Sustainable Entrepreneurship Theory is also among the most popular and is based on the idea that the business operations can resolve the market failures that lead to environmental degradation and be profitable (Salaheldeen et al., 2024). The challenges of ecological and societal problems are re-packaged as opportunities in innovation. The entrepreneurs are able to locate the inefficiencies in the resource utilization, inequalities in renewable sources of energy or unmet needs in sustainable operations, and come up with solutions that generate mutual benefit. Green entrepreneurship aligns with the concept of opportunity-based sustainability, where environmental constraints are perceived as inspirations to new business models and innovative ways of recombination's (Veleva, 2021).

The second needed framework is Triple Bottom Line (TBL) model, that establishes the performance measurement standards on a bigger scale, including environmental and social performance (Yasir et al., 2023). Initially suggested decades ago, TBL has acquired a new facet in the context of climate change and investment flows according to ESG (Al Halbusi et al., 2024). The TBL model is a green entrepreneurial internalisation approach to first phases of company ventures. They view environmental responsibility as an aspect of it and include ecological indicators like reduction of carbon footprint, minimisation of waste and resource efficiency in the strategic decision-making process. The social goals are also worked into the value propositions, including equitable hiring, empowering the community, and equal access to the basic services (Emon & Mazid-Ul-Haque, 2025).

The institutional theory helps to understand green entrepreneurship because it highlights the different impacts of regulatory, normative, and cultural-cognitive pressures in venture-making (Alwakid et al., 2021). Increased environmental standards, carbon taxes and renewable energy legislation are being implemented by governments and provide limitations and incentives to green innovation (Ahmed & Ahmed, 2026). The reputational benefits created by parallel normative demands of civic organizations, investors, and consumers compel corporations to be more eco-friendly (Yousaf et al., 2021). The green business model may be described in terms of the cultural-cognitive transformation of the younger generations that are more climate-conscious. Green entrepreneurship here involves changing institutional situations to promote financially viable behaviours, sometimes at the expense of environmental responsibility (Ahmed et al., 2026).

The alternative theoretical model is referred to as Stakeholder Theory that is grounded on the need to reconcile the interests of various stakeholders (Pauceanu et al., 2021). The networks green entrepreneurs need to work in are complicated due to a multifaceted nature of stakeholders that include investors, consumers, regulators, suppliers, workers, and local communities (M. K. Hasan et al., 2026). They found their sustainability and acceptability in the establishment of trust, transparency and value co-creation between various categories of people. This multidimensional approach to stakeholder engagement is presumably likely to facilitate the collaborative innovative processes, non-governmental organisations and participatory governance, so it will be less challenging to draw an analogy between green venture and profit-driven start-ups (Hasan et al., 2025).

Analytical distinction of green entrepreneurship and corporate social responsibility (CSR) is required. The current firms consider CSR to be an incidental practice that seeks to minimize reputational risk or a way of complying with the regulations. Green enterprises on the other hand are established based on sustainability. They have designed their purpose, operations, and income models in such a manner that environmental concerns have become central priorities and not peripheral concerns (Berrone et al., 2023). One such opportunity is a green start-up business model, which is largely based on the concept of a circular economy, since most of the characteristics of green start-ups, such as product service systems, recycling chains, and resource regeneration, are typically founded on the notion of a circular economy (Fu et al., 2023). Similarly, renewable energy, eco-design methodology and socially fair working practices are inherently integrated as compared to retrofitting.

Green entrepreneurship has four dimensions. Firstly, the aspect of environmental innovation involves technical development, organisational productivity, and development of sustainable products that will minimise the adverse effects on the environment. Second, the creation of social values is aimed at social participation in the community development, equal access and social inclusion. Third, long-term economic resilience understands that sustainable competitiveness is based on the adaptive capacity, resource efficiency, and responsible governance. Lastly, the systemic impact perspective that determines the green entrepreneur as those who aim to transform the business, influence policy debates, and redesign consumption patterns.

Figure 1. Integrated Conceptual Model of Green Entrepreneurship

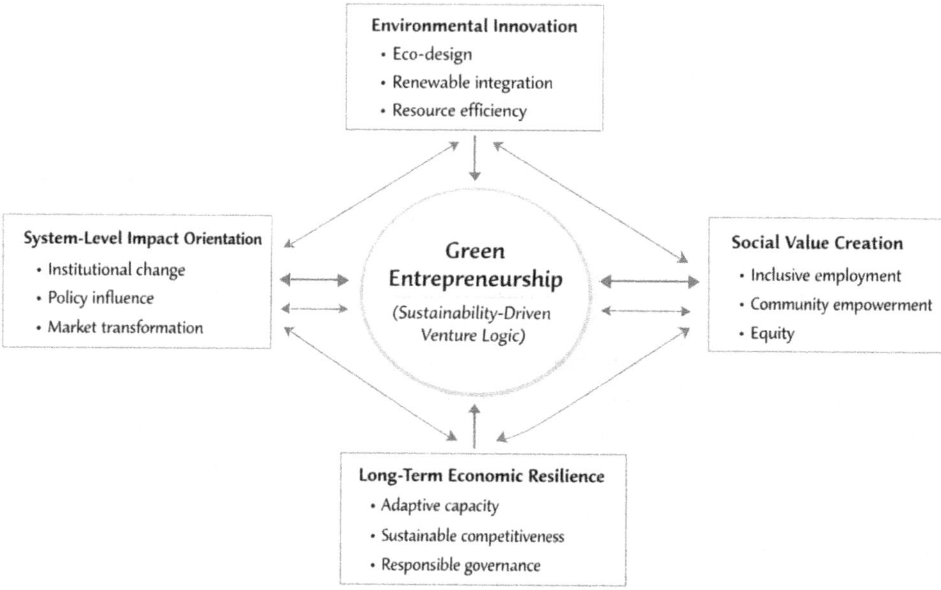

DRIVERS AND MOTIVATIONS FOR GREEN ENTREPRENEURSHIP

Green entrepreneurship is a not only a reaction to market opportunities, but a complex reaction to ecological, social, economic, and institutional pressures. Green space entrepreneurs are often driven by a set of core values, strategic goals, and empowering variables. These motives play a pivotal role in academic theorisation and policy-making because of their impact on the formation and sustainability of eco-innovative business (Singh et al., 2025). According to recent research, the motivation to go green is not universal and depends on the personal, societal, and technological contexts (Mondal et al., 2025b). The four main drives and motivations are outlined in this section as environmental awareness and ethical commitment, market opportunities, governmental and institutional encouragement, and technology advancements.

Environmental Awareness and Ethical Commitment

One of the main driving forces of green entrepreneurship is intrinsic drive. Several businesses are motivated by environmental concerns, moral responsibilities, and the goal of minimizing negative impacts on the environment. The increasing realization of the consequences of environmental degradation, resource consumption, and the loss of biodiversity has caused a sense of urgency, with some entrepreneurs taking to entrepreneurial activities (Reuther et al., 2023). Climate anxiety, especially among younger people, has turned into a major psychological driving force, and eco-innovators find opportunities in projects that have a direct impact on addressing sustainability concerns (Mondal et al., 2025a). Moreover, other elements of venture orientation are influenced by ethical commitment and pro-environmental principles. Ecological entrepreneurship puts the long-term well-being of the planet over short-term financial feasibility, making sustainability a part of the goal and the business strategy of the organization. The examples of the enterprises that depend on the availability of renewable energy or the introduction of the circular economy can be used as role models (Lazarte-Aguirre, 2024). In this respect, the cognitive perspective and moral framework by which eco-entrepreneurs envision opportunities and develop solutions is eco-consciousness and moral dedication.

Market Opportunities

Although the establishment of companies is controlled by basic values, the instrumental motive to exploit the market opportunities is a force to reckon with. The global movement toward the ecological, social, and ethical consumerism is noticeable, and more and more people consider it necessary to consume ecologically, socially, and morally responsible goods and services (M. M. Mia et al., 2022). The emerging business niches that can be ventured into are organic foods, renewable energy technology, sustainable fashion, eco-tourism, and low-carbon transportation. One of the best business opportunities is whereby the business conforms to the global environmental trends and regulations. Greater clean technology and sustainable solutions will be required to switch to ESG norms and corporate responsibility, which will result in unmet demand that can be offered by green entrepreneurs (Purwandani & Michaud, 2021). Those able to detect and react to market signals might gain a competitive advantage, such as an integrated set of environmental and financial incentives. The incentives in terms of opportunities are augmenting the intrinsic values within the environment that are shaping the strategic positioning and scaling opportunities of green initiatives.

Institutional and Policy Incentives

Green entrepreneurship is highly sensitive to external institutional forces that affect motivation. The policies and regulatory frameworks of the government, as well as the international agreements, are also encouraging the implementation of environmentally sustainable business models (Sarkar et al., 2021). The barrier to entry is lowered by the presence of renewable energy installations, green financing schemes favoured, tax incentives on sustainable practices, and subsidies on research and development of ecologically advanced technology, which increases the financial viability. The long-term outcomes of the decarbonisation and resource efficiency plan that enhances investor legitimacy and trust in green projects are reflected in international deals such as the Paris Agreement (Hameed et al., 2021). At the same time, the normative pressure will include the municipal carbon reduction goals, environmental laws, and compliance, whereas enterprises will look to pursue environmentally friendly activities on their own. The institutional support is the facilitating and motivating process that determines the magnitude of businesses and their emphasis on sustainable outcomes.

Technological Advancements

Green entrepreneurship is based on technological innovation which increases the feasibility of sustainability solutions and increases their scope. The renewable energy industry has access to cost-effective clean energy sources like solar photovoltaic systems and wind turbines (Yousaf et al., 2021). Internet of Things (IoT), artificial intelligence, big data analytics, and blockchain can improve the manufacturing process by turning it into an ecologically sustainable process, allowing real-time tracking of resources, and optimising supply chains. Advanced solutions such as innovations in biotechnology, sustainable materials, and waste-to-resource can help entrepreneurs develop goods and services that have fewer environmental impacts. Such innovations help in lowering the financial burdens of sustainable businesses by minimizing the technological and operational pressures, and by distinguishing competitive markets through innovation. The technology facilitators are not only advantageous but also motivating processes that allow entrepreneurs to come up with scalable solutions that are ecologically advantageous and able to provide financial self-sufficiency.

The interaction of inherent values, market dynamics, institutional incentives and technical facilitators forms a complex ecosystem of green entrepreneurship. The moral and cognitive drive to the development of the endeavour is the environmental consciousness and ethical commitment, and the structural and strategic drive to its development is the market potential, regulatory framework, and technology. Academics, educators, policymakers, and practitioners are the first to understand these factors in order to enhance sustainable business environments. According to personal values and the correspondence to the opportunity recognition, regulatory frameworks, and technological feasibility, the stakeholders can develop interventions, financing mechanisms, and educational strategies to improve the development of eco-innovators and their contribution to the society and environment.

STRATEGIES FOR GREEN INNOVATION

Green entrepreneurship is not just the sustainability agenda, but also the approaches of the entrepreneur to transform sustainability goals and environmental and social objectives into business value. In contrast to the traditional enterprises, green entrepreneurs involve sustainability as the core element of their business models, business operations, and value chains (Oduro et al., 2022; Singh et al., 2025). Green strategies are regarded as a compromise between the ecological responsibility and market competitiveness so that the ecological and social effects correspond to profitability and long-term sustainability. This part outlines four key strategies employed by green enterprises: circular economy models, eco-design and sustainable product development, sustainable supply chain integration, and data-driven sustainable approaches.

Figure 2. Integrated Strategies for Green Innovation

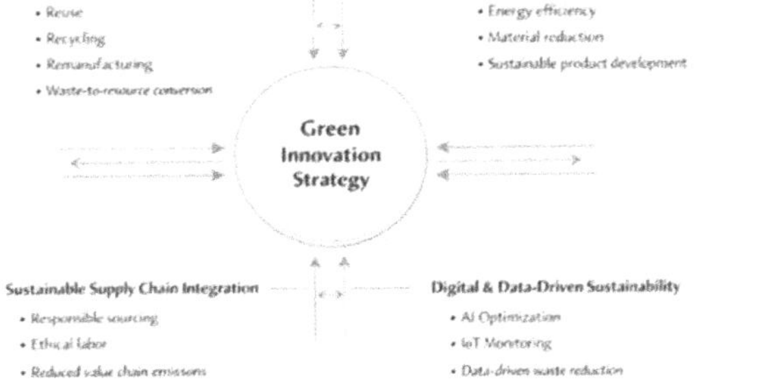

Circular Economy Models

Circular economy (CE) concepts are a prominent approach to green innovation, with its emphasis on resource efficiency, waste management, and lifetime management of products. Circular business models are contrasted with more traditional linear models of take-make-dispose because they focus on reuse, recycling, remanufacturing, and repurposing waste to form resources (Jiang et al., 2024). Some entrepreneurs employing the concepts of the circular economy tend to create products that are more durable, modular, and reparable, thus making materials more valuable at production-consumption stages. It is worth noting that businesses within the electronics, apparel and packaging industries rely on take-back products, product refurbishments or secondary-material markets, which are in effect resource loop-closures. Circular models generate economic benefit and their environmental footprint, such as cost savings through material savings, brand loyalty by environmentally conscious consumers, and other sources of revenue related to the product-as-a-service model (Al-Mamary, 2025). The ideas of a circular economy are the illustrations of the interconnectedness of environmental stewardship and business success.

Eco-Design and Sustainable Product Innovation

Eco-design is the other vital element of eco-ventures that involves giving consideration to the environment in the creation of products. It encompasses the energy consumption of products, their materials procurement, carbon footprint, and end life cycle disposal at the design phase instead of the sustainability retrofit of the products after manufacturing (Soomro et al., 2024). Lightweight materials, non-toxic substances, modular architecture, and manufacturing processes that are energy efficient are some of the elements of eco-design used by entrepreneurs. Besides affecting product quality, eco-design can enhance the competitive uniqueness by responding to the customer demands of sustainable products and responding to the ever-tightening environmental requirements. Sustainable product innovation brings about the technological improvement, which has led to the exploration of renewable materials, biomimetic design, and energy-efficient production processes, which have led to both environmental and economic outcomes (Zhang et al., 2022).

Sustainable Supply Chain Integration

The idea of sustainability is not only intrinsic to the company, but it is also a part of the supply chain that green entrepreneurs consider a strategic requirement. Responsible sourcing, ethical labour practices, and risk mitigations are also key issues among suppliers to warrant the viability and efficacy of sustainability claims that any venture may have (Silvério et al., 2025; Yasir et al., 2023). Green business ventures tend to partner with suppliers to create logistics that are resource-efficient, employ renewable energy, and sustainable packaging. Blockchain monitoring is an advanced traceability system that allows organisations to monitor environmental compliance, labour standards and carbon emissions throughout the entire value chain.

It will facilitate environmental performance, increase stakeholder trust, and reduce reputational issues, in addition to enhancing access to markets, and sustainability-focused certifications.

Digital and Data-Driven Sustainability

In green entrepreneurship efforts, technological innovation is increasingly playing a crucial role. Tools to optimise energy, predict demand, reduce waste, and improve the efficiency of processes include digital platforms, artificial intelligence (AI), the Internet of Things (IoT), and big data analytics (Arici & Uysal, 2022). As an example, predictive maintenance is optimised by AI in the industrial sector to optimise energy consumption and prevent resource wastage, and the sensors of internet of things allow real-time tracking of environmental and production parameters. Evidence-based business decisions can help entrepreneurs decide how to operate in line with the sustainability objectives, which can produce measurable ecological and economic benefits. The digital strategy increases the scalability of the effects, which allows enterprises to efficiently use their resources, improve supply chain visibility, and respond quickly to customer needs and laws.

CHALLENGES AND BARRIERS IN GREEN ENTREPRENEURSHIP

Although the potential of green entrepreneurship is immense in terms of environmental, social and economic benefits, the pressures on the entrepreneurs in the sector are very high and may disrupt the growth, survival and success of entrepreneurial activities. They are contextual barriers, financial, regulatory, market, and technical barriers, and the degree of their intensity depends on geographic, institutional, and economic factors (Salaheldeen et al., 2024; Singh et al., 2025). The interests of scholars, practitioners and policymakers to successful green innovation ecosystems should be considered in these barriers. All these still limit the growth of eco-ventures to new markets that lack sufficient resources, infrastructure, and other enabling frameworks (Mondal et al., 2025a).

Financial Constraints

One of the largest problems that green businesses encounter is financial constraint. Sustainable projects are costly to initiate as massive amounts of money are spent on sustainable technology, renewable energy systems and sustainable integration of the supply chain (Purwandani & Michaud, 2021). This would be a risky venture to the investors since they do not know the sources of revenue, payback time and regulatory requirements are not predetermined. The ultimate ending of this perception is that financial inequities exist and that the inequities are realized in the shape of stagnation in the possible growth, the reduced investment in research and development and the delays in development of the product. In order to solve this problem, numerous green financial instruments are available: impact investment funds, green bonds, and government-subsidised options, and they are not evenly spread around the globe (Derdabi & Dvouletý, 2025). It will be hard to operate since business people will be willing to bring together numerous sources of capital such as bootstrapping, grants and venture financing. As a result, the problem of financial limitations is among the most important strategic and practical challenges, which predetermines the speed and scale of green innovation and its scale in general.

Regulatory Complexity

Growth of green ventures is also associated with policy and regulatory issues. The environmental regulations are complicated, unfair and even inconsistent, not only on the local, national and international level (M. M. Mia et al., 2022). The strategies are bureaucratic and have administrative costs, vague permission process and long approval process that introduce uncertainties in the decision-making process. The regulatory system is not proactive but reactive in the meaning that it does not have incentive and standardisation which are conducive to sustainable corporate activities. The adherence to the changes regarding the emission levels, energy usage, or product certification can be a problem in various sectors, which do not have similar regulations (Yasir et al., 2023). The over-regulations are not only increasing the risks in operations, but are also threatening to discourage the new entrants to start sustainability-oriented businesses.

Market Acceptance

The other question that arises is the acceptability of the market even in those countries where technically processes and services of green goods are feasible. The location, culture, and level of income can determine the readiness of the customers to pay a price premium on environmentally friendly products (Hameed et al., 2021). In most cases, eco-products are not cheap as they are produced at high costs, with the use of sustainable resources or investment in technologies that could be applied to manipulate the prices. The belief in green businesses can be undermined by the ignorance of the environmental claims of the customers, the scepticism of the environmental claims, which has long been known as the greenwashing issue. It is at this point that a business person would be expected to invest in education, create certification and do some marketing to increase legitimacy and create adoption. An acute problem of the ratio of affordability to sustainability is the price-form based competition, and the most common price form is applied in the developing economy (Alwakid et al., 2021).

Technological and Infrastructure Limitations

One of the major issues is technical and infrastructure gap. The green solutions are based on a highly developed renewable technology, energy-saving systems, or internet-based monitoring systems that are unlikely to be implemented especially in underdeveloped countries (Yin et al., 2022). Lack of decent grid infrastructure, inaccessibility of renewable sources, and the high cost of green technology are only a few of the challenges that do not allow entrepreneurs to use their business model and effectively implement green improvements (Ersoy et al., 2022). Lack of technical skills and knowledge transfer systems could be an obstacle to the innovation and technology uptake.

AI or IoT linked solutions need to be implemented by trained personnel. Moreover, the demanded digital infrastructure is not only a question of the financial means of a small business or start-up, but most probably, also the technological means. These are the technical and infrastructural constraints and the operational and strategic constraints that green entrepreneurs are on the path of. Financial, regulatory, commercial and technical are some of the multi-faceted obstacles to the entrepreneurship of the green aspect, yet it has an innovative potential. The insufficient financial capabilities will make the innovation insufficient since it will not be in a position to provide the necessary capital and growth opportunities. The sophistication of regulations, increased compliance cost and operational risks will also be a problem. The familiarity with the consumers and their relative affordability will help in acceptance in the market, but poor technological and infrastructural factors will act as a barrier to the popularization of innovations. Governments should work together with business people, industry organizations and learning institutions to overcome such challenges. By detecting and eliminating these obstacles the stakeholders will be in a good position to offer conducive environment that will see the success and sustainability of the green enterprises which will translate to the maximisation of the ecological, social and economic impacts in the long term.

CASE STUDIES OF SUCCESSFUL GREEN VENTURES

Green entrepreneurship is not a mere concept, but an actual model that shows how companies can apply sustainability at the same time achieving economic and social outcomes. The case studies are useful in the context of the interdependence of innovation, market positioning, stakeholder engagement, and value generation that is driven by mission. In this section, the three internationally and nationally recognized green businesses, Tesla, Inc., Patagonia, and Grameen Shakti, will be analysed to clarify some of the strategies, challenges, and outcomes of sustainable businesses. These, they describe as scalable, stakeholder-incorporated, and imaginative business models, which can balance profitability with environmental and social responsibility.

Tesla, Inc.

Tesla, Inc. is an electric vehicle company and sustainable energy solution provider that was founded in 2003. The success indicates that technical innovation can result in disruptive interventions in the market and is consistent with sustainability objectives (J. Wang et al., 2021). The business strategy of Tesla includes the battery innovation, solar energy, and direct to consumer sales that offer synergies in energy production, storage, and consumption. The company has made substantial investments in research and development to boost battery performance, reduce the cost of production and expand the number of charging stations, which reflects its operational excellence and environmental responsibility (Palmié et al., 2024). The second area of concern of Tesla is brand positioning and customer experience as e-cars are not only perceived as environmentally friendly products but also as high-performance and fun options to the usual cars. This innovation, market strategy, and sustainability connection underscores the possibility of green companies to develop fast and pose threat to the established sectors.

Patagonia

Patagonia is a U.S. consumer-based outdoor apparel company, with a green entrepreneur who is also a leader in the industry. The company has a track record of sustainable sourcing, product repair programs, and corporate involvement (Shourkaei et al., 2024). The Patagonia Don't Buy This Jacket campaign changed the way people viewed the environmental footprint of their products and made people think of durability, repairs, and recycling as a better alternative to impulsive buying. Besides its marketing strategies, Patagonia incorporates sustainability in its supply chain processes such as sourcing organic cotton, fair employment, and reduced carbon footprint in its production process. The corporation also engages in campaigning and environmental programs, including funding grassroots conservation programs (Fürst & Akdağ, 2025). Ethical practices, environmental stewardship, and a traceable brand story make Patagonia demonstrate that commercial success and social and environmental responsibility can go hand in hand, creating an example of sustainable entrepreneurship in consumer-led industries.

Grameen Shakti

The Bangladeshi social business, Grameen Shakti, highlights the importance of green entrepreneurship to overcome energy poverty and support healthy socio-economic development. The organization was established in 1996 and is focused on building solar home systems (SHSs) in rural areas, which encourages the growth of the communities with limited access to renewable energy and cheap energy sources (M. A. Mia, 2022). The approach to Grameen Shakti involves a combination of technology provision, microfinance and community training, enabling households to adopt clean technologies as well as enabling local jobs and skill development. The idea is commercially viable and has made it possible to install millions of solar systems, which has reduced the consumption of kerosene, greenhouse gas emissions, and improved the standards of living. Grameen Shakti is a good example of how green entrepreneurship can be a transformational tool in developing nations through combining social empowerment and environmental innovations.

The three case studies show how green businesses can be flexible and adaptable in various sectors and areas. Tesla, Inc., the ethical consumption efforts of Patagonia, the supply chain responsibility and mission-driven marketing, and the socially inclusive green entrepreneurship of Grameen Shakti, which solves the energy poverty, are all examples of technological disruption and brand centered market acquisition. All these examples point to the success criteria, such as scalable innovation, stakeholder integration, mission-driven focus, and the ability to deliver environmental, social, and economic benefit. These analogies are important to scholars, practitioners and policymakers, as green entrepreneurship can become a transformative element that has strategic and operational impacts to sustainable company development.

POLICY AND INSTITUTIONAL SUPPORT FOR SUSTAINABLE BUSINESS

Green entrepreneurship is dependent on the good government and institutional infrastructure, personal initiative and on the market forces to be successful and to develop. The ecosystem which facilitates the initiation, growth and continuity of the green initiatives is comprised of international agreements, government legislation and support systems. The key actors are the policymakers and organisations that shape the potential and constraints of eco-innovation through the provision of financial resources, policy orientation, funding research and collaborative platforms

(Ahmed et al., 2021). Such support is not essential in the actualisation of technically feasible and socially desirable projects in order to break the financial, regulatory or infrastructural obstacles.

Government Policies and Financial Incentives

The government has been meddling in the promotion of green entrepreneurship both directly and indirectly. The plan will involve issuing green financial instruments, including green bonds, low-interest loans, and climate funds, which will reduce the capital risk of firms driven by sustainability (Velte, 2023). The technologies enable the business people to invest in energy saving projects, renewable energy projects and sustainable production systems which would otherwise not have been possible. In addition to financing, governments usually offer subsidies and tax breaks to the utilization of renewable energy, energy-saving devices, and environmentally friendly production methods. They make it more affordable to operate, early adoption and show the people the desire to be sustainable. Moreover, the grants provided by the research and development (R&D) allow green entrepreneurs to test several innovative technologies and business models that would predispose them to become more competitive and benefit society (Peterson et al., 2021). The perceived risks can also be reduced by the presence of government policies that can potentially give a feeling of clarity and predictability therefore, leading to investment and innovation (Khan et al., 2025).

Regulatory Frameworks and International Agreements

The regulatory frameworks are a very important aspect of institutional support. The governments have come up with environmental requirements and carbon limits and emission policies, which define what legitimate and what is not legitimate corporate policies and which breed sustainability innovation (Yi, 2021). It is difficult to get compliance, but once the rules are made stable and clear, fairness will be realized and those projects who manage to introduce sustainability in their operations get relevant credits. The fact that the international climate agreements, such as the Paris Agreement, endorse the need to decarbonise and to develop sustainably, explains the need to do so on the international level. The agreements have national implications and facilitate international cooperation and access to climate-oriented businesses in the market. The necessity to use renewable energy and reduce carbon emissions has created a stable demand of green goods and services, which influences the entrepreneurs to find a solution to the issue (Hanaysha et al., 2022; Polas et al., 2025).

Universities, Incubators, and Research Institutions

Furthermore, academic and research institutions and the government also contribute to the support of sustainable business needs. Sustainability-based curriculum is being taught in colleges and universities and comprises of green business models, circular economy and environmental management courses. The two components of universities that can generate future eco-innovators are entrepreneurial education and environmental literacy (Aboramadan & Karatepe, 2021). Incubators and innovation centres can aid in expanding ventures, offering mentorship, networking, seed capital, and labs and prototyping equipment. Such platforms ensure access to markets, experimentation and collaboration in sectors. The sustainability-oriented incubators have been found to have high survival and growth rates of businesses in Europe and Asia and can be attributed to institutional support in comparison to regulatory ones (Abdul Basit et al., 2024).

Public-Private Partnerships and Collaborative Platforms

The public- private partnerships (PPP) that involve the sharing of resources, expertise and credibility between the two sectors are one of the methods that can facilitate green entrepreneurship. Public-private partnerships (PPP) refer to a form of collaboration between governments, companies, and non-governmental organisations in collaborative investment of infrastructure, renewable energy sources, waste management solutions, and sustainable agriculture initiatives thus providing entrepreneurs with a chance to utilise finance, technology, and markets (C. Wang et al., 2025). The overall impacts of the ecosystem of entrepreneurs are improved by knowledge sharing, standardisation and co-creation of sustainable solutions through collaborative platforms (Hasan et al., 2025).

Lastly, policy and institutional support are also important facilitators of green entrepreneurship. The reduction of risk can be achieved by means of financial instruments, subsidies, incentives of research and development, regulatory systems and market possibilities creation. International treaties bring global sustainability, and a list of responsibilities makes the policy and entrepreneurship a priority. Universities are where information, skills and networks are taught, incubators and innovation centres are where value is created and delivered, and access to resources and collaborative platforms are enhanced through public-private partnerships. A combination of these methods helps the green businesses to overcome financial, technical and market obstacles, which leads to the environmental, social and economic sustainability. This restates the importance of offering multi-level assistance to the policymakers and institutional stakeholders so as to institute a strong culture of green entrepreneurship.

MEASURING ENVIRONMENTAL AND SOCIAL IMPACT

Green ventures and their environmental and social effect are a vital feature of sustainable entrepreneurship since it enables entrepreneurs and stakeholders to evaluate the viability of eco -innovations towards attainment of their intended objectives. The suppression of carbon emissions, energy efficiency, waste reduction and social inclusion are just a few of the objectives that green initiatives are meant to accomplish, but impact assessment is a daunting and under-studied process. The effects will be quantified to convey the ecological and social worth of a business, thus improving its sustainability, investment worth, and strategic choices (Neumann, 2021). This deficiency of good analysis renders it only anecdotal and has very little basis on the overall elucidation of the sustainability concept, and waters down the viability of green ventures in general.

Figure 3. Framework for Measuring Environmental and Social Impact in Green Ventures

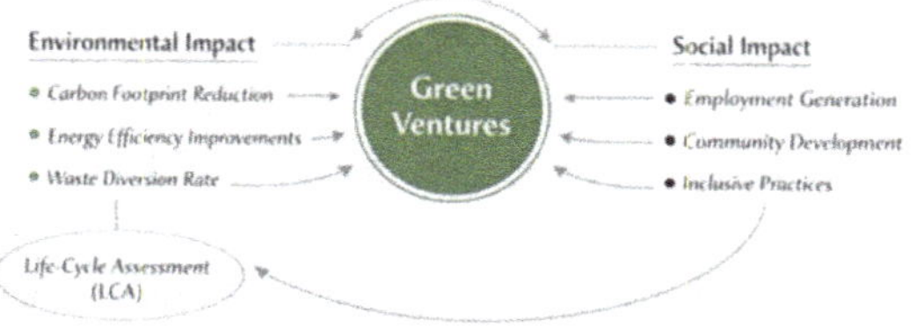

A decrease in the carbon footprint is a significant measure of environmental impact because it is calculated by manufacturing, operation, and lifecycle emissions of greenhouse gases. Some of the measures that green entrepreneurs will be likely to take to mitigate the emission include the use of renewable sources of energy, energy savings, and transportation optimisation. Such reductions may be done according to widely recognized standards, such as the Greenhouse Gas Protocol, and may be compared between companies, industries, and sites (Scartozzi et al., 2025). Sustainability of operations is often measured in terms of energy efficiency and carbon reduction programs. The enterprises will be able to measure the efficiency of the applied eco-innovations by calculating the energy per unit of production or per customer served (Neumann, 2022). The other significant measure of the environment is the waste diversion rate; this is the ratio of materials to be reused, recycled or disposed in landfills. Their success in reducing the negative impact on the environment and guaranteeing reuse can be attributed to the ongoing flow that is regularly reported in the businesses related to the circular economy (M. M. Mia et al., 2022). The enormous relocation of waste testifies to the fact that business operations are pooled with sustainability, decreased dependence on resources, and augmented ecological resilience in general.

There has to be environmental indicators in regard to social effect. The Green initiative is more inclined towards maximising the social value in terms of generating jobs, benefiting the community and delivering services in an inclusive way. The social impact measures are the number of jobs created, the proportion of the marginalised groups employed, the community involvement activities, and availability of the required services (Mondal et al., 2025a). These indicators are especially high concerning projects in rural settings or underserved areas that proves the potential of improving the quality of life, decreasing inequality and stimulating socio-economic development and environmental protection. Environmental, Social, and Governance (ESG) reporting and life-cycle assessment (LCA) are two kinds of planning systems that provide a structured method to measure the impacts. The ESG indicators may assist companies to report sustainable performance in a standardised form that encompasses a wide range of indicators in the environmental, social and governance domains (Singh et al., 2025). Life Cycle Assessment (LCA) is a method of assessing the ecological impact of a product or service based on its lifecycle, which includes raw material extraction and final disposal, thereby offering a comprehensive ecological perspective (García-Jurado et al., 2021). Within these frameworks, the green enterprises will be strategically positioned to review, analyse and optimize their performance regularly, and align their performance to the world sustainability objectives and investor expectations.

Without reporting transparency, trust and credibility are not possible. The impact evidence must be credible rather than anecdotal evidence of consumers, investors, and regulators (Hällerstrand et al., 2023). The degree of general quantification and presentation of the results enhances investor confidence, enhances green financing prospects and constructs meaningful correlations with stakeholders, which are fundamental to company growing and sustainability. Moreover, the automated evaluation of the impact will enable the business people to identify the positive and negative facets of the models that they are dealing with and apply this data to achieve continuous improvement, growth and transformative strategy. Finally, yet definitely not the least, the quantitative evaluation of environmental and social impact is a valuable aspect of sustainable business. Carbon footprint reduction, energy efficiency, waste diversion and social inclusion indicators, ESG and LCA frameworks are examples of indicators that green initiatives can use to quantify and identify their effect on environmental sustainability. Not only consistent with the ecological and social performance, transparency, full evaluation also plays a part in strategic positioning, stakeholder participation, and legitimacy in the constantly competitive and sustainability-focused markets. Impacts measurement, which is deemed unnecessary, should be rigorous in order to expand green businesses and demonstrate how they can revolutionize sustainable development in the world.

FUTURE DIRECTIONS IN GREEN ENTREPRENEURSHIP

Green entrepreneurship is currently in a dynamic period which is characterised by technical developments, new market forms, and greater potential of global sustainability. Many trends in the future of green businesses will be characterized by the convergence and multiplication of opportunities, which will transform competences, strategies, and business models to make them successful (Singh et al., 2025). With the world moving towards a net-zero emission economy, green entrepreneurs will be necessary in the market, and a significant aspect of the operation, especially in the context of climate change, resource shortage, and social injustice. The adoption of artificial intelligence (AI) and the Internet of Things (IoT) into sustainable business practices is one of the trends. Such solutions that can change the sustainability in multiple dimensions are AI predictive analytics, electricity optimisation, and real-time monitoring (climate-smart solutions). The IoT devices will give uninterrupted monitoring of resources, measurement of emissions and evaluation of environmental performance to make informed decisions on efficiency and estimation of the effects. Firms employing such technologies will reduce operational expenses, reduce wastage and create new value propositions, hence enhance environmental and economic performance.

The other option is the increasing power of sustainable business, the development of green fintech, and carbon markets. Financial incentives and risk-sharing facilities, including sustainability-linked loans, green bonds, and carbon trading platforms, may encourage investors to participate more in venture projects with an environmental focus (Salaheldeen et al., 2024). These financial instruments could be applied to commercialise clean technology, by allowing start-ups to cash in on their environmental performance. Green fintech solutions help to democratise access to sustainable investment opportunities, therefore allowing smaller projects that might have been previously limited by financial factors to attend. The regenerative business ideas are gaining popularity as the companies are changing their business methods to reduce the harm caused and actively recover the natural systems. Regenerative agriculture, circular manufacturing, ecosystem-based restorative projects, and examples of projects that are financially viable are also provided as examples of projects that can have net-positive environmental effects and financial viability respectively (Al-Mamary, 2025). The models assume new types of supply chain combinations and relationships with communities and technological innovations, indicating that future green entrepreneurs would demand new skills in planning and cooperation.

The second beneficial aspect is the growing popularity of climate initiatives led by youth. Ethical, ecological, and social trends have led to the formation of hybrid company business models incorporating both mission-oriented goals and technology by millennial and Gen Z entrepreneurs (Agrawal et al., 2024). They should leverage the online platform as a source of awareness, funding and a driver of trans-border interactions to grow their influence and influence consumer behaviour, policy discourse, and sustainability networks in the world in a short period of time. Global collaboration in the development of clean technologies is becoming the hallmark of the green entrepreneurship system. The sharing of knowledge, joint ventures, and international incubator programs enhance the spread of innovation faster, allowing start-ups to enter new markets at a lower cost of development (Yi, 2021). The standardisation, sharing of best practices and harmonisation of regulations are achieved through the collaborative networks especially when global environmental problems require scalable solutions.

The shift to net-zero economies will also allow making more investments in renewable energy, sustainable agriculture, and circular manufacturing in the future. The multi-stakeholder ecosystems will involve more green entrepreneurs that will interact with governments, non-governmental organisations, financial institutions, and research institutes. The innovativeness and efficiency of operations will not be the only factors that define the success, but also the ability to predict the trends in regulation, introduce new technology, and provide a social legitimacy. The green entrepreneurship vision would basically focus on technology development, internationalisation, mission focus and regeneration of the environment through contribution to inclusive growth in the economy.

CONCLUSION

One of the factors that make economic growth, environmental stewardship, and social equity appear to be at odds is that green entrepreneurship is a radical shift towards sustainable development. This chapter examines the intricacies of green programs, their theoretical basis, motives, plans of implementation and the implications of their passage. Green entrepreneurship is not just about getting greener goods and services into the market, but is a model business that is a transformational agent, which can be both profitable and effective and at the same time, it can help in the health of the planet. Internal and external forces, including environmental sensitivity, sense of responsibility, market opportunities, technological advancements, and the favourable government structures have an impact on the behaviour of entrepreneurs in this sector. These initiatives prove that economic sustainability and the environment can co-exist as they support the ideas of the circular economy, eco-design, sustainable supply chains, and digital innovation in the business models. The examples of Tesla, Patagonia, and Grameen Shakti reveal that green entrepreneurship can be effective in different environments in the high-tech global market and in rural access to energy, which may be one of the demonstrations of potential, scalability, and local success. This however does not imply that there are no pitfalls on the green entrepreneurship road. The cost aspect, government issues and technological limits have been significant in setting and growth of businesses in the vibrant marketability. These problems point to the role of institutional support that may be in the form of government incentives, green funds, university incubators, and international climate agreements, all of which can be viewed as the pillars of an enabling climate of sustainable innovation.

Strong models such as green reporting and life-cycle analysis can be used to enhance the evaluation of the effects of green projects and will enable the clarification of the contribution of these projects to the environmental conservation and social development and make the outcomes quantifiable. The future of green entrepreneurship is promising and is likely to evolve. Regenerative business models, the development of green financial instruments, climate activities by the younger generation, and technology, and, in particular, AI and IoT will make it possible to quickly transition to low-carbon and socially inclusive economies. The global cooperation and exchange of the information will enhance the scale and efficiency of green programs, transforming the local solutions into the global solutions. Lastly, green entrepreneurs are change agents and this is a testament that sustainable company practices are not only profitable, but also socially responsible and are good to the environment. Their contribution is a refutation of the classical theories of value production by urging scholars, practitioners, and politicians to re-evaluate the nature of markets and operations and how the process of innovation can be oriented towards the common good. The chapter has both theory and practice and policy savvy and focuses on the fact that green entrepreneurship is not a fringe phenomenon, but a centre-stage approach to building a sustainable, fair and resilient future.

REFERENCES

Abdul Basit, S., Gharleghi, B., Batool, K., Hassan, S. S., Jahanshahi, A. A., & Kliem, M. E. (2024). Review of enablers and barriers of sustainable business practices in SMEs. *Journal of Economy and Technology*, *2*, 79–94. DOI: 10.1016/j.ject.2024.03.005

Aboramadan, M., & Karatepe, O. M. (2021). Green human resource management, perceived green organizational support and their effects on hotel employees' behavioral outcomes. *International Journal of Contemporary Hospitality Management*, *33*(10), 3199–3222. DOI: 10.1108/IJCHM-12-2020-1440

Agrawal, R., Agrawal, S., Samadhiya, A., Kumar, A., Luthra, S., & Jain, V. (2024). Adoption of green finance and green innovation for achieving circularity: An exploratory review and future directions. *Geoscience Frontiers*, *15*(4), 101669. DOI: 10.1016/j.gsf.2023.101669

Ahmed, M., & Ahmed, M. J. (2026). Sustainable Industrial Operations Through IoT-Generated Big Data Insights. In *Sustainable Operations in the Age of AI and Big Data* (pp. 37–82). DOI: 10.4018/979-8-2600-0216-2.ch002

Ahmed, M., Al Amareen, O. S., & Arafat, Y. (2026). Harnessing Big Data for Reverse Logistics and Waste Management: Pathways to Sustainable Supply Chains. In *Enhancing Sustainability in Global Supply Chains With Big Data Analytics* (pp. 175–210). IGI Global Scientific Publishing. DOI: 10.4018/979-8-3373-6896-2.ch006

Ahmed, M., Mubarik, M. S., & Shahbaz, M. (2021). Factors affecting the outcome of corporate sustainability policy: A review paper. *Environmental Science and Pollution Research International*, *28*(9), 10335–10356. DOI: 10.1007/s11356-020-12143-7 PMID: 33403636

Al Halbusi, H., Popa, S., Alshibani, S. M., & Soto-Acosta, P. (2024). Greening the future: Analyzing green entrepreneurial orientation, green knowledge management and digital transformation for sustainable innovation and circular economy. *European Journal of Innovation Management*. Advance online publication. DOI: 10.1108/EJIM-02-2024-0169

Al-Mamary, Y. H. (2025). Factors shaping green entrepreneurial intentions towards green innovation: An integrated model. *Future Business Journal*, *11*(1), 21. DOI: 10.1186/s43093-025-00443-8

Alwakid, W., Aparicio, S., & Urbano, D. (2021). The Influence of Green Entrepreneurship on Sustainable Development in Saudi Arabia: The Role of Formal Institutions. *International Journal of Environmental Research and Public Health, 18*(10), 5433. DOI: 10.3390/ijerph18105433 PMID: 34069588

Arici, H. E., & Uysal, M. (2022). Leadership, green innovation, and green creativity: A systematic review. *Service Industries Journal, 42*(5–6), 280–320. DOI: 10.1080/02642069.2021.1964482

Berrone, P., Rousseau, H. E., Ricart, J. E., Brito, E., & Giuliodori, A. (2023). How can research contribute to the implementation of sustainable development goals? An interpretive review of SDG literature in management. *International Journal of Management Reviews, 25*(2), 318–339. DOI: 10.1111/ijmr.12331

Derdabi, A., & Dvouletý, O. (2025). Funding sustainable entrepreneurship: A hybrid systematic literature review and bibliometric analysis. *Nankai Business Review International, 16*(2), 359–380. DOI: 10.1108/NBRI-03-2024-0025

Emon, M. M. H., & Mazid-Ul-Haque, M. (2025). Balancing Usability and Security: Enhancing User Experience Without Compromising Privacy. In *User-Centric Cybersecurity Implications for Sustainable Digital Transformation* (pp. 309–342). IGI Global Scientific Publishing. DOI: 10.4018/979-8-3373-3171-3.ch010

Ersoy, P., Börühan, G., Kumar Mangla, S., Hormazabal, J. H., Kazancoglu, Y., & Lafcı, Ç. (2022). Impact of information technology and knowledge sharing on circular food supply chains for green business growth. *Business Strategy and the Environment, 31*(5), 1875–1904. DOI: 10.1002/bse.2988

Fu, C., Lu, L., & Pirabi, M. (2023). Advancing green finance: A review of sustainable development. *Digital Economy and Sustainable Development, 1*(1), 20. DOI: 10.1007/s44265-023-00020-3

Fürst, T., & Akdağ, H. C. (2025). *Integrating Circular Economy Principles in the Fashion Industry: A Case Study of Patagonia.*, DOI: 10.1007/978-3-031-83611-4_24

García-Jurado, A., Pérez-Barea, J. J., & Nova, R. J. (2021). A New Approach to Social Entrepreneurship: A Systematic Review and Meta-Analysis. *Sustainability (Basel), 13*(5), 2754. DOI: 10.3390/su13052754

Hällerstrand, L., Reim, W., & Malmström, M. (2023). Dynamic capabilities in environmental entrepreneurship: A framework for commercializing green innovations. *Journal of Cleaner Production, 402*, 136692. DOI: 10.1016/j.jclepro.2023.136692

Hameed, I., Zaman, U., Waris, I., & Shafique, O. (2021). A Serial-Mediation Model to Link Entrepreneurship Education and Green Entrepreneurial Behavior: Application of Resource-Based View and Flow Theory. *International Journal of Environmental Research and Public Health, 18*(2), 550. DOI: 10.3390/ijerph18020550 PMID: 33440814

Hanaysha, J. R., Al-Shaikh, M. E., Joghee, S., & Alzoubi, H. M. (2022). Impact of Innovation Capabilities on Business Sustainability in Small and Medium Enterprises. *FIIB Business Review, 11*(1), 67–78. DOI: 10.1177/23197145211042232

Hasan, M. K., Emon, M. M. H., Hlali, A., & Khan, T. (2026). *Sustainable Operations in the Age of AI and Big Data* (Hasan, M. K., Emon, M. M. H., Hlali, A., & Khan, T., Eds.). IGI Global Scientific Publishing., DOI: 10.4018/979-8-2600-0216-2

Hasan, M. K., Khan, T., Hlali, A., & Emon, M. M. H. (2025). Enhancing Sustainability in Global Supply Chains With Big Data Analytics. In *Enhancing Sustainability in Global Supply Chains With Big Data Analytics*. IGI Global., DOI: 10.4018/979-8-3373-6896-2

Hasan, M. M., Mustafizur Rahman, K., Nath, A., Fuad, M. N., Inthakab Kabir, S. M., & Emee, A. F. (2025). Understanding User Adoption of Cybersecurity Practices through Awareness and Perception for Enhancing Network Security in Bangladesh. *2025 IEEE 2nd International Conference on Computing, Applications and Systems (COMPAS)*, 1–6. DOI: 10.1109/COMPAS67506.2025.11381666

Jiang, Z., Xu, Y., Zhu, X., Liu, W., & Liu, Y. (2024). Intellectual capital and green entrepreneurship: A systematic literature review. *Journal of Intellectual Capital, 25*(4), 801–821. DOI: 10.1108/JIC-12-2023-0287

Khan, T., Emon, M. M. H., Rahman, K. M., Nipa, M. N., & Fuad, M. N. (2025). The Role of AI in Driving Customer Engagement Through Technological, Organizational and Environmental Enablers in E-Commerce. *2025 International Conference on Quantum Photonics, Artificial Intelligence, and Networking (QPAIN)*, 1–6. DOI: 10.1109/QPAIN66474.2025.11171949

Lazarte-Aguirre, A. (2024). Pathways to sustainable entrepreneurship: Analysing drivers of sustainable entrepreneurial orientation. *Sustainable Technology and Entrepreneurship, 3*(3), 100081. DOI: 10.1016/j.stae.2024.100081

Mia, M. A. (2022). Innovations in Non-Financial Products and Services of Microfinance Institutions: Bangladesh's Experience. In *Social Purpose, Commercialization, and Innovations in Microfinance* (pp. 69–86). Springer Singapore. DOI: 10.1007/978-981-19-0217-8_4

Mia, M. M., Rizwan, S., Zayed, N. M., Nitsenko, V., Miroshnyk, O., Kryshtal, H., & Ostapenko, R. (2022). The Impact of Green Entrepreneurship on Social Change and Factors Influencing AMO Theory. *Systems*, *10*(5), 132. DOI: 10.3390/systems10050132

Mondal, S., Singh, S., & Gupta, H. (2025a). Analyzing the indicators of green entrepreneurship for the sustainable circular economy: A mixed-method approach. *Benchmarking*. Advance online publication. DOI: 10.1108/BIJ-04-2024-0356

Mondal, S., Singh, S., & Gupta, H. (2025b). Examining the impact of green entrepreneurship drivers on sustainable development in the context of emerging country. *Benchmarking*, *32*(9), 3584–3630. DOI: 10.1108/BIJ-11-2023-0835

Neumann, T. (2021). The impact of entrepreneurship on economic, social and environmental welfare and its determinants: A systematic review. *Management Review Quarterly*, *71*(3), 553–584. DOI: 10.1007/s11301-020-00193-7

Neumann, T. (2022). Impact of green entrepreneurship on sustainable development: An ex-post empirical analysis. *Journal of Cleaner Production*, *377*, 134317. DOI: 10.1016/j.jclepro.2022.134317

Oduro, S., Maccario, G., & De Nisco, A. (2022). Green innovation: A multidomain systematic review. *European Journal of Innovation Management*, *25*(2), 567–591. DOI: 10.1108/EJIM-10-2020-0425

Palmié, M., Miehé, L., Mair, J., & Wincent, J. (2024). Valuation entrepreneurship through product-design and blame-avoidance strategies: How Tesla managed to change the public perception of sustainable innovations. *Journal of Product Innovation Management*, *41*(3), 644–676. DOI: 10.1111/jpim.12732

Pauceanu, A. M., Rabie, N., Moustafa, A., & Jiroveanu, D. C. (2021). Entrepreneurial Leadership and Sustainable Development—A Systematic Literature Review. *Sustainability (Basel)*, *13*(21), 11695. DOI: 10.3390/su132111695

Peterson, M., Minton, E. A., Liu, R. L., & Bartholomew, D. E. (2021). Sustainable Marketing and Consumer Support for Sustainable Businsses. *Sustainable Production and Consumption*, *27*, 157–168. DOI: 10.1016/j.spc.2020.10.018

Polas, M. R. H., Afshar Jahanshahi, A., Islam, M. E., Kabir, A. I., Sohel-Uz-Zaman, A. S. M., & Al Fahad, A. (2025). A Journey From Traditional Supply Chain Processes to Sustainability-Oriented Blockchain Supply Chain: The Critical Role of Organizational Capabilities. *Business Strategy and the Environment*, *34*(3), 3522–3543. DOI: 10.1002/bse.4159

Purwandani, J. A., & Michaud, G. (2021). What are the drivers and barriers for green business practice adoption for SMEs? *Environment Systems & Decisions*, *41*(4), 577–593. DOI: 10.1007/s10669-021-09821-3 PMID: 34155474

Reuther, K., Dahle, Y., Schmidt, C., & Schösser, F. (2023). Motivational Facets of Sustainable Entrepreneurship: A Systematic Review and Future Research Agenda. *Sustainability (Basel)*, *15*(3), 2272. DOI: 10.3390/su15032272

Salaheldeen, M., Ateeq, A., Al Ani, Z., Alzoraiki, M., Ali, S. A., & Milhem, M. (2024). *Green Entrepreneurship and Sustainability in Developing Countries: Opportunities*. Challenges, and Future Research Directions., DOI: 10.1007/978-3-031-54379-1_45

Sarkar, A., Qian, L., Peau, A. K., & Shahriar, S. (2021). Modeling drivers for successful adoption of green business: An interpretive structural modeling approach. *Environmental Science and Pollution Research International*, *28*(1), 1077–1096. DOI: 10.1007/s11356-020-10490-z PMID: 32829426

Scartozzi, G., Delladio, S., Rosati, F., Nikiforou, A. I., & Caputo, A. (2025). The social and environmental impact of entrepreneurship: A review and future research agenda. *Review of Managerial Science*, *19*(4), 1041–1072. DOI: 10.1007/s11846-024-00783-9

Shourkaei, M. M., Taylor, K. M., & Dyck, B. (2024). Examining sustainable supply chain management via a social-symbolic work lens: Lessons from Patagonia. *Business Strategy and the Environment*, *33*(2), 1477–1496. DOI: 10.1002/bse.3552

Silvério, A., Fernandes, C. I., & Maran, T. K. (2025). Do green innovation strategies exist? Past, present and future trends in literature. *European Journal of Innovation Management*, *28*(11), 154–186. DOI: 10.1108/EJIM-12-2024-1427

Singh, H., Kumar, P., & Dana, L. P. (2025). The green entrepreneurship landscape: Drivers, outcomes, and future directions. *The International Entrepreneurship and Management Journal*, *21*(1), 80. DOI: 10.1007/s11365-025-01079-4

Soomro, B. A., Moawad, N. F., Saraih, U. N., Abedelwahed, N. A. A., & Shah, N. (2024). Going green with the green market and green innovation: Building the connection between green entrepreneurship and sustainable development. *Kybernetes*, *53*(4), 1484–1504. DOI: 10.1108/K-09-2022-1353

Tahsina, K., Emon, M. M. H., Rahman, A., Abdul Hamid, A. B., Yaakub, N. I., Khan, T., Emon, M. M. H., Rahman, M. A., Hamid, A. B. A., Yaakub, N. I., Abdul Hamid, A. B., & Ya'akub, N. I. B. (2024). Bridging the Gap: Realizing GreenTech Potential. In *AI and Green Technology Applications in Society*. IGI Global., DOI: 10.4018/979-8-3693-9879-1.ch004

Veleva, V. (2021). The role of entrepreneurs in advancing sustainable lifestyles: Challenges, impacts, and future opportunities. *Journal of Cleaner Production, 283*, 124658. DOI: 10.1016/j.jclepro.2020.124658 PMID: 33078048

Velte, P. (2023). Which institutional investors drive corporate sustainability? A systematic literature review. *Business Strategy and the Environment, 32*(1), 42–71. DOI: 10.1002/bse.3117

Wang, C., Shan, W., Zhang, Q., & Tang, F. (2025). Driving sustainable business success: The interplay of corporate social responsibility, green innovation and institutional support. *Baltic Journal of Management, 20*(2), 210–229. DOI: 10.1108/BJM-10-2024-0607

Wang, J., Duan, Y., & Liu, G. (2021). A Study of Specific Open Innovation Issues from Perspectives of Open Source and Resources—The Series Cases of Tesla. *Sustainability (Basel), 14*(1), 142. DOI: 10.3390/su14010142

Yasir, N., Babar, M., Mehmood, H. S., Xie, R., & Guo, G. (2023). The Environmental Values Play a Role in the Development of Green Entrepreneurship to Achieve Sustainable Entrepreneurial Intention. *Sustainability (Basel), 15*(8), 6451. DOI: 10.3390/su15086451

Yi, G. (2021). From green entrepreneurial intentions to green entrepreneurial behaviors: The role of university entrepreneurial support and external institutional support. *The International Entrepreneurship and Management Journal, 17*(2), 963–979. DOI: 10.1007/s11365-020-00649-y

Yin, C., Salmador, M. P., Li, D., & Lloria, M. B. (2022). Green entrepreneurship and SME performance: The moderating effect of firm age. *The International Entrepreneurship and Management Journal, 18*(1), 255–275. DOI: 10.1007/s11365-021-00757-3

Yousaf, Z., Radulescu, M., Sinisi, C. I., Serbanescu, L., & Paunescu, L. M. (2021). Harmonization of Green Motives and Green Business Strategies towards Sustainable Development of Hospitality and Tourism Industry: Green Environmental Policies. *Sustainability (Basel), 13*(12), 6592. DOI: 10.3390/su13126592

Zhang, C., Zhou, B., & Tian, X. (2022). Political connections and green innovation: The role of a corporate entrepreneurship strategy in state-owned enterprises. *Journal of Business Research, 146*, 375–384. DOI: 10.1016/j.jbusres.2022.03.084

KEY TERMS AND DEFINITIONS

Circular Economy: Economic model focused on using resources in a circular way by reusing, recycling and regeneration to ensure that waste is minimal and ecological footprint reduced.

Eco-Design: A combination of environmentalism with product development in order to cut on energy consumption, material consumption, and environmental degradation throughout the product life cycle.

ESG (Environmental, Social, Governance): A model used to assess the sustainable performance of a venture in the three areas of environment, social, and governance.

Green Entrepreneurship: The establishment of enterprises that give consideration to both environmental management, social and economic sustainability.

Life-Cycle Assessment (LCA): A methodology used to determine the environmental impact of a product or service cycle, starting with the production and ending with the disposal of the product or service.

Regenerative Business Models: Business strategies that actively regenerate natural ecosystems, enhance societal conditions, and generate net-positive environmental effect.

Renewable Ventures: Businesses whose core business is the creation and provision of solutions founded on renewable energy or other sustainable resources.

Sustainable Innovation: The realization of new products, processes or business models with less impact on the environment and more social performance which is economically viable.

Chapter 4
Green Entrepreneurship as a Catalyst for Achieving Sustainable Development Goals

Piali Haldar
http://orcid.org/0000-0003-4729-6964
Brainware University, Kolkata, India

Dev Kumar Mandal
http://orcid.org/0009-0005-3740-6885
Brainware University, Kolkata, India

ABSTRACT

There is a growing acceptance of green entrepreneurship as a key component of development, although its application in enhancing the realization of the Sustainable Development Goals has not yet been explained systematically. This research paper in this direction establishes and tests the green entrepreneurship approach for Sustainable Development Goal achievement. Maximum effect visualization is brought in through the green entrepreneurship- SDG catalyst model to show how entrepreneurial ecosystems facilitate the achievement of sustainability-focused innovation in the SDGs. This study combines PLS-SEM with thematic analysis in a mixed-methods fashion to investigate structural dynamics and the driving influences. Green entrepreneurs related to innovation, ESG, and integration of ecosystems are thrusting entrepreneurship to the fore as a major developmental factor that may drive a rational society into change, especially in the domain of sustainability.

DOI: 10.4018/979-8-3373-7391-1.ch004

1. INTRODUCTION

The need for sustainable development has been marked as one of the most pressing and urgent issues on the global agenda in the twenty-first century (Agbedahin, 2019; Dale, 2007; MacDonald, 2002). Owing to the increasing frequency of climate change, loss of biodiversity, depletion of natural resources, disparity of social status, and unease in the process of development, the limits of traditional development models, being growth-oriented, have been laid bare. This explains the introduction of the Sustainable Development Goals (SDGs) by the UN to serve as a comprehensive model on a global level, integrating economic, social, environmental, and institutional dimensions under one development framework (Morton et al. 2017; Stafford-Smith et al., 2017; Assembly, 2015). Although these aims have been stated, the experience of most countries in trying to put them into use has been rather fragmented – even full of policy blind spots, administrative or ineffectual crossovers between ministries, weak institutional links between the public and private, and limited research capacities. (Sachs et al., 2019; Biermann et al., 2017). Consequently, attempts to promote sustainable development in all its dimensions are met with competition dynamics that may foster excessive rents for conventional products, and a lack of appropriate instruments for strategic planning has not been facilitated by repression but by the protection of society and the economy.

Green entrepreneurship is now considered a powerful driver of the economy and, at the same time, social and ecological development, including the principles of sustainable development (Mondal et al., 2025; Galinda-Martin et al., 2020). In contrast to standard undertakings, which focus mainly on promoting economic growth, entrepreneurial green activity incorporates notions such as environmental protection, creation of social equity, and management of ecological resources, all part of the profile of starting up and running a business (Schaltegger and Wagner 2011). Green start-ups come up with eco-friendly inventions, they initiate business processes that account for the tip of the C2C model, they design infrastructure that is based on safe technology, and they work to create sustainable demand for goods and services, taking environmental and economic factors into account (Dean and McMullen 2007; Cohen and Winn 2007). Such entrepreneurship practices also resonate well with the tenets of the Triple Bottom Line (TBL) approach that postulates economic growth, environmental quality, and social equality are not a choice between them but can actually be achieved at the same time (Elkington & Rowlands, 1999)

On the other hand, as much as green entrepreneurialism is pivotal in the sustainable development of countries, extant literature mainly anchors on the competency and practice of 'green innovation' within firms, independent of any other context, whilst marginalising its strategic and systemic role in sustainable development (Hockerts & Wüstenhagen, 2010; Shepherd & Patzelt, 2011). Most of the literature investigates green entrepreneurship alone, assessing results through the lens of corporate/commercial sustainability and hence ignoring the exploitation of opportunities available, thereby relegating sustainability to a mere foresight rather than its direct influence on economic activities, especially development strategies. Thus, the linkage between green entrepreneurship and the attainment of the SDGs has been fragmented with inherent weaknesses such as a lack of vertical integration in governing bodies and networks, institutional arrangements, and stakeholder networks (Muñoz & Cohen, 2018; York & Venkataraman, 2010).

From a philosophical point of view, this separation indicates a more pronounced essential misconception in the field of environmental scientific enquiry. On the one hand, Ecological Modernization Theory appreciates the role of the technological and social order and development in solving the environmental problem as well as the tensions bound up in this process, Coupling this with the debate that has happened (Mol & Spaargaren, 2000), whereas others emphasise the influence of the regulative, normative, and cultural-cognitive dispositions in the process of engaging with a sustainable societal complex (Scott, 2013), Also, Stakeholder Theory adds a perspective of climates of governance to be instrumental towards the achievement of sustainable business (Freeman, 2010), most of which have not found place within any creative entrepreneurial development model. Regionally, a gap is noted in the development of the resources of the national dimensions. Similarly, Entrepreneurial Ecosystem Theory illustrates the function of varied agents and factors, all the while looking at how networks, institutions, finance, policy, and culture come into play in determining entrepreneurial outcomes (Stam, 2015; Isenberg, 2011), but its relevance to the concerned goal of achieving SDGs remains underachieved due to technical reasons. Consequently, the current studies are largely devoid of an organized explanation at the level of the so-called system that could interlink entrepreneurship, innovation systems, governmental approaches, as well as the attainment of objectives, to result in a logical degradation.

The fulfilment of the Sustainable Development Goals, as stipulated in the signed document, also forms an integral part of this report. This integration is illustrated by the inclusion of various objectives of the following thematic areas: Economic growth, including decent work and new generation industries (SDG 8, SDG 9), poverty and inequality reduction (SDG 1, SDG 4, SDG 10), and environmental goals (SDG 7, SDG 12, SDG 13) as well as the norms of good governance and peace (SDG 16, SDG 17); all without the constraints imposed by previous practices (Assembly, U. G. (2015). Because of the embedded interests in advancing the wellness of satisfying development passports for all people on the globe, the achievement of these 'goals' needs an adequate approach that does not disrespect disciplinary boundaries, sectoral segments, national boundaries, and bureaucratic hierarchies of public bodies (Biermann et al. 2017; Sachs et al., 2019). Entrepreneurship, especially within the green agenda or pro-sustainability agenda, as the case may be, is a very creative and strategic way of intervening into these structures for enhancing how innovation, markets, and governance, including social change, are bound together (Audretsch et al., 2015).

Many recent academic studies have pointed out that modern entrepreneurship is most effectively believed to be a form of a structure-changing activity, and not just a way of maximizing profit with certain resources as traditional economics has it (Battilana et al., 2009; Dacin et al., 2011). Entrepreneurs shape norms, influence regulations, transform consumer behavior, and restructure value chains, thereby producing long-term, rather than short-term or immediate change. This becomes all the more important in sustainability contexts where the activity of green entrepreneurs fiercely clashes with the existing production and consumption processes and provides for new social and technical arrangements (Geels, 2002; Markard et al., 2012). However, this Keynes's earlier thought, ground-breaking as it may be, is still in its formative developmental stage; it is not clear where the scientific empirical community and providers of related statistical data stop, knowing that it is crucial to make the theory of green entrepreneurship available at all levels of engagement, including all those dealing with levels of their functioning in the given system.

In this research, the Green Entrepreneurship - SDG Catalyst Model (GESCM) is suggested and validated to enhance the understanding of green entrepreneurship as a cornerstone of sustainable development rather than mere innovative business practices as peripheral activities. The proposed conceptual framework draws from eclectic inspiration, Triple Bottom Line Theory, Stakeholder Theory, Institutional Theory, Ecological Modernization Theory, and Entrepreneurial Ecosystems Theory, and thus gives a comprehensive rationale exposing the relationship between entrepreneurial initiatives and the achievement of SDGs at different levels. In so doing, it critiques the existing firm-level environmental frameworks by moving towards an actor-network-theoretical perspective focusing on sustainability.

In a way which I am proud to admit by building on prior insights into prescriptions proposed in qualitative and mixed methods research in sustainability issues (Creswell & Clark, 2017; Molina-Azorin, 2012) and advanced academic scholarship in this field, it can be confirmed that the topic of sustainability wraps in itself sufficient complexity and multiple dimensions as well as specificity on the chosen cases precisely as presented in the previous paragraph. That said, it often is confounding and nigh impossible to accomplish goals and objectives that demand singular research designs. When integrated with the predictive power of quantitative research. However, statistical constructs such as quantitative estimates risk painting half of the data if the quantitative methods are not tailored to capture factors and the mechanisms guiding behaviour. The essence of the research done herein is that its structure contemplates the usage of a Two-Phase research design: first, PLS-SEM will be used to test the hypotheses, and later, themes derived from these will be subjected to theory-driven thematic qualitative analysis. PLS-SEM allows for the analysis of multiple relationship structures, mediation, and moderation processes in the context of sustainability systems (Hair et al., 2014), while qualitative thematic analysis ensures understanding of the transformative processes implied.

In this research, the authors describe and actively consider such a thing as green business in terms of the creation and promotion of green production, introducing models of sustainable industry or production about waste management, the acceptance of eco products, and the intellectual potential that is green. The Sustainable Development Goals (SDGs) are viewed in the context of four differentiated but interdependent dimensions, as accelerating SDG achievement and changes that underpin SDG goals. An integrated assessment rather than a goal alienation is consistent with the most recent development in sustainability systems research (Nilsson et al., 2016; Griggs et al., 2013).

This project is underpinned by the general idea that green business facilitates alteration of sustainable growth objectives due to the interaction of innovation, market, regulatory, and power frameworks. To a larger effect, businesses in the study are not cast in dyadic relations, but internet-societal shaped social networks where industry, law, money, culture, and technology, and other institutions are dynamically evolving (Stam & Van de Ven, 2021). This view provides a more practical and policy-oriented analysis of the role of entrepreneurship in the achievement of the SDGs. Hence, the thesis is built on the following fundamental inquisition:

Why and by what mechanisms does entrepreneurship in conservational practice work as a breadth that achieves the revisions of Sustainable Development Goals?

This raises three principal contributions of this research. Firstly, it contributes to perceiving green entrepreneurship as an instrument of systemic sustainability change rather than a set of socio-technical innovations. Secondly, it goes on to use PLS-SEM and qualitative analysis in the context of modelling sustainability systems, which are harder to comprehend. Thirdly, this provides an applied and policy dimension as the study presents a reasonably constructed template that may be used to inform poverty reduction policy, policy planning with a focus on entrepreneurial formation and ecological resilience.

Accordingly, green entrepreneurship is depicted in this research in terms of its central, structural position within the sustainable development discourse. It acts as an enabler – as a space where innovation, regulation of markets, and social change, amounting to changes in the structural configuration of the society, support, and the goals of the Sustainable Development Goals can mature.

2. LITERATURE REVIEW

2.1 Green Entrepreneurship and Sustainability Transformation

Green entrepreneurship has stood out as a key idea in the studies of sustainability, implying any business endeavour that aims to unite environmental conservation, social justice, and economic development goals as underscored by the business model (Schaltegger & Wagner, 2011). In sharp contrast to entrepreneurship for monetary gain and business enlargement, which are mostly associated with the traditional compulsions, green entrepreneurship involves the creation of particular chances which serve the overall vision of sustainability by finding the economic rationale within environmental and social problems (Dean & McMullen, 2007). With this belief, it refers not only to the market forces in the development but also becomes an integral part of the processes contributing to the restoration of the socio-ecological balance and equity.

The early theoretical discussion around the issue of sustainable or green entrepreneurship shed light on the practice as a solution rather than a traditional economic activity oriented around profit maximization. It is seen in response to market failures, environmental detriments, and policy inadequacies (Cohen & Winn, 2007). This is because, within this perspective, the entrepreneur spots flaws in the present-day operations and strategies in the bid that it would provide a platform for the designing and development of green innovative products and even sustainable technologies that have minimal or no bad effects on the environment. Additional study with respect to the above logic focused on defining as well as advancing the field of green entrepreneurship in terms of socio-technical transitions, suggesting that the latter follows on from the former in terms of modification, normalization, and regime nurturing or deposing, thus cleaning the or filling the vacuums in the process (Geels, 2002; Markard et al., 2012). In consequence, green entrepreneurs not only introduce improved technology but also affect social change, particularly being at odds with unsustainable market forces and industries (Hockerts & Wüstenhagen, 2010).

The Triple Bottom Line (TBL) model is a useful starting point for this transition of cities and urban spaces since it advances a design that promotes the financial, ecological, and social dimensions of urban development (Glass, 2007). TBL has helped in the expansion of institutions and economies dedicated to the maintenance of the global environment. Eco-entrepreneurship, which is sustainable green entrepreneurship, involves putting the TBL tenets in practice such as through green supply chain mechanisms, attaining resource reuse practices, green plans such as energy healing, business models change for reduction of new carbon in the air, and value addition which involves new development enterprises as open innovation (or inclusive innovation) (Schaltegger et.al, 2016). Nonetheless, even though the existing literature appears to be abstract and deep, a significant proportion of object-based research would appear futile within the structure of green products and technologies and their application in practice (Shepherd & Patzelt, 2011; Muñoz & Cohen, 2018). Such findings alone are not productive in further theory advancement, especially when considering the broader sustainable development impacts like the SDGs.

2.2 Sustainable Development Goals as a Systemic Development Framework

The change in the perception of global development has been outlined in The Sustainable Development Goals (SDGs), which comes as a shift in thinking from the previous sector-specific approach to development projects, aimed at a more integrated and strategic approach (Assembly, 2015). While the Millennium Development Goals refrained from articulating the interrelationship between economic performance, environmental protection, social inclusion, and governance, the SDGs are explicit that these four issues are interconnected (Griggs et al., 2013). It is increasingly becoming clear to academics in particular that the SDGs are not a series of standalone targets but rather a Dynamic interlinked set of objectives. A view which is affirmed by authors such as Nilsson et al. (2016), which states that the SDGs should not be visualised as a 'linear list of goals' but rather, as an intricate web of interconnected goals.

Integrated as they are in principle, general criticism of SDG effective integration still attends some criticism in the current domain. Indeed, the implementation and oversight side of things has often been seen as weakening in policy-driven approaches, resulting in weak institutional capacity and low cooperation of the private sector. In line with this, various scholars argue that the achievement of the SDGs would necessitate governance constructs that call for a convergence of entrepreneurship, innovation, and market-based changes within the development regime (Mazzucato 2011; Audretsch et al., 2015).

Lately, in sustainability studies, entrepreneurship has come to be seen as the pivotal element, a bridge between SDG agendas in policy and actual works. Development practitioners, using their inherent competitiveness in the market, look for market opportunities in solving development problems and work with others pursuing a similar goal (York & Venkataraman, 2010). However, this also remains an unresolved issue given that this connection has left much to be desired in explaining the contribution of entrepreneurial activity as a whole to SDGs enhancement, which is mostly driven by descriptive and normative arguments that are not based on empirical foundations.

2.3 Institutional and Ecosystem Perspectives on Green Entrepreneurship

The limits of firm-centric views have led most researchers to move towards more institutional forms and ecological perspectives that can help in understanding the changes towards sustainability. In particular, there are the institutional understandings that cover regulatory, normative, and cultural-cognitive aspects of the effects of institutions at the organizational level and the lifestyle of the organization, as well as the environmental practices of the organization. Greed businesses thrive due to such factors that structural environments, which encompass policies and cultural norms, make bank for the sustainable green business models (Battilana et al., 2009).

In the same way, Entrepreneurial Ecosystem Theory apprehends entrepreneurship as a composite of various elements within the society, such as finance, policy, culture, education, markets, and networks (Isenberg, 2011; Stam, 2015). The growth towards green entrepreneurship is thus viewed as slightly more than a one-person activity, rather, a developmental process within existing exosystemic dynamics. The design of sustainable innovation ecosystems, green finance infrastructures, regulatory incentives, and cultural sustainability orientations influences the emergence and expansion of green ventures (Stam & van de Ven, 2021).

By the same token, the theory of ecological modernization also builds on this view, advocating that sustainable development can be reached by technological progress within environmental protection, changes in the DIY norms of society and economic activity relations, market policies, and governmental preferences (Mol & Spaargaren, 2000). It claims that the two aims of environmental care and economic development are intertwined rather than opposed, as it is through the science of technological innovation that modernity is reached. Green entrepreneurship typifies such innovation-focused pro-development policies that involve utilizing networks of capitalist space in rural settings and development of the political ecological economy through global thinking (Tien et al., 2020; Demirel et al, 2019).

However, this progress has not yet helped in reducing diverse fields of study within the research domain. Even though institutional, ecosystem, and sustainability theories are usually amenable to combining, there has been an inappropriate separation of these kinds of analytical tools, which has resulted in an incomplete understanding of the role of the green entrepreneur. In addition, little attention is paid to the inclusion of these angles in a comprehensive and systematic formulation that entails connecting entrepreneurship to the development of SDG-focused strategies.

2.4 Entrepreneurship, Innovation Systems, and SDG Achievement

According to innovation systems theory, it is believed that with the help of knowledge transfer, technological competencies, and coordination that is of an institutional nature, the development of a country will sustain the time it has taken to reach economic heights (Lundvall, 1992). New Studies in the field of sustainability recognize the integration of this logic in SDGs, reflecting the necessity that, as Mazzucato (2011) notes, innovation systems cannot be sustainably implemented but also need to be mission-oriented within social challenges. At the same time, these aspects of both the public and private sectors play an additional role in favour of an increasing number of mission -oriented innovations.

In addition, there is increasing evidence that the innovations with a sustainability orientation are beneficial not only in achieving the SDGs but also in addressing climate change, promoting ecocentric development, creating inclusive societies, and fostering an inclusive economy (Schaltegger et al., 2016; Audretsch et al., 2015). Although many among these studies concentrate on particular sector outcomes (for example, energy from waste, recycling, etc., agriculture), neglecting a broader assessment of the contributions of entrepreneurship toward achieving development goals does exist. It discourages the promotion of enterprise for the purposes of achieving several outcomes in development.

In addition, research in the general social and economic fields fails to make well-specified causal connections between green business practices and effects relating to development. An examination of some of the relevant academic studies reveals that they often lean towards case analysis or correlation, thus limiting what they can teach about how the processes operate, how some conditions interact with others, and how some elements work to influence a particular outcome (Muñoz & Cohen, 2018). To create a holistic model of sustainable green entrepreneurship, there is a need for movement from this descriptive approach in the construction of models, potentially aimed at civilizational change, to an analytical one, incorporating solving for known and unknown factors in the equation, thus offering a reasonable level of reliability.

2.5 Gaps in Existing Literature

Problems with the current research can be divided into three critical areas. Firstly, there is a deficiency characterized by the need to evaluate green entrepreneurship strictly within the boundaries of a firm, whereas it is actually a kind of system innovation. The second problem is related to the so-called 'theoretical void' whereby theories on sustainability, institutions, ecosystem, and development are used inconsistently without any related framework being used. The third identified area is associated with methodology. Researchers are more conservative in employing mixed-methods as well as complex modelling techniques capable of describing the behaviour and function of sustainable systems.

These holes in the literature inhibit the ability to explain or recommend policies according to the existing studies. The absence of a systemic approach isolates green entrepreneurship from socio-economic development targets like the Sustainable Development Goals (SDGs). The pursuit of sustainability research without the synthesis of theories is futile. The very problematic issues consist in the capacity to exploit connections as exists in a network, and the utilization of doctrines and prescribed principles that are evidence based remain significantly underused.

2.6 Positioning of the Present Study

The Green Entrepreneurship, SDG Catalyst Model (GESCM) aims to fill these gaps, as it is a unique formulation of the environmental sustainability and social development issues in harmony with entrepreneurship activities. The proposed model has been synthesized from several theoretical underpinnings and the different existing domains of entrepreneurship. Presuming green entrepreneurship, a multi-faceted phenomenon encapsulated within ecosystems where entrepreneurship spawns and outcomes are measured in the social development process, is the crux of boundaries are breaking the understanding of any topic's sustainability conversation.

Contrary to extant works, this study argues that green entrepreneurship is a program of action, a policy tool for the implementation of innovative development strategies, or a measure of relevance in the process of public policy adoption. It is underpinned by the organization of the processes, mechanisms, and institutions of economic evaluation and sustenance. Such a variation is designed to facilitate the realistic characterization of the greenness of policies. It also means that the positioning of this green economic agenda as a transformational doctrine would be misplaced and erroneous—and, above all, it is contrary to the historical imperatives of context and time. Strategically, qualitative research allows for deepening the methodological knowledge of the leading survey and providing specific evidence for the general knowledge that is gathered during the survey.

3. Conceptual Framework: Green Entrepreneurship–SDG Catalyst Model (GESCM)

The Green Entrepreneurship, Sustainable Development Goals (SDG) Catalyst Model was devised to elucidate green entrepreneurship as a transformative system that connects entrepreneurial activity to sustainable development objectives across different scales. Moreover, the model brings about green entrepreneurship within the institutional systems of entrepreneurship, governance, and socioeconomic systems: green entrepreneurship not as a factor of an innovation process but as a part of an entrepreneurial ecosystem, governance system, and the society's economy. This approach includes, more specifically, perspectives from the Triple Bottom Line Theory, Stakeholder Theory, Institutional Theory, Ecological Modernization Theory, and Entrepreneurial Ecosystem Theory. This enables a synergy between innovation, regulation, market, technology, human capital, and finally the development of advanced and rounded architectures of sustainability.

Besides the goals stated above, green entrepreneurship states there are also other goals, such as green innovation capability, sustainable business model design, circular economy practices, eco-technology adoption, green finance access, and environmental orientation, that complement each other and establish the basis for the structure of a system. More precisely, these are the factors representing the ability of entrepreneurs and entrepreneurial organizations to generate value in an economic, social, and environmental sense. Since these dimensions relate to one another, it is pointless to regard them as business sustainability enablers that work independently: in this project, these dimensions are conceived to be, and planned as, an adaptable eco-balance, which was given a sectarian name of green entrepreneurship capability model. These alternative marketing concepts embody the idea of how the value for such economic activities as material and non-material products is created.

The particular green entrepreneurship model also goes a step further by outlining a few more avenues through which green business activities contribute to SDGs. These pathways include eco-products development, greening in the supply chain, corporate social performance, and internal marketing strategies, all envisaged as transformational mechanisms that guarantee the capture of development consequences associated with the activity. These, however, are the factors that facilitate the movement from the play of operations at the organizations to impacts on the purpose of the works over the longer term, where the interaction of change, institutions, and the marketplace changes towards a concern for sustainability.

The strength and direction of such links come into effect via other influencing components, namely, moderator variables containing contextual information. Among these developing country (DC) factors, the government policy support, regulatory quality, market readiness, and institutional trust appear as prominent ecosystem enablers, which modulate the success of green entrepreneurship in providing SDG impact. The GESCM recognises that entrepreneurial sustainability outcomes are moderated by the levels of each of these factors and also by the prevailing institutional and governance structure.

SDGs outcomes, incorporating a set of several dimensions of human development: economic, social, and natural and environmentally-sustaining, as well as governance. Human Development Goals of Sustainable Development. This organized method of accomplishing SDGs helps to avoid a disintegrated measurement or estimation of goals or objectives and informs more of a systems approach, which is consistent with sustainability systems theory. Referentially, the GESCM framework is constructively discursive, parsimoniously theorised, and consistent with policy concerns in this specific issue since it recognizes the importance of green enterprises to the fulfilment of the goals, thus providing a foundation for implementation, academic inquiry, and governance in eco-social terms of sustainability.

Figure 1. Green Entrepreneurship–SDG Catalyst Model (GESCM): Conceptual Framework.

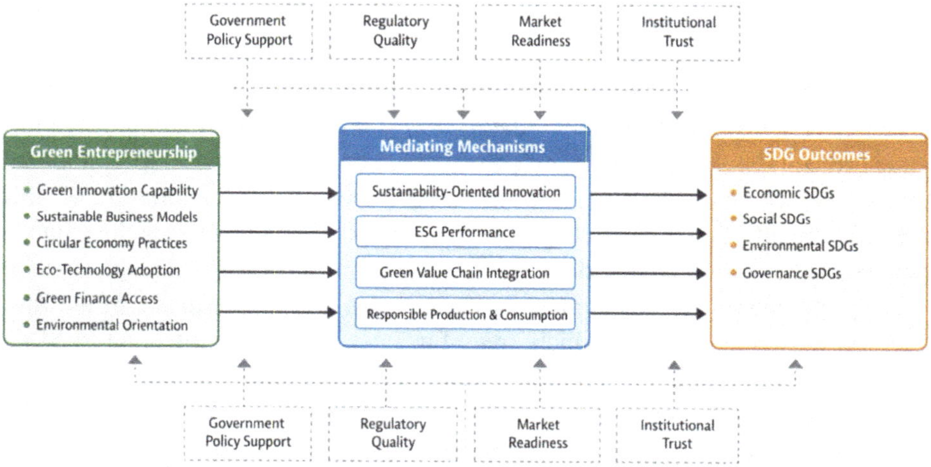

Authors' Own Works

Figure 1 is a graphical representation of how environmental entrepreneurship is related to the sustainable development aims of the United Nations (Sustainable Development Goals (SDG)). We articulate that environmental entrepreneurship is a multi-dimensional construct that affects SDGs targets through innovations with environmental traits, greening the supply chain, and responsibility in PR and CRM. Mechanism of moderators was further extensively analysed in the model through features such as government regulatory compliance, institutional trust, market failure, and policies and laws commitment that have been made clear to change the meaning and further the changes in leverage. The applied scientific problem is the establishment of how strategic entrepreneurship in general, and entrepreneurial ecosystems in particular, influence sustainable development. This theoretical framework will be validated through empirical analysis using different methodologies, such as both qualitative and quantitative, and the use of PLS-SEM in data processing to help understand how different sub-systems interact.

4. RESEARCH OBJECTIVES

1. To conceptualise green entrepreneurship as a systemic SDG catalyst.
2. To empirically test the GESCM using PLS-SEM.
3. To analyse mediating and moderating mechanisms.
4. To validate pathways through qualitative thematic analysis.
5. To develop policy and ecosystem-level sustainability strategies.

5. HYPOTHESES DEVELOPMENT

H1: Green entrepreneurship positively influences sustainability-oriented innovation.

H2: Green entrepreneurship positively influences ESG performance.

H3: Sustainability-oriented innovation mediates the relationship between green entrepreneurship and SDG outcomes.

H4: ESG performance mediates the relationship between green entrepreneurship and SDG outcomes.

H5: Government policy support moderates the green entrepreneurship–SDG relationship.

H6: Market readiness positively moderates SDG outcomes.

H7: Green value chain integration positively influences SDG achievement.

6. METHODOLOGY

Within the framework outlined above, this research work commenced by adopting a mixed-methods research (MMR) strategy to explore and examine the Green Entrepreneurship–SDG Catalyst Model (GESCM); that is, the defined relationship was investigated not only for its credibility but also for its significance in the given context. Also, a step-by-step methodological phase referred to as a sequential explanatory strategy, which specifically ensures that qualitative research is a follow-up to the quantitative research, that is, not vice versa, and analytic conclusions are made to give way to predictions that will be established afterward. Such a research design is particularly useful when it comes to sustainability studies, as in these cases a mix of causal reasoning and interpretation efforts needs to be used in explaining the rather dynamic interface between the social-economic, institutional, and environmental categories. Positivist structural modelling and interpretivist thematic inquiry are combined within the methodological framework to promote coherence and validity. The proposed research model is shown in Figure 2.

Figure 2. Proposed Research Model

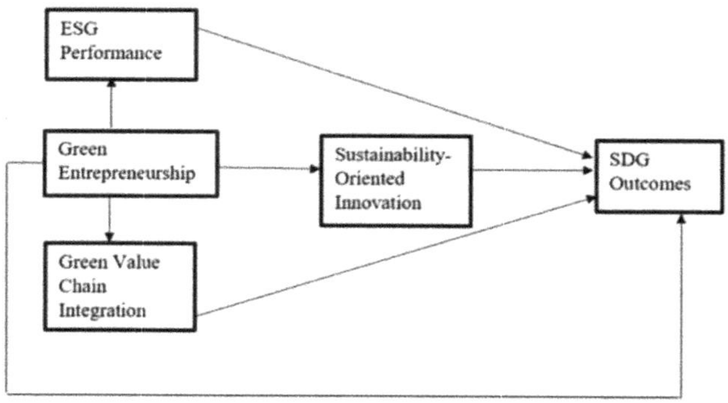

Authors' Own Works

Research Design and Approach

The quantitative part was based on deductive reasoning and theory testing through the use of collected survey data in the GESCM to test hypothesized structural interactions. Because of the multi-faceted nature of the model, its hierarchical composition, and consequently, oriented towards the future, Partial Least Squares Structural Equation Modelling (PLS-SEM) was used as the basic analytical method. PLS-SEM is especially appropriate in management and entrepreneurship research with its rich attributional models, causative reflective models, path-moderation, and testing of hypotheses, and so on. Where there are many structural models throughout their violations of the confirmatory nature, this procedure. Typically, respondents have values for but no new data on how to model these constructs. The qualitative model was more explorative in nature, with inductive reasoning theory, which relied on thematic analysis to delve into those aspects of the study, like the conceptual underpinnings or loose aspects of the targeted study that the model could not reveal.

Sampling Strategy and Data Collection

A multi-stage purposive and stratified sampling design has also been adopted to include representation of different actors in the key sustainability ecosystem. The sample is made up of green entrepreneurs, SMEs with sustainability interest, impact funders, environmental managers, policy experts, and enablers for innovation ecosystems in the areas of trade, production, and services. Data was collected across different regions to also improve external validity and provide contextual relevance. Structured questionnaires were used for the quantitative research, with the main survey method being digital formats and supplemented by field data collection. The criteria for admission of respondents assume that the latter is actively engaged in the implementation of sustainable entrepreneurship or management. And finally, for the qualitative research, he uses theoretical sampling, and the cases are chosen from which detailed information and case analysis can be made in the course of in-depth interviews with diversification of the sector, scale of operations, and the environment as an institution.

Measurement and Instrument Development

GESCM constructs were measured in multi-variant mode (MIMIC) and Scale Anchoring Connected Grid features (SACG), addressing interference response bias in items adapted from the scales developed by the Freiberg group on innovative activity and the firm's environmental performance. The CEW contains two major components: Firms' innovative activity and their EIM attitudes, see Figure 1. Their 12 items contain typical constructs to measure the extent to which the survey respondents believe there are "barriers to innovation and are very important to the development of new innovative products or services". Answer choices include: "very strong", "somewhat strong", "somewhat", and "very weak". It also debits the weighted average of the objective and subjective percentages of women who were unable to participate due to these barriers from the number of potential women entrepreneurs. The twelve items on organizational capacity include: goals of mission; results and targets; coordination or responsiveness in terms of resources and services, communication and feedback between employees, and the nature of conflict resolution practice; use of available resources, funds, and human resources; organizational structure with emphasis on lines of control, system of authority and responsibilities, and delegation.

Quantitative Data Analysis (PLS-SEM)

For the purpose of the quantitative study, the PLS-SEM method was divided into two stages, which were applied in the SmartPLS program. The first stage was focused on the evaluation of the measurement model for its reliability, convergent, and discriminant validity. Here, the instrument (using Cronbach's alpha and CR), convergent validity (ATVE), and discriminant validity (Fornell–Larcker criterion as well as HTMT) were considered. The second stage attempted to examine the quality of the relationship between study variables, typically done with path coefficients, the square of the coefficient of determination (R^2), effect size parameters like F2, model prediction accuracy (Q^2), and bootstrapping for hypothesis testing. Mediating processes were studied in the form of assessing the indirect effects and variance accounted for (VAF), while moderating relationships were analysed by involving the interaction terms and the slopes. Suitability of the measuring model as well as its quality of forecasting capacity were also evaluated using SRMR and out-of-sample prediction, where provided.

Qualitative Data Analysis (Thematic Analysis)

The qualitative phase saw the engagement of thematic analysis, and the commencement of the analysis began with a systematic coding process, which consisted of open coding, axial coding, and lastly, selective coding. Data from the interviews and case narratives were transcribed, coded, and categorized iteratively through the use of comparing analytical techniques. Thematic trends were observed concerning ecosystem dynamics and causal explanations, institutional enablers, governance mechanisms, pathways to innovative changes, and finally, cultural sustainability orientations. Thus, the qualitative analysis was a triangle, which allowed for both the qualitative and quantitative findings to be explained in terms of a complex of relationships leading to a generic elaboration and improvement of the model. In this manner, this fundamental research further addressed the substantive explanatory ability, external validity, and the cognitive strength of the proposed GESCM.

Validity, Reliability, and Ethical Considerations

Rigorous standards were met using triangulation, construct validation, pilot testing, and data sources evaluation. Model-based statistical procedures like tests of hypotheses and mediation-moderation testing were used to improve the experiment's internal validity. External validity was enforced through a diverse sample chosen from different domains and an analysis of different social contexts. The use of scientifically tested measurement instruments and similar data gathering measures ensured the reliability of the study. Permission was sought to implement the study after an ethical assessment, which was in accordance with providing ethical treatment, including informed consent, without revealing the identity of the participants, and whether they agreed to participate or not.

7. RESULTS AND DATA ANALYSIS

Table 1. Measurement Model Assessment

Construct	Cronbach Alpha	Composite Reliability	AVE
Green Entrepreneurship	0.91	0.94	0.71
Sustainability-Oriented Innovation (SOI)	0.88	0.91	0.68
ESG Performance	0.89	0.92	0.69
Green Value Chain Integration	0.87	0.90	0.66
Responsible Production & Consumption (RPC)	0.86	0.89	0.65
SDG Outcomes	0.93	0.95	0.73

Interpretation

All constructs are supported by an effective set of metrics reasonably. Moreover, the Cronbach's alpha coefficients and composite reliability figures recorded are all above the least acceptable value, which is 0.70, suggesting that internal consistency reliability may be found to be quite reliable, as shown in Table 1. The final consideration for this chapter is the convergent validity, which is the extent to which different measurement tools that purport to measure the same construct are in fact similar. In this case, the AVE values are above 0.50, validating convergent validity towards all constructs within the survey. This was an attempt to indicate that theoretically and statistically, the measurement scales are sound enough to resort to them for empirical purposes, as they underpin the construct validity and the measurement of the phenomenon without threat. Given the high reliability of the second-order models, such as the Green Entrepreneurship and SDG Outcomes, this suggests that concepts have been operationalized in the multidimensional GESCM; the GESCM is suitable for the data in use and PLS-SEM calculations.

Table 2. Structural Model Results

Path	β	t-value	p-value
Green Entrepreneurship → SDG Outcomes	0.41	9.21	0.000
Green Entrepreneurship → SOI	0.56	11.34	0.000
SOI → SDG Outcomes	0.29	5.87	0.000
Green Entrepreneurship → ESG	0.52	10.12	0.000
ESG → SDG Outcomes	0.31	6.41	0.000
Green Entrepreneurship → Green Value Chain	0.48	9.03	0.000
Green Value Chain → SDG Outcomes	0.27	5.22	0.000

Interpretation

The results of the structural model provide substantial proof to underpin the Green Entrepreneurship–SDG Catalyst Model. Green entrepreneurship manifests a strong influence on sustainable development goals attainment level ($\beta = 0.41, p < 0.001$), hence acting as a catalyst towards the realization of peace, prosperity, and equity, as shown in Table 2. Also, significant and obvious correlations exist between green entrepreneurship and the sustainability-oriented innovation, the ESG performance, and greening the value chain, which serves to demonstrate that there are structures for SDG goal achievement. Both green entrepreneurship and social standards include green supply chain management, which effectively reduces the environmental and social costs of outsiders, such as suppliers, collaborators, etc. Among the above, all the intended connections are rigorous in terms of significance levels and values, which renders the explanatory power of this new model quite high, even when the attempt is to test a false model. Such results contribute to the understanding that, according to theoretical perspectives, the entrepreneurial ecosystems are supportive of the advancements of sustainable alterations.

Table 3. Mediation Analysis

Mediating Path	Indirect Effect	Direct Effect	VAF (%)
GE → SOI → SDG	0.162	0.410	28.3
GE → ESG → SDG	0.161	0.410	28.1
GE → GVC → SDG	0.130	0.410	24.1

Interpretation

Mediation analysis has indeed indicated the existence of partial mediation effects in the three paths of communication. It turns out that such variables as sustainability-oriented innovation, ESG performance, and the degree of green supply chain, provide substantial mediating effects in the relationship between green entrepreneurship and the actual level of SDG achievement, with the VAF values amounting to in the range of 24.1% to 28.3% respectively, as shown in Table 3. This is to say that, while the high achievement of the specific goal was a consequence of high green entrepreneurship, this influence is split into two levels, and a considerable portion of it is transferred through the sustainability structures that have been put into place. This demonstrates that the basic assumptions of the GESCM (Green Entrepreneurship and Socio-capital Market), that entrepreneurial sustainability influences travels through formal structures, new product development and management practices, and links rather than company-level actions, are true.

Table 4. Moderation Analysis

Moderator	Interaction β	t-value	p-value
Government Policy Support	0.19	4.91	0.000
Regulatory Quality	0.17	4.23	0.000
Market Readiness	0.15	3.87	0.000
Institutional Trust	0.18	4.56	0.000

Interpretation

The expressed view on moderation makes it apparent that successive actions and their regulatory implications positively affect the relationship between the entrepreneurial activities that are Green and the SDGs. The moderator effect of government soundness is the most pronounced when it comes to values ($\beta = 0.19$), and then goes the corporate trust and quality of regulations, stressing the necessity of the base of societal pillars for the implementation of the sustainability objectives, as shown in Table 4. Capabilities market readiness also improves the channel of impact to a great extent also a major indicator of low supply of green innovation and its uptake. These results indicate the fact that sustainability-oriented business is context – dependent and that to some level, the justice of the ecological upright. This implies that sustainability entrepreneurship outcomes are more intensified when operating under normative or legal or marketplace systems that facilitate pro-ecoentrepreneurial law supporting behaviour.

8. DISCUSSION

The objective of the current research is the theoretical refinement and empirical verification of the model of the phenomenon of Green Entrepreneurship – the SDG Catalyst Model (GESCM). The priority task is to determine how Green Entrepreneurship operates within a structure and during the achievement of the SDGs. These results conclusively back this aim and competently validate all of the suggested assumptions, demonstrating how green entrepreneurship is more than a form of sustainability at the firm level but acts as a creation of a cross-cut sustainable system in the parameters of the entrepreneurial environment, governance structure, and innovation system. The analysis also offers strong evidence that there is a significant and positive impact of green entrepreneurship on SDG achievement, which is in line with the model's core assumption and the main aim of the study overall, that is, the fact that entrepreneurship is a key force in the era of sustainable development, without being subordinated.

Although inconclusive, the first hypothesis positing an affirmative association between green entrepreneurship and the SDG could be seen as evidence supportive of the notion that entrepreneurial orientation covering sustainability aspects involves the creation of cross-sectoral gains, including the economic, social, environmental, and governance aspects. It is consistent with some theories of systems and sustainable change that substantial change does not come from changing policies, but rather from the innovations and changes in personalities within institutions. The size of the coefficient and its significance in practice seem to confirm that Green Entrepreneurs significantly contribute to the industrial development as they can influence Green Socio-Economic Interfaces at the level of the system.

The large body of research has only recently been initiated, and more research has to be conducted to confirm these assumptions empirically. The strong empirical support for Hypotheses 2 and 3, linking green entrepreneurship to sustainability-oriented innovation and, subsequently, to SDG outcomes, provides evidence for the innovation-mediated sustainability pathway embedded in the GESCM. These results justify the model's theoretical integration of Ecological Modernization Theory and innovation systems theory by demonstrating that sustainability transformation is driven by structured innovation processes rather than ad hoc environmental initiatives. The mediation effects confirm that innovation operates as a translation mechanism through which entrepreneurial activity becomes institutionalized into development outcomes, thereby fulfilling the research objective of identifying causal sustainability transmission situations.

Furthermore, supporting the validation of both hypotheses 4 and 5 as regards the role ESG performance plays as a mediator of the remit of this institutional mechanism, contacts positively with the governance-centred logic of the model. The analysis points out that ESG is not just a set of costs and benefits or financial analysis of your project, but in fact a critical component of boards and their sub-committees, which is also a major component in converting the sustainability orientations and goals to development delivery accountability. The ESG performance is one of the components of the IC that aligns most effectively with the As' Kind of Performative Behaviour. The finding directly validates the inclusiveness of the Stakeholder Theory and Institutional Theory in the model, reinforcing the fact that sustainability is achieved through created and enforced norms. As such, through the liberal paradigm, arguably, the built environment can be reshaped according to the SDG goals, rather than creating these in turn.

There is much prior support for Hypotheses 6 and 7, as these hypotheses outline that green value chain integration acts as a mediating variable in the sustainable development transformation. By demonstrating that the value chain integration performs as a mechanism for transformation based on empirical evidence, this research shifts the sustainability impact from individual firms' functioning to the network. Such an outcome is consistent with the theory of ecological energy, which explains those who carry out entrepreneurial activities and the framework of the Circular Economy Strategy. This exploration assists the model in a meaningful way, provides the concept of the ecosystem model, and verifies the purpose of the study, which is to surpass the sustainable models of the company's attributes.

It is important to point out that the direct and indirect effects of the mediating variables under consideration mediate the impact of green entrepreneurship on sustainable development goals. This juxtaposition of two pathways serves to confirm the catalytic theory of the GESCM, in which entrepreneurship, on one hand, helps in stimulating different aspects of the market effect, and it is dependent on system development at the same time. This discovery will help the improvement and the practical use of sustainable development by bridging the gap between the two already existing structures or patterns of agency and development.

The empirical test of the moderating hypotheses is valuable in several ways. One of these is its ability to enhance the understanding of the exosystemic perspective of the model. Thus, the interaction terms deduced from anything-by-anything models, government policy support, regulatory quality, market readiness, and AU institutional trust, suggest that entrepreneurship in the manner intended has more to do with a range of institutional configurations than with the overarching societal structure in which it takes place and how supports and restrictions tell on the outcome. These findings help in meeting the research objective of finding out the situations under which green entrepreneurship is most and least effective in achieving the SDG. This is also in line with institutional economics and governance, which is to say that development outcomes are shaped by a combination of regulated and spontaneous processes.

From a theoretical point of view, it may be concluded that the GESCM can be considered as an integrative model, as it is successful in combining several different definitional approaches. The results of the research proved to be consistent with the synthesis of the 'Triple Bottom line' theory, the Theory on Stakeholders, the Theory of Institutional Change, the Idea of Ecologization of Modernization Processes, and the Theory of Entrepreneurial Activity – all these trends are united by one so-called 'sustainable development' model. This synthesis of theories is designed to solve the division of labour in the theory of sustainability research, and it serves the aim of the research by working out a system-level model of sustainable development that integrates several theories of growth and development together.

In general, the results of the conducted studies fully support the assumptions made and the purposes of the research as mentioned in the research design. This is because enterprises' activity, the core of green entrepreneurship, changes other aspects (innovation, governance, and market contours), which is difficult to attain and, in the end, contributes to stability. Such key outcomes tend to reframe the importance of entrepreneurship in relation to global sustainability governance and achievement of the SDGs, leading the way to the development of a framework that is sound in theory, yet practiced in reality. The GESCM in this regard marks a stride down the path of sustainability studies as it quits visualization of green business development and turns to developing a model of development where actors are causal, and transformations are systemic and policy-oriented, thereby suggesting directions for further empirical research, policy-making, and environmental projects for SDG attainment.

9. IMPLICATIONS

The results of the research are very important and should be looked into further from both a theoretical and managerial point of view, beyond the limits of the recent discourse on sustainable development. It aims towards providing a way forward as to how green entrepreneurship can be harnessed as a strategic tool in the realization of Sustainable Development Goals (SDGs) and tackles the enabling roles of such administered and unmeasured systems as institutions, networks, and economic systems towards the promotion of green entrepreneurship such that the practice is reframed from an environment enhancing tool located at the fringes of economic development, to an integral and dominant part of any national development system.

Theoretical Implications

At a conceptual level, the research will contribute to the literature on sustainability and entrepreneurship by treating green entrepreneurship not only as a narrow innovation in an individual firm, but as a software aimed at system-level transformation. Further research can refine the above argument with the GESCM, which offers itself as the structural component of a universal sustainability theory that will go beyond the existing models of corporate social responsibility, environmental innovation, ESG consideration, etc. This structure of the model facilitates subsequent research to access transition to sustainability from a number of levels, recognizing it as a 'co-evolutionary' development of all markets, structures, regulating bodies, and ecosystems in existence. Particular opportunities will also be found in the areas of complexity, sustainability, or systems science modernisation, and also in development economics, as the focal concepts aiming to posit green entrepreneurship as an active component of systemic transformation towards sustainable development at the global level.

Policy and Governance Implications

This implies that policymakers need to adjust the future SDG ecosystem design trend, moving away from an overemphasis on emission-reducing mechanisms alone, to a broader architecture that facilitates an SDG achievement for engine regulation to an ecologically enabling innovation policy. Instead of coercing the industry to observe environmental and resource use standards adequate to eco-efficiency objectives, build green innovation systems with intelligent components, governments should focus more on ensuring comprehensive, supportive environments. However, those who find a new way of thinking win in the market, as entrepreneurs can take advantage of opportunities when others regard them as problems. Future SDG designs should incorporate green entrepreneurial strategies at their very core, including their integration in the country's development program, trade and industrial policies, and climate change strategies. Public innovation will also depend on public, extracted, and available resources, managing private entrepreneurship, since this will also approach relying entirely on the traditional tax and other regulatory mechanisms would not suffice to achieve all the objectives set out in the new agenda.

Managerial and Entrepreneurial Implications

For the entrepreneurs and company leaders themselves, the findings show that it is time to stop doing sustainability projects separately and integrate such projects into the business strategy. The green businesses of tomorrow will have to come up with business models that seek to achieve ESG, address circular economy issues, and incorporate SDG-specific objectives within their strategy rather than treating these as additional responsibilities. Since there is increasing evidence that the competitive success of a firm might be attributed to its achievement of sustainable development goals (SDGs), it is expected that firms will be focusing on developing a sustainability system integration that cuts across innovation, governance, financial, and social value creation. Therefore, change is necessary in terms of hiring entrepreneurs, future generations of young executives are being raised differently, and creating companies' education and leadership programs need to become more advanced in the direction of SDG attainment, systemic organization, and sustainability development as the points of relevant competence.

Financial and Investment Implications

The concept elaborated above also contains useful clues for future developments in the area of sustainable finance. As it has been proven, the role that green entrepreneurship plays, on the system's level as well as for the economy, the growth of impact investments, green bonds, ESG financial products, and SDG-related markets can be expected. Capital will begin to be invested not only for financial purposes, but also for the benefit of socially set goals, and the game of development will also move towards financing the human aspects of life instead of the fear of moral degradation. In these countries, the financial sector will evolve in a way that real lending will account for most of the capital, and network/corporate finance will be simply for facilitating operations between banks.

Societal and Developmental Implications

At the societal level, the GESCM sees green entrepreneurship as a tool for fair and inclusive development, with the potential for communities and the disadvantaged themselves to accomplish their objectives, which have innovative, democratic, and environmentally-benign aspirations without the need for other third-party professionals. The emergence of future development trajectories will escalate in dependence on the so-called "bottom-up" sustainability model, in which development actors include, but are not limited to, communities, social enterprises, and grassroots innovations within the actions of Sustainable Goals. This means development has ceased to be a form of action by the state or by the international community and is now understood and applied as a participatory and business-like activity.

Future-Oriented Strategic Implication

As we move forward in time, the coming ten years or so will see an overwhelming confluence of forces of green entrepreneurship, digital technologies, climate innovation-led, and the ensuing governance restructuring. Therefore, the Global Entrepreneurship and Sustainability Centre for Muslims (GESCM) is not only a response to this question, but it also presents a kind of road map profiling the future of the Islamic society. This is a logical evolution of aggressive green entrepreneurship incorporating sustainable development, which moves away from the current stand-alone growth model of single economic sectors. That means that transitioning towards models of sustainable economic development is no longer limited to environmental considerations, nor is it all about the policy to be adopted by countries. It becomes a project within an economy to create a new entrepreneurial system.

10. CONCLUSION

This paper seeks to take the conversation on sustainability and entrepreneurship in a new direction. Particularly, the research proposes the Green Entrepreneurship - SDG Catalyst Model (GESCM), and it is claimed that green entrepreneurship is a systemic transformation needed for the achievement of the Sustainable Development Goals. There is a transition from the firm sustainability and compliance-based view of green entrepreneurship, and this work therefore treats green entrepreneurship as an institutionalized process that induces change in innovation systems, policy networks, entrepreneurial environments, as well as development structures. The study provides sound conclusions by deploying explanatory, predictive, and descriptive approaches to entrepreneurship development. There are, in the main, qualitative methodologies and secondary data collection in the form of document reviews. The patterns of entrepreneurial activities are moulded by broader social institutions.

The study proves that deploying green startups is a useful method that would drive the realization of the SDGs, as it works both through structural impact and softening methods such as technological innovation for sustainability, ESG performance indicators, and green supply chain development. The two cascaded structures show that sustainability change is not about stand-alone socio-economic development initiatives but rather about the inter-linkage of entrepreneurial behaviour, organization, market, and governance. Equally, the examination of interaction effects pushes the argument further that sustainable development achievements hinge on the type of supporting policies, the level of effectiveness of the rules and institutions, the level of interpersonal relations, and societal readiness. Such conclusions thereby spot the importance of development strategies at the level of an ecosystem.

By synthesizing the issues that such theories raise, the GESCM proposes a complete understanding of the change by suggesting a common framework, which helps in gathering the concepts of transformation elaboration from numerous theoretical perspectives. This research repositions entrepreneurship as the central subject in the global concurrence on sustainability and the construction of business models that advance the goals of sustainable development. Rather, the remnants of the already adopted approaches exist in a non-compliant manner to the ideas of environmental protection.

At the end of the day, the study positions green entrepreneurship not only as a technological revolution but also as one of the most effective instruments for achieving strategic social goals in the 21st century – one of the central areas of innovative activity, institutional change, and social resistance. And it is in companies that must face increasing climate risks, social disparities, and environmental emergencies that focus will arise towards GESCM, which offers a top-down perspective in illustrating how to build green development within this system, as opposed to bottom-up with entrepreneurs and no policy interventions.

11. LIMITATIONS AND FUTURE SCOPE

This particular study, despite its theoretical and empirical content sets should be considered as limited as it serves as provide areas for future study. The first limitation is the focus on only one point in time, which does not allow to analyse changes over time in green entrepreneurship, SDG transitions, and other aspects. It makes sense to carry out longitudinal and panel data studies as transitional motions are a part of sustainably developing systems. The second issue is that social action structures used in the model have a multi-actor aspect, but their percentage since there is a larger dependence on the collection of data from instruments. Questionnaires are self-administered, and they lend themselves to various types of biases, including social desirability, purposive, and recall biases. In addition, there is a provision made in the plan that future research, whenever needed to circumvent the individual aspects of all the determinants of the Oracle brand through their contents, should include the use of objective sustainability indicators, ESG ratings, policy indices, and SDG performance metrics to strengthen the measurement construct.

Finally, in the case of GESCM, while this CRM makes assumptions in its systematic structure, adjustments for varying institutional contexts, regions, and levels of development are not really included. Scholars in the near future can conduct research to explore the applicability of the proposed concepts and approaches in GESCM to cross-national and cross-cultural contexts involving different levels of governance. Comparative studies between developed and developing economies can help bring out the nuances of the context. Lastly, future researchers can consider how digital technologies, as well as AI that have brought about sustainability and climate-tech entrepreneurship, are merged within this framework, for the analysis and prediction of the next generation of development enclosing systemic perspective. These extensions will allow the model of GESCM to progress and become a more elastic tool for the development of long-term and short-term sustainable development research objectives, which are research objectives or policy development over a long period of time.

REFERENCES

Agbedahin, A. V. (2019). Sustainable development, Education for Sustainable Development, and the 2030 Agenda for Sustainable Development: Emergence, efficacy, eminence, and future. *Sustainable Development (Bradford)*, *27*(4), 669–680. DOI: 10.1002/sd.1931

Assembly, U. G. (2015). Transforming our world: the 2030 Agenda for Sustainable Development.

Audretsch, D. B., Lehmann, E. E., & Paleari, S. (2015). Academic policy and entrepreneurship: A European perspective. *The Journal of Technology Transfer*, *40*(3), 363–368. DOI: 10.1007/s10961-014-9359-6

Battilana, J., Leca, B., & Boxenbaum, E. (2009). 2 how actors change institutions: Towards a theory of institutional entrepreneurship. *The Academy of Management Annals*, *3*(1), 65–107. DOI: 10.5465/19416520903053598

Biermann, F., Kanie, N., & Kim, R. E. (2017). Global governance by goal-setting: The novel approach of the UN Sustainable Development Goals. *Current Opinion in Environmental Sustainability*, *26*, 26–31. DOI: 10.1016/j.cosust.2017.01.010

Cohen, B., & Winn, M. I. (2007). Market imperfections, opportunity and sustainable entrepreneurship. *Journal of Business Venturing*, *22*(1), 29–49. DOI: 10.1016/j.jbusvent.2004.12.001

Creswell, J. W., & Clark, V. L. P. (2017). *Designing and conducting mixed methods research*. Sage publications.

Dacin, M. T., Dacin, P. A., & Tracey, P. (2011). Social entrepreneurship: A critique and future directions. *Organization Science*, *22*(5), 1203–1213. DOI: 10.1287/orsc.1100.0620

Dale, A. (2007). *At the edge: Sustainable development in the 21st century* (Vol. 6). UBC press.

Dean, T. J., & McMullen, J. S. (2007). Toward a theory of sustainable entrepreneurship: Reducing environmental degradation through entrepreneurial action. *Journal of Business Venturing*, *22*(1), 50–76. DOI: 10.1016/j.jbusvent.2005.09.003

Demirel, P., Li, Q. C., Rentocchini, F., & Tamvada, J. P. (2019). Born to be green: New insights into the economics and management of green entrepreneurship. *Small Business Economics*, *52*(4), 759–771. DOI: 10.1007/s11187-017-9933-z

Elkington, J., & Rowlands, I. H. (1999). Cannibals with forks: The triple bottom line of 21st century business. *Alternatives Journal*, *25*(4), 42.

Freeman, R. E. (2010). *Strategic management: A stakeholder approach.* Cambridge university press. DOI: 10.1017/CBO9781139192675

Geels, F. W. (2002). Technological transitions as evolutionary reconfiguration processes: A multi-level perspective and a case-study. *Research Policy*, *31*(8-9), 1257–1274. DOI: 10.1016/S0048-7333(02)00062-8

Glass, A. (2007). Understanding generational differences for competitive success. *Industrial and Commercial Training*, *39*(2), 98–103. DOI: 10.1108/00197850710732424

Griggs, D., Stafford-Smith, M., Gaffney, O., Rockström, J., Öhman, M. C., Shyamsundar, P., Steffen, W., Glaser, G., Kanie, N., & Noble, I. (2013). Sustainable development goals for people and planet. *Nature*, *495*(7441), 305–307. DOI: 10.1038/495305a PMID: 23518546

Hair, J. F. (2014). *A primer on partial least squares structural equation modeling (PLS-SEM).* sage.

Hockerts, K., & Wüstenhagen, R. (2010). Greening Goliaths versus emerging Davids—Theorizing about the role of incumbents and new entrants in sustainable entrepreneurship. *Journal of Business Venturing*, *25*(5), 481–492. DOI: 10.1016/j.jbusvent.2009.07.005

Isenberg, D. J. (2011). *The Entrepreneurship Ecosystem Strategy as a New Paradigm for Economic Policy: Principles for Cultivating Entrepreneurship. Babson Entrepreneurship Ecosystem Project. Babson Park.* Babson College.

Lundvall, B. A. (1992). *National systems of innovation: towards a theory of innovation and interactive learning* (Vol. 242). Pinter.

MacDonald, M. (2002). *Agendas for Sustainability: Environment and development into the 21st century.* Routledge.

Markard, J., Raven, R., & Truffer, B. (2012). Sustainability transitions: An emerging field of research and its prospects. *Research Policy*, *41*(6), 955–967. DOI: 10.1016/j.respol.2012.02.013

Mazzucato, M. (2011). The entrepreneurial state. *Soundings*, *49*(49), 131–142. DOI: 10.3898/136266211798411183

Mol, A. P., & Spaargaren, G. (2000). Ecological modernisation theory in debate: A review. *Environmental Politics*, *9*(1), 17–49. DOI: 10.1080/09644010008414511

Molina-Azorin, J. F. (2012). Mixed methods research in strategic management: Impact and applications. *Organizational Research Methods, 15*(1), 33–56. DOI: 10.1177/1094428110393023

Mondal, S., Singh, S., & Gupta, H. (2025). Examining the impact of green entrepreneurship drivers on sustainable development in the context of emerging country. *Benchmarking, 32*(9), 3584–3630. DOI: 10.1108/BIJ-11-2023-0835

Morton, S., Pencheon, D., & Squires, N. (2017). Sustainable Development Goals (SDGs), and their implementation: A national global framework for health, development and equity needs a systems approach at every level. *British Medical Bulletin, 124*(1), 81–90. PMID: 29069332

Muñoz, P., & Cohen, B. (2018). Sustainable entrepreneurship research: Taking stock and looking ahead. *Business Strategy and the Environment, 27*(3), 300–322. DOI: 10.1002/bse.2000

Nilsson, M., Griggs, D., & Visbeck, M. (2016). Policy: Map the interactions between sustainable development goals. *Nature, 534*(7607), 320–322. DOI: 10.1038/534320a PMID: 27306173

Sachs, J. D., Schmidt-Traub, G., Mazzucato, M., Messner, D., Nakicenovic, N., & Rockström, J. (2019). Six transformations to achieve the sustainable development goals. *Nature Sustainability, 2*(9), 805–814. DOI: 10.1038/s41893-019-0352-9

Schaltegger, S., Hansen, E. G., & Lüdeke-Freund, F. (2016). Business models for sustainability: Origins, present research, and future avenues. *Organization & Environment, 29*(1), 3–10. DOI: 10.1177/1086026615599806

Schaltegger, S., & Wagner, M. (2011). Sustainable entrepreneurship and sustainability innovation: Categories and interactions. *Business Strategy and the Environment, 20*(4), 222–237. DOI: 10.1002/bse.682

Scott, W. R. (2013). *Institutions and organizations: Ideas, interests, and identities.* Sage publications.

Shepherd, D. A., & Patzelt, H. (2011). The new field of sustainable entrepreneurship: Studying entrepreneurial action linking "what is to be sustained" with "what is to be developed". *Entrepreneurship Theory and Practice, 35*(1), 137–163. DOI: 10.1111/j.1540-6520.2010.00426.x

Stafford-Smith, M., Griggs, D., Gaffney, O., Ullah, F., Reyers, B., Kanie, N., Stigson, B., Shrivastava, P., Leach, M., & O'Connell, D. (2017). Integration: The key to implementing the Sustainable Development Goals. *Sustainability Science, 12*(6), 911–919. DOI: 10.1007/s11625-016-0383-3 PMID: 30147763

Stam, E. (2015). Entrepreneurial ecosystems and regional policy: A sympathetic critique. *European Planning Studies*, *23*(9), 1759–1769. DOI: 10.1080/09654313.2015.1061484

Stam, E., & Van de Ven, A. (2021). Entrepreneurial ecosystem elements. *Small Business Economics*, *56*(2), 809–832. DOI: 10.1007/s11187-019-00270-6

Tien, N. H., Hiep, P. M., Dai, N. Q., Duc, N. M., & Hong, T. T. K. (2020). Green entrepreneurship understanding in Vietnam. *International Journal of Entrepreneurship*, *24*(2), 1–14.

York, J. G., & Venkataraman, S. (2010). The entrepreneur–environment nexus: Uncertainty, innovation, and allocation. *Journal of Business Venturing*, *25*(5), 449–463. DOI: 10.1016/j.jbusvent.2009.07.007

Chapter 5
Green Entrepreneurship and the SDGs:
Conceptual Insights From Emerging Economies

Gurpreet pal Kaur
http://orcid.org/0000-0001-7475-3548
Lovely Professional University, India

Mushtaq Ahmed Shah
http://orcid.org/0000-0002-3177-9622
Lovely Professional University, India

ABSTRACT

Green entrepreneurship is becoming a key tool for achieving the UN SDGs in emerging economies that seek growth while tackling environmental degradation and social inequality. This chapter explores how green entrepreneurship links innovation, ecological sustainability and inclusive development using secondary data from research and reports by UNDP, UNEP, and the World Bank. The findings show strong contributions to SDG 7, 9, 12, and 13 through renewable energy, circular economy models, and sustainable production. The chapter concludes that expanding green finance, strengthening institutions, and promoting sustainability education are vital for building resilient, low-carbon, and inclusive economies.

1. INTRODUCTION

Sustainable development is now of global concern in the twenty-first century as countries are experiencing increased problems that revolve around climate change,

DOI: 10.4018/979-8-3373-7391-1.ch005

environmental degradation, and inequality. UN Sustainable Development Goals (SDGs) offer a template that unites economic, social and environmental targets in order to promote the global well-being. Recent research highlights that entrepreneurship is one of the most important mechanisms in this transition, which allows creating innovation and sustainable growth (Soliman et al., 2023). In this framework, green entrepreneurship as the combination of ecological accountability and economic potential has become the focus of interest as a key means to achieve the SDGs, particularly in emerging and developing economies (Badjeena et al., 2024; Prasetyo et al., 2023; Nuringsih et al., 2022). Besides contributing to innovation, green entrepreneurs are also known to solve local sustainability issues by socially inclusive and environmentally conscious business models (Ilesanmi, 2024; Kaur & Kaur, 2019).

Green entrepreneurship includes the creation and running of enterprises that lead to environmental sustainability and societal developments as well as being economically feasible. Based on the idea of the triple bottom line, people, planet and profit, it supports economic development, which supports the ecological and social integrity. Research indicates that green start-ups have been adopting the sustainability concept in their business strategy, which has facilitated economic growth through eco-innovation, circular economy, and minimizing the extent of resources wasted (Shah & Singh, 2026; Sharma & Subba, 2025). This model is especially crucial in the case of emergent economies where countries aim to achieve the intended balance between industrialization and environmental protection by introducing educational and sustainable policy interventions (Alao et al., 2023). Women entrepreneurs also lie at the core of this change, as they have become at the forefront of renewable energy, sustainable agriculture, and waste management despite the challenges of insufficient funding and gender discrimination (Gupta, 2025). Furthermore, the implementation of circular bioeconomy and green business models in industries proves that profitability is possible to correspond with sustainability and make green entrepreneurship one of the pillars of global development strategy (Basile et al., 2025).

Green entrepreneurship can be seen to adhere to the Sustainable Development Goals (SDGs) in a number of the most important objectives. Companies that are involved in renewable energy are active in achieving SDG 7 (Affordable and Clean Energy), and those that move to the use of circular economy should accommodate SDG 12 (Responsible Consumption and Production). On the same note, new business models through which pollution and carbon emissions can be addressed promote SDG 13 (Climate Action) (Sharma and Subba, 2025). Green entrepreneurs can be considered drivers of sustainable change by increasing the efficiency of resources and responsible innovation and transforming conventional industries into regenerative systems (Khymych, 2026). In spite of this opportunity, regardless of financial constraints, weak institutional frameworks, and poor levels of environmental literacy, green entrepreneurship continues to grow slow in emerging economies (Badjeena et al., 2024). However, despite the growing recognition of its importance, existing literature largely provides descriptive accounts of green entrepreneurship and its alignment with SDGs, with limited attention to the underlying mechanisms through which entrepreneurial activities generate measurable sustainability outcomes. This indicates a clear research gap in understanding the causal pathways linking green entrepreneurship to SDG achievement, particularly in the context of emerging economies characterized by institutional constraints and resource limitations. Moreover, the chapter adopts a conceptual perspective but previously lacked explicit theoretical grounding. To address this limitation, the present study is guided by an integrated framework combining institutional theory, sustainable entrepreneurship theory, and innovation ecosystem perspectives, which together explain how regulatory environments, entrepreneurial behavior, and innovation systems interact to influence sustainability outcomes.

Given the above discussion, this study will look at the role of green entrepreneurship in assisting the emerging economies to realize the SDGs. Specifically, the study seeks to answer how and through what mechanisms green entrepreneurship contributes to SDG outcomes. It concentrates on three primary objectives, i.e., how it will contribute to the SDGs achievement, institutional and policy systems through which it can be facilitated and strategic opportunities and challenges, which will make the future of sustainable entrepreneurship.

2. REVIEW OF LITERATURE

Green entrepreneurship is a notion that has arisen as an imperative solution to the challenges of sustainability at the global scale such as environmental downgrades, social disparity, and economic disturbances. It incorporates environmental friendliness and social inclusivity into the essence of business strategy, which takes the classical profit-driven perspective of entrepreneurship. New research term, green entrepreneurship is one of the key drivers of sustainable development, as the pursuit of solutions based on markets to create economic, social, and environmental value and positions it (Sołoducho-Pelc, 2020). Researchers note that it coincides with the concept of the triple bottom line, people, planet, and profit, and the fact that entrepreneurial activity can contribute to economic development and the state of the environment at the same time (Gu et al., 2022). Moreover, green entrepreneurship is perceived as a way of advancing environmental awareness and value-based innovation in the upcoming entrepreneurs, which adds to the importance of sustainable economic transformation (Nuringsih, 2021).

The green entrepreneurship is firmly theoretical in the fact that the definition of sustainable development as developed by the Brundtland Commission (1987) states: sustainable development is to meet the needs of the present without disrupting the potential of the future generation to meet their needs. This model has defined sustainability as a multidimensional target that has involved economic, social, and environmental balance (Hummels and Argyrou, 2021). Based on this background, the entrepreneurship is more and more accepted as a transformational process of attaining sustainable progress, especially by creating environmentally friendly innovations and responsible business strategies (Szopik-Depczyńska et al., 2021). Green entrepreneurs as a change agent implement renewable energy sources, environmentally friendly technologies, and circular business models as direct contributors to the United Nations Sustainable Development Goals (SDGs) (Pandikar et al., 2024).

From a theoretical perspective, green entrepreneurship can be better understood through multiple complementary lenses, including institutional theory, which emphasizes the role of regulatory and governance structures, and innovation ecosystem theory, which highlights the interaction between firms, policymakers, and knowledge institutions. The integration of these perspectives enables a more comprehensive understanding of how entrepreneurial activities are shaped by contextual factors and contribute to sustainability outcomes.

The connection between green entrepreneurship and Sustainable Development Goals (SDGs) has been the subject of widely stressed scholarship in recent years. Green entrepreneurship pursues directly several major goals, such as the SDG 7 (Affordable and Clean Energy) through renewable energy projects, SDG 9 (Industry, Innovation, and Infrastructure) through the development of sustainable industrialization and green technologies, SDG 12 (Responsible Consumption and Production) through projects of the circular economy, and SDG 13 (Climate Action) through carbon and ecosystem restoration projects (Raman et al., 2025). It is demonstrated that through sustainable entrepreneurial ecosystems, environmental requirements may be matched to the business opportunities, allowing economic resilience and innovativeness to thrive in low-carbon transitions (Khymych, 2025). In addition, these green ventures are becoming progressively essential in the development of the emerging economies towards the SDGs as they combine environmental and economic goals to catalyze the inclusive and regenerative growth (Stanković et al., 2024).

However, existing studies largely emphasize the alignment between green entrepreneurship and SDGs in a descriptive manner, with limited empirical evidence explaining the causal mechanisms through which these contributions materialize. This indicates a gap in understanding how specific entrepreneurial activities translate into measurable environmental and social outcomes

Green entrepreneurship in emerging economies can be considered one of the key players in resolving the two problems of industrial growth and environmental destruction. These regions are also known to have entrepreneurs that tend to innovate in resource-constrained environments and use the local materials and sustainable technologies to lead to eco-inclusive development (Attah & Yonkor, 2025). The green venture experience in India proves that the combination of technological innovation and social impact in a sustainable business model can prove effective and lead to poverty reduction and access to clean energy (Sutariya and Arora, 2023). Likewise, off-grid solar projects in Sub-Saharan Africa have brought more energy and economic empowerment, which directly contributes to SDG 7 (Affordable and Clean Energy) and SDG 1 (No Poverty) (Rumbayan et al., 2025). These attempts highlight the role of green entrepreneurship as an inclusive contributor to economic development through the empowerment of communities, job creation, as well as facilitation of the movement towards resilient, low-carbon economies (Majumdar, 2025).

While these case-based insights are valuable, the literature often lacks systematic comparative analysis across regions, which limits the generalizability of findings. Greater integration of cross-country evidence is therefore required to strengthen analytical robustness. Policies and institutional encouragement are put together as one of the key factors helping in the encouragement of green entrepreneurship through the establishment of enabling environment of sustainable business development. Incentive, infrastructure and capacity-building schemes are examples of state efforts that promote sustainability via innovation, as observed in Startup India and National Action Plan on Climate Change (NAPCC) in India, which combines environmental concerns with entrepreneurial growth (Bhatnagar et al., 2022). Internationally, governments have been arranging the financial and technical support to drive the green transition process in developing economies through the help of programs like the UNEP Green Economy Initiative, as well as the Climate Investment Funds by the World Bank (Sharma & Subba, 2025). Nevertheless, research shows that there are still weak points such as uneven implementation of policies, institutional coordination, and access to sustainable financing processes (Anjanappa, 2023). These loopholes emphasize the importance of more powerful governance and innovation of finances in order to actually achieve potential of green entrepreneurship.

A new corpus of literature identifies the increasing significance of green finance and impact investment in the promotion of sustainable entrepreneurship. Green bonds, carbon credits, and sustainability-linked loans are some of the financial instruments that have become critical in terms of providing capital that is directed towards environment-related ventures (Sharma & Subba, 2025). But emerging economies are usually struggling to scale up such financial instruments because of the lack of awareness among investors, regulatory loopholes and the perceived risk

(Saeedi & Ashraf, 2024). Simultaneously, green finance is changing the way digital technologies, such as Artificial Intelligence (AI), Blockchain, and the Internet of Things (IoT) are being used to increase transparency, facilitate project monitoring, and minimize inefficiencies in transactions (Shah & Uddin, 2023; Ahmad et al., 2025). They do not only enable responsible capital flows but also enable entrepreneurs in developing economies to overcome the structural challenges, maximize their operations, and scale sustainable solutions more easily (Sosa & Ivanova, 2025). Despite these advancements, limited attention has been given to evaluating the effectiveness and implementation challenges of such financial and technological mechanisms, particularly in weak institutional contexts, thereby highlighting another important research gap.

Although the literature on green entrepreneurship is growing, it has a lot of research gaps. Empirical data on its direct effect on the targets of particular Sustainable Development Goal (SDG) are limited as well, especially in emergent economies, where systematic long-term evaluations of both environmental and social performance are limited (Raman et al., 2025). Additionally, the relationships between policy systems, institutional abilities, and entrepreneurial innovation in how sustainable ecosystems can be evolved are under-researched and most studies focus on developed countries (P. Singh et al., 2025). The other significant gap is the absence of uniform measures to determine the successes of green businesses other than financial measures (Offiong et al., 2025a). Moreover, the impact of socio-cultural, gender, and behavioural factors affecting the adoption of green entrepreneurship in resource-limited environments is not well studied (Gupta, 2025). Furthermore, issues related to causality, endogeneity, and attribution of sustainability outcomes to entrepreneurial activities remain largely unexplored in the existing literature, limiting the robustness of current findings

The chapter is structured based on three main goals. To begin with, it examines the role of green entrepreneurship in enhancing the realization of Sustainable Development Goals (SDGs) in the emerging economies through integrating the entrepreneurship with both environmental and social agendas. Second, it looks at the policy and institutional frameworks that facilitate and support the existence of green entrepreneurial ecosystems with a special focus on the role of governance and financial mechanisms in facilitating sustainability-led innovation. Third, it determines the most critical issues and strategic prospects of improving green innovation and inclusive economic development, especially in the collaboration of policy measures and capacity-building. Combined, these goals highlight the role of entrepreneurial innovation in generating sustainable change and a model on how to incorporate environmental, social, and economic aspects in national development policy to promote the SDGs.

3. METHODOLOGY

This book chapter uses both theoretical and empirical approaches based on the conceptual and descriptive research design to summarize the theoretical and empirical considerations of the nature of green entrepreneurship in supporting the Sustainable Development Goals (SDGs) in the emergent economies. The complex dynamics between the entrepreneurial innovation, institutional forces, and the sustainability policy mechanisms are the issues that are highly applicable to the conceptual approach (Raman et al., 2025). The literature review is based on peer-reviewed literature and institutional reports and other international organizations, including the UNDP, UNEP, World Bank, and OECD, as well as national plans, such as the National Action Plan on Climate Change in India and Startup India (Bhatnagar et al., 2022). The thematic content analysis allows the study to determine recurring patterns, opportunities, and barriers that define green entrepreneurship in resource-constrained environments like India, Kenya, and Brazil (Sosa & Ivanova, 2025). Furthermore, the analysis involved systematic identification and categorization of themes related to institutional factors, innovation mechanisms, and sustainability outcomes.

The theoretical framework will combine knowledge on sustainable development theory and innovation management to describe the impact of policy support and entrepreneurial behaviour on the sustainability outcomes, which interact (Singh et al., 2025). In addition, institutional theory and innovation ecosystem perspectives are incorporated to strengthen the analytical foundation of the study. Despite the lack of primary empirical data, the study gives a comprehensive basis of analysis to the future research and policy formulation. However, it is acknowledged that the conceptual nature of the study limits empirical validation and raises potential concerns related to causality and indigeneity. It can be used as a theoretical framework to build evidence-based interventions and evaluation methods that reinforce the green entrepreneurial ecosystems that are consistent with global sustainability agenda.

4. GREEN ENTREPRENEURSHIP AND SDG NEXUS

The association of the green entrepreneurship and the Sustainable Development Goals (SDGs) is the crucial direction in terms of global sustainability development as illustrated in Figure 1. Green entrepreneurship is a facilitator and facilitator of SDGs because its strategy is to entrench ecological responsibility and social inclusiveness in business innovation (Sharma & Subba, 2025). In the developing world, with the rise of industry usually at the expense of the environment, it offers radically new, market-driven, solutions that centralize growth and ecological management (Raman et al., 2025). Green entrepreneurs are moving sustainable economic growth through eco-innovation, sustainable production, and community-based practices that support the global endeavours to ensure environmental resilience in the long term (Bhatnagar et al., 2022). More specifically, the contribution of green entrepreneurship to SDGs can be understood through key causal mechanisms, including innovation diffusion, resource efficiency, inclusive business models, and sustainability governance, which together translate entrepreneurial activities into measurable environmental and social outcomes (Bandna et al., 2025).

Green entrepreneurship has a major role to play in different aspects of the Sustainable Development Goals (SDGs), especially SDG 7 (Affordable and Clean Energy). Green ventures increase the availability of sustainable energy sources like solar, wind, and biogas and minimize the dependence on carbon (Rumbayan et al., 2025). M-KOPA Solar has been successful in Kenya in its example, in an exercise to create pay-as-you-go solar systems that have supplied clean and affordable electricity to more than one million off-grid households in the country, contributing to energy inclusion as well as poverty reduction (Majumdar, 2025). On the same note, solar businesses within the National Solar Mission in India have increased the use of renewable energy and created jobs and empowered the economy (Bhatnagar et al., 2022). Such examples demonstrate that green entrepreneurship is both a factor in stimulating environmental sustainability and inclusive development of growing economies.

Figure 1. Green Entrepreneurship and SDG Nexus.

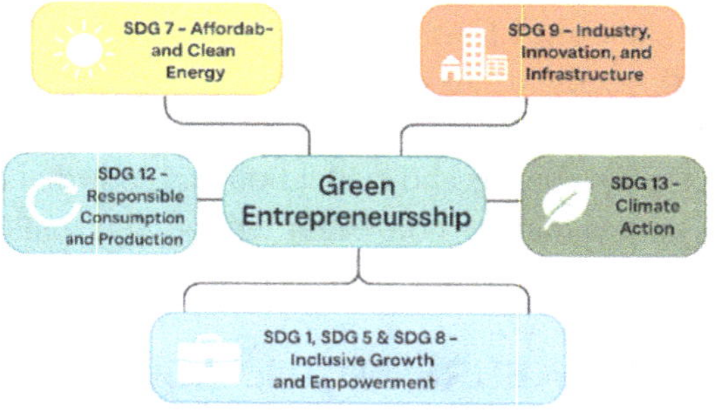

In addition to increasing the access to energy, green entrepreneurship is critical to the implementation of SDG 9 (Industry, Innovation, and Infrastructure) through sustainable industrialization and robust production systems. Green ventures incorporate sustainability into the manufacturing and supply chains questioning the traditional, resource-consuming models of industries (S. N. Sharma & Subba, 2025). The case of India-based Ather Energy, which specializes in electric mobility, and local suppliers, which are associated with Tesla Energy in South Asia, portray the role of clean technology innovation in promoting low-carbon transformation of industries (Alamandi, 2025). They do not only reduce environmental impact by combining digital tools, circular economy, and resource-efficient processes, but also offer scalable blueprints of how similar industrial development can take place in emerging markets (Sosa & Ivanova, 2025). These examples illustrate how innovation-driven mechanisms enable the transition toward low-carbon industrial systems, thereby linking entrepreneurial activity with measurable SDG outcomes such as reduced emissions and improved resource productivity.

Green entrepreneurship is also important in the development of SDG 12 (Responsible Consumption and Production), whereby it promotes business models that are based on waste management, recycling, and sustainable product development. Nowadays, the green business cannot be defined without such initiatives of the circular economy when waste materials are recycled into new production cycles (Kaur & Shah, 2026). One company that can be considered an example of this transition in India is Bare Necessities, which achieved zero waste operation through ethical sourcing, sustainable packaging, and consumer education to transform the market (S. N. Sharma & Subba, 2025). Recreating the approaches of production and changing consumer behaviour, these ventures do not only reduce the environmental footprints but also encourage the wider implementation of responsible and circular business practices (Khymych, 2025).

Green entrepreneurship is also part of the development SDG 13 (Climate Action) through enhancing low-carbon technologies, carbon capture, sustainable agriculture. The climate-related businesses are among the first to come up with strategies that reduce greenhouse gases and ensure resilience to the environment (Raman et al., 2025). SMEs that do organic farming, renewable building materials and water conservation also make a contribution to national and global climate targets (Sosa & Ivanova, 2025). BioSense in India is a good example of this idea; it combines digital agriculture with sustainability Data-driven tools help optimize the use of fertilizers and water and reduce ecological footprints, which increase farm productivity (Alamandi, 2025). Such sector-specific examples demonstrate the operational pathways through which green entrepreneurship contributes to climate mitigation and adaptation outcomes.

Regarding socioeconomic perspective, green entrepreneurship contributes to inclusive and equitable growth by enhancing SDG 1 (No Poverty), SDG 5 (Gender Equality), and SDG 8 (Decent Work and Economic Growth) at the same time. It helps to make the just transition to a sustainable low-carbon economy by creating green jobs, empowering the marginalized group, particularly women and the rural population (Gupta, 2025). Green businesses that are led by women are highly transformative as they incorporate innovation and uplift the community together with green responsibility. Examples of such initiatives include programs of solar entrepreneurship run by the SELCO Foundation in India that empower women to be renewable energy micro-entrepreneurs, thus connecting gender empowerment and sustainable development (Raman et al., 2025).

In addition to their contributions to the economy and the environment, the green entrepreneurs have an indispensable institutional and cultural role to play in the process of promoting sustainability. They are change agents, who by doing so confront the paradigms of how development has always been by demonstrating that profitability of business can be ecologically and socially oriented (Khymych, 2025). Their companies are a frequent testbed of policies, and they drive government innovations in governance, regulatory decisions and corporate sustainability behaviors (S. N. Sharma & Subba, 2025). This interaction of the grassroots entrepreneurship and macro-level policy reform creates the impact of systemic influence of the green entrepreneurship in defining the national and global agendas of sustainability (P. Singh et al., 2025).

In developing economies, where the institutional frameworks are not yet fully developed, the domain of green entrepreneurship and the SDGs coincidence depend on the presence of a strong support system that encompasses consistent policies, focused funding, and innovation based on education. The examples of the policy tools like the Sustainable Finance Framework in India and the Atal Innovation Mission can be viewed as national initiatives attempting to integrate sustainability into the development of entrepreneurship (Bhatnagar et al., 2022). Cooperative coalitions between government bodies, universities, and business investors also make it possible to exchange knowledge, build capacity, and disseminate green innovation (Khymych, 2025). Besides, the consideration of sustainability in higher education institutions and startup incubation initiatives fosters the future generations of eco-friendly entrepreneurs, which reinforces sustainable development in the long term (Raman et al., 2025).

Although it has the transformative potential, the role that green entrepreneurship plays in the achievement of SDGs in most developing parts of the world is limited by the systemic factors like the lack of financing, poor institutional governance, and poor environmental awareness (Anjanappa, 2023). Market pressures in the short term and the lack of alignment of policies usually discourage the investment in sustainable innovation, which is why it is necessary to combine entrepreneurship policies with ESG (Environmental, Social, and Governance) frameworks and create clear mechanisms of impact measurement. In this context, impact measurement frameworks and sustainability reporting mechanisms are essential to evaluate the actual contribution of green entrepreneurship to SDGs, thereby addressing concerns related to attribution and accountability. The critical barriers and corresponding policy interventions necessary to scale Green Entrepreneurship are summarized in Table 1.

Table 1. Mechanisms of Green Entrepreneurship and Alignment with Core SDGs

GE Mechanism	Relevant SDG(s)	Catalytic Action/Impact Pathway	Emerging Economy Context Evidence
Green Innovation (Technology/Process)	SDG 7, 13, 9, 12	Enhancing energy efficiency, low-carbon solutions, industrial modernization	Illustrative evidence suggests potential reduction in emissions through green technologies in emerging economies
Inclusive Business Models	SDG 1, 8, 5	Job creation, empowerment, reduced inequality	Indicative outcomes include employment generation and improved income opportunities, particularly for women
Sustainable Supply Chains & Circularity	SDG 12, 6	Waste reduction, circular resource use	Emerging practices highlight improvements in resource efficiency and waste management systems
Transparent Sustainability Reporting	SDG 17	Accountability, monitoring sustainability performance	Growing adoption of ESG reporting enhances transparency and stakeholder trust

The connection between green entrepreneurship and SDGs can be said to be multidimensional, referring to technological, social, and ecological aspects. Green business leaders not only innovate, but transform the nature of business, to become a systemic change agent, which further advances objectives like access to clean energy, responsible production, and climate resiliency, and inclusive economic development (Sharma & Subba, 2025). In the case of emerging economies, strengthening this link is one of the possible ways to balance economic growth with environmental management, with green entrepreneurship emerging as a strategic pillar of sustainable and fair world development (Khymych, 2025).

5. POLICY FRAMEWORK AND REGULATIONS

Policy support and the institutional structures that allow sustainable business ecosystems highly influence the development and prosperity of the green entrepreneurship. These mechanisms are highly important in the emerging economies to face the issues of the environment and development, as well as to encourage circular and sustainable business (Zhaksybayeva et al., 2024). Green ventures are scalable and resilient with effective governance, such as access to green finance and they can be coordinated by institutional actions (Elf et al., 2025). Sustainability-based policies can be aligned with entrepreneurship; in addition to stimulating innovations, they can be used to improve long-term environmental and societal payoffs (Mamash et al., 2025). Moreover, the availability of finance, technology, market preparedness, etc. is enhanced by institutional and regulatory support, and SMEs can take green strategies and grow sustainably (V. K. Singh et al., 2024; Rashid et al., 2025). However, the effectiveness of these policy mechanisms varies significantly across emerging economies due to differences in institutional capacity, governance quality, and regulatory enforcement, highlighting the need for context-specific policy design and implementation.

On the global front, a number of frameworks have been formulated to facilitate sustainable entrepreneurship in terms of financial and institutional cooperation as shown in Figure 2. The Green Economy Initiative (GEI) by the United Nations Environment Programme is just one example of putting the concept of sustainability within the economic policy making and investment strategy (Chirambo, 2020). On the same note, other efforts like the World Bank Climate Investment Funds (CIF) and the Global Environment Facility (GEF) have created resources to encourage climate-sensitive innovation, especially in the developing economies (Mendez & Houghton, 2020). These transitions are identified as being central to the role of small and medium-sized enterprises (SMEs) since the environmental and social performance of these organizations has a direct impact on achieving the Sustainable Development Goals (SDGs). Nevertheless, these global efforts must work based on the robustness of domestic institutions and the extent or ability of domestic policies to translate international sustainability models into practical results (Durst and Gerstlberger, 2020). This indicates that while global frameworks provide strategic direction, their success is contingent upon effective localization, institutional coordination, and alignment with national development priorities.

Figure 2. OECD Policy Pillars for Emerging Economies

Sustainability in the entrepreneurship promotion has been enshrined in policy and institutional mechanisms in India. New opportunities have been generated by the National Action Plan on Climate Change (NAPCC) and its sectoral missions on renewable energy, water, and sustainable agriculture to develop innovation by the private sector (Chakraborty and Karandikar, 2025). The science, technology, and innovation ecosystem is reinforced by programs like the Startup India, the Atal Innovation Mission (AIM) as well as the support provided to startups in terms of fiscal incentives, mentorship, and incubation networks additionally in accordance with the Sustainable Development Goals (SDGs) (Surana et al., 2020). In a similar way, such mechanisms as the National Clean Energy Fund (NCEF) contribute to increased investment in renewable projects and allow more easily entering the world of green entrepreneurs (N. Sharma et al., 2025). On the state level, Kerala has an example of decentralized programs, which include the Responsible Tourism Mission initiative and the Renewable Energy Policy project in Maharashtra, where subnational programs transform sustainability principles into enterprise models (Ahluwalia, 2019).

Financial institutions are central to the development of green entrepreneurship by incorporating the concept of green finance and ESG (Environmental, Social, and Governance) approaches. The emergence of green bonds, impact investments, and sustainability-linked loans has offered new avenues of financing of environmentally friendly projects (Bhatnagar et al., 2022). Responsible investment in India was promoted by the Reserve Bank of India (RBI and the Securities and Exchange Board of India (SEBI) because they have required corporations to disclose ESG and sustainability reports (Chipalkatti et al., 2025). Nevertheless, the research indicates that institutional uncertainty and divided policy frameworks are the reasons why adoption of green banking is not even after regulation (Chandran et al., 2025). In addition, while ESG frameworks and green finance instruments are expanding rapidly, their implementation remains uneven due to regulatory fragmentation, lack of standardized reporting practices, and limited awareness among stakeholders, particularly in developing economies. As part of the growing focus on climate-compatible projects and clean technologies globally, financial institutions like the European Investment Bank and Asian Development Bank have begun giving preference to finance sustainable entrepreneurship (Kaakandikar, 2025).

However, in most of the developing economies, poor implementation of environmental policies, inconsistencies in policy and the lack of coordination between agencies still remains a challenge to successful implementation of sustainability programs. Further inhibition of the accessibility of green finance and the institutions support mechanisms is also caused by bureaucratic complexity and a lack of awareness among SMEs (Chandran et al., 2025).

To overcome the current issues, researchers focus on multi-stakeholder governance approaches, which refers to the combination of governments, investors, academia, and civil society that facilitate coherence in policies and knowledge exchange in sustainable entrepreneurship (Forcadell & Aracil, 2019). This type of collaboration improves the level of innovation and transparency and makes sure the principles of sustainability are embedded in both institutional and business practices (Berniak-Woźny et al., 2025). Incorporating sustainability education and trainings in institutions of higher learning can also develop green innovators and match the academic outputs with Sustainable Development Goals (SDGs) (Schimperna et al., 2025). Also, the implementation of impact measurement frameworks can be used to assess the contribution of green enterprises to the sustainable development of the countries, enhancing accountability and policymaking that is supported by evidence (Raman et al., 2025).

To sum it up, robust policy and institutional systems are imperative to cultivate the robust green entrepreneurship ecosystems. Given that the emerging economies need to align their national strategies with international sustainability objectives and develop institutions that are driven by innovation, it will become possible to transform entrepreneurship in these nations into a vehicle of inclusive and sustainable development (Saxena, 2025).

6. STRATEGIC OPPORTUNITIES AND CHALLENGES

Although there is an increasing recognition of green entrepreneurship as a strategic instrument of attaining the Sustainable Development Goals (SDGs), it has been found to experience the entrenched financial, structural, and institutional obstacles to its growth in the emerging economies. According to the recent researches, the policy frameworks and the institutional assistance have been getting better, but the scalability of green ventures is limited due to poor fragmented governance and the lack of uniformity in regulations enforcement (Sharma et al., 2025). This indicates a persistent gap between policy intent and implementation outcomes, which constrains the effective scaling of green entrepreneurial initiatives.

One of the main challenges is the problem of low access to finance. Green businesses are sometimes costly upfront costs (research, clean technologies, and eco-friendly infrastructure) which discourage conventional lenders. Small-scale and early-stage projects are often underfunded due to insecure returns in the long payback period, which banks and investors consider these projects to be high-risk. The problem of green credit instruments, including sustainability-linked loans and risk-sharing, makes this financing gap even worse (Sosa & Ivanova, 2025). Moreover, poor investor understanding of the benefits of environmental sustainability and lack of uniform ESG performance indicators undermine confidence in measuring the solvency of sustainable startups. These financial constraints highlight the need for standardized sustainability metrics and risk-sharing mechanisms to improve investor confidence and capital allocation efficiency.

Policymaking and institutional discrepancies are also of equal importance. In most developing countries the environmental laws are either not enforced well or are spread out in various ministries and agencies and this creates confusion to the entrepreneurs. Bureaucratic complexity and overlapping jurisdictions are some of the factors that reduce the efficiency of the approval processes, thereby limiting the implementation of green projects. Studies have pointed out that a poor level of coordination between national industrial policies and sustainability framework creates loopholes that do not necessitate green innovation.

The third prominent barrier is knowledge and capacity deficit. Most of the potential entrepreneurs in the emerging markets do not have the technical and managerial skills to create viable sustainable business models. An article on sustainable innovation management underlines that without proper preparation (training and institutional) the spread of green technologies, in particular in such spheres of renewable energy and waste recycling, and water savings, is weak (Alamandi, 2025). Low consumer awareness regarding environmentally friendly products and enduring price sensitivity still limit the growth in the market on the demand side. This demonstrates that both supply-side (skills and capabilities) and demand-side (consumer awareness and affordability) constraints jointly hinder the adoption of green entrepreneurship.

Figure 3. Strategic challenges in SDGs

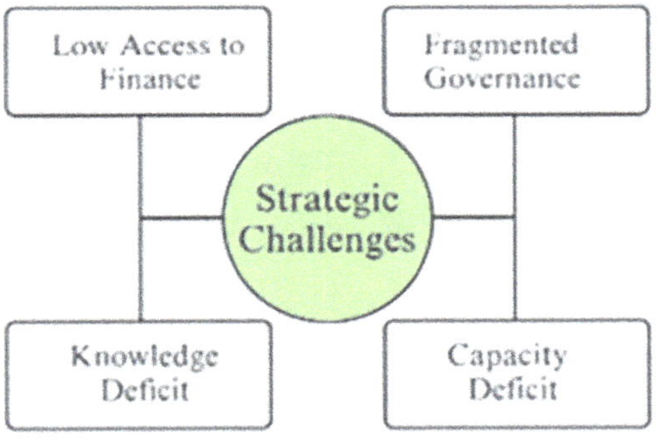

In spite of these systemic barriers, strategic opportunities are appearing in large numbers. Environmental, Social, and Governance (ESG) models and green capital market mechanisms (green bonds, carbon credits, and impact investment funds) have started to widen the access to sustainable capital markets across the world

(Dhar et al., 2026). FinTech and GreenTech development are moving in parallel with the development of artificial intelligence (AI), blockchain, and the Internet of Things (IoT), making the field of green entrepreneurship more transparent, efficient in environmental monitoring, and less costly to run a transaction (Offiong et al., 2025b). These technological advancements also enable improved impact measurement, traceability, and transparency, thereby addressing key challenges related to accountability and performance evaluation.

Another opportunity offered by the increasing power of the circular economy is the possibility of recovering resources, valorising waste, and designing sustainable products. The innovations can be seen especially in incubator models of connecting startups and smart city sustainability agendas, which proves the significance of a multi-stakeholder approach to using local governments, research institutions, and private investors (Berniak-Wozy et al., 2025).

To bridge knowledge and financing gaps between governments and international development agencies, policy instruments are actively being designed towards building a public-private partnership (PPP) (Shah & Ghayas, 2022), green accelerator and sustainability incubator. These initiatives are based on focusing on capacity-building, training green skills, and women inclusion so that women-led and communal-based businesses could take advantage of the green shift (Sharma et al., 2025). Such collaborative models enhance ecosystem coordination and facilitate knowledge transfer, which are critical for scaling sustainable innovations in emerging economies.

Finally, the road toward sustainable development of the emerging economies depends on a coherent policy which combines policy reform, market incentives, and technological development. It is crucial to strengthen the capacity of governance, increase green finance, and promote innovation-based institutions to make the green entrepreneurship an engine of inclusive and low-carbon development (Alamandi, 2025).

7. IMPLICATIONS

The green entrepreneurship is viewed through the prism of the Sustainable Development Goals (SDGs), which is why the phenomenon is characterized by its transformative possibilities as more than an economic activity it is a structural force of sustainable development and inclusive growth in the emerging economies (Watson et al., 2023). Green entrepreneurship reinforces the traditional concept of success by integrating the environmental and social responsibility into the innovations that predetermines the ecological sustainability and social justice (Tiuncika & Bormane, 2024). This development is a systemic reorientation to the green form of industrialization and fair ways of development (Saxena, 2025). This highlights the role of green entrepreneurship as a system-level catalyst that integrates economic growth with environmental and social objectives.

In a theoretical perspective, this change supports the triple bottom line paradigm advanced by Elkington (1997) in which the environmental and social impact are the cornerstone of business success coupled with profit. Modern studies combine institutional theory, focusing on the importance of the governance structures and regulatory framework in establishing entrepreneurial behaviour, with the innovation theory, which predicts the emergence of creativity and sustainable technological diffusion in resource-constrained settings (Koe et al., 2024). This intersection implies that sustainability-oriented entrepreneurship thrives in the context when the institutions are favourable, policies are adaptable, and the entrepreneur capabilities are deployed successfully (Caro-Gonzalez, 2024). This integrated theoretical perspective strengthens the understanding of how multi-level factors influence sustainable entrepreneurial outcomes.

Implications of the policy are enormous. Policymakers are encouraged to shift to dynamic ecosystem governance by following the principles of ESG as they are being incorporated into the national entrepreneurship strategies, and there is an extension of access to green finance through the use of public- private mechanisms. These adaptive frameworks are required to enhance the global sustainability goals and local entrepreneurial activities in alignment with the impact measurement frameworks (Steiner and Makarenko, 2026). n addition, the development of standardized impact measurement frameworks is essential to ensure accountability and effective evaluation of policy outcomes.

To academicians and practitioners, the challenge of integrating sustainability in any entrepreneurship education and incubation program is crucial in creating the future generation of green innovators. The introduction of environmental ethics, responsible production models, and inclusive innovation into the curriculum can stimulate ethical leadership and make sure that an entrepreneurial venture will make a meaningful contribution to the SDGs (Sánchez-Hernandez et al., 2025). Furthermore, strengthening the linkage between academia, industry, and policy institutions can enhance knowledge transfer and practical implementation of sustainable innovations.

8. CONCLUSION

Green entrepreneurship has been an innovative solution in the implementation of the Sustainable Development Goals (SDGs) and more in the emerging economies where the most urgent solution is the inclusive and low-carbon growth. Green entrepreneurs are the agents of economic and environmental sustainability by connecting innovation, policy and sustainability. More importantly, their contribution can be understood through key mechanisms such as innovation diffusion, resource efficiency, and inclusive business models that translate entrepreneurial activities into measurable sustainability outcomes. Their full potential will be realized though, however, more powerful institutional structures, available green finance and general environmental literacy.

However, it is acknowledged that the conceptual nature of this study limits empirical validation and raises concerns related to causality and impact attribution, which should be addressed in future research. Further studies are required in the following areas that would help create impact measurement models, study the gender and regional aspects of green entrepreneurship, and understand the role of digital technologies in accelerating the process of sustainability-related business change in various economic settings. Overall, the study contributes by providing an integrated conceptual framework that links green entrepreneurship with SDG outcomes, offering insights for policymakers, researchers, and practitioners to strengthen sustainable development strategies in emerging economies.

REFERENCES

Ahluwalia, I. J. (2019). Urban governance in India. *Journal of Urban Affairs*, *41*(1), 83–102. DOI: 10.1080/07352166.2016.1271614

Ahmad, F., Boumaiza, A., Sanfilippo, A., & Al-Fagih, L. (2025). A Detailed Comprehensive Role of Digital Technologies in Green Finance Initiative for Net-Zero Energy Transition. *Advanced Energy and Sustainability Research*, *6*(10), 2500066. DOI: 10.1002/aesr.202500066

Alamandi, M. (2025). Sustainable Innovation Management: Balancing Economic Growth and Environmental Responsibility. *Sustainability (Basel)*, *17*(10), 4362. DOI: 10.3390/su17104362

Alao, O. E., Alao, P. O., & Elijah, T. M. (2023). Developing the entrepreneurial skills of Nigerian business education students for sustainability: Policy and practice imperatives. *Contemporary Educational Researches Journal*, *13*(4), 251–263. DOI: 10.18844/cerj.v14i4.8965

Anjanappa, J. (2023). Assessing Barriers to Scale-up Adaptation Finance for India. SSRN *Electronic Journal*. DOI: 10.2139/ssrn.4489053

Attah, E., & Yonkor, E. D. (2025). Social Entrepreneurship and Sustainable Development Goals. SSRN *Electronic Journal*. DOI: 10.2139/ssrn.5550899

Badjeena, B. P., Ali, E., Wonyra, K. O., & Tamou, K. (2024). Green entrepreneurship: Opportunities and challenges for the transition to a circular economy in Togo, West Africa. *World Development Sustainability*, *5*, 100181. DOI: 10.1016/j.wds.2024.100181

Bandna, P. K. (2025). *Hussain, I., Shah, M. A., & Bhalla, M.* Principles and Frameworks for Sustainable Finance., DOI: 10.1002/9781394311682.ch5

Basile, V., Capobianco, N., & Vona, R. (2025). Business model development in the circular bioeconomy: A focus on the fashion-textile industry. *Journal of Cleaner Production*, *494*, 144944. DOI: 10.1016/j.jclepro.2025.144944

Berniak-Woźny, J., Sliż, P., & Siciński, J. (2025). Empowering Smart Cities Through Start-Ups: A Sustainability Framework for Incubator-City Collaboration. *Systems*, *13*(4), 219. DOI: 10.3390/systems13040219

Bhatnagar, M., Taneja, S., & Özen, E. (2022). A wave of green start-ups in India—The study of green finance as a support system for sustainable entrepreneurship. *Green Finance*, *4*(2), 253–273. DOI: 10.3934/GF.2022012

Caro-Gonzalez, A. (2024). *Transformative Governance for the Future: Navigating Profound Transitions*. Springer Nature Switzerland., DOI: 10.1007/978-3-031-43132-6

Chakraborty, S., & Karandikar, A. (2025). Policies driving India's innovation-driven growth in science and technology: Pathway to progressive excellence over the past decade and roadmap to Viksit Bharat-2047. *Proceedings of the Indian National Science Academy. Part A, Physical Sciences*, *91*(1), 1–8. DOI: 10.1007/s43538-025-00436-9

Chandran, R., Chandran, M. C. S., Achuthan, K., & Sahib, P. R. (2025). Theoretical perspectives on green banking adoption in India: Regulatory uncertainty, institutional barriers, and policy solutions. *Discover Sustainability*, *6*(1), 581. DOI: 10.1007/s43621-025-01406-3

Chipalkatti, N., Prasuna, A., Rishi, M., & Siva Kumar, S. N. V. (2025). ESG disclosure scores and Indian banks: A search for relevance. *Cogent Economics & Finance*, *13*(1), 2552874. DOI: 10.1080/23322039.2025.2552874

Chirambo, D. (2020). Principles for Enhancing Earth System Governance and Sustainable Development Through Informality. *International Journal of Entrepreneurship and Governance in Cognitive Cities*, *1*(1), 47–67. DOI: 10.4018/IJEGCC.20200101.oa1

Dhar, B. K., Roshid, M., Dissanayake, S., Chawla, U., & Faheem, M. (2026). Leveraging FinTech and GreenTech for long-term sustainability in South Asia: Strategic pathways toward Agenda 2050. *Green Technologies and Sustainability*, *4*(1), 100263. DOI: 10.1016/j.grets.2025.100263

Durst, S., & Gerstlberger, W. (2020). Financing Responsible Small- and Medium-Sized Enterprises: An International Overview of Policies and Support Programmes. *Journal of Risk and Financial Management*, *14*(1), 10. DOI: 10.3390/jrfm14010010

Elf, P., Owen, R., Lyon, F., & Da Gama Torres, H. (2025). Developing sustainable entrepreneurial finance ecosystems in an emerging market context: The role of keystone actors in managing competing institutional logics. *Venture Capital*, •••, 1–26. DOI: 10.1080/13691066.2025.2496192

Forcadell, F. J., & Aracil, E. (2019). Can multinational companies foster institutional change and sustainable development in emerging countries? A case study. *Business Strategy & Development*, *2*(2), 91–105. DOI: 10.1002/bsd2.45

Gu, W., Pan, H., Hu, Z., & Liu, Z. (2022). The Triple Bottom Line of Sustainable Entrepreneurship and Economic Policy Uncertainty: An Empirical Evidence from 22 Countries. *International Journal of Environmental Research and Public Health*, *19*(13), 7758. DOI: 10.3390/ijerph19137758 PMID: 35805416

Gupta, R. (2025). Women-Led Green Entrepreneurship: Motivators and Challenges. SSRN *Electronic Journal*. DOI: 10.2139/ssrn.5517519

Hummels, H., & Argyrou, A. (2021). Planetary demands: Redefining sustainable development and sustainable entrepreneurship. *Journal of Cleaner Production*, *278*, 123804. DOI: 10.1016/j.jclepro.2020.123804

Ilesanmi, J. (2024). Importance of Eco-Entrepreneurship as a Tool for Climate Action and LowCarbon Transition in Developing Countries: A Case Study of Nigeria. *Journal of Sustainable Development Law and Policy (The)*, *15*(2), 298–327. DOI: 10.4314/jsdlp.v15i2.11

Kaakandikar, R. (2025). THE THREE PILLARS OF BUSINESS: A GUIDE TO INTEGRATED MARKETING, FINANCE & HR PRACTICES. SSRN *Electronic Journal*. DOI: 10.2139/ssrn.5161493

Kaur, G. P., & Shah, M. A. (2026). Artificial Intelligence in Circular Economy and Green Logistics. *Advances in Computational Intelligence and Robotics*, •••, 87–114. DOI: 10.4018/979-8-3373-5946-5.ch004

Kaur, P., & Kaur, D. S. (2019). Green entrepreneurship in India: A study of select green businesses. *International Journal of Applied Research*, *5*(3), 369–376. DOI: 10.22271/allresearch.2019.v5.i3d.10782

Khymych, O. (2025). EU Insights on Innovative Entrepreneurship Ecosystems Following Sustainable Development Goals. In Steiner, B. E., & Makarenko, I. (Eds.), *Bridging Governance, Public Support, Innovation, and Transparency* (pp. 103–131). Springer Nature Switzerland., DOI: 10.1007/978-3-031-94082-8_5

Khymych, O. (2026). EU Insights on Innovative Entrepreneurship Ecosystems Following Sustainable Development Goals. In Steiner, B. E., & Makarenko, I. (Eds.), *Bridging Governance, Public Support, Innovation, and Transparency* (pp. 103–131). Springer Nature Switzerland., DOI: 10.1007/978-3-031-94082-8_5

Koe, W.-L., Nordin, N. M., & Othman, R. (2024). Fostering sustainable entrepreneurial intention: The role of institutional factors. *Management & Marketing*, *19*(1), 32–50. DOI: 10.2478/mmcks-2024-0003

Majumdar, P. (2025). Illuminating the Path to Sustainability Analysing Global Electricity Access for Achieving SDG 7. *American Journal of Information Science and Technology*, *9*(1), 42–59. DOI: 10.11648/j.ajist.20250901.15

Mamash, A., Iyiola, K., & Aljuhmani, H. Y. (2025). The Role of Circular Economy Entrepreneurship, Cleaner Production, and Green Government Subsidy for Achieving Sustainability Goals in Business Performance. *Sustainability (Basel)*, *17*(9), 3990. DOI: 10.3390/su17093990

Mendez, A., & Houghton, D. P. (2020). Sustainable Banking: The Role of Multilateral Development Banks as Norm Entrepreneurs. *Sustainability (Basel)*, *12*(3), 972. DOI: 10.3390/su12030972

Nuringsih, K. (2021). ROLE OF GREEN ENTREPRENEURSHIP IN RAISING THE EFFECT OF GREEN VALUE TOWARD SUSTAINABLE DEVELOPMENT. *International Journal of Economics, Business, and Entrepreneurship*, *3*(2), 29–46. DOI: 10.23960/ijebe.v3i2.69

Nuringsih, K., Mn, N., & Rosa, J. A. (2022). Mendorong Green Entrepreneurial Intention Melalui Green Economy dan Green Entrepreneurial Orientation. *Jurnal Ekonomi*, *27*(3), 417–438. DOI: 10.24912/je.v27i3.1203

. Offiong, U. P., Szopik-Depczyńska, K., & Ioppolo, G. (2025a). FinTech Innovations for Sustainable Development: A Comprehensive Literature Review and Future Directions. *Sustainable Development*, sd.70068. DOI: 10.1002/sd.70068

. Offiong, U. P., Szopik-Depczyńska, K., & Ioppolo, G. (2025b). FinTech Innovations for Sustainable Development: A Comprehensive Literature Review and Future Directions. *Sustainable Development*, sd.70068. DOI: 10.1002/sd.70068

Pandikar, E., Affandi, I., Disman, D., & Sundawa, D. (2024). Harmonizing Economic Principles, Islamic Values, and Entrepreneurial Attitudes for a Sustainable Environment. *Yupa: Historical Studies Journal*, *6*(2), 188–197. DOI: 10.30872/yupa.v6i2.3739

Prasetyo, P. E., Azwardi, A., & Kistanti, N. R. (2023). Gender equality and social inclusion (GESI) and institutions as key drivers of green entrepreneurship. *International Journal of Data and Network Science*, *7*(1), 391–398. DOI: 10.5267/j.ijdns.2022.9.008

Raman, R., Ray, S., Das, D., & Nedungadi, P. (2025). Innovations and barriers in sustainable and green finance for advancing sustainable development goals. *Frontiers in Environmental Science*, *12*, 1513204. DOI: 10.3389/fenvs.2024.1513204

Rashid, M., Anser, M. K., Shah, S. T. H., Nabi, A. A., Ahmad, I., & Zaman, K. (2025). Fostering entrepreneurship: Analyzing the influence of access to finance, innovation investment, educational attainment, infrastructure development, and regulatory environment. *Future Business Journal*, *11*(1), 140. DOI: 10.1186/s43093-025-00557-z

Rumbayan, M., Kindangen, J., Sambul, A., Sompie, S., & Cross, J. (2025). Solar energy implementation in rural communities and its contributions to SDGs: A systematic literature review. *Unconventional Resources*, *6*, 100180. DOI: 10.1016/j.uncres.2025.100180

Saeedi, M., & Ashraf, B. N. (2024). The Role of Technology in Promoting Green Finance: A Systematic Literature Survey and the Development of a Framework. *Journal of Risk and Financial Management*, *17*(10), 472. DOI: 10.3390/jrfm17100472

Sánchez-Hernández, M. I., Rabazo-Martín, A., Rodriguez-Rivero, E., & Guerrero-Cáceres, J. M. (2025). The Convergence of the Fourth Sector and Generation Z's Biospheric Values: A Regional Empirical Case Study in Spain. *WORLD (Oakland, Calif.)*, *6*(2), 83. DOI: 10.3390/world6020083

Saxena, D. S. (2025). Corporate Social Responsibility as a Strategic Tool for Sustainable Growth: A Comparative Study of Startups in India and Southeast Asia. *Journal of Asia Entrepreneurship and Sustainability*, •••, 108–116. DOI: 10.53555/jaes.v21i2.35

Schimperna, F., Schimperna, M., Gigli, S., & Manzari, A. (2025). Sustainability and higher education: Exploring ESG drivers of university performance through a multi-stakeholder lens. *International Journal of Information and Operations Management Education*, *8*(1), 74–96. DOI: 10.1504/IJIOME.2025.148369

Shah, M. A., & Ghayas, A. (2022). Impediments to Public-Private Partnership Projects In Aftermath of Covid-19 Pandemic. *Parikalpana: KIIT Journal of Management*, *18*(1), 85. DOI: 10.23862/kiit-parikalpana/2022/v18/i1/212347

Shah, M. A., & Singh, A. (2026). Examining the Impact of Circular Economy Practices and Brand Reputation on Financial Performance. *Circular Economy and Sustainability*, *6*(1), 2. Advance online publication. DOI: 10.1007/s43615-026-00751-3

Shah, M. A., & Uddin, F. (2023). Leveraging Blockchain Technology in the Construction Industry. *Advances in Business Information Systems and Analytics*, •••, 50–65. DOI: 10.4018/978-1-6684-7808-0.ch004

Sharma, N., Trivedi, M., & Choudhary, M. (2025). From tradition to transform: SDGs and the role of the Indian knowledge system in india's growth through ESE (Environment, Social, and Economic) factors. *Discover Sustainability*, *6*(1), 1110. DOI: 10.1007/s43621-025-01905-3

Sharma, S. N., & Subba, R. (2025). Entrepreneurship and Sustainability: Analyzing the impact of Green Startups on Economic Development. *Innovation and Green Development*, *4*(4), 100280. DOI: 10.1016/j.igd.2025.100280

Singh, P., Daga, S., Yadav, K., & Nguyen, P. M. (Eds.). (2025). *Advancing the SDGs in Developing and Emerging Economies: Volume II: Sustainable Development Challenges*. Springer Nature Switzerland. DOI: 10.1007/978-3-031-95103-9

Singh, V. K., Keshari, A., Singh, D., Singh, P. C., & Gautam, A. (2024). Green export strategies and SMEs export performance: Mediating roles of innovation, readiness, and activities. *Journal of Innovation and Entrepreneurship*, *13*(1), 87. DOI: 10.1186/s13731-024-00451-y

Soliman, S., Elkholy, S. M. A., & Elkharbotly, M. M. Y. (2023). EVALUATION OF ENVIRONMENTALLY-FRIENDLY ENTREPRENEURSHIP PROJECTS) FIELD STUDY. *Journal of Environmental Sciences (China)*, *52*(8), 29–55. DOI: 10.21608/jes.2023.213379.1532

Sołoducho-Pelc, L. (2020). Sustainable Entrepreneurship Utopian Idea or a New Business Model for the 21st Century? In Michałkiewicz, A., & Mierzejewska, W. (Eds.), *Contemporary organisation and management. Challenges and trends* (pp. 205–219). Wydawnictwo Uniwersytetu Łódzkiego., DOI: 10.18778/8220-333-2.12

Sosa, M., & Ivanova, A. (2025). Innovation and Disruptive Technologies for Sustainable and Climate Finance. *Modern Economy*, *16*(09), 1401–1419. DOI: 10.4236/me.2025.169065

Stanković, S., Ilić, B., & Rabrenović, M. (2024). Using the Composite EEPSE Green Economy Index to Assess the Progress of Emerging Economies in Achieving the Sustainable Development Goals. *Problemy Ekorozwoju*, *19*(1), 78–88. DOI: 10.35784/preko.5751

Steiner, B. E., & Makarenko, I. (Eds.). (2026). *Bridging Governance, Public Support, Innovation, and Transparency: A Combined Approach to Sustainable Development in Europe*. Springer Nature Switzerland., DOI: 10.1007/978-3-031-94082-8

Surana, K., Singh, A., & Sagar, A. D. (2020). Strengthening science, technology, and innovation-based incubators to help achieve Sustainable Development Goals: Lessons from India. *Technological Forecasting and Social Change*, *157*, 120057. DOI: 10.1016/j.techfore.2020.120057

Sutariya, J., & Arora, D. G. (2023). Empowering Rural Economies: The Role Of Microfinance Institutions In Transforming The Financial Landscape Of Rural Communities. *Educational Administration: Theory and Practice*, *29*(03). Advance online publication. DOI: 10.53555/kuey.v29i3.9991

Szopik-Depczyńska, K., Cheba, K., Vikhasta, M., & Depczyński, R. (2021). New form of innovations related to the environment—A systematic review. *Procedia Computer Science*, *192*, 5039–5049. DOI: 10.1016/j.procs.2021.09.282

Tiuncika, L., & Bormane, S. (2024). Sustainable Management of Manufacturing Processes: A Literature Review. *Processes (Basel, Switzerland)*, *12*(6), 1222. DOI: 10.3390/pr12061222

Watson, R., Nielsen, K. R., Wilson, H. N., Macdonald, E. K., Mera, C., & Reisch, L. (2023). Policy for sustainable entrepreneurship: A crowdsourced framework. *Journal of Cleaner Production*, *383*, 135234. DOI: 10.1016/j.jclepro.2022.135234

Zhaksybayeva, N., Serikkyzy, A., Baktymbet, A., & Yousafzai, S. (2024). Circular shifts: Insights into kazakhstan's circular business ecosystem. *Cogent Business & Management*, *11*(1), 2431652. DOI: 10.1080/23311975.2024.2431652

Chapter 6
Green Entrepreneurship and Sustainable Development in India:
Emerging Innovation Pathways and Inclusive Business Models for a Greener Economy

M. Hariharan
http://orcid.org/0009-0000-3953-3582
SASTRA (Deemed to be) University, India

D. Indhumathi
http://orcid.org/0009-0000-1720-3996
SASTRA (Deemed to be) University, India

ABSTRACT

Green entrepreneurship has emerged as a vital approach for balancing economic growth with environmental sustainability in rapidly developing economies such as India. This chapter uses an integrative conceptual and policy-oriented review to examine how green enterprises promote sustainable development. Drawing on academic studies, policy reports, and industry cases, it explores innovation, inclusive business models, and policy support across sectors including renewable energy, waste management, sustainable manufacturing, and agriculture. The analysis highlights the role of institutional frameworks and entrepreneurial ecosystems while identifying challenges related to financial viability and policy dependence. The chapter contributes to global debates on sustainable entrepreneurship in emerging economies.

DOI: 10.4018/979-8-3373-7391-1.ch006

1. INTRODUCTION

1.1 Sustainability Issues in "Emerging Economies"

These issues of climate change, environmental degradation, resource depletion and social inequality are now playing an increasing role in global economic development. In several developing countries, economic growth has been boosted, especially in cities, but as a result of this industrialization and urbanization there has been a significant increase of pollution, carbon emissions, waste production and ecological imbalance. Emerging economies thus have a critical challenge to achieve economic development, social inclusion and environmental sustainability (Banerjee, 2003; UNEP, 2020).

India is a major case in point for this sustainability quandary. The country is one of the fastest growing economies in the world, with the growth of energy demand, industrial growth, urbanization and rising consumption levels. These growths are not only driving economic development but also causing environmental challenges such as air pollution, water scarcity, solid waste management issues, and climate change risks (Government of India, 2015; Central Pollution Control Board, 2021). Thus, sustainable development is now a key national policy focus of policymakers, industries, and entrepreneurial ecosystems.

The increasing focus on sustainability is strongly connected to the worldwide shift in economic systems towards sustainability. The United Nations Sustainable Development Goals (SDGs) (United Nations, 2015) are international agreements that promote the integration of economic development and environmental protection and social equity (SDGs) at the country level. In this context, companies are now more and more required to implement cleaner production techniques, renewable energy solutions, circular economy and sustainable operation strategies (Elkington, 1997).

In the traditional industrial paradigm, productivity and profitability were the main focus with little regard for long-term ecological impacts. But the evolution of regulatory systems, technological innovations and a growing consciousness of the environment have helped to speed up the move to sustainable business. These changes have opened up new possibilities for entrepreneurial individuals who can find solutions that are both economically and environmentally viable and relevant to markets (Hart & Milstein, 1999).

In developing countries, financial resources, institutional weaknesses, lack of technology, and poor infrastructure are the factors that can hinder sustainability transition. While playing a crucial role in employment and industrial activity, small and medium-sized enterprises (MSMEs) often do not benefit from sustainable financing, cutting-edge technologies, and innovation ecosystems (OECD 2021; Ministry of Micro, Small and Medium Enterprises 2021). The structural problems illustrate the need for business models that are both environmentally responsible and economically viable.

In this context, the development of green entrepreneurship has become an important mechanism in supporting the sustainable development. Green enterprises foster sustainable industrial change, create employment, improve resource use and innovation for the environment (Dean & McMullen, 2007; Cohen & Winn, 2007). The growing importance of entrepreneurship for sustainability is thus a sign of the growing intertwining of innovation, environmental management, and inclusive economic development.

1.2 Green entrepreneurship is a sustainable development strategy.

Green Entrepreneurship is defined as the initiation and operations of business activities that include environmental sustainability as an integral component of their products, operations and strategies. Green entrepreneurship goes beyond the traditional entrepreneurial approach, which is primarily economic, and targets the simultaneous creation of economic, environmental and social values (Schaltegger, 2002). Businesses that consider sustainability therefore try to achieve a balance between profit and taking care of the environment and society.

As sustainable economic systems are more and more gaining weight, green entrepreneurship is also gaining in importance. The necessity of more than just regulatory solutions to address environmental challenges has become evident to governments, industries and international organizations alike. Entrepreneurial innovation is essential for the ability to create scalable and market-oriented sustainability solutions (York & Venkataraman, 2010). Thus, green entrepreneurs are not only helping to protect the environment but also to modernize industries, develop technologies, and ensure long-term economic stability.

The green entrepreneurship shows strategic significance in India because of the growing environmental concerns and the growth of demand for green products and services in India. Opportunities for entrepreneurs have increased in renewable energy, sustainable agriculture, waste management, use of eco-friendly packaging, electric mobility and green construction (Gupta & Sharma, 2023; Sarkar & Ghosh, 2022). Technology innovation, policy supports and consumer preferences are on the rise in these sectors.

The benefits of green entrepreneurship to sustainable development are numerous. Green enterprises create innovation, job opportunities and industrial diversification from an economic perspective. They are beneficial for the environment, in terms of greener technologies, use of renewable energy, resource efficiency, and circular economy. A socially oriented enterprise can contribute to the development of the community, inclusion of rural people and the availability of ecologically responsible products and services (Hockerts & Wüstenhagen, 2010). This multidimensional contribution will be in line with the Triple Bottom Line approach that focuses on economic, environmental and social sustainability (Elkington 1997).

Government initiatives and policies that promote sustainability have also contributed to the growth of green entrepreneurship in India. Schemes like Startup India, Make in India and renewable energy development have been promoting innovative ventures and green startups (DPIIT, 2025). Sustainability-oriented entrepreneurial ecosystems have been further bolstered by financial incentives, incubation centres and technological support systems. Yet, with the progress of policy, implementation challenges, funding problems and regulatory issues remain a constraint on the scaling-up of many green businesses.

Advancements in technology have also contributed to the rise in sustainability-based entrepreneurship. Artificial Intelligence, Internet of Things (IoT), Blockchain-based supply chains, Renewable energy systems and Smart waste management technologies are some of the developing technologies that are influencing Sustainable business operations (Ramasamy & Choudhury, 2023). These innovations will also increase their resource efficiency, minimize operational waste and improve environmental monitoring capabilities, which will further strengthen the competitiveness of green enterprises.

Yet there are some structural and operational problems that remain to further undermine the sustainability of green ventures in emerging economies. Businesses that prioritize sustainability often face challenges such as high operating costs, low awareness of the market, poor infrastructure and financial returns (Mishra & Singh, 2024). Likewise, poor institutional co-ordination and ill-defined regulations can hinder sustainability efforts.

The linkage of innovation capability, policy support and business sustainability is therefore of great importance. Policy incentives could be used to drive more entrepreneurial engagement, but sustainability will rely on enterprises' capacity to build sustainable business models, market agility, and efficiency. Green entrepreneurship is thus no longer only considered to be an environmental program, but a strategic tool for sustainable economic transition and inclusive development.

1.3 Research Problem and Objectives

Despite the growing academic and poliy interest in green entrepreneurship, the current literature still shows some limitations in analysis, especially in the context of emerging economy. Numerous studies have led to descriptive reports on the practice of sustainability without in-depth consideration of the dynamic nature of the linkages between entrepreneurial innovation, institutional support, policy ecosystems, market dynamics and sustainable outcomes. In addition, there is a lack of cross-sectoral integration of the literature and an absence of the integrated consideration of the contribution of sustainability-oriented enterprises to economic, environmental and social transformation.

In India, studies on green entrepreneurship often highlight the opportunities and policies for green businesses without offering much discussion on the constraints of operation, the constraints of scale and institutional inefficiencies that present a barrier to sustainability-focused businesses. Likewise, the analytical attention on the part of MSMEs, technological innovation and entrepreneurial ecosystems to support sustainable industrial transitions is still lacking. These gaps contribute to the limited practical and theoretical knowledge about the effectiveness of green entrepreneurship in sustainable development in the long run.

This chapter thus seeks to analyse the pathways of innovation, inclusive business models, institutional supports and sustainability issues of green entrepreneurship in India and its contribution towards sustainable development. The chapter also examines the impacts of policy frameworks, technological innovations and entrepreneurial sustainability and explores some key challenges for entrepreneurial growth and scalability related to the green sector.

The main aims of the chapter are:

- To explore the contribution of green entrepreneurship for sustainability in India.
- To understand how new innovation paths form in sustainability related sectors.
- To assess the impact of policy and institutional environment on green enterprises.
- To find the main problems of the scalability and sustainability of greens ventures.
- To offer managerial and policy suggestions on boosting entrepreneurship for sustainability.

1.4 Structure of the Chapter

The chapter is organized into eight major sections. Following the introduction, the second section discusses the methodological approach and analytical framework adopted for the study. The third section critically reviews existing literature and identifies major research gaps. The fourth and fifth sections analyze emerging innovation pathways, sustainable business models, and market dynamics in green entrepreneurship. The sixth section evaluates policy support mechanisms and entrepreneurial ecosystems influencing sustainability-oriented enterprises. The seventh section discusses major challenges, limitations, and future research directions. Finally, the concluding section summarizes the major findings and presents managerial and policy implications related to sustainable entrepreneurship and innovation in India.

2. ANALYSIS AND METHODOLOGY

2.1 Research Design

The chapter uses integrative and analytical review approach to analyze the relationship between green entrepreneurship and sustainability oriented innovation with regard to the issue of sustainable development in India. The use of the integrative review method is suitable since it allows for the convergence of multidisciplinary sources of information related to entrepreneurship, sustainability, innovation management, environmental policy and business transformation (Creswell & Creswell, 2018). The integrative review type is more apt to be critical and to synthesize, compare and interpret conceptually across the various studies than the traditional descriptive review.

The chapter is mostly based on secondary data gathered from academic journals, government reports, sustainability frameworks, policy documents, international institutional publications and industry analyses. Database sources of literature included the journals indexed in Scopus, Google Scholar, ScienceDirect, Springer, Emerald, Wiley and sustainability-related institutional publications. Recent studies on green entrepreneurship, circular economy practices, innovation on renewable energy, sustainable business models, and transitions towards sustainable development of MSMEs were prioritized.

Analytical focus of the chapter is to understand the role of entrepreneurial innovation in the context of environmental sustainability, economic development and social inclusion in India. The chapter also examines how institutional support systems, technological innovation and market factors impact the scalability and sustainability of green companies.

2.2 Analytical Framework

The chapter is based on three conceptual approaches: the Triple Bottom Line approach, Sustainable Innovation Theory and Institutional Theory. These frameworks together enable to analyse from a sustainability perspective on entrepreneurship and business transformation.

According to Triple Bottom Line (Elkington, 1997), economic, environmental and social sustainability are all key business goals that must be achieved concurrently. This view is especially relevant for green entrepreneurship as sustainability driven businesses should account for profitability, while at the same time being environmentally responsible and creating social value.

Sustainable Innovation Theory underscores the importance of innovation in the area of cleaner production systems, technological developments and resource utilization efficiency (Nidumolu et al., 2009). Green entrepreneurs frequently need to innovate their technologies and processes in order to create environment friendly products and services that can solve sustainability problems and remain competitive to the market.

Institutional Theory aims to understand how regulation, policy landscapes, market designs and institutional facilitation shapes entrepreneurial actions and sustainability transitions (Hockerts, 2017). In emerging economies, institutions are a key determinant of successful, scalable sustainability-oriented business.

By incorporating these frameworks, a comprehensive understanding of green entrepreneurship can be achieved by linking sustainability goals, innovation potential, and institutional support. This analytical framework is helpful to assess innovation pathways, business models, policy ecosystem and operational barriers of green enterprises in India.

2.3 Scope and Limitations

The chapter is majorly concentrating on sustainability driven entrepreneurship and innovation context in India. Specific focus is placed on the areas of renewable energy, sustainable manufacturing, waste management, sustainable agriculture, green technologies and circular economy. The study also explores policy measures, entrepreneurial ecosystems, and institutional support aspects that impact green enterprise development.

The chapter however does have some drawbacks. The study is mainly descriptive, secondary data based and literature synthesis so that it doesn't contain the process of empirical field analysis and quantitative validation. Furthermore, the dynamic nature of sustainability policies and technological developments can affect other entrepreneurship trends, which are not covered in the presented review. However, the chapter offers a detailed analytical insight into the opportunities, challenges and strategic relevance of green entrepreneurship in India despite of these limitations.

3. LITERATURE REVIEW AND RESEARCH GAPS

3.1 Evolution of Green Entrepreneurship

Over the last 20 years, green entrepreneurship has undergone an enormous development when it was more and more included in economic and industrial development strategies due to the growing emphasis on sustainability issues. Initially, ecopreneurship came from considerations of environmentally-sensitive business operations and protecting the environment (Paquin, 1998). The definition of green entrepreneurship, however, must be extended now to look at it as a larger system that enables innovation-driven economic transition, social integration and sustainable industrial growth in contemporary sustainability literature.

Environmental market failures offer innovative entrepreneurship opportunities for innovations focusing on sustainability, as shown by Dean & McMullen (2007). Likewise, Cohen and Winn (2007) pointed out that inefficiencies in resources utilization and ecological aspects could trigger creative ideas that may lead to new viable business models that could create economic and ecological value. These visions moved the paradigm of entrepreneurship beyond profit and profit making to focus on interventions from the quest of making economic systems more sustainable.

Later studies further developed the idea and added sustainability considerations and integration of innovation management and institutional development. Hockerts and Wüstenhagen (2010) argued that for sustainability transitions, cooperation between the old and the new businesses, i.e., established industries and emerging green enterprises, is needed. Similarly, York and Venkataraman (2010) pointed out the necessity of entrepreneurial innovations in combating environmental uncertainty and challenges in resource management.

Therefore, green entrepreneurship as a strategy to a sustainable economic transformation rather than just an environment-friendly business approach is increasingly acknowledged in the literature. Sustainability-focused businesses are now linked with new renewable energy projects, the implementation of a circular economy, sustainable agriculture, waste management, sustainable manufacturing, and relevant technologies for digital sustainability.

3.2 Sustainable Business Models and Innovation

Renewable business models are increasingly in the focus of recent reports and debates concerning green business and industrial change. Bocken et al. (2014) proved that the purpose of sustainable business models is to generate value through embedding environmental stewardship in production systems, through the supply chain and consumer engagement. Sustainability business models focus, in contrast to traditional business models, on the efficient use of resources, minimization of waste and long-term ecological resilience.

Often too, the literature makes mention of the growing significance of circular economy principles in the development of sustainable businesses. Ghisellini et al. (2016) stated that the systems of Circular economy are focused on recycling, reuse, remanufacturing and sustainable resource utilization. These practices relieve pressure on the environment, and provide new entrepreneurship and market possibilities.

The application of technological innovation makes sustainable business transformation even stronger. For Nidumolu et al. (2009), one of the most important factors responsible for innovation and long-term competitiveness is sustainability. These new technologies range from renewable energy solutions to machine learning, supply chain systems and smart waste systems, which offer businesses the ability to be more efficient in their business operations while minimising their environmental impact.

But a few studies suggest that the process of business change for sustainability is stagnant in emerging economies. MSMEs are commonly constrained by technology and finance in terms of innovation adoption and scaling up (OECD, 2021). While innovation and sustainability brings market opportunities, for many businesses sustainability investments are difficult to reconcile with financial sustainability.

3.3 Policy Ecosystems and Institutional Support

The institutional and policy support mechanisms are crucial for the development of green entrepreneurship. These are often sources of sustainability-focused businesses relying on, such as for instance, regulations incentivizing their operation, financing, incubation systems, and technological infrastructure.

The government policy like Startup India, renewable energy policy, development of MSMEs etc. has prompted sustainability-based innovations in India (DPIIT, 2025). The green economy start-up ecosystems have expanded thanks to renewable energy incentives, incubator programs for startups and digital entrepreneurship programs.

However, there are a few institutional restrictions on the development of green enterprises that were also identified from the available literature. Sustainability policies' effectiveness can be limited due to regulatory complexity, fragmented implementation and lack of coordination between public and private institutions (World Bank, 2022). Likewise, green startups continue to struggle with access to finance because they require significant money investments at the beginning, and they need to wait long periods before returning money.

International comparative studies suggest that countries with robust support networks for green innovations, security in policy regimes and continued funding for green economy exhibit higher levels of green innovation and sustainable entrepreneurship. EU circular economy policies and the Chinese green energy systems serve as a case in point for the robustness of a coordinated policy approach for supporting a shift towards sustainable industry (OECD, 2018).

3.4 Research Gaps

Despite the significant growth and development of the literature on green entrepreneurship, some gaps of analysis and conceptualization persist. One, most of the literature in the field is descriptive and has a focus on sustainability practices, where the interplay between innovation capability, institutional ecosystems and sustainability of businesses in the longer term is not examined.

Second, there is reduced studies specific to the difficulties involved in introducing scalability issues to sustainability-focused MSMEs in emerging economies. Research products of the past often highlight opportunities and policy options, and fail to analyse operational constraints, market restrictions, and institutional inefficiencies for the development of green enterprise.

Third, between the research fields of entrepreneurship and economy, ecology and society, there is still limited integration of the dimensions of economic, ecological and social sustainability outcomes. Various studies have discussed the different dimensions of sustainability apart from considering them as interdependent and investigating their joint effects on entrepreneurial performance and industrial transformation.

Lastly, the comparative and policy-oriented analysis is still limited in context of India. Some systematic reviews have been published on the policies and green innovation programs, but the implementation effectiveness, long-term entrepreneurial resilience and legal-coordinating problems in implementing policies have not been sufficiently analyzed. The research gaps indicate a need to explore and understand the phenomenon of green entrepreneurship and sustainable development with an integrated and analytical approach in emerging economies like India.

4. EMERGING INNOVATION PATHWAYS IN INDIA

4.1 Renewable Energy Entrepreneurship

Sustainability-driven entrepreneurship in renewable energy has become one of a major contributors and has been one of the greatest contributors in India for the innovation in sustainability in India. Growing demand for energy, climate change and the desire to minimize reliance on fossil fuels have spurred investment in solar, wind, bioenergy and decentralized renewable energy systems. People who enter the entrepreneurial world in the energy sector find plenty of opportunities thanks to the government measures for ensuring clean energy transition and the lower costs of renewable technologies (IRENA, 2022).

With backing from policy (including institutional) environments, private investment, and the need for clean energy solutions, solar energy entrepreneurship has grown at a rapid pace. Entrepreneurs are constantly innovating solar micro-grids, rooftop solar, smart energy management technology and decentralised rural electrification solutions. These innovations help to reduce emissions, to increase energy availability and to support sustainable industrial development. Renewable energy companies create job opportunities in jobs such as manufacturing, installation, maintenance, and technologies.

Renewable Energy businesses still experience the following structural barriers although they have great potential to grow. Scalability and long-term sustainability are often hampered by requirements of a high capital budget, funding cumbersomeness, and technological reliance and policy uncertainty. For smaller players, infrastructure and the limited reach of certain markets can pose a challenge to compete with the large companies. Moreover, the lack of uniformity and delays in subsidy payments can lead to low investor confidence in the subsidy framework of a sustainable energy market (Sarkar & Ghosh, 2022).

4.2 Sustainable Manufacturing and Green Packaging

With industries trying to minimize the impact on the environment while at the same time sustaining their operation and competitiveness, sustainability has become a growing focus on sustainable manufacturing. Energy Efficiency, Cleaner Production, Waste Minimization, Sustainable Sourcing and Environmentally Responsible Supply Chain Management are the features of emphasis in green manufacturing practices. With the advent of environmental regulations, consumer awareness, and international environmental standards, Indian industries are slowly incorporating sustainability into their manufacturing processes.

In the context of rising ecological and plastic pollution issues, the innovative element in packaging materials is increasingly relevant. Entrepreneurs are creating packaging that is biodegradable, recyclable, reusable and using plants to produce packaging systems that have less impact on the environment. Variations of these are being integrated in the food processing, retail, logistics and e-commerce sectors more and more.

Technological innovation is a very important lever for sustainable manufacturing transformation. The technologies of digital automation, smart monitoring systems, resource optimisation technologies and environmentally friendly production methods help to boost productivity and cut resource use. Manufacturing companies that focus on sustainability thus not only help protect the environment but also participate in industrial upgrading and sustainability, helping to provide long-term competitiveness.

But there is a significant variance at the industry level in the process of sustainable manufacturing transitions. Technical and financial constraints for the use of improved green production systems remain a challenge for many MSMEs. Transitions in smaller industrial companies (SMEs) are often hindered by high implementation costs, lack of technical skills, and the lack of institutional support (Selvan & Rajan, 2023).

4.3 Integrating sustainable agriculture into entrepreneurship

The agricultural sector is a significant sector of the Indian economy and is still one of the places where entrepreneurship for sustainability can be considered. The rising concerns of the environment associated with the use of pesticides and fertilizers in agriculture, degradation of soil, water shortages and climatic fluctuations have facilitated the development of sustainable agriculture and the organic business landscape. Entrepreneurs are nourishing increased innovative solutions in the field of agriculture which are environmentally friendly and also contribute to the conservation of environment thereby enhancing the well-being of the farmers and agricultural growth in the rural areas.

The emphasis of the organic farming enterprises is on the use of nature friendly food production, sustainable irrigation systems, natural methods of cultivation and biofertilizers. These business provide soils betterment, biodiversity protection and low reliance on chemicals. Moreover, with a growing demand for organic and health-conscious goods, organic agriculture enterprises are now finding greater market opportunities for sustainability (Singh & Kumar, 2023).

Technological development is also impacting sustainability in agriculture. The use of precision agriculture technologies, smart irrigation systems, digital agriculture platforms, and renewable energy-powered agriculture boosts productivity and mitigates environmental effects. Digital platforms are now being used more and more by green entrepreneurs to expand their supply chain management capabilities, increase market access and enhance resource efficiency.

Although the opportunities are increasing for sustainable agriculture enterprises the enterprises are still having some problems in their operations. Limited awareness of farmers, complexity of certification, high transition cost, and small market structures, are some of the factors that hinder the profitability and marketability of organic agriculture enterprises. Limited infrastructure and policy support in rural areas also have a long-term impact on the sustainability of green enterprises focusing on agriculture.

4.4 Innovation for the Circular Economy and Waste Management

With growing waste generation, limited resources and environmental problems, it is now pertinent to attend a growing significance of the entrepreneurship of the circular economy. Circular economy practices are more associated with the "take, use, recycle and use again" and "use and sustain" models as compared to the traditional "take, use, and discard" ones (Ghisellini et al., 2016). This may provide opportunities for business model innovators to design and develop business models that are environmentally sustainable and resource efficient.

Plastic recycling firms, electronic waste recycling units, Industrial waste management recycling, and composting technologies, are all emerging waste management startups in India that are emerging nowadays. This is some business that helps in sustaining the environment, managing the city's usage and helping in producing renewable energy. Waste collection systems, material tracking and the efficiency of materials being recycled has been enhanced further through digital technologies.

Innovation by entrepreneurs is also beneficial for the creation of jobs and the joining of people into the informal sector in the context of the circular economy. There are several sustainability oriented enterprises, which work with waste collectors, recycling cooperatives and local communities to build efficient management of wastes and enhance social inclusion.

Structural obstacles to implementing circular economy exist, however, such as poor waste-separation infrastructure, insufficient awareness amongst the population, insufficient enforcement of regulations and insufficient waste-separation-trained infrastructure. Another reason for the financial sustainability remains problematic for many waste management start-ups is the volatility in the waste recycling market, and operating expenses (Central Pollution Control Board, 2021).

4.5 Digital Green Technologies and Smart Sustainability

Digital transformation has taken a huge stride in recent years concerning entrepreneurship that has been proactively oriented to sustainability. The advent of new technologies such as artificial intelligence, the Internet of Things (IoT), blockchain, cloud and data-analytics are used in growing ways within green business. These technologies enhance environmental monitoring, operational efficiency, resource optimisation and sustainability reporting.

The number of companies involved in green tech startups continues to create intelligent transportation systems, digital waste management systems, smart energy solutions, and carbon monitoring applications alongside the solutions that are more environmentally friendly in the supply chains. The innovations boost sustainable industrial practices and make the organisation more competitive and scalable.

Digital platforms can also improve consumer's connection and accessibility to the market for sustainability-minded businesses. Green businesses can leverage platforms such as e-commerce systems, digital marketing tools, and online sustainability platforms to build their customer base and raise awareness on sustainable products and services.

While digital sustainability transitions progress with technological development, they are limited by infrastructure deficits, digital technology affordability, cyber security and a lack of digital accessibility. Malaysia's medium-sized businesses, which have fewer technical and financial resources, may find it challenging to implement advanced digital systems. (Ramasamy & Choudhury, 2023). Thus, although there are many sustainability opportunities associated with the use of digital technologies, layers of institutional support are needed with technological accessibility to make this widely adopted among entrepreneurs.

Table 1. Emerging Green Innovation Pathways in India

Sector	Major Innovation Pathways	Sustainability Contribution	Key Challenges
Renewable Energy	Solar energy systems, wind power, decentralized energy solutions	Reduction in carbon emissions and promotion of clean energy	High capital investment and policy uncertainty
Sustainable Manufacturing	Green production systems, energy-efficient technologies, eco-friendly materials	Reduced industrial pollution and improved resource efficiency	High implementation cost and technological barriers
Organic Agriculture	Biofertilizers, precision farming, sustainable irrigation systems	Soil conservation and reduced chemical dependency	Certification complexity and market limitations
Circular Economy and Waste Management	Recycling systems, waste-to-energy technologies, material recovery	Waste reduction and sustainable resource utilization	Infrastructure gaps and low public awareness
Green Packaging	Biodegradable and recyclable packaging solutions	Reduction in plastic pollution and environmental impact	Higher production costs and limited scalability
Digital Green Technologies	Smart monitoring systems, IoT-enabled sustainability tools, digital platforms	Improved environmental monitoring and operational efficiency	Digital infrastructure limitations and affordability issues

5. INCLUSIVE BUSINESS MODELS, MARKET DYNAMICS AND SUSTAINABILITY OUTCOMES

5.1 Sustainability-Oriented Business Models

Sustainability Models are generating greater significance in the current context of business ecosystems. Green business models are different from the usual business model in that they build in a long-term economic focus that is linked with social inclusion and the environment. These models focus on resource efficiency, ethical production systems, sustainable supply chains and on creating value from the perspective of stakeholders (Bocken et al., 2014).

Circular economy and inclusive business models are becoming commonplace within green enterprises because they offer a solution to environmental and operational challenges that generate resilience. The circular business models emphasize on minimizing waste, maximizing reuse, maximizing extension of the useful life, and recycling. Inclusive business models make instead an attempt to engage underserved groups, rural producers, women entrepreneurs and informal workers into sustainability business chains. All these can be used to support environmental sustainability and social development.

India is notable for the increased visibility of 'sustainability-oriented' business models, such as renewable energy providers, organic farmers, sustainable textiles, eco-friendly packaging and waste management companies. There are several startups that innovate and engage the community to develop low cost and scalable solutions. The companies prove that making environmental conservation and business competitiveness work can occur when proper innovative approaches and business efficiency are followed.

It's a significant challenge for numerous green businesses to balance profitability and sustainability, though. Sustainable production systems may necessitate increased capital, more sophisticated technologies, certification and environmentally-conscious supply chains, etc. All these can lead to higher operating expenses and lower immediate profits, especially for the MSMEs with limited capital. As a result of this, some sustainable companies are struggling to ensure their sustainability from business continuity.Due to this, many sustainable companies have a weak business continuity despite their environmental and social goals.

5.2 Market Dynamics and Consumer Behaviour

Market dynamics are critical factors in influencing growth and sustainability of green entrepreneurship. There is a growing awareness of the environment, climate issues and consumer preference for "environmental" products and services in the urban market, which has driven an increase in demand. Consumers are increasingly favoring products connected within them to renewable energy, organic production, sustainable packaging, ethical sourcing, and environmentally friendly production methods.

Consumers in the middle class in cities, younger populations and those connected to the digitalities are more willing to practice sustainable consumption. This change has taken all over the world and helped companies embrace sustainability in their name, promotion, and product definitions. More firms are incorporating green certification in their supply change, eco-labels in their marketing and sustainability reporting processes to boost consumer confidence and market positioning.

The transformation to digitization has further facilitated market expansion for sustainability oriented growth. Use of ecommerce platforms, digital payment systems and social media marketing fuels market availability for enterprises that are green, and helps startups better target eco-minded purchasers. Digital platforms also ensure visibility on sustainable sourcing, environmental performance and ethical production standards.

Although awareness of green products is rising, consumption of green products is not consistently high in all areas and income groups. In developing countries, price sensitivity is still a major barrier, as products with environmental benefits are more costly than conventional ones. However, several green enterprises have suffered from lack of consumer awareness, availability of the product and varying sustainability standards, which also affect market penetration.

This poses more difficulties for the rural and semi-urban markets where lack of awareness about sustainable consumption, reduced purchasing power, and absence of the infrastructure is a challenge. Thus, there is growth in sustainability related markets, and more mainstream customers will adopt these products if they become more affordable, better awareness is promoted and they are more available.

5.3 Sustainability Outcomes and Economic Impact

The green entrepreneurship fosters sustainable development in various economic, environmental and social aspects. Sustainability businesses contribute, in terms of the economy, in industrial diversification, innovation based growth, job creation and entrepreneurial development. Companies and startups in the green economy sector (renewable energy, recycling, organic farming and sustainable manufacture) generate new opportunities for investment and foster the development of new industrial ecosystems.

On the environmental aspect, green businesses help curb pollution, use renewable resources, manage to become "clean"" producers, and lower carbon emissions. The cycles of using and reusing resources and materials in a circular way are able to encourage higher efficiency in waste management and sustainable use of resources. In addition, the renewable energy sector contributes to low-carbon transitions by decreasing reliance on fossil fuels and encouraging the use of renewable energy sources.

Socially, inclusive GB models support rural development and engagement, women's empowerment, and enhance livelihood opportunities. Numerous pursuing enterprises work with local manufacturers, self-help organizations, waste management laborers and rural communities to make economically inclusive and socially inclusive economies. These partnerships help to make communities more resilient, and contribute to the larger sustainability goals.

The sustainability effects of green enterprises, however, are not homogenous throughout industries. However, there are cases in which some companies focus on communicating a green message without having meaningful sustainability actions in place, giving rise to issues of "greenwashing" and below par accountability for sustainability in enterprises. Likewise, long-term environmental gains of some technologies may rely on the need of effective regulation, lifecycle management, and institutional oversight.

The relationship between sustainability and profitability therefore remains complex. Sustainability business models can provide long-term competitive benefits, but there is a cost and risk to the operation and finances of enterprises when they are being implemented. In the long run, firms must navigate a balance between corporate social responsibility, competitiveness, adaptation to new technologies, and economic stability.

6. POLICY, INSTITUTIONAL SUPPORT, AND ENTREPRENEURIAL ECOSYSTEMS

6.1 Policy Support for Green Entrepreneurship

Government policy has a key influence on the development of entrepreneurial ecosystems for sustainability. Climate responsibility, a focus on renewable energy, digitalization and new entrepreneurship have gained in relevance to promote green entrepreneurship in India. The government's policies like Startup India, Make in India, Digital India, Renewable energy development, etc. have contributed to a conducive and nurturing environment for innovation and sustainability (DPIIT, 2025).

Sustainability programs and regulations, notably in the field of environmental protection and renewable energy, as well as environmental sustainability industrial policies, enabled entrepreneurship in fields as wide as the solar sector, the electric mobility, waste management, sustainable manufacturing, and organic agriculture. An offering of economic support such as incentives, tax exemption, technology subsides and support systems for green enterprises are further provided in the promotion of green enterprise development.

Sustainability ecosystems also benefit from institutional support like the startup incubators, technology parks, innovation centers and entrepreneurship development programmes. Seeking to support sustainability-oriented innovation and green technology commercialization, more and more universities, research institutions and private companies work together.

Yet, execution of the expansion of policy is heterogeneous across regions and sectors. There are delays in several sustainability initiatives for various reasons including administrative complexity, lack of institutional coordination and inadequate monitoring mechanisms. However, smaller companies may experience obstacles in getting government assistance due to the rules and red tape involved, documentation needs and lack of knowledge of government schemes.

6.2 Financing and Investment Ecosystems

Having access to finance continues to be the key driver of the sustainability and scalability of green enterprises. Many sustainability-driven businesses are initially capital intensive, and investing in technology, infrastructure implementation, certification and research are all vital parts of their set-up. As a result, access to finance has a strong impact on the growth of entrepreneurs and their innovation capacity.

Indian entrepreneurial ecosystems have been getting smaller and browner with the gradual increase in green financing mechanisms such as impact investment, venture capital, sustainability linked loan, and blended models. Enterprises with sustainability in mind are quickly gaining investor attention as they see them as compelling long-term growth opportunities to generate not only financial returns, but social returns as well.

However, funding is still a problem for many startups and MSMEs. The characteristics of the market demand, long payback periods, and regulatory uncertainty make green enterprises more challenging to invest in traditional finance companies. Consequently, it is often difficult for smaller businesses which operate sustainably to access long-term and affordable financing.

In addition, due to limited working capital, some opportunities for innovation and business expansion remain unrealized as well. During the early life of growth stages, many green startups heavily depend on their investors, whether personal or through grants. This reliance can have a negative impact on the stability and scaling aspects of the operation, especially in the competitive sustainability markets.

6.3 Entrepreneurial Ecosystems and Institutional Challenges

Good entrepreneurial ecosystems need to be coordinated between governments, industries, investors, education and tech providers. Robust institutional frameworks facilitating innovation diffusion, knowledge sharing, financing and market integration are essential to enterprises that are working towards and building sustainability.

India's startup ecosystem shows significant growth in recent times, specifically in the digital space and sustainability driven areas. Innovation networks and digital entrepreneurship platforms for collaborative innovation are growing in importance and are currently deployed for the benefit of renewable energy startups, climate technology and circular economy businesses in particular.

Nonetheless, weaknesses in the institutions are continuing to have a negative impact on the sustainability of entrepreneurs. The implementation of policies varies widely across regions, extensive regulatory complexity, infrastructure issues and differences in approach restrict the scalability of enterprises. In many rural areas and smaller cities, people have limited access to technological infrastructure and incubation technology, as well as to skilled employees and sustainability-oriented investment networks.

Comparative international experiences show that countries with an ecosystem of sustainability, a sense of long-term policy stability, and institutional coordination have more advanced degrees of green innovation and industrial transformation (OECD, 2018). Hence, enhancing institutional partnership and policy coherence will continue to play a crucial role in promoting the long-term sustainability of Green entrepreneurship in India.

7. CHALLENGES, LIMITATIONS, AND FUTURE DIRECTIONS

7.1 Financial and Operational Challenges

The major challenge is the upfront investment of environmentally sustainable technologies, renewable energy devices, waste management facilities and green production methods. Economically, many startups as well as small and medium enterprises (MSMEs) may lack some investment in operational sustainability to implement their sustainability measures, especially in the early stages of growth.

On the other hand, traditional financial institutions consider green enterprises as high-risk businesses because they are subject to changeable market demands, long return periods, and changing regulations. Thus, there is an impediment to the entrepreneurs to avail finance of reasonable cost, long-term credit facilities, and venture capital support. Finance continues to be generally not equally accessible across sectors and regions (OECD, 2021), but this is starting to change with the implementation of green financing initiatives and the emergence of impact investment models.

The other challenges hinder operational scalability and sustainability of the enterprise. Creating products in a sustainable manner often entails technological expertise, greened supply chains, certification processes, and ongoing innovation. Smaller Companies in particular may not have technical capacity and available managerial resources to operate efficiently/continuously and stay competitive in the fast changing markets.

7.2 Technological and Infrastructure Barriers

Another big question that has been posed as a problem for green entrepreneurship in emerging economies is technological accessibility. Many advanced sustainability technologies, digital monitoring systems, renewable energy infrastructure and resource-efficient production processes come with a high upfront and maintenance cost. Many MSMEs therefore struggle to adopt technological innovations despite recognizing their long-term benefits.

Furthermore, the ability of sustainability transitions to be effective is constrained by infrastructure constraints. For businesses focused on sustainability, poor transport networks and transportation services, unreliable energy supply, inadequate recycling facilities, and sluggish internet connections often pose challenges to operational efficiency. Infrastructure gaps have been a significant issue and can hinder the spread of green enterprises outside cities and urban areas, especially in rural and semi-urban areas.

Moreover, insulation from other countries' systems and components could make operations more costly and stifle homegrown innovation. The—sustainability-related—sectors are still based upon widely international technologies, which are increasing the financial and supply chain weaknesses.

7.3 Regulatory and Market Limitations

The regulatory complexity and institutional fragmentation still remain as a barrier in the process of Entrepreneurial development in sustainable way. Several government initiatives promotes green innovation, and policy effectiveness is hampered by inconsistencies in execution and time delays. Business owners often run into delays in various elements of licensing, environmental clearance, certification and also availability of subsidies.

The potential scaleability of green enterprises is also constrained by markets. Sustainable products purchases are not equally understood among different demographic and regional groups. The price is a common determinant for buying and selling products, especially in developing countries where eco-sustainable products are sometimes seen as high cost alternatives. Consequently, there are problems more often with increasing market demands and stable revenue obtaining in many enterprises.

Further, the lack of a common sustainability metric and certification may also decrease consumer trust and transparency. Some businesses have undertaken superficial sustainability marketing without making substantive efforts for sustainability, which invokes worry about greenwashing and ineffective accountability frameworks.

7.4 Scalability and Long-Term Sustainability

For many green businesses, sustainability in the long term is a key issue on their agenda. While a number of start-ups launch novel solutions for sustainable practices, growth of these into larger markets can be challenging for a number of reasons including financial constraints, operational requirements and institutional barriers. Sustainable business initiatives often have to revisit technology solutions, introduce policy adjustments, and develop new markets if they are to compete.

The linkage of sustainability and profitability can introduce strategic complexities as well. For green enterprises, a compromise must be found between environmental responsibility and feasibility and profitability in the market. In addition to a robust sustainability goal, doubts about consumer demand, high operational costs, and infrastructure challenges can also hinder long-term business sustainability.

Regional disparities contribute to the sustainability of businesses. High entrepreneur green activity is correlated with digital infrastructure, investments and institutions in urban areas that is more developed than in rural or less developed areas. Thus, the overall growth path towards sustainability is still uneven in India geographically.

Table 2. Major Challenges Affecting Green Entrepreneurship in India

Challenges	**Impact on Green Enterprises**	**Possible Strategic Solutions**
Financial Constraints	Limited scalability and delayed business expansion	Expansion of green financing and impact investment
Technological Limitations	Reduced innovation adoption and operational efficiency	Technology transfer and digital infrastructure support
Regulatory Complexity	Delays in implementation and compliance difficulties	Simplification of environmental regulations
Infrastructure Deficiencies	Operational inefficiencies and regional disparities	Investment in sustainable infrastructure systems

continued on following page

Table 2. Continued

Challenges	Impact on Green Enterprises	Possible Strategic Solutions
Market Uncertainty	Inconsistent consumer demand and profitability issues	Consumer awareness campaigns and green branding
Limited Institutional Coordination	Weak policy implementation and fragmented support systems	Stronger collaboration between government and industries
Low Consumer Awareness	Reduced adoption of sustainable products and services	Sustainability education and awareness initiatives
Scalability Challenges	Difficulty in achieving long-term sustainability	Business incubation and entrepreneurial ecosystem support

7.5 Future Directions

Technological innovation, digital transformation and policy integration will likely shape future sustainability transitions more. New technologies like artificial intelligence, blockchain-tracing supply chain, Internet of Things (IoT) and smart energy systems will have a positive impact on the efficiency of green businesses and will enhance their environmental monitoring capabilities as well.

Policy frameworks and their support for renewable energy, implementation of circular economy, green financing and sustainable industrial development will still be important influencing factors on the entrepreneurial ecosystem. Improving institutional coordination and establishing a stable policy process can boost the trust of the investors and enterprise size.

The future research concerns empirical assessment of sustainability impacts, comparative international studies, scalability of the MSME's, creation and application of digital sustainability ecosystems, and innovation driven business transformation. To broaden the knowledge base of green entrepreneurship in emerging economies, future studies that further investigate the concept of rural sustainability entrepreneurship, inclusive green business models, and long term environmental performance measurement would be valuable.

8. CONCLUSION AND MANAGERIAL IMPLICATIONS

In recent years, green entrepreneurship has become a more prominent tool for sustainable economic development, the conservation of the environment, and the transformation of industries based on innovations and businesses in both developed and developing nations. The rise of environmental concerns, climate change risks, resource scarcity and a fast growing entrepreneurial ecosystem have pushed governments, industry and entrepreneurs to follow a more sustainable roadmap that can bring balance between environmental protection and economic growth. The emerging dimensions in entrepreneurship, sustainability, are closely allied with the current global development trend that is heading for low-carbon development, circular economy systems, consumption of renewable energy and socially inclusive business development.

The strategic relevance of green entrepreneurship in the Indian context is rising with the increasing environmental stress, rapid urbanization, technological developments, and the growth of the startup ecosystem. While economic expansion and innovation have brought significant opportunities for industrial development and advancement, the economy has also increased the environmental risks related to pollution, waste production, resource scarcity, and climate vulnerabilities in India. Under these circumstances, there has been an urgent demand for models and techniques that are entrepreneurial, can facilitate the economic development, and minimize environmental degradation and maintenance of sustainable resource use.

This chapter shows that the green entrepreneurship is a way of supporting sustainable development on a multi-level economy-environment scenario. Green businesses involved in renewable energies, sustainable production chains, waste management, ecodesign of goods and services, organic farming, IT and digital technologies for sustainability and eco-innovation can offer new sources of innovation, employment, industrial diversification, and resource efficiency. Renewable energy ventures promote low-carbon adjustments and lessen reliance on non-subsistent fossil fuels, while circular economy ventures refine the recycling framework or enhance waste decrease and sustainable material use. Like this, sustainable agricultural enterprises help to encourage environmentally responsible farming practices and economical development in the rural areas.

Technological innovation is also identified as a key factor to support entrepreneurship with a focus on sustainability, with particular emphasis on the analysis. Technologies like Artificial Intelligence, blockchain-based supply chains, Internet of Things (IoT), data analytics, intelligent monitoring systems, and digital sustainability platforms are becoming more and more popular and facilitate operational efficiency, environmental monitoring, and resource optimization. So, in the context of digital transformation, green enterprises can gain competitiveness and performance in green business. Technology-based business models have also enhanced business and market access, consumer engagement and visibility of environmentally responsible production systems.

Table 3. Managerial and Policy Implications for Strengthening Green Entrepreneurship

Stakeholders	Key Responsibilities	Strategic Recommendations
Entrepreneurs	Adoption of sustainable business practices	Integrate sustainability into long-term strategic planning
Policymakers	Development of supportive sustainability ecosystems	Improve green financing and policy implementation
Financial Institutions	Support sustainability-oriented investment	Expand sustainability-linked loans and impact investments
Research Institutions	Promote innovation and sustainability research	Strengthen industry–academia collaboration
Consumers	Encourage sustainable consumption patterns	Increase demand for eco-friendly products and services
Industries	Improve operational sustainability and resource efficiency	Invest in cleaner production technologies and circular systems

Another significant chapter's conclusion is that inclusive business models and models for sustainability have become a greater part of business relevance. Social and ethical responsibility, whether with respect to community involvement, ethical procurement, inclusion of the rural population and/or involving stakeholders in the decision-making process is a core part of the operating style of many green businesses. These help in building sense of environmental sustainability and social development through providing employment, skill development, women participation and fostering livelihood opportunities. In turn, this amount of integration between the environmental and the economic and social aspects of sustainable development, makes green entrepreneurship a valuable support for broader sustainable development goals.

However, the chapter also offers a few insights into the structural, operational and institutional barriers to the development and sustainability of green enterprises. One of the major constraints is financial shortfalls, especially for start-ups and MSMEs. Establishing a sustainable business can be expensive due to the upfront costs of modern technology, infrastructure, certification systems and production that consider the environment. But most businesses have some trouble in accessing cost-effective funding because of high perceived investment risk, uncertain length of recovery periods and lack of institutional support mechanisms.

Limited technology and infrastructure technology further hinders sustainability transitions in emerging economies. Green technologies, digital infrastructures, talents and innovation ecosystems are less accessible for smaller companies, that is one of the reasons why they are not skilled in implementing sustainable production systems. Lack of infrastructure in the supply, transportation, recycling and digital network sectors also compromises the efficiency in operating systems and the scalability of businesses, especially those in rural and semi-urban areas.

The effectiveness of entrepreneurial ecosystems towards sustainability is still limited by regulatory complexity and disjointed institutional coordination. Several Government support schemes and incentives have been put in place to promote development of renewable energy, start-up innovation and sustainable industrialization but these are often inadequate to achieve the policy benefits the Government is seeking due to constraints in implementation. Entrepreneurs do not like participating in the sustainability sectors due to the various factors, such as awareness of support schemes, a lack thereof, or restrictions and inconsistencies in the processes and regulations.

The chapter further illustrates that barriers are still affecting a green business expansion from a marketing perspective. While consumer awareness has grown significantly, especially among younger and urban consumers, the use of products that are good for the environment has only been introduced patchily across income levels and geographical regions. However, green products and services are less accepted in the market because of price sensitivity, lack of access to the product, lack of sustainability knowledge in the product and uncertainty about the reliability of the product. These market conditions generate further business difficulties for sustainability-minded businesses seeking to become profitable and competitive in the long-term.

Policy and institutional environments are thus critical to support sustainable entrepreneurship in India. The government's policies, like Startup India, Renewable Energy, Digital Innovation and MSME development, have also given boost to entrepreneurial opportunities in sustainably focused sectors. Additionally, entrepreneurial ecosystems have become possible through incubation centers, research collaborations, green financial programs and innovation systems. To enhance scalability and operational resilience of green enterprises, however, there is an urgent need to establish a stronger institutional linkage, long-term policy stability, financial accessibility, and infrastructure development in regions.

Managerially, sustainability can be used in the strategic planning, organization's culture, innovation process and in the process of organizational management, it is not a branding or a compliance procedure. Conclusions for entrepreneurs and business leaders: Resource efficiency, cleaner production systems, technological adaptation, sustainable supply chain and collaborative innovation strategies will be the most important. Those all serve as actions that will contribute to competitiveness in the longer term. Sustainability-minded organizations need to also consider how to coexist with financial stability and ability to change or adapt in the volatile current market.

Managers should also understand that the innovation linked to sustainability can have long-term strategic benefit due to more efficient work processes, more enduring relationships with stakeholders, a better reputation, and increased trust among consumers. Investors, regulators, consumers and international markets are now more positively inclined towards businesses practicing environmentally care. The attitude about businesses practicing environmentally responsible practices has turned positive so far. Hence, incorporating sustainability into operations should be viewed as a strategic investment.

Governments need to increase the level of support mechanisms for green entrepreneurship by streamlining the regulatory process, scaling up the green finance space, enhancing sustainability infrastructure and making sustainability technology accessible for MSMEs and Start-ups on a policy level. Industry-specific policies promoting renewable energy, sustainable production and waste management innovation, and circular economy can further speed up the energy, manufacturing, waste management, and circular economy sustainability transition respectively. Besides, the promotion of entrepreneurial education, sustainability awareness raising and industry–academy cooperation will facilitate the construction of innovation ecosystem and the sustainable industrial transformation.

The chapter further points to the need for increased cooperation between governments, private industry, financial institutions, research institutions and start-ups, and local communities. Enabling collaboration and exchange of knowledge, allowing access to financing, bringing technical innovation and ensuring the implementation of sustainability in multi-stakeholder partnerships exist in all sectors. Cooperation is vital to addressing structural constraints, enhancement of the scalability and as a whole to solving the challenge of sustainability oriented enterprises.

On the whole, green entrepreneurship will be one huge stride toward the sustainable industrial restructuring, economic inclusiveness, and the environment-friendly development of emerging economies like India. There are various financial, technological, institutional, and market-related barriers that persist in implementation and scalability, but opportunities to deliver long-term environmental and economic sustainability abound, such as sustainability oriented innovation, supportive policy and institutional ecosystems, digital innovation, and adaptability of entrepreneurs. The future development of green entrepreneurship will rely on a combination of businesses, policy makers, investors and institutions that are able to work together and dynamically respond to innovation that is able to achieve eco-friendly sustainability transitions that are compatible with economic development, ecological stewardship and social inclusion.

REFERENCES

Banerjee, S. B. (2003). Who sustains whose development? Sustainable development and the reinvention of nature. *Organization Studies*, *24*(1), 143–180. DOI: 10.1177/0170840603024001341

Bocken, N. M. P., Short, S. W., Rana, P., & Evans, S. (2014). A literature and practice review to develop sustainable business model archetypes. *Journal of Cleaner Production*, *65*, 42–56. DOI: 10.1016/j.jclepro.2013.11.039

Central Pollution Control Board. (2021). *Management of municipal solid waste in India*. Ministry of Environment, Forest and Climate Change.

Cohen, B., & Winn, M. I. (2007). Market imperfections, opportunity and sustainable entrepreneurship. *Journal of Business Venturing*, *22*(1), 29–49. DOI: 10.1016/j.jbusvent.2004.12.001

Creswell, J. W., & Creswell, J. D. (2018). *Research design: Qualitative, quantitative, and mixed methods approaches* (5th ed.). Sage.

Dean, T. J., & McMullen, J. S. (2007). Toward a theory of sustainable entrepreneurship. *Journal of Business Venturing*, *22*(1), 50–76. DOI: 10.1016/j.jbusvent.2005.09.003

DPIIT. (2025). *Startup India annual report 2024–25*. Government of India.

Elkington, J. (1997). *Cannibals with forks: The triple bottom line of 21st century business*. Capstone.

Ghisellini, P., Cialani, C., & Ulgiati, S. (2016). A review on circular economy: The expected transition to a balanced interplay of environmental and economic systems. *Journal of Cleaner Production*, *114*, 11–32. DOI: 10.1016/j.jclepro.2015.09.007

Government of India. (2015). *National action plan on climate change*. Ministry of Environment, Forest and Climate Change.

Gupta, V., & Sharma, A. (2023). Sustainable agriculture and green entrepreneurship in India. *Asian Journal of Sustainable Development*, *12*(2), 89–105.

Hart, S. L., & Milstein, M. B. (1999). Global sustainability and the creative destruction of industries. *Sloan Management Review*, *41*(1), 23–33.

Hockerts, K. (2017). Sustainable entrepreneurship: Past contributions and future directions. *Journal of Small Business Management*, *55*(1), 1–24.

Hockerts, K., & Wüstenhagen, R. (2010). Greening Goliaths versus emerging Davids: The role of incumbents and new entrants in sustainable entrepreneurship. *Research Policy, 39*(4), 481–492.

IRENA. (2022). *Renewable energy market analysis.* International Renewable Energy Agency.

Ministry of Micro, Small and Medium Enterprises. (2021). *MSME annual report 2020–21.* Government of India.

Mishra, P., & Singh, R. (2024). Green innovation strategies in Indian MSMEs. *Journal of Cleaner Production, 379*, 135150.

Nidumolu, R., Prahalad, C. K., & Rangaswami, M. R. (2009). Why sustainability is now the key driver of innovation. *Harvard Business Review, 87*(9), 56–64.

OECD. (2018). *Business models for the circular economy: Opportunities and challenges for policy.* Organisation for Economic Co-operation and Development.

OECD. (2021). *Financing SMEs and entrepreneurs 2021: An OECD scoreboard.* OECD Publishing.

Ramasamy, C., & Choudhury, A. (2023). Digital solutions and sustainability in Indian startups. *Technology in Society, 74*, 102241.

Sarkar, S., & Ghosh, P. (2022). Renewable energy entrepreneurship and social impact in India. *Energy Policy, 167*, 113024.

Schaltegger, S. (2002). A framework for ecopreneurship. *Greener Management International, 38*(38), 45–58. DOI: 10.9774/GLEAF.3062.2002.su.00006

Selvan, S., & Rajan, P. (2023). Sustainable packaging innovations in India. *Journal of Environmental Innovation and Societal Transitions, 48*, 65–82.

Singh, H., & Kumar, B. P. (2023). Organic agriculture and sustainable rural entrepreneurship in India. *International Journal of Agricultural Sustainability, 21*(3), 201–219.

UNEP. (2020). *Emissions gap report 2020.* United Nations Environment Programme.

. United Nations. (2015). *Transforming our world: The 2030 agenda for sustainable development.*

World Bank. (2022). *Sustainable entrepreneurship and innovation: Global trends and policy recommendations.* World Bank.

York, J. G., & Venkataraman, S. (2010). The entrepreneur–environment nexus: Uncertainty, innovation, and allocation. *Journal of Business Venturing*, *25*(5), 449–463. DOI: 10.1016/j.jbusvent.2009.07.007

KEY TERMS AND DEFINITIONS

Circular Economy: An economic system focused on recycling, reuse, remanufacturing, and sustainable resource utilization to reduce waste generation.

Eco-Innovation: Innovation aimed at reducing environmental harm through sustainable technologies and operational practices.

Green Entrepreneurship: Entrepreneurial activities that integrate environmental sustainability into business operations, products, and strategic objectives.

Green Technology: Technological solutions designed to improve environmental sustainability and resource efficiency.

MSMEs: Micro, Small, and Medium Enterprises contributing significantly to employment generation and industrial development.

Sustainable Development: Development that meets present needs without compromising the ability of future generations to meet their own needs.

Sustainable Innovation: The development of products, services, or processes that generate economic value while minimizing environmental impact.

Triple Bottom Line: A sustainability framework emphasizing economic, environmental, and social performance simultaneously.

Chapter 7
Green and Social Entrepreneurship in Tunisia:
Dynamics, Circular Economy Models, and Innovations in Support of the SDGs

Nizar Mtibaa Mtibaa
http://orcid.org/0009-0005-4427-0680
Faculty of Economic Sciences and Management, Tunisia

Sami Boudabbous Boudabbous
Faculty of Economic Sciences and Management, Tunisia

ABSTRACT

This chapter investigates the dynamics of green and social entrepreneurship in Tunisia through a multiple case study of four circular initiatives operating in textile recycling, plastic valorization, regenerative agriculture, and organic waste treatment. Using an interpretive qualitative approach supported by methodological triangulation, the analysis identifies shared mechanisms such as frugal innovation, resource circularity, organizational hybridization, and territorial embeddedness. The findings show substantial contributions to SDGs 8, 12, 13, and 15, while highlighting the role of these ventures in compensating for institutional voids in an emerging context. Overall, the chapter demonstrates how small circular enterprises can generate systemic sustainability impacts under conditions of structural constraint

DOI: 10.4018/979-8-3373-7391-1.ch007

INTRODUCTION

The 21st century has been marked by a global awareness of the urgency of environmental issues and social inequalities, reflecting itself in the adoption of the United Nations 2030 Agenda for Sustainable Development. These goals, which call for universal action to eradicate poverty, protect the planet, and promote inclusive prosperity, place innovation and entrepreneurship at the heart of the necessary transformations, echoing the work of Schaltegger and Wagner (2011) on the interactions between sustainable entrepreneurship (SE) and sustainable innovation.

In this context, SE, which integrates economic, environmental, and social dimensions, is emerging as a strategic and rapidly expanding field of research. Green and social entrepreneurship thus appear as essential levers of ecological and socio-economic transition, particularly in developing countries facing intertwined environmental, social, and institutional challenges. Green entrepreneurship can be defined as the creation of businesses that seek to solve environmental problems through innovative, environmentally friendly, and economically viable solutions (Schaper, 2002). Conversely, social entrepreneurship focuses on addressing societal issues by mobilizing market mechanisms to generate social value while ensuring economic sustainability (Mair and Martí, 2006).

This research domain is embedded within an integrative theoretical framework that combines institutional logic theory, the "institutional voids" approach, and the perspective of shared value creation (Stephan et al., 2026; Gupta & Antony, 2026). In emerging economies, these frameworks help explain the rise of hybrid organizations that simultaneously pursue economic performance, social impact, and environmental sustainability (Polloni, 2026; Battilana et al., 2012; George et al., 2021). More specifically, the "institutional voids" perspective (Mair & Marti, 2009; Khanna & Palepu, 2010) highlights the role of entrepreneurs as institutional substitutes capable of compensating for market failures and weak regulatory systems. Recent research further confirms that impactful entrepreneurial initiatives significantly contribute to economic resilience and sustainable innovation in such fragile contexts.

Within this conceptual landscape, the circular economy (CE) has emerged as a central operational model. It is defined as a regenerative system aimed at minimizing waste and maximizing resource value through closed-loop production and consumption (Kirchherr et al., 2017; Ellen MacArthur Foundation, 2023). First, CE seeks to extend resource lifecycles, reduce waste generation, and optimize raw material use. Simultaneously, frugal innovation, understood as the development of simple, cost-effective solutions adapted to resource-constrained environments, constitutes a key transformation lever in such contexts (Hossain, 2021). The integration of these approaches within green and social entrepreneurship enables the emergence of hybrid circular economy models, particularly relevant in developing countries.

Moreover, the Sustainable Development Goals (SDGs), adopted by the United Nations General Assembly in 2015, provide a comprehensive global framework to guide public policies, economic strategies, and private initiatives toward inclusive and sustainable development (United Nations, 2015). They are also widely used as a reference for assessing the social, environmental, and institutional impact of organizations. In this perspective, the SDGs constitute a normative framework for evaluating entrepreneurial contributions to sustainable development (UN, 2023).

At the national level, Tunisia presents a particularly relevant context for analyzing these dynamics. Approximately 80% of SDG targets are integrated into national development strategies, reflecting a relatively advanced level of institutional alignment (OECD, 2025). However, this integration remains only partially operationalized at the firm level.

Empirically, the Tunisian entrepreneurial ecosystem has experienced notable growth. According to the Global Startup Ecosystem Report (2024), the ecosystem reached a value of $241 million between 2021 and 2023, representing a growth rate of 205%. Additionally, more than 1,100 startups certified under the Startup Act generated nearly $300 million in combined revenue, with fundraising exceeding $24 million in 2024 (Startup Tunisia, 2024; CDC, 2024).

Despite this dynamism, green entrepreneurship remains marginal. Only 3.78% of Tunisian startups operate in green economy sectors such as waste management, sustainable agriculture, and renewable energy (Managers, 2023). Furthermore, only 15% to 16% of startups integrate circular economy practices, indicating a still limited but gradually increasing adoption (Startup Tunisia, 2022). This situation contrasts sharply with Tunisia's structural challenges, including waste management issues, more than 2.6 million tons of municipal waste generated annually, and high energy dependence (World Bank, 2023; ANGED, 2022).

The ecosystem supporting green entrepreneurship is nevertheless evolving, with more than 17 support structures and 9 specialized mentoring programs (Managers, 2023), alongside initiatives such as Greenov'i and GreenTech, which aim to finance innovative projects in ecological transition sectors. However, persistent institutional, financial, and cultural barriers continue to hinder the large-scale development of these models.

In this context, green and social entrepreneurship emerges as a strategic lever for addressing socio-economic challenges, particularly in a country where unemployment remains around 15.6%, with significant gender and regional disparities (World Bank, 2023; UNDP, 2024). Entrepreneurs can thus be viewed as "institutional repairers," contributing to the structuring of circular value chains and addressing unmet social and environmental needs.

Despite the growing interest in these issues, the literature remains fragmented, especially in the Global South context. There is a notable lack of integrative analyses explicitly linking green and social entrepreneurship, circular economy models, and measurable contributions to the SDGs within the Tunisian setting.

Therefore, this chapter aims to fill this gap by analyzing how Tunisian companies engaged in green and social entrepreneurship reconcile economic viability, innovation, and sustainable impact, while contributing to the structuring of circular value chains and the achievement of the SDGs within a transitional institutional environment.

Table 1. The 17 SDGs (The United Nations, 2015)

SDG	Label	Objective
SDG 1	No poverty	End extreme poverty in all its forms
SDG 2	Zero hunger	Ensure food security and promote sustainable agriculture.
SDG 3	Good health and well-being	Enable all people to live healthy lives and promote well-being.
SDG 4	Quality education	Ensure inclusive and equitable quality education.
SDG 5	Gender equality	Achieve gender equality and empower all women and girls.
SDG 6	Clean water and sanitation	Ensure access to safe and affordable drinking water and sanitation for all.
SDG 7	Affordable and Clean Energy	Ensure access to affordable, reliable, sustainable, and modern energy for all.
SDG 8	Decent Work and Economic Growth	Promote sustained, inclusive, and sustainable economic growth, full and productive employment, and decent work for all.
SDG 9	Industry, Innovation, and Infrastructure	Build resilient infrastructure, promote inclusive and sustainable industrialization, and foster innovation.
SDG 10	Reduced Inequalities	Reduce inequality within and among countries.
SDG 11	Sustainable Cities and Communities	Make cities inclusive, safe, resilient, and sustainable.
SDG 12	Responsible Consumption and Production	Ensure sustainable consumption and production patterns.
SDG 13	Climate action	Take urgent action to combat climate change.
SDG 14	Life below water	Conserve and sustainably use the oceans, seas, and marine resources.
SDG 15	Life on land	Protect and restore terrestrial ecosystems, combat desertification, and halt biodiversity loss.
SDG 16	Peace, Justice and Strong Institutions	Promote peaceful and inclusive societies, provide access to justice for all and build effective institutions.
SDG 17	Partnerships for the Goals	Strengthen the means of implementation and revitalize the global partnership for SD.

Researchers have pointed out the primordial role of SE as a driver of innovation and socio-environmental transformation, particularly in transition economies (Hall et al., 2010; Shepherd and Patzelt, 2011). It also underlines the strategic role of hybrid models, which are capable of combining economic performance, social impact, and environmental preservation simultaneously (Cohen and Winn, 2007; Battilana et al., 2012; Nguyen and Kinda, 2024). However, research on CE (Ellen MacArthur Foundation, 2015, 2023; Geissdoerfer et al., 2017) and frugal innovation (Radjou and Prabhu, 2015; Pansera, 2018) provides evidence that resource optimization and waste recovery are major levers for strengthening local sustainability, particularly in emerging contexts. However, little research exists on how such dynamics concretely come about within these countries of the Global South, even less so within the Maghreb region, where the ecological transition remains hampered by institutional, technical, and socio-economic constraints (UNEP, 2024; OECD, 2025).

In this context, issues of pollution, waste management, energy vulnerability, and unemployment among young people raise, in Tunisia, the importance of economic models capable of combining innovation, inclusion, and sustainability. Green and social entrepreneurs thus assume their role of "institutional repairers" by intervening in environments characterized by institutional voids (Mair and Martí, 2009; Khanna and Palepu, 2010) and by mobilizing local resources to help satisfy social needs that are insufficiently addressed.

Despite the increasingly high relevance of SE, and despite the efforts of Tunisia to integrate the Circular Economy and the SDGs, there is a remarkable literature gap: the absence of an integrated analysis that explicitly correlates, in a Tunisian context, the dynamics of green and social entrepreneurship, the CE models implemented, and their measurable impact on the SDGs.

The central issue is, therefore, to understand how, in this fragile institutional context and increasing societal and environmental pressure, companies involved in green and social entrepreneurship in Tunisia manage to generate impact and structure circular value chains while ensuring economic viability.

The purpose of this chapter is threefold:

- Descriptive objective: Describe the institutional dynamics and challenges particular to the emergence and development of green and social entrepreneurship in Tunisia.
- Purpose of analysis: This will analyze the kinds of CE models these entrepreneurs adopted and what social and technological innovations came as a result.

Evaluative Objective: Assess the potential contribution of these entrepreneurial initiatives to selected targets of SDG, including SDGs 8, 9, 12, and 13, and present an integrative analytical framework.

These will make explicit the added value of this type of entrepreneurship and provide informed recommendations for decision-makers and practitioners.

Within this perspective, this chapter is part of the approach whose relevance is based on the need to understand the specific mechanisms of green and social entrepreneurship in Tunisia, a country where, despite the growing contribution to SD Goals, circular initiatives remain under-documented. This work intends, through a multiple case study, to analyze how four Tunisian companies, respectively Koun, NextFood Tunisia, Eco-R, and Biodôme, integrating circular practices, manage to create social, economic, and environmental value in a difficult context.

To answer this question, the chapter is divided into four complementary sections. Firstly, the Literature Review conceptually situates the key concepts based on certain theoretical contributions. The second describes the methodological approach adopted, supported by qualitative triangulation and a multiple case study (Yin, 2018; Miles and Huberman, 2003; Eisenhardt, 1989). Then, the third section describes the empirical results from the interviews, observations, and documents analyzed, emphasizing mechanisms of action and circular practices. Finally, the fourth section presents a critical discussion based on the literature, ending by identifying the contributions, limitations, and future research directions.

1. LITERATURE REVIEW

1.1. Scientific field and theoretical positioning

This research is located within the interdisciplinary context of SE, which draws knowledge from entrepreneurship, corporate social responsibility, and environmental sciences (Modaffari & Beck, 2026; Schaltegger and Wagner, 2011; Hall et al., 2010). It leverages research on social entrepreneurship (Mair and Martí, 2006), studies on hybrid models (Battilana et al., 2012), emerging literature on the Circular Economy as an operational framework for sustainability (Ellen MacArthur Foundation, 2015, 2023; Geissdoerfer et al., 2017), approaches to frugal innovation (Radjou and Prabhu, 2015; Pansera, 2018), and analyses of institutional voids (Mair and Martí, 2009; Khanna and Palepu, 2010) as means to understand the specific dynamics characterizing the Global South context.

These different traditions constitute a theoretical background from which one can raise questions about how, why, and under what conditions socially and environmentally oriented enterprises emerge and create an impact in constrained contexts.

1.2. Central concepts: operational definitions used in the study

The study of green and social entrepreneurship requires a cross-disciplinary theoretical approach, rooted in the literature on SE, the CE, and institutional systems (Budumuru & Paruchuru, 2025). For the sake of analytical consistency throughout this chapter, we have adopted the following operational definitions:

SE is an integrative concept that differs from conventional entrepreneurship in its triple objective: economic, environmental, and social (the "Triple Bottom Line"; Elkington, (1998). Recent literature tends to view green entrepreneurship and social entrepreneurship not as separate entities, but as interdependent dimensions of SE, particularly relevant in developing countries where environmental and social challenges are intrinsically linked (Littlewood, 2022; Benavides-Sánchez et al., 2025).

Table 2. The differences between Green, Social, and Sustainable entrepreneurship

Dimension	Main Objective	Value Created	Relevant Theoretical Framework
Green	Reduction of environmental impact	Ecological value: pollution reduction, resource conservation	Environmental Economics, Industrial Ecology
Social	Addressing an unmet social need	Societal value: inclusion, employment, access to essential services	Stakeholder Theory, Social Justice Theory
Sustainable	Balance and long-term integration of the three dimensions	Integrated value economic, social, and environmental coherence and durability	SE Theory

1.3. The Circular Economy as a Business Model for Sustainable Entrepreneurship

The CE has evolved from a waste management concept to a macroeconomic model aimed at decoupling economic growth from the consumption of finite resources (Ferasso et al., 2020; Geissdoerfer et al., 2017). For SE, the CE provides a set of operational strategies (the "R-strategies": Reduce, Reuse, Recycle, Repair, Remanufacture, etc.) that enable environmental and social objectives to be achieved (Lieder and Rashid, 2016; Jabbour et al., 2020).

In the Tunisian context, the transition to CE is imperative in view of landfill saturation and the cost of importing raw materials (Trabelsi, 2024). Recent studies highlight that the adoption of circular models by Tunisian SMEs is a lever for green job creation and innovation (ICU, 2025). However, the academic literature still lacks a systematic analysis of the specific types of circular models implemented by Tunisian entrepreneurs and their social impact.

1.4. The Role of the Institutional Context in the MENA Region

Institutional theory posits that organizations adopt practices not only for reasons of efficiency, but also to comply with the expectations of their environment (legislative, normative, cultural) (DiMaggio and Powell, 1983). In Tunisia, the entrepreneurial ecosystem is characterized by an evolving regulatory framework (Social and Solidarity Economy Act), financing challenges, and a strong influence from international actors (EU, GIZ, UNDP) who actively promote green entrepreneurship (CGDR, 2013). Any analysis of the dynamics of SE in Tunisia must therefore consider institutional pressure and the mechanisms by which entrepreneurs navigate the constraints and opportunities of this environment.

1.5. Strategic Alignment with Sustainable Development Goals (SDGs)

The CE has evolved from a waste management concept into a macroeconomic model targeted at decoupling economic growth from the consumption of finite resources (Geissdoerfer et al., 2017; Ferasso et al., 2020). For SE, the CE provides a set of operational strategies-the "R-strategies" of Reduce, Reuse, Recycle, Repair, Remanufacture, etc.-through which environmental and social objectives can be achieved (Jabbour et al., 2020; Lieder and Rashid, 2016).

In the Tunisian context, it is imperative to make the transition to CE in view of landfill saturation and the cost of importing raw materials (Trabelsi, 2024). Recent studies underline that adoption of circular models by Tunisian SMEs represents a lever of green job creation and innovation (ICU, 2025). However, academic literature still lacks any systematic analysis regarding the specific types of the circular models implemented by Tunisian entrepreneurs and their social impacts.

1.4. The Role of the Institutional Context in the MENA Region

Institutional theory postulates that organizations take on practices not solely because of reasons tied to efficiency but also because of the demands of their environment-legislative, normative, and cultural (DiMaggio and Powell, 1983). In Tunisia, the entrepreneurial ecosystem is marked by an emerging regulatory framework (Social and Solidarity Economy Act), confrontation with financial hurdles, and a powerful influence wielded by international actors at play within the country (EU, GIZ, UNDP) that strongly advocate for green entrepreneurship (CGDR, 2013).

It is thus impossible to study the dynamics in the field of SE in Tunisia without considering institutional pressure and the mechanisms through which entrepreneurs navigate the constraints and opportunities of this environment.

1.5. Strategic Alignment with Sustainable Development Goals (SDGs)

The SDGs create a shared language and measurement framework for evaluating business contributions toward SDs (Van Zante and Van Tulder, 2018; Raman et al., 2022). The following SDGs have relevance for green and social entrepreneurship:

- SDG 8: Decent work and economic growth through the creation of green and inclusive jobs.
- SDG 9: Industry, innovation, and infrastructure through the creation of clean technologies and innovative business models.
- SDG 12 (Responsible consumption and production): through the adoption of CE.
- SDG 13 (Climate action) by reducing greenhouse gas emissions. The academic challenge is not limited to declaring an intention but rather formulating a serious analytical framework that quantifies or qualifies the real contribution of these initiatives in terms of the specific SDG targets.

2. THEORIES AND MODELS

2.1. Sustainable entrepreneurship and green entrepreneurship

Schaltegger and Wagner (2011) define SE as the pursuit of economic opportunities that simultaneously create economic, social, and environmental value (triple bottom line). Cohen and Winn (2007) show that market imperfections (pollution, uninternalized externalities) generate green entrepreneurial opportunities. These theoretical frameworks explain why private actors invest in recycling, renewable energy, or regenerative agriculture: they capture opportunities created by institutional or environmental failures.

2.2. Hybrid models and social enterprises

The literature on hybrid organizations distinguishes between the tensions and management strategies of market logic and social logic. Battilana et al. (2012) highlight the benefits and challenges of hybrids (legitimacy, governance, financing).

Mair and Martí (2006) show that social entrepreneurship lies at the intersection of value creation and social change.

2.3. Circular economy (CE)

The CE (Ellen MacArthur Foundation, 2013; Geissdoerfer et al., 2017) proposes closing material loops (reduce, reuse, recycle). In research, CE is both a normative framework and an operational toolbox for business models based on waste recovery. The literature identifies circular business models (product-service, reuse) and shows their potential for job creation and environmental impact reduction, while highlighting the challenges of scale and governance.

2.4. Frugal innovation

Radjou and Prabhu (2015) and Pansera (2018) characterize frugal innovation as the development of simple, inexpensive solutions adapted to local constraints. This concept is particularly relevant for explaining the spread of artisanal circular solutions in resource-constrained contexts.

2.5. Institutional voids and entrepreneurial ecosystems

The theory of "institutional voids" (Mair and Martí, 2009; Khanna and Palepu, 2010) suggests that the absence or weakness of market institutions (regulation, infrastructure, financing) creates both barriers and opportunities for social entrepreneurship. Recent studies emphasize the role of ecosystems (incubators, NGOs, donors) in compensating for these voids (OECD, 2024).

3. PREVIOUS EMPIRICAL STUDIES AND THEIR CONTRIBUTION

Empirical studies conducted in various international contexts shed light on sustainability- oriented entrepreneurial dynamics and constitute an essential analytical basis for positioning the Tunisian case in a global perspective. For developed economies, Hall et al. (2010), through several case studies conducted in the United States and Europe-in particular, in the renewable energy and waste management sectors-have demonstrated that the entrepreneurs who are committed to SD very often occupy the niches neglected by traditional players, while mobilizing innovative strategies able to answer to environmental market failures. Another work, that of Shepherd and Patzelt (2011), could present, from empirical analyzes conducted in

Germany and the United States, how intrinsic motivations, empathy, the sense of community, and ecological responsibility were driving the commitment into SE, showing that green entrepreneurs are animated by a vision surpassing the strictly economic logics.

Relevant dynamics also emerge from research on hybrid organizations conducted in more structured institutional contexts, such as the United States. Battilana et al. (2012), in a multiple case study of ten American social enterprises, show that managing tensions between social mission and economic viability depends on participatory and adaptive governance mechanisms. This organizational hybridization, typical of dual-mission models observed in several OECD countries, requires a delicate balance between market norms and social requirements.

Empirical studies of the CE conducted in various industrialized and emerging countries, notably by the Ellen MacArthur Foundation (2015, 2023), have documented models of value chain transformation in the plastics, textiles, agribusiness and organic waste sectors. Based on sectoral analyses and hundreds of cases in the European Union, China, Brazil and South Africa, this work demonstrates that circularity rests on localised resource loops (reuse, repair, recycling) but remains highly dependent on the existence of a favourable institutional framework. In turn, research by the OECD (2024) - based on surveys and case studies in South-East Asia and Latin America - confirms that SMEs face similar regulatory constraints, lack of green financing and absence of tax incentives despite very different economic contexts.

Frugal innovation, on the other hand, has been a subject of an important body of empirical research carried out in severe resource-constrained environments. Radjou and Prabhu (2015) have shown, through case studies in India, Brazil, and South Africa, that material constraints are a powerful driver of innovation, leading to simple, low-cost solutions focused on the basic needs of local populations. More recent work, such as that of Pansera and Sarkar (2016), based on ethnographic surveys in India, Kenya, and Pakistan, has been able to confirm that the most robust frugal innovations very often grow from marginalized communities rather than formal institutions and are part of deeply localized territorial dynamics.

Finally, research on entrepreneurship in contexts of institutional vacuums, notably the famous study by Mair and Martí (2009) on Grameen Bank in Bangladesh, demonstrates how social entrepreneurs play an institutional substitution role in environments where public infrastructure is either absent or failing. Guided by an immersive qualitative approach, this study shows how entrepreneurs become creators of alternative rules, standards of the market, and new trust mechanisms capable of sustaining populations excluded from the economic system.

Thus, empirical work conducted in various international contexts-developed countries, emerging economies, and institutionally fragile environments-all converge on the idea that SE is based simultaneously on strong social motivations, hybrid models, frugal innovation strategies, and a capacity for structural adaptation in the face of regulatory constraints. These lessons provide an essential frame of reference for analyzing and understanding the specific characteristics of the Tunisian initiatives studied in this chapter.

4. METHODOLOGY

4.1. Epistemological choice and methodological approach

In this study, we favored an exploratory qualitative approach (Yin, 2018), justified by the emerging nature of green and social entrepreneurship in the Tunisian context, where institutional dynamics, citizen initiatives, and sustainable entrepreneurial practices remain poorly documented.

This epistemological stance is in line with the constructivist-interpretive perspective, according to which social reality is constructed through the experiences, representations, and interactions of actors (Perter et al, 1966; Charmaz, 2014).

This research is based on a multiple case study strategy, examining four companies with social and environmental impact (Koun, Eco-R, NextFood Tunisia, and Biodôme) in order to compare their trajectories, rationales for action, and sustainable innovation strategies.

This method, considered one of the most robust in qualitative research applied to management (Stake, 1995; Eisenhardt and Graebner, 2007), promotes understanding of the phenomenon in its real context and the generation of theoretical frameworks based on empirical observations.

Selection criteria

In accordance with the recommendations of Yin (2018) and Eisenhardt and Graebner (2007), four selection criteria guided the choice of cases:

Table 3. Selection criteria

Criterion	Description	Methodological Reference
Thematic relevance	The companies explicitly belong to the field of green and social entrepreneurship, integrating sustainability and circular-economy practices.	Yin (2018), Stake (1995)
Sectoral diversity	The cases cover various sectors: textile recycling, plastic management, circular agriculture, and organic-waste processing.	Eisenhardt (1989)
Territorial and social embeddedness	The companies operate in different regional contexts, enabling analysis of the links between SE and local development.	Miles et al. (2018)
Contribution to the SDGs	Each case illustrates concrete contributions to at least three major SDGs (8, 12, 13) through measurable actions.	UN (2024), Schaltegger and Wagner (2011)

These business cases were selected based on criteria of relevance, representativeness, and sectoral diversity.

This choice stems from a purposeful sampling strategy typical of qualitative case-study research (Eisenhardt, 1989). In an exploratory approach, the goal is not statistical representativeness but analytical relevance: selecting cases that allow for an in-depth understanding of an emerging phenomenon and illustrate its contextual diversity (Yin, 2018; Stake, 1995).

Table 4. Characteristics of a company

Company	Sector of Activity	Main Objective
Koun	Textile recycling	Socio-economic integration of vulnerable women within a circular-economy model
NextFood Tunisia	Circular agriculture	Sustainable production and reduction of agricultural waste
Eco-R	Plastic recycling	Recovery of plastic waste and reduction of urban pollution
Biodôme	Organic-waste processing	Transformation of organic waste into energy and agricultural resources

These cases therefore embody, to varying degrees, the foundational dimensions of green and social entrepreneurship in Tunisia, namely:

- the creation of multiple forms of value (economic, social, and environmental),
- the integration of circular-economy principles,
- territorial and community embeddedness,
- direct contribution to the SDGs.

4.2. Sample and Data Collection Methods

4.2.1. Methodological triangulation

The research employed a triangulation of sources and methods (Denzin, 1978), combining three main tools:

- Semi-structured interviews,
- Direct observations,
- Document analysis.

This triangulation ensures the credibility and internal validity of the results.

a) Smi-structured interviews

Semi-structured interviews constitute the primary source of qualitative data for this research. They were chosen for their flexibility, exploratory depth, and their ability to reveal the subjective meaning of practices and lived experiences of the actors (Kvale and Brinkmann, 2009).

Sixteen interviews were conducted between 2023 and 2024 with founders, managers, and key personnel from the four selected companies, as shown in the following table.

Table 5. Distribution of Interviews Conducted with the Studied Companies

Company	Number of Interviews	Profile of Respondents
Koun	4	Founder, production manager, social trainer, marketing manager
NextFood Tunisia	5	Co-founder, agronomist engineer, RandD manager, project coordinator, sales manager
Eco-R	4	Founder, technical director, logistics manager, workshop supervisor
Biodôme	3	Co-founder, technical manager, partnerships manager

Each interview lasted between 60 and 90 minutes and was recorded with the informed consent of the respondents.

The interview guides were designed around four main themes:

5. Entrepreneurial motivations and values (social, ecological, economic dimensions);
6. Sustainability strategies and circular innovation;

7. Institutional constraints and enablers (financing, regulatory framework, support networks);
8. Assessment of social and environmental impact (links with the SDGs).

These interviews played a crucial role in the empirical construction of the conceptual model by revealing the logics of frugal innovation and the territorial dynamics specific to green and social entrepreneurship in Tunisia.

The specific objectives of the interviews vary across sectors but converge toward understanding the articulation between innovation, sustainability, and social inclusion.

b) Direct observation

Direct observation was an essential complement to the interviews.

In line with the recommendations of Yin (2018) and Stake (1995), it allows us to understand the phenomenon in its natural context and to analyze behaviors, interactions, and routines that actors do not always explicitly articulate in their discourse.

The importance of this method in research lies in its ability to reveal the embodied and contextualized dimension of SE: gestures, tools, human interactions, and the materiality of work play an essential role in understanding the CE in action.

c) Documentary analysis

resorting to documentary analysis was an attempt to complement the interviews and observations and to provide a macroscopic and contextual reading of the phenomenon under study.

According to Bowen (2009), the analysis of official, institutional, or media documents helps to reinforce the external validity of the study and to situate local practices within broader political and economic frameworks.

The documents consulted included:

- institutional reports (UN, OECD, Ellen MacArthur Foundation, 2023–2024);
- scientific and professional publications on sustainable and circular entrepreneurship;
- internal documents (activity reports, action plans, impact assessments);
- specialized media articles (economic journals, social innovation platforms).
- Company newsletters

This sort of analysis made it possible to recontextualize each case study within the Tunisian sustainability ecosystem; compare the discourse of stakeholders with national and international institutional guidelines (Agenda 2030, National Green Growth Strategy); and document regional trends in SD in North Africa.

As a result, the documentary analysis ensures consistency between the micro (companies), meso (ecosystems), and macro (public policies) levels, reinforcing the explanatory and comparative scope of the research.

This documentary analysis, along with the methods already mentioned, namely semi-structured interviews and observation, are not used in isolation, but in a complementary and integrated manner.

Their articulation makes it possible to grasp the complexity of the sustainable entrepreneurial phenomenon; highlight the consistency between discourse, practices, and policies; and promote a holistic understanding of the Tunisian dynamics of green and social entrepreneurship.

Drawing on this methodological triangulation, the research responds to the call made by Schaltegger and Wagner (2011) and Cohen and Winn (2007) to explore the contextual and systemic dimensions of SE, going beyond purely economic approaches to include social, territorial, and ecological aspects.

4.2.2. Data processing and analysis

The data that were collected were processed using the thematic analysis method (Miles and Huberman 2003; Braun and Clarke 2006). All interviews were fully transcribed and thereafter manually analyzed using mixed thematic coding, combining first, an approach that is deductive in nature, based on the conceptual framework of SE and the CE (Schaltegger and Wagner, 2011; Cohen & Winn, 2007); and second, an inductive approach: allowing categories to emerge from the empirical data (Glaser and Strauss, 1967). This dual logic enables one to articulate theory and fieldwork, following the principle of grounded theory.REF

Coding was done in three main stages, based on the model devised by Braun and Clarke (2006):

Familiarization: Transcripts to be read and re-read, annotated in detail.

- Initial coding: Identifying the relevant units of meaning (key words, phrases, ideas);

Thematic grouping involves classifying codes into major categories and subthemes according to entrepreneurs' logic of action, values, and impacts.

The main categories of analysis that have been identified include:

- Entrepreneurial motivations and values (social, ecological, economic logics);
- Sustainable and circular innovation strategies.

- Participatory governance and hybridization of models;
- Institutional and financial constraints;
- Development levers and ecosystem dynamics;
- Socio-environmental impact and contribution to SDGs.

These themes were then cross-referenced between cases to identify convergences and divergences in the practices observed (comparative case analysis; Eisenhardt and Graebner, 2007).

This table is organized around the conventions of qualitative analysis (Miles and Huberman, 2003; Braun and Clarke, 2006) and identifies the chief categories with their emerging sub-themes and typical units of meaning extracted from the actors' discourse. (See Appendix 1)

5. RESULTS AND ANALYSIS

This section presents the research findings in a progressive and structured manner. In accordance with qualitative analysis practices based on multiple case studies, the analysis follows an intra-case approach, then a cross-case approach, before identifying the underlying mechanisms of action and finally the contributions to the SDGs.

5.1. Intra-Case Analysis

5.1.1. Koun: Textile Recycling and Social Inclusion

The collected data show that Koun operates at the intersection of CE and social entrepreneurship, transforming textile waste into reusable products while professionally integrating women in vulnerable situations. The observed workshops reveal an organizational model based on learning by doing, capacity building, and co-production, corresponding to a capability-building logic commonly found in social enterprises operating in institutionally fragile contexts.

The community dimension is central: the enterprise uses textiles not only as a material to recycle but also as a means of economic and social rehabilitation.

Koun embodies a hybrid model in the sense described by Battilana et al. (2012), combining social purpose (empowerment, economic autonomy) and environmental value creation (waste reduction, textile circularity). The strong collective participation and territorial anchoring confirm the company's ability to act as an "institutional repairer" in an environment marked by structural voids. This model illustrates a form of SE in which material circularity is accompanied by social circularity grounded in inclusion and skills development.

5.1.2. NextFood Tunisia: Circular and Regenerative Agriculture

NextFood Tunisia implements agricultural practices including composting, recycling of residues, reduction of inputs, and optimization of water resources. Field observations reveal production systems aligned with regenerative agriculture principles, where each organic flow is reintroduced into the production cycle.

This "zero waste" logic reflects a nuanced understanding of Tunisian agro-environmental constraints and a capacity to adapt high-tech solutions into frugal and context-appropriate versions.

NextFood illustrates a model of frugal innovation (Radjou and Prabhu, 2015) applied to agriculture, where creativity and ingenuity compensate for limited financial, technological, and institutional resources. The enterprise manages to reconcile economic performance with ecological sustainability, confirming the idea that circular initiatives can be resilience levers in semi-arid environments. The case thus validates research on CE applied to regenerative agriculture, where organic flows are revalorized as productive inputs.

5.1.3. Eco-R: Plastic Recovery

Eco-R positions itself as a major actor in circular plastic-waste management. Interviews reveal a rationalized process: mobilization of formal and informal collection networks, sorting, mechanical transformation, and production of recycled materials for industry. Observations confirm a productive and intensive model where each step aims to reduce losses and optimize material yield.

Eco-R embodies an industrial circularity model consistent with typologies identified by the Ellen MacArthur Foundation (2015, 2023): loop closing through material regeneration, value recovery through transformation, and industrial symbiosis via partnerships with manufacturing companies.

This case demonstrates how an SME in an emerging economy can convert urban waste streams into high value-added economic resources, confirming the relevance of "business sustainability" models in developing contexts. It also illustrates entrepreneurs' capacity to compensate for institutional failures by structuring alternative value chains.

5.1.4. Biodôme: Organic Waste Treatment and Renewable Energy

Biodôme develops a model based on anaerobic digestion of organic waste to produce biogas and compost. On-site observations show a biological valorization infrastructure built around energy recovery and the production of agricultural amendments, forming a local ecosystem in which agriculture, energy, and environment reinforce each other.

Biodôme illustrates an advanced form of organic circularity aligned with the "biological loop" logic in circularity models (Geissdoerfer et al., 2017). It demonstrates the feasibility of local symbiosis linking waste treatment, renewable energy production, and sustainable agriculture.

The enterprise also embodies systemic frugal innovation, using accessible, modular, low-cost technologies that can deliver high environmental impact in institutionally constrained contexts. This model suggests that biological valorization can be a credible alternative to energy dependence and chemical fertilizers in countries of the Global South.

These intra-case analyses show that the four enterprises deploy distinct yet convergent circular and social logics aimed at addressing institutional, economic, and environmental constraints in Tunisia through sustainable innovation. They illustrate specific configurations of SE aligned with research on hybrid organizations, CE, and frugal innovation.

5.2. Cross-Case (Thematic) Analysis

The cross-case analysis reveals several structural regularities across the four initiatives, highlighting common mechanisms in green and social entrepreneurship in emerging contexts.

5.2.1. Motivations and Values: A Shared Normative and Territorial Orientation

The comparison shows that all entrepreneurs share a strong normative orientation rooted in solidarity, environmental responsibility, and contribution to collective well-being.

In line with Shepherd and Patzelt (2011), intrinsic motivations such as empathy, moral sense, and territorial commitment play a central role in the emergence of sustainable initiatives.

Across the four cases, profit-seeking appears secondary to social (inclusion, empowerment, community cohesion) and environmental impact (reduction, valorization, regeneration). This shared axiological orientation explains the coherence of entrepreneurial trajectories and confirms the vocational nature of SE in the Global South.

5.2.2. Frugal Innovation: Creativity as a Response to Scarcity

The second transversal theme concerns the central role of frugal innovation. Facing material, financial, and institutional constraints, entrepreneurs develop simple, modular, easily replicable solutions, consistent with Radjou and Prabhu (2015) and Pansera and Sarkar (2016).

In waste management, circular agriculture, or energy production, these enterprises rely on accessible technologies adapted to local capacities, combining low cost, operational efficiency, and territorial anchoring.

This ingenuity under constraint constitutes a distinctive competence enabling economic viability despite limited institutional support, confirming the relevance of resource bricolage in precarious environments.

5.2.3. Circular Economy as a Structural Logic: Shared Value Loops

The cross-case analysis shows that all four enterprises use circularity as their main value-creation logic. Whether it concerns textiles, plastics, agricultural residues, or organic waste, they operate according to circular principles (reduce, reuse, recycle), consistent with the Ellen MacArthur Foundation (2015, 2023) and Geissdoerfer et al. (2017).

Circularity generates not only material recycling but also economic loops (resource reintegration), social loops (skills building, inclusion), and environmental loops (emissions reduction, input substitution).

In emerging contexts, circularity becomes both an ecological strategy and an economic resilience mechanism.

5.3. Hybrid Models: Reconciling Market Logic with Socio-Ecological Mission

The four cases illustrate hybrid organizational models combining business logic and socio-environmental missions, consistent with Battilana et al. (2012).

This hybridization appears through:

- economic models based on waste valorization, inclusion or training mechanisms,
- community or cross-sector partnerships,
- participatory governance practices.

Hybridization emerges as a structural response to institutional voids (Mair and Martí, 2009), enabling partial self-financing and social cohesion while generating new forms of context-adapted value.

The cross-case analysis thus highlights patterns that transcend sectoral differences. It shows that SE in Tunisia rests on a structural triptych: strong normative values, frugal innovation, and circular logic, supported by organizational hybridization. These results confirm existing literature while revealing dynamics specific to emerging contexts.

5.3.1. Identified Mechanisms of Action

The cross-analysis of the four case studies highlights several mechanisms that explain how these enterprises simultaneously generate economic, social, and environmental impacts. Although deployed differently across sectors, these mechanisms converge toward a common model of green and social entrepreneurship characteristic of emerging contexts.

5.3.2. Resource Loop: Converting Waste into Economic Opportunities

The first mechanism corresponds to transforming waste flows into economic resources, a central process in circular thinking (Ellen MacArthur Foundation, 2015; Geissdoerfer et al., 2017).

Eco-R turns collected plastic into recycled pellets; Biodôme converts organic matter into biogas and compost; Koun transforms textile scraps into value-added artisanal products.

This "value recovery" mechanism highlights entrepreneurs' capacity to reconfigure depreciated flows into marketable assets, generating economic benefits while reducing ecological footprint.

5.3.3. Productive Inclusion: Empowerment Through Skills Development

The second mechanism is the creation of socio-economic opportunities for vulnerable groups through training and learning processes.

This mechanism is most visible in Koun, where women undergo a trajectory of empowerment based on technical training, workshop production, and integration into the value chain.

It reflects the capability-building logic (Sen, 1999; Nussbaum, 2009) and the role of social entrepreneurship as a lever for inclusion (Mair and Martí, 2006). Productive inclusion thus strengthens economic autonomy and resilience, confirming the systemic nature of the generated social impact.

5.4. Territorial Synergies: Cooperation and Local Anchoring as Efficiency Levers

The third mechanism concerns territorial partnerships and inter-organizational cooperation. Biodôme and NextFood, in particular, rely on synergies with farmers, municipalities, companies, NGOs, and incubators, enabling optimized resource circulation and shared constraints. This corresponds to territorial embeddedness and local symbiosis described in circular ecosystem research (Korhonen et al., 2018; OECD, 2024). These synergies enhance operational efficiency and contribute to resilient local value chains based on horizontal exchanges rather than vertical market logics.

5.5. Frugal Innovation: Designing Lean and Adaptive Solutions

The fourth mechanism corresponds to the use of frugal innovation as an adaptation strategy to economic, technological, and institutional constraints (Radjou and Prabhu, 2015; Pansera and Sarkar, 2016).

Eco-R, NextFood, and Koun develop accessible, modular, low-cost production systems capable of functioning despite uncertainty or limited resources.

Frugal innovation becomes a strategic lever for reducing costs and ensuring operational sustainability, revealing that local ingenuity is a key resource in Southern contexts.

Together, these mechanisms show that green and social entrepreneurship relies on a unique articulation between material circularity, social inclusion, territorial anchoring, and frugal innovation. Their combined effect enables the studied enterprises to generate significant systemic impact despite the institutional and economic constraints characteristic of the Tunisian context.

Contribution to the Sustainable Development Goals (SDGs)

The cross-case analysis of the four enterprises reveals a significant and multidimensional contribution to the SDGs, in line with the UN's 2015 action framework. The impact generated by these companies manifests economically, socially, environmentally, and territorially, illustrating the capacity of circular and hybrid models to produce systemic effects in institutionally constrained contexts.

SDG 8 — Decent Work and Economic Growth

The enterprises contribute directly to SDG 8 by generating inclusive forms of employment and creating new economic opportunities in often marginalized territories. Koun and Eco-R, in particular, create direct jobs in collection, sorting, transformation, and production activities.

Koun also stands out for its training programs targeting vulnerable women, enabling the development of transferable technical skills and sustainable socio-economic empowerment. This mechanism aligns with the logic of capacity building and productive inclusion, consistent with international recommendations for inclusive growth.

SDG 12 — Responsible Consumption and Production

All four initiatives explicitly contribute to SDG 12 by reconfiguring resource flows according to CE principles. Through the valorization of textile waste (Koun), plastic (Eco-R), agricultural residues (NextFood), or organic waste (Biodôme), these enterprises reduce pressure on natural resources and create local alternatives to linear production chains.

This focus on circularity exemplifies resource recovery and closed-loop production models, as described by the Ellen MacArthur Foundation (2015, 2023). Their contribution to SDG 12 is therefore structural and forms the core of their economic model.

SDG 13 — Climate Action

Impact on SDG 13 occurs through two main mechanisms:

1. Reduction of CO_2 emissions related to recycling, observed at Eco-R and Koun;
2. Energy substitution and biological valorization, exemplified by Biodôme, which converts organic waste into biogas, reducing fossil fuel use.

These activities contribute to climate mitigation by reducing the volume of waste sent to landfills and promoting renewable energy use. They illustrate the link between circularity and climate resilience promoted by the 2030 Agenda.

Related SDGs: Specific Highlights

SDG 5: Gender Equality (Koun)

Koun significantly impacts SDG 5 by promoting the economic inclusion of vulnerable women. Its training and professional integration model directly contributes to socio-economic empowerment and the reduction of gender inequalities.

SDG 7: Affordable and Clean Energy (Biodôme)

Biodôme contributes to SDG 7 by producing renewable energy from anaerobic digestion. This model reduces dependence on fossil fuels and provides a local, accessible, and sustainable energy alternative.

SDG 11: Sustainable Cities and Communities (Eco-R)

Eco-R contributes to SDG 11 by promoting sustainable urban waste management, improving public space cleanliness, and strengthening local collection and valorization circuits. The enterprise enhances urban resilience and residents' quality of life.

Overall, the four studied cases do not merely produce isolated environmental impacts; they simultaneously contribute to several key SDGs, demonstrating the systemic reach of green and social entrepreneurship in emerging countries. Their activities confirm the relevance of circular and hybrid models as levers for ecological transition and socio-economic inclusion.

Table 6. Summary of SDG Contributions by Enterprise

SDG	SDG Description	Koun	NextFood Tunisia	Eco-R	Biodôme
SDG 8	Decent Work and Economic Growth	Inclusive employment (vulnerable women) Training and integration	Creation of sustainable agricultural jobs	Jobs in sorting and recycling	Jobs in organic waste management
SDG 12	Responsible Consumption and Production	Textile reuse Artisan CE	Circular agriculture Zero waste	Plastic recycling Reduction of urban waste	Organic waste valorization
SDG 13	Climate Action	Reduction of landfill waste → lower emissions	Reduction of agricultural inputs and emissions	CO_2 reduction through plastic recycling	Green energy production (biogas)

continued on following page

Table 6. Continued

SDG	SDG Description	Koun	NextFood Tunisia	Eco-R	Biodôme
SDG 15	Life on Land	Reduction of textile pollution in soils	Soil protection Regenerative agriculture	Reduction of illegal plastic dumping	Reduced organic pollution Protection of agricultural soils
SDG 5	Gender Equality	Strong female inclusion	—	—	—
SDG 7	Affordable and Clean Energy	—	—	—	Renewable energy production (biogas)
SDG 11	Sustainable Cities	Reduction of textile waste	Sustainable urban compost management	Reduction of urban plastic pollution	Reduction of urban organic waste

As shown in the following table, we can conclude that:

- All four enterprises contribute strongly to SDGs 12 and 13, confirming that the CE and climate mitigation are central pillars of their economic and ecological models.
- **Koun** stands out for its major contribution to SDG 5, placing female inclusion at the heart of its social action.
- **Biodôme** distinguishes itself through its direct contribution to SDG 7 by producing renewable energy from organic waste.
- **NextFood Tunisia** plays a key role in SDG 15 by implementing circular and regenerative agricultural practices.
- **Eco-R** contributes significantly to SDGs 11 and 12 by reducing plastic pollution, strengthening urban sustainability.

6. RESULTS DISCUSSED IN LIGHT OF THE LITERATURE

6.1. Circular Economy as a Central Driver: Confirmation and Reinterpretation of the Literature

The results show that the four studied enterprises base their economic model on the valorization of waste (textiles, plastics, organic, and agricultural).

This observation confirms the work of Schaltegger and Wagner (2011) and Cohen and Winn (2007), which argue that SE emerges where environmental inefficiencies or "market imperfections" exist.

In the Tunisian context:

- **Eco-R** valorizes over 150 tons of plastic, demonstrating that waste becomes an economic resource.
- **Biodôme** converts organic waste into biogas, illustrating a complete circular loop.
- **Koun** transforms textile waste into artisanal products, adding a social dimension.

While the literature often describes circularity as a "global" strategy, the Tunisian field shows that it primarily responds to local constraints: lack of raw materials, low purchasing power, technological limitations.

Thus, the studied model reinforces the thesis of contextualized circularity, embedded in local territories (Geissdoerfer et al., 2017).

6.2. Hybridization of Business Models: Observation Consistent with Battilana et al. (2012)

The four enterprises combine:

- A commercial logic (revenue generation)
- With a social or environmental mission (inclusion, pollution reduction, sustainability)

This aligns with the concept of **hybrid organizations** (Battilana et al., 2012), which posits that social impact emerges when actors combine economic strategy with social purpose.

Examples:

- **Koun** employs and trains vulnerable women while producing marketable goods.
- **NextFood** combines profitable agriculture with ecological regeneration.

Unlike Western hybrid models, often technologically advanced or institutionally supported, Tunisian models are frugal and self-sustaining, showing that hybridization can emerge in response to institutional gaps, as highlighted by Mair and Martí (2006).

6.3. Frugal Innovation as a Structuring Feature: Validation of Recent Work

The data show that Tunisian entrepreneurs develop solutions that are:

- Simple
- Low-cost
- Adapted to their environment
- Co-constructed with local communities

This confirms the concept of frugal innovation described by Radjou and Prabhu (2015) and further developed by Pansera (2018).

Field examples:

- **NextFood** uses agricultural techniques based on organic waste recycling without costly technology.
- **Koun** relies on an artisanal model based on local know-how.
- **Eco-R** optimizes its machinery to reduce energy costs.

The literature notes that frugal innovation is particularly common in emerging countries. In Tunisia, it is not only an economic choice but also a philosophy of adaptation, allowing sustained impact despite limited funding.

6.4. The Role of "Institutional Voids": Verification of Mair and Martí (2006)

The study reveals that the enterprises operate where the state or market are deficient:

- Lack of effective municipal waste management systems (**Eco-R**, **Biodôme**)
- Absence of integration programs for women (**Koun**)
- Lack of support for regenerative agriculture (**NextFood**)

These findings confirm the institutional voids theory: when institutions are weak, social entrepreneurs become regulators and repair agents.

However, the study nuances the literature by showing that entrepreneurs do not simply "fill a void" but create new collective practices through partnerships with:

- Municipal authorities
- Local NGOs
- Social incubators (Lab'ess, Impact Partner, etc.)

6.5. Measurable Contribution to the SDGs: Alignment with Hall et al. (2010)

The analyzed cases show a clear and measurable contribution to the SDG, confirming that green and social entrepreneurship can produce tangible social, economic, and environmental impacts even in emerging country contexts.

Table 7. Contribution of Enterprises to the SDGs

Enterprise	Main SDGs
Koun	SDG 5, SDG 8, SDG 12
Eco-R	SDG 12, SDG 13, SDG 11
NextFood Tunisia	SDG 2, SDG 12, SDG 15
Biodôme	SDG 7, SDG 11, SDG 13

These results confirm the analyses of Hall et al. (2010), showing that SE can contribute simultaneously to multiple SDGs, especially in emerging countries.

The literature emphasizes that such contributions usually require a supportive ecosystem. However, this study shows that impact is achieved despite a fragile institutional environment, reinforcing the idea that SE can act as a compensatory, or even substitutive, agent for insufficient public policies.

CONCLUSION

This chapter explored the dynamics of green and social entrepreneurship in Tunisia through a multiple-case study of four enterprises applying CE principles. Using an interpretive qualitative methodology, including semi-structured interviews, direct observations, and document analysis, the study highlighted the action logics, innovation mechanisms, and hybridization forms characterizing these enterprises operating in often fragile institutional contexts.

The results demonstrate that the studied organizations generate measurable socio-environmental value through a combination of frugal innovation, territorial embeddedness, and circularity implemented in artisanal and community-based ways. They also show remarkable resilience, based on the hybridization of economic models and the integration of social and environmental missions into entrepreneurial strategies.

In doing so, this chapter confirms the relevance of several existing theoretical frameworks:

- Viability of circularity in emerging contexts
- The structuring role of frugal innovation in Southern economies
- The importance of hybrid models as a lever for sustainability

At the same time, the results nuance some dominant literature approaches:

- CE does not necessarily rely on advanced technologies but can develop from simple, local, community-based solutions.
- SE can emerge despite the absence of robust institutional frameworks, questioning the assumption that institutional voids always hinder sustainable innovation.

Major Contributions of the Chapter

1. Original Empirical Contribution

This chapter is the first in-depth analyses of four Tunisian initiatives integrating the CE: Koun, NextFood Tunisia, Eco-R, and Biodôme. Through 16 interviews, direct observations, and systematic document analysis, it provides unique qualitative data, detailed descriptions of local circular practices, understanding of hybrid business models in the Maghreb context, and a mapping of enablers and obstacles faced by these enterprises. This empirical richness helps reduce the gap in studies on SE in North Africa and the Global South, largely absent from mainstream literature.

Theoretical Contribution

The chapter proposes an integrated reading of green and social entrepreneurship, articulating three theoretical pillars often studied separately:

- **Circular economy** as a structuring logic for value chains
- **Frugal innovation** as a strategy to adapt to financial and technological constraints
- **Hybrid business models** combining social mission and economic viability

This theoretical articulation allows the conceptualization of a "Tunisian model of entrepreneurial sustainability", characterized by:

- Local waste valorization
- Community mobilization
- Technological frugality

- Simultaneous socio-environmental value creation

This contribution enriches existing paradigms by showing that circular dynamics can emerge "out of necessity", not only in industrialized contexts.

Methodological Contribution

The multiple-case study approach combines semi-structured interviews, field observations, documentary data, and abductive thematic analysis which provides a rich, nuanced, and contextualized understanding of sustainable entrepreneurial practices. This methodology, rarely used in Tunisian research, can serve as a reference for future studies exploring hybrid models, social innovation ecosystems, and local circular practices.

Limits of the Study

Still, this research suffers from some limitations that constrain its scope:

1. The number of the selected case (though adequate for in-depth analysis) limits the statistical generalization of the results.
2. Data rely heavily on self-reported interviews, which might produce self-presentation or desirability bias.
3. The absence of quantitative measures of environmental or social impact limits objective comparison across companies or with other national contexts.
4. This piece of research was conducted during a specific socio-economic period (2023–2024), marked by political and economic tensions that could influence observed dynamics.

Future Research

This work opens several research avenues for other researchers who wish to:

- Expand the sample to other sectors in green energy, ecotourism, and sustainable agriculture to test for transferability of identified mechanisms.
- Longitudinally study development regarding green entrepreneurial models for a number of successive years, including scaling capacity.
- Include quantitative methods wherever possible: measuring carbon impact, inclusion indicators, cost-benefit analysis, which can complement the qualitative results and reinforce conclusions.

- Make international comparisons between countries of the Maghreb and Sub-Saharan Africa to test the specificity of entrepreneurial sustainability models in the Global South and highlight potential structural or cultural factors in common.

REFERENCES

ANGED. (2022). Rapport sur la gestion des déchets en Tunisie.

Battilana, J., Lee, M., Walker, J., & Dorsey, C. (2012). In search of the hybrid ideal. *The Academy of Management Annals*, *6*(1), 51–96.

Benavides-Sánchez, E. P., Moya-Clemente, I., & Pérez-Sánchez, M. (2025). Bibliometric analysis and systematic literature review of the relationship between sustainable development goals and sustainable entrepreneurship over time. *Discover Sustainability*, *6*(1), 1–18. DOI: 10.1007/s43621-024-00572-0

Bowen, G. A. (2009). Document analysis as a qualitative research method. *Qualitative Research Journal*, *9*(2), 27–40. DOI: 10.3316/QRJ0902027

Braun, V., & Clarke, V. (2006). Using thematic analysis in psychology. *Qualitative Research in Psychology*, *3*(2), 77–101. DOI: 10.1191/1478088706qp063oa

Budumuru, U. R., & Paruchuru, M. (2025). Tracing the evolution of ecosystems in social entrepreneurship: Perspectives on innovation and sustainability. *Sustainable Futures : An Applied Journal of Technology, Environment and Society*, *9*, 100645. DOI: 10.1016/j.sftr.2025.100645

CDC. (2024). Global Startup Ecosystem Report – Tunisia insights.

CGDR. (2013).La Dynamisation de l'Entrepreneuriat Social en Tunisie.

Charmaz, K. (2014). Constructing grounded theory.

Cohen, B., & Winn, M. I. (2007). Market imperfections, opportunity and sustainable entrepreneurship. *Journal of Business Venturing*, *22*(1), 29–49. DOI: 10.1016/j.jbusvent.2004.12.001

Denzin, N. K. (1978). *The Research Act: A Theoretical Introduction to Sociological Methods* (2nd ed.). McGraw-Hill.

DiMaggio, P. J., & Powell, W. W. (1983). The iron cage revisited: Institutional isomorphism and collective rationality in organizational fields. *American Sociological Review*, *48*(2), 147–160. DOI: 10.2307/2095101

DiMaggio, P. J., & Powell, W. W. (1983). The iron cage revisited: Institutional isomorphism and collective rationality in organizational fields. *American Sociological Review*, *48*(2), 147–160. DOI: 10.2307/2095101

Eisenhardt, K. M. (1989). Building theories from case study research. *Academy of Management Review*, *14*(4), 532–550. DOI: 10.2307/258557

Eisenhardt, K. M., & Graebner, M. E. (2007). Theory building from cases: Opportunities and challenges. *Academy of Management Journal*, *50*(1), 25–32. DOI: 10.5465/amj.2007.24160888

Elkington, J. (1998). *Cannibals with forks: The triple bottom line of 21st century business*. New Society Publishers.

Ellen MacArthur Foundation. (2015).Towards a circular economy: Business rationale for an accelerated transition.

Ellen MacArthur Foundation. (2023). Circular Economy Overview.

Ferasso, M., Beliaeva, T., Kraus, S., Clauss, T., & Kailer, N. (2020). Circular economy business models: The state of research and avenues ahead. *Business Strategy and the Environment*, *29*(8), 3006–3021. DOI: 10.1002/bse.2554

Geissdoerfer, M., Savaget, P., Bocken, N. M., & Hultink, E. J. (2017). The Circular Economy–A new sustainability paradigm? *Journal of Cleaner Production*, *143*, 757–768. DOI: 10.1016/j.jclepro.2016.12.048

George, G., Merrill, R., & Schillebeeckx, S. (2021). Digital sustainability and entrepreneurship. *Journal of Business Venturing*, *36*(1).

GIZ. (2020).Améliorer la protection du climat à travers l'économie circulaire en Tunisie.

Gupta, P., & Antony, A. (2026). Institutional voids and financial markets: an institutional theory perspective. *Qualitative Research in Financial Markets*, 1-31.

Hall, J. K., Daneke, G. A., & Lenox, M. J. (2010). Sustainable development and entrepreneurship: Past contributions and future directions. *Journal of Business Venturing*, *25*(5), 439–444. DOI: 10.1016/j.jbusvent.2010.01.002

Hossain, M. (2021). Frugal innovation: A review and research agenda. *Journal of Cleaner Production*, •••, 182.

ICU. (2025).GREENSTEP Project: Embracing the Green Transition for Small and Medium-sized Enterprises.

Jabbour, C. J. C., Seuring, S., de Sousa Jabbour, A. B. L., & Jugend, D. (2020). Stakeholders, innovative business models for the circular economy and sustainable performance of firms in an emerging economy facing institutional voids. *Journal of Environmental Management*, *273*, 111105.

Khanna, T., & Palepu, K. (2010). *Winning in emerging markets*. Harvard Business Press.

Kirchherr, J., Reike, D., & Hekkert, M. (2017). Conceptualizing the circular economy. *Resources, Conservation and Recycling*, *127*, 221–232. DOI: 10.1016/j.resconrec.2017.09.005

Korhonen, J., Honkasalo, A., & Seppälä, J. (2018). Circular economy: The concept and its limitations. *Ecological Economics*, *143*, 37–46. DOI: 10.1016/j.ecolecon.2017.06.041

Kvale, S., & Brinkmann, S. (2009). Interviews: Learning the craft of qualitative research interviewing. sage.

Lieder, M., & Rashid, A. (2016). Towards circular economy implementation: A comprehensive review in context of manufacturing industry. *Journal of Cleaner Production*, *115*, 36–51. DOI: 10.1016/j.jclepro.2015.12.042

Lieder, M., & Rashid, A. (2016). Towards circular economy implementation: A comprehensive review in context of manufacturing industry. *Journal of Cleaner Production*, *115*, 36–51. DOI: 10.1016/j.jclepro.2015.12.042

Littlewood, D., Ciambotti, G., Holt, D., & Steinfield, L. (2022). Special issue editorial: Social innovation and entrepreneurship in Africa. *Africa Journal of Management*, *10*(2), 1–10. DOI: 10.1080/23322373.2022.2071579

Mair, J., & Marti, I. (2006). Social entrepreneurship research: A source of explanation, prediction, and delight. *Journal of World Business*, *41*(1), 36–44. DOI: 10.1016/j.jwb.2005.09.002

Mair, J., & Martí, I. (2006). Social entrepreneurship research: A source of explanation, prediction, and delight. *Journal of World Business*, *41*(1), 36–44. DOI: 10.1016/j.jwb.2005.09.002

Mair, J., & Marti, I. (2009). Entrepreneurship in and around institutional voids. *Journal of Business Venturing*, *24*(5), 419–435. DOI: 10.1016/j.jbusvent.2008.04.006

Mair, J., & Marti, I. (2009). Entrepreneurship in and around institutional voids: A case study from Bangladesh. *Journal of Business Venturing*, *24*(5), 419–435. DOI: 10.1016/j.jbusvent.2008.04.006

Managers. (2023). Écosystème entrepreneurial vert en Tunisie.

Miles, M. B., & Huberman, A. M. (2003). *Qualitative Data Analysis: A Sourcebook of New Methods* (2nd ed.). SAGE Publications.

Modaffari, G., & Beck, T. (2026). From Corporate Social Responsibility to Social Entrepreneurship: A Bibliometric Approach. *Corporate Social Responsibility and Environmental Management*, *33*(2), 2005–2017. DOI: 10.1002/csr.70259

Nussbaum, M. C. (2009). Creating capabilities: The human development approach and its implementation. *Hypatia, 24*(3), 211–215. DOI: 10.1111/j.1527-2001.2009.01053.x

OECD. (2025). *Mind the SDG data gaps: Insights from the OECD SDGs Hub. OECD Policy Insights on Well-being, Inclusion and Equal Opportunity, No. 20.* OECD Publishing.

Pansera, M. (2018). Frugal or fair? The unfulfilled promises of frugal innovation. *Technology Innovation Management Review, 8*(4), 6–13. DOI: 10.22215/timreview/1148

Pansera, M., & Sarkar, S. (2016). Crafting sustainable development solutions: Frugal innovations of grassroots entrepreneurs. *Sustainability (Basel), 8*(1), 51. DOI: 10.3390/su8010051

Patzelt, H., & Shepherd, D. A. (2011). Recognizing opportunities for sustainable development. In *Entrepreneurship & Sustainability – Business Solutions for the 21st Century*. DOI: 10.1111/j.1540-6520.2010.00386.x

Polloni, E. (2026). Public, private and hybrid organizations collaborating for social sustainability.

Radjou, N., & Prabhu, J. (2015). Frugal Innovation: How to Do More With Less.

Raman, R., Subramaniam, N., Nair, V. K., Shivdas, A., Achuthan, K., & Nedungadi, P. (2022). Women entrepreneurship and sustainable development: Bibliometric analysis and emerging research trends. *Sustainability (Basel), 14*(15), 9160. DOI: 10.3390/su14159160

Schaltegger, S., & Wagner, M. (2011). Sustainable entrepreneurship and sustainability innovation: Categories and interactions. *Business Strategy and the Environment, 20*(4), 222–237. DOI: 10.1002/bse.682

Schaltegger, S., & Wagner, M. (2011). Sustainable entrepreneurship and sustainability innovation: Categories and interactions. *Business Strategy and the Environment, 20*(4), 222–237. DOI: 10.1002/bse.682

Schaltegger, S., & Wagner, M. (2011). Sustainable entrepreneurship and sustainability innovation: Categories and interactions. *Business Strategy and the Environment, 20*(4), 222–237. DOI: 10.1002/bse.682

Schaper, M. (2002). The essence of ecopreneurship. *Greener Management International, 2002*(38), 26–30. DOI: 10.9774/GLEAF.3062.2002.su.00004

Sen, A. (1999). *Freedom. Development.* Oxford University Press.

Stake, R. E. (1995). *The Art of Case Study Research*. SAGE Publications.

Startup Tunisia. (2022, 2024). Rapports annuels.

Stephan, U., Uhlaner, L. M., & Stride, C. (2026). Institutions and social entrepreneurship: A hierarchy of institutions to revisit institutional voids, support, and configurations. *Journal of International Business Studies*, *57*(1), 4–25. DOI: 10.1057/s41267-025-00829-4

Trabelsi, E. (2024). Transition to sustainable environment and economic growth in Tunisia. *Journal of Environmental Management*, •••, 2772–655X.

UNDP. (2019). Rapport National Volontaire sur la mise en œuvre des ODD en Tunisie.

UNEP. (2023). *SwitchMed in Tunisia*. Policy and Strategy.

Van Zanten, J., & Van Tulder, R. (2018). Multinational enterprises and the Sustainable Development Goals: An institutional approach to corporate engagement. *Journal of International Business Policy*, *1*(3-4), 208–233. DOI: 10.1057/s42214-018-0008-x

World Bank (2023). Tunisia Economic Monitor.

Yin, R. K. (2018). *Case Study Research and Applications: Design and Methods* (6th ed.). SAGE Publications.

APPENDIX 1

Table 8. Summary of thematic coding of Semi-structured interviews

Main Category	Identified Sub-Themes	Examples of Meaning Units (Representative Quotes)	Companies Concerned
1. Entrepreneurial Motivations and Values	– Sense of community and social usefulness – Environmental commitment – Search for meaning and territorial impact	"We wanted to create an activity that makes sense for the community, not just profit." "Reusing also means giving people a second life, not only objects." "Our mission is to act where no one else intervenes." "Protecting the environment is a responsibility, not a choice." "This project was born from a need to contribute to the territory, not to do traditional business."	Koun, Eco-R, Biodôme
2. Sustainable Innovation Strategies	– Frugal and local innovation – Integration of the circular economy – Cooperation with public actors and NGOs	"We innovate with few resources but many ideas." "Our waste becomes raw materials for other actors." "Every constraint becomes an opportunity for us to invent." "The local context pushes us toward simple, effective, and sustainable solutions." "We co-construct our solutions with on-the-ground partners."	NextFood, Eco-R, Biodôme
3. Governance and Organizational Model	– Participatory leadership – Training and social inclusion – Hybridization of the economic model	"Everyone participates in decision-making, even the workers." "Our model relies on valuing people as much as materials." "We learn together, we decide together, that's our strength." "For us, the social and the environmental are not separate." "Our organization must remain flexible to uphold our dual mission."	Koun, NextFood
4. Obstacles and Constraints	– Limited access to green financing – Regulatory instability – Low institutional recognition – Cultural challenges	"Banks still don't understand our model." "The lack of a legal framework for social enterprises slows us down a lot." "We navigate within a system that was not designed for us." "Mentalities evolve slowly, especially regarding environmental issues." "Administrative procedures slow us down more than the work itself."	All

continued on following page

Table 8. Continued

Main Category	Identified Sub-Themes	Examples of Meaning Units (Representative Quotes)	Companies Concerned
5. Levers and Success Factors	– Support from incubators – Local cooperation–Community awareness	"Thanks to incubators, we learned how to structure our projects." "Our connection with the local community gives us strong legitimacy." "Partnerships helped us move from ideas to action." "Without the support of neighborhood youth, we would never have been able to move forward." "The trust of local actors is our most precious capital."	Koun, NextFood
6. Impact on the SDGs	– SDG 8: employment and inclusion – SDG 12: circularity – SDG 13: climate – SDG 5: gender	"Every ton recycled is a step for the climate and one more job." "Our work directly contributes to the SDGs, even if few people know it." "We see the impact in people's lives and in the cleanliness of the neighborhood." "We contribute to the future without always having the means." "Environmental and social progress go hand in hand that's our conviction."	All
7. Forward-Looking Vision and Support Needs	– Need for a clear legal framework – Green financing – International cooperation	"There must be a real legal status for social enterprises in Tunisia." "We want to cooperate with other Maghreb countries to share our practices." "Without appropriate financing, our impact will remain limited." "The future lies in South-South alliances, not only North-South." "Tunisia needs to seriously invest in the circular economy."	NextFood, Eco-R, Biodôme

Chapter 8

Entrepreneurial Accounting for Sustainable Development:

Linking Green Innovation, ESG Reporting, and SDG Impact Measurement

Rimi Gusliana Mais
http://orcid.org/0000-0002-2625-0601
Sekolah Tinggi Ilmu Ekonomi Indonesia Jakarta, Indonesia

Munir Munir
http://orcid.org/0009-0006-4464-5136
Sekolah Tinggi Ilmu Syari'ah Al-Manar Jakarta, Jakarta, Indonesia

Ririn Widyastuti Wulaningsih
http://orcid.org/0009-0008-1593-7521
Universitas Bung Karno, Indonesia

Rahmat A. Yuliansyah
Sekolah Tinggi Ilmu Ekonomi Indonesia Jakarta, Indonesia

Erita Oktasari
Universitas Bung Karno, Indonesia

Muhammad Ibnu Sholeh
http://orcid.org/0000-0003-0841-3101
STAI Kh Muhammad Ali Shodiq Tulungagung, Jawa Timur, Indonesia

ABSTRACT

This chapter explores the transformative role of Entrepreneurial Accounting for Sustainable Development (EASD) in aligning financial systems with sustainability transitions through the integration of green innovation, ESG reporting, and SDG impact measurement. Entrepreneurial accounting reconceptualizes conventional financial practices by embedding multi-capital value creation, environmental management accounting (EMA), and impact-weighted approaches into decision-making

DOI: 10.4018/979-8-3373-7391-1.ch008

frameworks. Empirical evidence from Southeast Asia highlights how adaptive governance, green budgeting, and digital trust technologies—including AI and blockchain—enhance transparency, accountability, and scalability in sustainability performance. The study presents a unified framework connecting non-financial indicators, global disclosure standards (IFRS S1–S2, GRI), and policy instruments to foster verifiable, outcome-based entrepreneurship. Ultimately, EASD emerges as a strategic governance mechanism that harmonizes public responsibility, private innovation, societal value, accelerating progress toward the SDGs.

INTRODUCTION

Sustainable development has progressively altered the function of accounting in both private and public sector entities. In addition to its traditional financial management role, accounting is now anticipated to promote environmental sustainability, social responsibility, and the production of long-term value. Entrepreneurs, investors, governments, and regulatory bodies face increasing demands to exhibit not only financial performance but also quantifiable contributions to climate resilience, social inclusiveness, and the Sustainable Development Goals (SDGs).

Simultaneously, conventional accounting systems predominantly focus on historical financial reporting and short-term economic outcomes. Such approaches frequently lack adequacy for assessing sustainability-focused innovation, especially in scenarios characterised by environmental uncertainties, transition hazards, and prolonged social consequences. As organisations progressively embrace green technologies, ESG reporting frameworks, and sustainable finance instruments, there arises a necessity for accounting methodologies that can amalgamate financial and non-financial aspects into a cohesive governance framework.

Recent advancements in global sustainability standards, specifically IFRS S1–S2 and the updated GRI Universal Standards, demonstrate a wider institutional shift towards the provision of decision-useful sustainability disclosures. Nonetheless, significant obstacles persist. Numerous organisations persist in encountering challenges in systematically assessing social and environmental consequences, incorporating sustainability indicators into managerial decision-making, and assuring the integrity of ESG-related information. These problems are particularly pronounced for entrepreneurial organisations and public sector innovators in emerging economies, where resource constraints and institutional capacity deficiencies frequently hinder implementation.

This chapter presents Entrepreneurial Accounting for Sustainable Development (EASD) as a cohesive governance paradigm that connects green innovation, ESG reporting, and SDG impact assessment. This chapter reframes sustainability reporting from a mere disclosure activity to entrepreneurial accounting as a strategic tool for harmonising innovation, responsibility, and the development of long-term societal value. This chapter analyses how accounting systems can facilitate more transparent, adaptive, and outcome-oriented approaches to sustainable development by integrating sustainability accounting literature, public financial management reforms, impact measurement methodologies, and emerging digital governance tools.

This chapter adopts a qualitative integrative review and normative-analytical approach. It synthesizes recent peer-reviewed literature (2020–2025), international regulatory standards (IFRS S1–S2, GRI), public financial management (PFM) reforms, and emerging digital governance research to construct a conceptual framework for Entrepreneurial Accounting for Sustainable Development (EASD). Rather than conducting primary empirical testing, the chapter develops a theory-informed synthesis that integrates sustainability accounting, environmental management accounting (EMA), impact monetization methodologies (IWA and SROI), and digital trust technologies (AI and blockchain).

The analytical method follows three steps:

(1) comparative review of global sustainability reporting standards and impact measurement frameworks;
(2) conceptual integration of entrepreneurial theory, institutional theory, and multi-capital accounting;
(3) normative development of a governance-oriented EASD framework linking firm-level innovation, public budgeting, and SDG measurement.

This methodological clarification positions the chapter not as a descriptive review, but as a structured conceptual advancement aimed at bridging theory, governance mechanisms, and operational sustainability accounting practices.

The discourse is structured into five interrelated sections. The chapter initially redefines entrepreneurial accounting in the context of modern sustainability transitions, then analysing the integration of green innovation into accounting and control systems. The next sections examine the significance of ESG reporting, SDG impact assessment, and public-sector governance frameworks in enhancing sustainable accountability. The chapter finishes by suggesting policy and institutional strategies to promote Entrepreneurial Accounting for Sustainable Development across various organisational and regional contexts.

Executive Summary: Key Contributions of This Chapter

a. Introduces Entrepreneurial Accounting for Sustainable Development (EASD) as governance mechanism rather than a reporting too
b. Integrates IFRS S1–S2, GRI, EMA, IWA, and SROI into a unified framework
c. Examines digital technologies as assurance infrastructures
d. Proposes phased implementation for SMEs and developing economies
e. Provides policy roadmap linking green budgeting and SDG finance

1. REDEFINING ENTREPRENEURIAL ACCOUNTING IN THE ERA OF SUSTAINABILITY

Entrepreneurial accounting transforms accounting from a retrospective record-keeping role into a proactive function that stimulates value creation across economic, social, and environmental sectors. In sustainable contexts, entrepreneurs, including start-ups and intrapreneurs within public agencies, encounter Knightian uncertainty, path-dependent institutions, and changing disclosure frameworks (e.g., ISSB's IFRS S1–S2). Accounting must extend beyond the management of financial capital to facilitate the discovery, validation, and scaling of green breakthroughs (e.g., circular models, low-carbon technologies) through decision-useful metrics, narrative explanations, and trustworthy assurance. Recent research indicates that environmental management accounting (EMA) is evolving from a focus on eco-efficiency cost accounting to a strategic tool for innovation decisions and long-term positioning, thereby affirming accounting's function in facilitating sustainability strategy rather than solely quantifying it (Swalih, Chithra, & Raj, 2024).

Circular economy transitions simultaneously reveal the limitations of conventional management control systems and necessitate dialogic, multi-capital strategies that incorporate flows, stocks, and stakeholder effects throughout product life cycles (Aureli et al., 2023). The acceleration of this shift has been facilitated by standard-setting. IFRS S1–S2, endorsed by IOSCO and frequently cited by regulators, incorporates governance, strategy, risk management, and metrics/targets components that integrate sustainability with corporate performance and capital allocation. For entrepreneurial entities, these prerequisites institutionalize scenario analysis, transition planning, and risk-opportunity quantification as standard management practices, so enhancing the comparability and investability of green enterprises.

However, the quality of disclosure remains inconsistent, since risk narratives frequently surpass opportunity quantification, underscoring the necessity for improved controls, foundational data systems, and integration with operational decision-making (Business Strategy and the Environment, 2024). A subsequent redefinition pertains to impact. Impact-Weighted Accounts (IWA) advocate for the monetization of product and operational impacts to convert social-environmental externalities into decision-relevant metrics, whereas Social Return on Investment (SROI) promotes blended-value reasoning for programmatic interventions (Serafeim & Trinh, 2020; Corvo et al., 2022).

By utilizing digital trust tools such as blockchain for provenance and immutability, and AI/analytics for anomaly detection and near-real-time insights entrepreneurial accounting can transition incentives from output compliance to outcome attainment (Mulligan et al., 2024). Recent advancements in Public Financial Management (PFM) within the public sector position budgeting, performance systems, and procurement as mechanisms that integrate and amplify entrepreneurial sustainability solutions for the Sustainable Development Goals (SDGs). From this perspective, entrepreneurial accounting is a cross-sector competency that integrates standardized ESG reporting with impact monetization, digital assurance, and public financial management mechanisms to expedite progress towards the Sustainable Development Goals (SDGs).

1.1 The Evolution from Traditional to Entrepreneurial Accounting

Historically, traditional accounting methods were developed to facilitate stewardship, financial oversight, and adherence to regulations. Their main focus was on documenting historical transactions, assuring the accuracy of financial data, and safeguarding investor interests through uniform reporting protocols. Although these roles are crucial, they are increasingly viewed as inadequate in the realm of sustainability transitions, where organisations must concurrently address long-term environmental risks, social consequences, and uncertainties associated to innovation.

In the past decade, accounting study and professional practice have progressively transitioned towards more expansive notions of organisational value creation. This movement signifies an increasing acknowledgement that financial performance alone insufficiently captures organisational resilience, climatic vulnerability, stakeholder legitimacy, or long-term developmental impact. As sustainability issues increasingly permeate corporate governance and public policy, accounting systems are transitioning from solely retrospective tools to strategic mechanisms that shape planning, investment decisions, and organisational transformation.

The rise of Entrepreneurial Accounting signifies this wider institutional and management shift. Entrepreneurial accounting transcends just financial measurement by integrating predictive evaluations, non-financial metrics, and sustainability-focused performance assessments into organisational decision-making. In this setting, accounting serves not just as a control mechanism but also as a facilitating infrastructure that promotes experimentation, innovation, and adaptive governance amid uncertainty.

Recent advancements in sustainable reporting standards have expedited this change. The implementation of IFRS S1 and IFRS S2 created a cohesive worldwide framework that connects governance, strategy, risk management, and sustainability KPIs. These guidelines promote the integration of climate-related risks, transition planning, and sustainability possibilities into core managerial and financial operations, rather than addressing them as isolated reporting tasks. The updated GRI Universal Standards enhanced stakeholder-focused disclosure practices by highlighting organisational effects on society and the environment.

This institutional change has also impacted management accounting methods. Environmental Management Accounting (EMA), originally centred on identifying environmental costs and analysing eco-efficiency, is progressively utilised to facilitate strategic decision-making, promote green innovation, and enhance long-term sustainability planning. Accounting methodologies linked to circular economy models now prioritise life-cycle analysis, resource recirculation, and multi-stakeholder collaboration over traditional short-term efficiency metrics. These advancements illustrate the gradual adaptation of accounting processes towards more systemic and sustainability-focused value generating methods.

The increasing significance of impact-oriented measurement has broadened the scope of entrepreneurial accounting. Methodologies like Impact-Weighted Accounts (IWA) and Social Return on Investment (SROI) seek to convert environmental and social consequences into more pertinent analytical formats. Despite their methodological complexity and occasional contention, these approaches exemplify a broader trend toward incorporating societal outcomes into the assessment of organisational performance and investment decisions.

In practice, these extensive sustainability transitions have prompted organisations to implement more defined impact-oriented accounting models. IWA converts product externalities into monetary values suitable for incorporation into financial statements, whereas SROI offers counterfactual and valuation frameworks for social and environmental programs both pertinent to entrepreneurial enterprises and public-private collaborations aimed at achieving SDG outcomes (Serafeim & Trinh, 2020; Corvo et al., 2022).

The digital layer is revolutionizing data pipelines: blockchain architectures augment traceability and tamper-resistance within supply chains; AI enhances classification, outlier detection, and narrative analysis, facilitating more precise and timely guidance for innovators and investors (Mulligan et al., 2024). Collectively, these advancements transform accounting from merely documenting the past to actively shaping the future, establishing it as an entrepreneurial asset that directs capital towards viable low-carbon, inclusive, and circular solutions.

1.2 Entrepreneurship, Innovation, and Accountability

Entrepreneurship is intrinsically linked to experimentation, uncertainty, and the identification of opportunities. In sustainability-focused contexts, entrepreneurial endeavours encounter heightened expectations for accountability, transparency, and quantifiable societal impact. Investors, regulators, communities, and public institutions today anticipate that organisations will not only innovate but also illustrate how such innovation contributes to environmental preservation, social inclusion, and sustainable developmental goals.

This conflicting expectation presents a significant governance difficulty. Entrepreneurial entities are frequently urged to embrace flexibility, swift adaptation, and risk-taking, whereas sustainability governance systems prioritise comparability, consistent disclosure, and performance verification. Consequently, organisations often find it challenging to reconcile exploratory innovation with the accountability demands of ESG reporting and SDG-focused evaluation frameworks.

Entrepreneurial accounting is crucial in this context as it offers methods for converting innovative activity into more organised and verifiable forms of organisational accountability. Instead of confining accountability to financial outcomes, entrepreneurial accounting broadens organisational assessment to encompass wider aspects of value creation, such as environmental efficiency, stakeholder influence, and long-term sustainability resilience.

Recent sustainability disclosure frameworks have bolstered this transition. IFRS S1–S2 progressively include sustainability-related governance, risk evaluation, and strategy planning into organisational reporting frameworks, prompting companies to link entrepreneurial endeavours with clearer performance metrics. Concurrently, comprehensive stakeholder-oriented frameworks like the GRI Standards highlight the societal impacts of organisational actions, thereby broadening accountability from investors to a larger array of stakeholder groups.

This transformation alters the operational function of management accounting systems within organisations. Environmental Management Accounting (EMA), circular economy accounting, and carbon management accounting are progressively utilised not solely for compliance reporting, but for assessing resource efficiency, product redesign, supplier sustainability, and low-carbon investment strategies. In this setting, accounting systems integrate into the innovation process by shaping organisational project prioritisation, resource allocation, and assessment of long-term sustainability trade-offs.

The increasing focus on effect measurement enhances the responsibility aspect of entrepreneurial endeavours. Methods like Impact-Weighted Accounts (IWA) and Social Return on Investment (SROI) strive to enhance the visibility of environmental and social effects inside organisational assessment frameworks. Despite ongoing methodological constraints, particularly concerning valuation assumptions, attribution logic, and data comparability, these frameworks illustrate the increasing institutional pressures on organisations to exhibit quantifiable sustainability achievements rather than mere symbolic ESG promises.

From a governance standpoint, entrepreneurial accountability increasingly relies on the veracity of sustainability information. Organisations are consequently compelled to enhance internal controls, data quality systems, and assurance procedures that can provide dependable non-financial reporting. This advancement is especially significant in situations when issues related to greenwashing, selective disclosure, and inconsistent ESG indicators persistently erode stakeholder trust and investment confidence.

In addressing these accountability concerns, organisations are progressively implementing digital technology to enhance the dependability, traceability, and timeliness of sustainability-related information. Blockchain improves provenance, substantiates chain-of-custody assertions for recycled materials, and facilitates tokenized incentives; AI aids in anomaly detection, KPI predictions, and thematic analysis of narrative disclosures. A comprehensive study associates these technologies with policy-relevant sustainability objectives, such as ESG data integrity and market trust (Mulligan et al., 2024). In the public sector, public financial management changes (program budgeting, results-based financing, SDG tagging) enhance absorptive capacity to expand impactful initiatives via procurement and grants, while ensuring accountability for public funds (Manes Rossi et al., 2024).

In summary, entrepreneurial accounting serves as the intersection of exploration and accountability: it aligns experiments with standardized disclosures, multi-capital metrics, and impact assertions that endure audit and public examination thus enhancing the credibility, financial viability, and societal legitimacy of entrepreneurial solutions to the Sustainable Development Goals (SDGs).

1.3 Theoretical Underpinnings of Sustainable Entrepreneurial Accounting

Sustainable entrepreneurship accounting utilizes several theoretical perspectives. Stakeholder theory asserts that firms generate value by reconciling the interests of various stakeholders; entrepreneurial accounting actualizes this by incorporating non-financial stakeholder outcomes (e.g., labor safety, community welfare, biodiversity) into metrics and disclosures that are relevant for decision-making. Institutional theory elucidates the dissemination of practices through coercive (regulatory standards), normative (professionalization), and mimetic (benchmarking) forces, hence elucidating the swift adoption of ISSB-aligned disclosures and the development of sector-specific playbooks concerning material issues. The resource-based and dynamic capabilities frameworks validate investments in data, analytics, and assurance capabilities as strategic assets that empower organizations to identify and expand sustainability possibilities more rapidly and at reduced capital expenditures.

These theories are implemented using specific measurement frameworks. IWA addresses stakeholder and institutional requirements by translating externalities into a format comprehensible to capital markets; SROI's theory of change and counterfactual reasoning correspond with stakeholder significance and public accountability, particularly in social entrepreneurship and public–private partnerships (Serafeim & Trinh, 2020; Corvo et al., 2022). Research on EMA and circular accounting indicates that dialogic controls, which facilitate contestation, learning, and iterative goal revision, are more suitable for innovation in uncertain environments than solely diagnostic controls; they also correspond with institutional pluralism in sustainability, necessitating the reconciliation of diverse logics (economic, social, environmental) (Aureli et al., 2023; Jorgensen et al., 2023).

From an information economics perspective, standardized sustainability disclosures mitigate information asymmetry and agency costs, whilst scenario analysis and transition plans serve as credible indicators of managerial quality and flexibility. Recent data indicates diversity in disclosure quality and the necessity for enhanced opportunity metrics, advocating for the ongoing development of advice, safe-harbor experiments, and assurance processes (Business Strategy and the Environment, 2024; Dias et al., 2024).

Ultimately, socio-technical systems perspectives validate blockchain and AI as infrastructural complements to standards, augmenting verifiability, comparability, and timeliness; systematic reviews suggest these technologies can bolster policy objectives by enhancing data integrity, chain-of-custody, and auditability essential prerequisites for markets to incentivize authentically sustainable entrepreneurial models (Mulligan et al., 2024). Theoretical perspectives collectively suggest that entrepreneurial accounting transcends basic assessment; it constitutes an institutional framework for the discovery, discipline, and dissemination of innovations linked with the Sustainable Development Goals.

1.4 The Role of Accountants as Sustainability Innovators

Accountants are progressively functioning as architects of entrepreneurial education rather than mere passive record-keepers. In sustainability transformations, they (i) establish controls that harmonize exploration and discipline, (ii) develop data and measurement systems for multi-capital performance, (iii) convert impacts into financial metrics, and (iv) facilitate credible disclosures that unlock capital and foster public trust. Empirically, EMA's strategy shift illustrates the increasing impact of accountants on product design, supplier selection, and capital budgeting roles that were previously marginal to conventional accounting (Swalih et al., 2024). In circular contexts, accountants collaboratively develop dialogic control systems that integrate life-cycle considerations, reverse logistics, and materials recirculation into objectives and incentives; without this reconfiguration, companies find it challenging to transition from incremental eco-efficiency to radical resource decoupling (Aureli et al., 2023; Jorgensen et al., 2023).

As disclosure specialists, accountants implement IFRS S1–S2 regulations and integrate cross-functional inputs (risk, operations, strategy) into cohesive narratives and decision-relevant indicators. Research examining the "fast-lane" of climate reporting indicates variability in disclosure quality and emphasizes the accountant's role in enhancing opportunity metrics, internal controls, and assurance preparedness (Business Strategy and the Environment, 2024; Dias et al., 2024). Impact monetization broadens their scope: through the application of IWA and SROI, accountants transform vague externalities into quantifiable, verifiable figures that investors, lenders, and public funders can evaluate facilitating results-based finance, SDG-linked instruments, and outcome-focused procurement (Serafeim & Trinh, 2020; Corvo et al., 2022).

Digital competencies have become essential. Systematic evidence associates blockchain with policy-relevant sustainability outcomes, such as traceability and tamper-resistant records, while AI facilitates anomaly detection and narrative analysis-skills that accountants can leverage to improve the integrity and efficiency of ESG/impact reporting (Mulligan et al., 2024). Public sector PFM changes linking budgets to SDG targets necessitate accountants to develop tagging systems, performance frameworks, and procurement criteria that direct resources towards viable entrepreneurial solutions (Manes Rossi et al., 2024). Accountants ultimately transform into sustainability innovators by integrating standards, impact methodologies, and digital frameworks into a unified measurement and control system that mitigates uncertainty, aligns incentives, and expedites capital allocation toward high-impact initiatives.

This development enhances the professionalism of sustainability entrepreneurship, rendering it more attractive for investment, governance, and scalability. Having established the theoretical and institutional foundations of entrepreneurial accounting, the next section operationalizes these insights by examining how green innovation can be embedded within accounting frameworks and management control systems.

These achievements collectively demonstrate the evolution of entrepreneurial accounting from standard reporting functions to a more expansive role in governance and strategic coordination. Sustainability-focused accounting systems progressively link innovation processes, organisational responsibility, and public policy goals via integrated performance assessment and reporting procedures. This part explores the operationalisation of green innovation within accounting and management control frameworks, after the establishment of the conceptual and institutional foundations of Entrepreneurial Accounting for Sustainable Development.

2. INTEGRATING GREEN INNOVATION INTO ACCOUNTING FRAMEWORKS

Green innovation has emerged as a vital element of modern sustainability transitions. Organisations in both the business and public sectors are progressively investing in renewable energy systems, low-carbon technology, circular production methods, and sustainable supply chains. The efficacy of such innovation relies not solely on technological prowess, but also on organisations' capacity to consistently measure, assess, and manage sustainability-related performance in a manner pertinent to decision-making.

Conventional accounting systems frequently fail to account for the comprehensive value produced by green innovation. Traditional financial reporting standards were mostly intended to assess short-term economic success and operational efficiency, rather than long-term environmental sustainability or social effect. Consequently, numerous sustainability-focused investments, especially those related to circular economy initiatives, resource efficiency programs, or climate adaption methods, are challenging to evaluate only through financial metrics.

This constraint has enhanced the significance of sustainability-focused accounting systems that may include environmental, social, and economic factors into managerial decision-making. Recent advancements in Environmental Management Accounting (EMA), carbon management accounting, and circular economy accounting illustrate the evolution of accounting methods from compliance-focused measurement to more strategic and innovation-enhancing roles. Organisations are increasingly utilising sustainability accounting systems to monitor environmental costs and to inform product design, supplier assessment, investment prioritisation, and long-term transition planning.

Sustainability innovation concurrently introduces novel types of organisational complexity. Green technologies frequently entail unpredictable returns, extended investment timelines, fluctuating regulatory environments, and interconnected stakeholder dynamics. Circular economy projects necessitate that organisations assess resource flows, product life cycles, waste recovery systems, and collaborative value networks that transcend conventional organisational boundaries. Therefore, accounting systems must evolve to be more adaptable, proactive, and proficient in facilitating cross-functional collaboration amid uncertainty.

Recent study underscores the necessity for cohesive accounting frameworks that amalgamate financial metrics with environmental data, life-cycle assessments, carbon evaluations, and impact-driven performance indicators. In this overarching trend, techniques like Material Flow Cost Accounting (MFCA), Life Cycle Assessment (LCA), and carbon management accounting increasingly serve as interrelated elements of sustainability governance systems rather than as standalone technical instruments.

Simultaneously, governments and public institutions are enhancing the function of accounting in sustainability governance via green budgeting efforts, sustainable procurement frameworks, and public financial management reforms linked to the Sustainable Development Goals (SDGs). These advancements illustrate that accounting transcends mere organisational reporting, increasingly functioning as a coordinating mechanism that links entrepreneurial innovation, regulatory responsibility, and sustainable development policy goals.

Digital technology significantly expedite this shift. Artificial intelligence, blockchain technology, and sophisticated analytics tools are progressively incorporated into sustainable accounting frameworks to enhance data traceability, reporting uniformity, and performance validation. However, these technologies provide governance difficulties including interoperability, technological complexity, energy consumption, and data reliability, especially for smaller organisations and emerging nations. Consequently, digitalisation need to be perceived not as a replacement for governance, but as a facilitating framework that enhances transparent and accountable sustainability management practices.

In this context, the subsequent subsections analyse the operationalisation of green innovation via distinct accounting frameworks and management control systems, encompassing eco-efficiency measurement, circular economy accounting, sustainable cost management, and green budgeting mechanisms.

2.1 Green Technologies and Eco-Efficiency Metrics

Green technologies-renewable energy, electrification, precision process controls, and sophisticated materials-transform cost structures and risk profiles. Technological adoption generates value only when accompanied by metrics that differentiate efficiency from impact. Eco-efficiency metrics, such as energy or emissions intensity per output, are essential yet inadequate; organizations are progressively augmenting them with transition-aligned KPIs, including abatement cost curves, avoided emissions per unit of capital expenditure, and internal carbon price coverage, to prioritize projects in capital allocation. Evidence suggests that companies implementing Environmental Management Accounting (EMA) to assess resource and emissions intensities realize cost and performance improvements, indicating a transition from short-term compliance to strategic positioning (Swalih et al., 2024).

Figure 1. Entrepreneurial Accounting Integration Pathway: Green Innovation, ESG Reporting, and SDG Impact Measurement

Source: *Author's adaptation based on IFRS Foundation (2025), OECD (2024), and Swalih et al. (2024).*

This diagram illustrates the integrative process in entrepreneurial accounting where Green Innovation initiatives generate sustainability data that inform ESG Reporting, which in turn enables measurable SDG Impact Assessment. The arrows represent the accountability flow linking innovation, disclosure, and outcome evaluation within sustainable development governance.

At the macro–meso level, studies on eco-innovation efficiency employing frontier approaches reveal heterogeneous efficiency and club convergence, underscoring the significance of managerial and institutional competencies in transforming technology into quantifiable benefits (Henriques et al., 2025). The CMA enhances eco-efficiency through the incorporation of scenario analysis and internal carbon budgets into management control systems. A recent synthesis contends that CMA enhances openness and accountability solely when integrated into governance frameworks and underpinned by dependable activity data (Abhishek et al., 2024). In manufacturing and logistics, MFCA reveals concealed expenses associated with waste, rework, and leakage by correlating physical flows with financial losses; when combined with LCA/CFP, MFCA facilitates the comparison of technological options based on unit economics and life-cycle implications (Iqbal et al., 2024).

Empirical research in small and medium-sized enterprises indicates that resource-efficiency initiatives such as energy and water conservation, renewable energy integration, materials reduction, and recycling are associated with enhanced performance, implying that eco-efficiency and eco-innovation are concurrently influenced by managerial practices and learning (Majid et al., 2023). To avert metric myopia, entrepreneurial accounting must include (i) process-level eco-efficiency (intensities), (ii) outcome/impact (absolute reductions versus counterfactuals), and (iii) finance-relevant indicators (EBITDA effects, capital expenditure payback under carbon-price scenarios). This triangulation conforms to standardized reporting (IFRS S1–S2; GRI) while maintaining the value of innovation options the capacity for technology to provide non-linear performance as ecosystems (grids, supply chains) develop. In conclusion, eco-efficiency metrics are essential; nevertheless, the advancement rests in impact-oriented, finance-related measurements that guide green technology towards scalable decarbonization and resilience.

2.2 Accounting for the Circular Economy

Accounting for Circular Economy must monitor inventories and flows within open-loop value chains evolving into closed-loop systems. Recent studies highlight the inadequacies of conventional control systems in Circular Economy contexts and advocate for dialogic methodologies that facilitate experimentation, collaboration among partners, and life-cycle considerations (Aureli et al., 2023). This involves broadening cost objects and responsibility centers beyond the factory gate: design-for-remanufacture, reverse logistics, secondary materials markets, and product-as-a-service models necessitate the assessment of retained value (material quality, embedded energy) and subsequent uses.

Resource accounting (materials, energy, quality attributes) assumes a prominent role. A field study of a digitalized waste-management system illustrates how resource accounting information, along with digital tracking, can promote higher-value recovery and guide pricing, contracting, and investment decisions (Jorgensen, Pedersen, & Skard, 2023).

MFCA implements this principle by quantifying losses in non-product output in monetary terms; when integrated with LCA, it enables managers to prioritize CE initiatives based on environmental and financial returns (Iqbal et al., 2024). Circular transitions, from a governance standpoint, interface with public instruments such as extended producer responsibility, circular economy-oriented procurement, and standardization. Green public procurement (GPP) initiatives and municipal pilots increasingly emphasize durability, repairability, recycled content, and take-back schemes; case studies and review evidence indicate potential while highlighting deficiencies in measurement and verification capabilities (Andersson, 2024; Bhandari et al., 2025). For accountants, this necessitates the establishment of rules that facilitate multi-actor value generation, shared assets, and performance-based contracts that incentivize retained value and the minimization of waste.

Table 1. Comparative Overview of Green Accounting Frameworks

Framework	Focus	Measurement Dimension	Applicability	Example Use
EMA	Resource & Energy Efficiency	Quantitative	Public & Private	Cost & Emission Tracking
CMA	Carbon Externalities	Monetary	Corporate	Carbon Pricing Integration
MFCA	Waste & Resource Flow	Physical–Monetary	Manufacturing	Circular Economy
SROI	Social Value Creation	Monetized Outcomes	NGO/Public	SDG-linked Investments

Source: Author's adaptation based on Swalih et al. (2024), Aureli et al. (2023), and Corvo et al. (2022).

This table presents a comparative summary of key green accounting frameworks Environmental Management Accounting (EMA), Carbon Management Accounting (CMA), Material Flow Cost Accounting (MFCA), and Social Return on Investment (SROI) highlighting their respective focus, measurement dimensions, applicability, and practical examples across sectors. Conceptually, CE accounting prioritizes intertemporal value retention and system boundary decisions over period expenses. Dialogic controls promote stakeholder discourse regarding boundary delineations (e.g., the locus of recovery), valuation methodologies (market versus replacement cost), and the management of quality deterioration in secondary loops.

The research agenda emphasizes interoperable data standards for secondary materials, guarantee of chain-of-custody and recycled content (perhaps utilizing blockchain), and impact-linked incentives that align private circular economy investments with public benefits (Aureli et al., 2023; Jorgensen et al., 2023). CE accounting enables entrepreneurial entities to identify and seize value within loops, converting circular methods into quantifiable, finance-related performance metrics.

2.3 Sustainable Cost Management and Green Budgeting

Sustainable cost management enhances conventional cost discipline by incorporating environmental restrictions into pricing and directing capital towards transition paths. At the firm level, this encompasses: (i) internal carbon pricing and shadow pricing influencing hurdle rates; (ii) eco-design cost models that assess durability and repairability trade-offs; and (iii) supplier scorecards with scope-3 ramifications. The CMA literature consolidates drivers (regulatory pressure, investor scrutiny), mechanisms (carbon budgets, marginal abatement costing, scenario analysis), and outcomes (risk transparency, capital reallocation), while cautioning against isolated implementations devoid of governance integration (Abhishek et al., 2024).

At the systemic level, green budgeting links entrepreneurial initiatives to public funding. The 2024 OECD survey indicates that around two-thirds of OECD nations implement aspects of green budgeting, integrating environmental objectives into budget development, tagging, appraisal, and oversight (OECD, 2024). An accompanying article in the OECD Journal on Budgeting outlines institutional mechanisms (legal mandates, budget classification, spending reviews) and warns that confidence relies on methodological consistency and scrutiny by parliament and Supreme Audit Institutions (Blazey & Lelong, 2022). This architecture generates demand-side signals through procurement and results-based compensation for entrepreneurs, while enhancing fiscal transparency about climate alignment.

Organizations can create sustainable cost maps that connect (a) internal cost drivers (energy, materials, waste), (b) policy levers (taxes, standards, subsidies), and (c) budgetary hooks (program tags, performance indicators) to blend private and public logics. EMA/MFCA discern efficiency potential; CMA transforms them into budget-relevant solutions (e.g., emissions reduction per monetary unit). When procurement incorporates CE/GHG requirements, cost models must consider the whole cost of ownership and end-of-life value. Empirical deficiencies persist: the OECD emphasizes the restricted measurement of GPP impact and budget tagging, indicating a necessity for accountants to develop attribution-aware evaluations across programs (OECD, 2024; 2025).

Sustainable cost management that is proficient in public financial management allows governments, state-owned enterprises, and suppliers to attract financing for abatement and circularity. The way forward: (i) synchronize internal carbon budgets and eco-design cost models with green budget tags; (ii) implement results-based or impact-linked procurement; and (iii) institutionalize verification of environmental classifications. These measures convert cost systems into allocation mechanisms for decarbonization and resilience.

2.4 Case Studies in Public and Private Sectors

Private sector digitized resource accounting for circular economy. A field study on a digitalized municipal waste system demonstrates how resource accounting information captured and disseminated via digital platforms-restructured incentives among collectors, processors, and municipalities, enhancing high-value recovery and informing pricing and contracting (Jorgensen et al., 2023). The instance exemplifies a replicable pattern: when flow-based measurements and quality attributes (e.g., contamination rates, material grade) are quantified and monetized, companies access new profit opportunities in reuse and remanufacturing while mitigating environmental impacts.

Private sector-CMA as a regulatory framework. Companies utilizing CMA alongside internal carbon budgets and scenario-tested KPIs increased openness in investment decisions and better preparedness for sustainability disclosures; yet, efficacy depended on governance integration and data quality (Abhishek et al., 2024). This highlights the importance of accountants in developing decision-grade carbon ledgers and facilitating cross-functional accountability.

Public sector-sustainable budgeting and procurement. Ministries of finance in OECD nations are implementing green budget labeling, conducting spending evaluations, and establishing program classifications to align expenditures with environmental objectives (OECD, 2024). Simultaneously, instances of green public procurement in European municipalities illustrate how demands for durability, repairability, and recycled content can stimulate supplier innovation while exposing deficiencies in verification and life-cycle costing (Andersson, 2024). These public instruments generate market demand for entrepreneurial solutions but require measuring capabilities to assess outcomes (e.g., mitigated emissions, preserved material value).

Intersectoral learning. Efficiency programs based on EMA in manufacturing have influenced municipal circular economy pilots and vice versa: the integration of MFCA and LCA enables both companies and cities to pinpoint leakage spots and prioritize interventions according to dual materiality (financial and environmental) (Iqbal et al., 2024; Swalih et al., 2024). When governments integrate green budgeting with results-based financing, private entities can expand solutions based on verifiable achievements, so mitigating the danger of greenwashing and enhancing access to funding. These stories collectively demonstrate that the use of entrepreneurial accounting stacks (EMA/MFCA/CMA + digital trust + green budgeting) enables firms to transform sustainability aspirations into viable, verifiable, and scalable actions in both public missions and competitive marketplaces.

The integration of green innovation within accounting systems naturally extends into disclosure and accountability mechanisms. The following section therefore examines how ESG reporting frameworks transform entrepreneurial sustainability initiatives into verifiable, investable information.

Mini Case Box: Indonesia's Green Sukuk and Sustainability Accountability

Indonesia's sovereign green sukuk program exemplifies the integration of sustainability-focused accounting, public financial management, and ESG accountability systems within the framework of a growing economy. The green sukuk framework has been utilised to finance projects aimed at environmental sustainability, including renewable energy development, sustainable transport, climate resilience infrastructure, and waste management efforts.

The program uniquely incorporates sustainability reporting and effect verification into public financial governance processes. Government agencies must categorise qualifying expenditures based on environmental objectives and furnish regular reports on climate-related results. This reporting framework enhances transparency, allowing investors and global stakeholders to assess the environmental integrity of financed projects.

The Indonesian example illustrates many implementation issues typically encountered by developing economies. This include challenges in institutional coordination, constraints in data harmonisation, and the technical intricacies related to effect measurement and ESG assurance. Nonetheless, the green sukuk effort demonstrates how innovative accounting procedures can facilitate the convergence of public finance, sustainability reporting, and investment governance focused on the Sustainable Development Goals in developing market contexts.

2.5 Implementation Challenges for SMEs and Developing Economies

Despite its strategic potential, EASD implementation presents significant barriers for small and medium-sized enterprises (SMEs) and organizations operating in developing economies. Unlike large corporations, SMEs often lack specialized sustainability personnel, digital infrastructure, and financial resources necessary to implement blockchain-based traceability systems or AI-driven ESG analytics. Compliance costs associated with IFRS S1–S2 alignment, assurance preparation, and impact monetization can be proportionally burdensome.

Empirical studies suggest that SMEs prioritize short-term liquidity and survival over long-term sustainability integration, particularly in contexts of regulatory uncertainty or limited investor demand. Moreover, fragmented data systems and limited interoperability reduce the feasibility of advanced ESG data management systems in emerging markets.

A phased "roadmap" approach is therefore recommended:

Phase 1 – Foundational Controls:

Basic EMA adoption, simplified carbon accounting, materiality mapping aligned with GRI.

Phase 2 – Strategic Integration:

Internal carbon pricing, supplier sustainability scorecards, gradual alignment with IFRS S1–S2 governance components.

Phase 3 – Advanced Digitalization:

Selective blockchain verification for high-risk supply chains; AI-based anomaly detection; integration into green-financing instruments.

For developing economies, international development banks and regional taxonomies (e.g., ASEAN sustainable finance initiatives) may play a catalytic role by subsidizing transition costs and standardizing reporting templates. Without such incremental and context-sensitive pathways, EASD risks becoming aspirational rather than operational.

Table 2. Illustrative Cost–Benefit Dimensions of EASD Implementation

Dimension	Short-Term Costs	Long-Term Benefits
IFRS S1–S2 Alignment	Staff training, data system upgrades	Improved capital access, investor confidence
Carbon Management Accounting	Data collection, scenario modeling	Risk mitigation, transition resilience
Blockchain Traceability	Infrastructure, technical integration	Fraud reduction, supply-chain transparency
Impact Monetization (IWA/ SROI)	Valuation modeling complexity	Enhanced funding eligibility, outcome-based financing

Source: Developed by the authors based on synthesis of recent sustainability accounting and reporting literature, including IFRS Sustainability Disclosure Standards (IFRS S1 and IFRS S2), Global Reporting Initiative (GRI) Standards, Environmental Management Accounting (EMA) frameworks, Impact-Weighted Accounts (Harvard Business School), Social Return on Investment (SROI) methodologies, and emerging research on blockchain-enabled ESG verification (2020–2025)

This table illustrates that while transition costs are non-trivial, long-term strategic advantages include enhanced credibility, financing access, and governance integration. Table 2 presents an illustrative cost benefit framework for the implementation of Entrepreneurial Accounting for Sustainable Development (EASD). The table synthesizes insights from sustainability reporting standards, transition risk literature, and impact measurement research to demonstrate that while adoption entails measurable short-term costs, the strategic benefits are structural and long-term in nature.

IFRS S1–S2 Alignment.

Compliance with international sustainability disclosure standards requires investments in staff training, governance restructuring, data infrastructure upgrades, and internal control systems. However, empirical capital market research suggests that improved disclosure quality reduces information asymmetry, enhances investor trust, and lowers cost of capital. Thus, the short-term administrative burden is offset by improved access to sustainable finance and enhanced reputational capital.

Carbon Management Accounting.

The introduction of carbon accounting systems involves data collection mechanisms, lifecycle assessment tools, and climate scenario modeling aligned with transition pathways. Although implementation can be resource-intensive, these systems strengthen enterprise risk management by identifying exposure to regulatory shifts, carbon pricing mechanisms, and stranded asset risks. Over time, such integration enhances organizational resilience and strategic positioning within low-carbon transitions.

Blockchain Traceability.

Blockchain-enabled ESG verification requires infrastructure development, interoperability adjustments, and technical expertise. Initial integration costs may be significant, particularly for SMEs. However, blockchain systems improve auditability, reduce fraud risks, enhance supply-chain transparency, and increase stakeholder confidence in non-financial disclosures. The long-term benefits lie in strengthened governance credibility and reduced monitoring costs.

Impact Monetization (IWA/SROI).

Impact valuation methodologies require sophisticated modeling, counterfactual reasoning, and data harmonization across financial and non-financial metrics. These processes may increase analytical complexity and consulting costs. Nevertheless, monetized impact metrics enable outcome-based financing mechanisms, improve eligibility for blended finance and green bonds, and allow organizations to communicate value creation beyond traditional profit metrics.

Conceptual Implication

The cost–benefit structure demonstrates that EASD should not be evaluated solely through immediate compliance expenditures. Instead, it represents a governance transformation investment, where early-stage implementation costs contribute to long-term financial stability, regulatory readiness, stakeholder trust, and sustainable competitive advantage. This reinforces the argument that entrepreneurial accounting is not merely a reporting extension but a strategic reconfiguration of organizational value measurement.

3. ESG REPORTING AND ENTREPRENEURIAL ACCOUNTABILITY

Over the past decade, ESG reporting has transformed from a predominantly voluntary disclosure practice into a more formal governance mechanism that impacts investment decisions, regulatory monitoring, and organisational accountability. sustainable reporting is increasingly recognised not merely as a communication tool for bolstering business legitimacy, but as an integral component of a wider institutional shift towards more transparent and quantifiable sustainable governance.

This shift has been expedited by increasing worldwide apprehensions about climate risk, social inequality, resource scarcity, and the enduring resilience of economic systems. Investors, regulators, public institutions, and civil society organisations increasingly demand that organisations illustrate the integration of sustainability considerations into strategic planning, risk management, and operational decision-making processes. Consequently, ESG reporting frameworks significantly influence how organisations delineate corporate responsibility and assess long-term success.

This transition holds significant ramifications for entrepreneurial organisations. Sustainability-focused innovation frequently entails uncertainty, experimentation, and extended investment timelines, whereas ESG governance systems prioritise consistent disclosure, comparability, and quantifiable responsibility. Entrepreneurial organisations are under growing pressure to convert creative sustainability activities into credible and verifiable organisational reports that meet the demands of investors, regulators, and broader stakeholders concurrently.

In this setting, entrepreneurial responsibility transcends traditional financial reporting to encompass wider systems of sustainable governance. Organisations are increasingly required to elucidate not only the sustainability efforts they implement but also the manner in which these programs produce quantifiable environmental and social results. Thus, ESG reporting is intricately linked to organisational legitimacy, investor credibility, and access to sustainable financing methods.

Recent global sustainability reporting standards, specifically IFRS S1–S2 and the updated GRI Universal Standards, embody this institutional shift. These frameworks promote the incorporation of sustainability-focused governance, risk management, strategic planning, and performance measures into conventional organisational reporting systems. Simultaneously, they reveal considerable implementation issues, such as data fragmentation, inconsistent measurements, inadequate assurance procedures, and disparate institutional capacities among jurisdictions.

The increasing significance of sustainability accountability has concurrently heightened apprehensions about greenwashing and superficial disclosure techniques. Organisations often announce extensive sustainability pledges without adequate evidence of implementation quality or verifiable impact results. This difficulty is notably critical in swiftly growing ESG marketplaces, where discrepancies in non-financial data and inadequate verification procedures persistently erode stakeholder trust and hinder comparison among organisations.

The efficacy of ESG reporting increasingly relies on the calibre of organisational governance processes that underpin sustainability information. Internal controls, assurance procedures, impact evaluation methodology, and digital traceability systems are increasingly essential for credible sustainability accountability. ESG reporting serves not just as an external responsibility but also as an integral component of a comprehensive governance framework that connects organisational transparency, sustainability performance, and enduring institutional trust.

In this context, the subsequent subsections analyse the development of global ESG frameworks, the impact of digital technologies on ESG data management, governance issues in the public sector, and the growing significance of transparency in social entrepreneurship and SDG-focused accountability systems.

3.1 Global ESG Frameworks and Standards

A pragmatic synthesis for entrepreneurs and public innovators entails harmonizing two complementing frameworks: (1) investor-materiality through IFRS S1–S2 and (2) impact materiality via GRI. IFRS S1 mandates the provision of decision-useful sustainability information that may reasonably impact investors' evaluations; IFRS S2 necessitates climate-specific disclosures encompassing governance, strategy (including transition plans), risk management, and metrics/targets, such as Scope 1–3 emissions where relevant. These standards formalize prospective studies (e.g., scenarios) and associate them with enterprise value, improving comparability and access to finance for green enterprises. GRI's Universal Standards (effective 1 January 2023) offer a comprehensive framework for impact reporting (GRI 1/2/3 and sector standards), promoting due diligence-compliant disclosure of an organization's most significant effects on the economy, environment, and society.

Recent cross-firm studies reveal that the quality of climate disclosures is inconsistent, with companies providing more comprehensive information on risks than on opportunities or quantitative transition pathways-this imbalance diminishes the use of such disclosures for innovation financing. Concurrent bibliometric analyses on greenwashing caution that, without stringent governance and verification, an increase in disclosure volume may obscure inadequate impact performance, highlighting the necessity for standardized coherence and verifiable measures. To ensure policy coherence, public financial management (PFM) innovations, particularly green budgeting, are integrating environmental objectives throughout the budget cycle and generating a demand for standardized, verifiable disclosures.

The practical approach is a dual-materiality bridge: Align GRI impact themes with IFRS S1–S2 investor-relevant risks and opportunities, establish common indicators and controls, and integrate them into performance and compensation frameworks. This bridge improves funding preparedness (banks, impact investors, procurement) and mitigates the potential for greenwashing by standardizing narratives, measurements, and audit trails.

Strengthening Assurance and Preventing Greenwashing

An increasing body of literature highlights the paradox of disclosure expansion without proportional impact improvement. Automated ESG reporting systems may unintentionally facilitate sophisticated greenwashing if verification mechanisms remain weak.

To mitigate this risk, EASD must incorporate:

1. Independent third-party assurance
2. Clear counterfactual impact logic
3. Audit trails for non-financial data
4. Harmonization between investor-material and impact-material standards

Auditing non-financial information should move beyond checklist verification toward substantive testing of assumptions, scenario plausibility, and outcome attribution.

3.2 Digital Transformation in ESG Data Management

Digital transformation is progressively altering the methods by which organisations gather, validate, and disseminate sustainability-related information. As ESG reporting mandates expand and become increasingly data-driven, numerous organisations encounter escalating challenges in sustaining reporting uniformity, data integrity, and prompt verification within intricate operational and supply-chain contexts.

In response to these problems, organisations are implementing various digital technologies such as artificial intelligence, blockchain systems, advanced analytics, and automated reporting platforms to enhance ESG data management operations. These technologies have significant opportunity to enhance data traceability, anomaly detection, reporting efficiency, and sustainability verification. Nonetheless, its implementation raises new governance issues pertaining to technical complexity, interoperability, algorithmic transparency, and energy usage.

Figure 2. ESG Data Value Chain

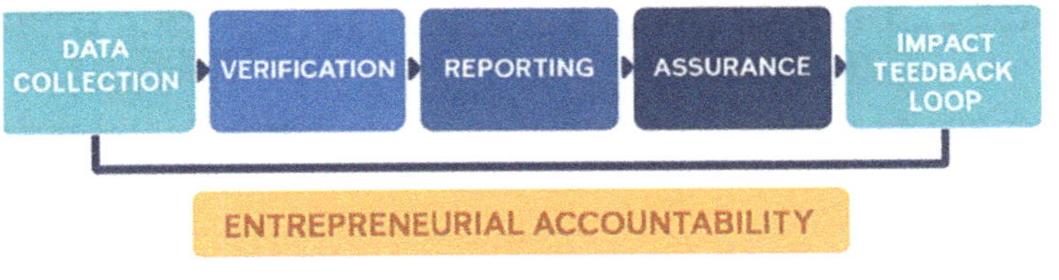

Source: *Author's adaptation based on IFRS Foundation (2025), OECD (2024), and Mulligan et al. (2024).*

This schematic flow illustrates the sequential process of ESG data management beginning with Data Collection, followed by Verification, Reporting, Assurance, and culminating in the Impact Feedback Loop. The overarching layer of Entrepreneurial Accountability ensures governance, transparency, and continuous improvement across all stages. Ongoing market frictions discrepant provider estimates, limited SME data, and disputed scopes persistently hinder allocators, as highlighted by asset-manager surveys and market analyses.

Digital transformation must therefore be linked to standards (IFRS S1–S2, GRI) and controls (access management, segregation of tasks, audit trails) to enhance the quality of evidence from sensor/ERP to disclosure. A functional stack: (i) data ingestion and lineage tracking; (ii) rules engines to uphold standards and calculate metrics; (iii) governance of AI models; (iv) cryptographic proofs or blockchain anchoring for essential assertions; and (v) exports prepared for assurance. This stack mitigates information asymmetry, enhances market trust, and implements entrepreneurial responsibility by connecting project-level evidence to investable, comparable disclosures.

While blockchain and artificial intelligence offer promising mechanisms for enhancing ESG data integrity, their implementation is not cost-neutral nor environmentally neutral. Blockchain infrastructures particularly proof-of-work systems may involve significant energy consumption, potentially contradicting decarbonization objectives. Even energy-efficient architectures require technical expertise and interoperability standards that may exceed SME capabilities.

Similarly, AI-driven ESG analytics depend on high-quality datasets and algorithmic transparency. Without robust governance, automated classification and predictive tools may institutionalize biased assumptions or amplify greenwashing through sophisticated narrative optimization. Therefore, digital tools should be framed as enabling infrastructures rather than substitutes for governance. Their deployment must be accompanied by: energy-efficiency assessments, algorithmic transparency policies, independent assurance mechanisms, cost–benefit evaluation prior to adoption. A realistic EASD framework balances technological innovation with governance maturity and institutional readiness.

3.3 Public Sector ESG Disclosure and Governance Challenges

Public-sector organizations encounter unique limitations: numerous mandates, dispersed outputs, and fragmented data systems across various agencies and levels of government. Recent research in Financial Accountability & Management highlights that attaining the SDGs necessitates public financial management reforms that integrate sustainability into budgeting, performance, and supervision; otherwise, transparency remains merely symbolic. Green budgeting has proliferated swiftly approximately two-thirds of OECD nations reported implementing measures by

2022, such as tagging, carbon budgets, and environmental spending reviews yet methodological uniformity and impact assessment continue to be inconsistent.

Disclosure frameworks derived from the private sector (GRI; emerging ISSB alignment) can enhance transparency but require adaptation for public-value generation and service provision. Analyses of public-sector sustainability reporting indicate persistent deficiencies in capabilities ineffective data collection, inadequate integration with strategy, and irregular external assurance resulting un inconsistent or superficial reporting. Furthermore, regulatory fluctuations, such as judicial challenges to climate regulations in particular jurisdictions, introduce uncertainty for state-owned firms and sub-national governments attempting to establish harmonized baselines.

A viable progression integrates PFM instruments (program budgeting, results-based finance, climate audits by SAIs) with standards-based reporting: (i) SDG-tagged programs aligned with GRI impacts and ISSB risk/opportunity registers; (ii) procurement specifications (repairability, recycled content) documented through verifiable chain-of-custody; and (iii) citizen-facing dashboards that align budget, outputs, and outcomes. Such arrangements transform ESG disclosure from "reporting about" to "governing for" sustainability aligning financial decisions, operational controls, and public accountability. This governance transition enables public entrepreneurs (agencies, SOEs) to scale green solutions by linking funding and procurement to verifiable environmental and social performance.

3.4 Social Entrepreneurship and Impact Transparency

Social enterprise relies on clear and credible effect assertions to attract mixed finance and public backing. Two synergistic methodologies have garnered prominence. Social Return on Investment (SROI) formulates a theory-of-change framework, delineates outcomes with stakeholders, and quantifies social and environmental value through proxies; a systematic review synthesizes its conceptual progress and persistent limitations (attribution, deadweight, valuation choices), highlighting the necessity for methodological rigor and validation. Impact-Weighted Accounts (IWA) convert product, employment, and environmental externalities into monetized entries that accompany financial statements, facilitating comprehension for investors and enabling comparative analysis between alternatives.

At the ecosystem level, bibliometric and empirical research on greenwashing cautions that amplifying impact narratives without substantiated proof undermines confidence; thus, stringent criteria and third-party validation are necessary for social initiatives that claim to achieve SDG results. Digital trust layers can enhance security: blockchain can ensure the integrity of beneficiary and delivery-data provenance (e.g., last-mile health/education), while AI can identify abnormalities in outcome registries; nevertheless, both necessitate governance to mitigate bias and privacy concerns. Allocators are shifting their focus from demonstrating to enhancing impact: systematic studies of impact investing contend that investors must integrate measurement with changes in practice (such as pricing externalities and outcome-linked contracts) to realize their commitments.

A pragmatic transparency framework for social enterprises and public-private collaborations encompasses: (i) dual reporting (GRI/ISSB) for governance and risk management; (ii) an impact assessment methodology (SROI or IWA) tailored to the specific use-case and data accessibility; (iii) transparent methodologies and assumptions (valuation sources, counterfactuals); and (iv) assurance mechanisms (peer review, audit, or verification through digital evidence). This framework mitigates information asymmetry, enhances comparability, and facilitates access for social entrepreneurs to both concessional and commercial capital transforming credible impact into viable investment opportunities.

Table 3. ESG Accountability Components within Entrepreneurial Accounting

Component	Primary Function	Governance Contribution	Key Challenge
IFRS S1–S2	Investor-oriented sustainability disclosure	Risk and strategy integration	Implementation consistency
GRI Standards	Stakeholder impact reporting	Broader accountability transparency	Data comparability
EMA/CMA	Operational sustainability measurement	Resource and carbon management	Organizational integration
IWA/SROI	Impact monetization	Outcome-oriented evaluation	Valuation complexity
Blockchain Systems	Traceability and verification	Data integrity enhancement	Technical scalability
AI Analytics	ESG data processing and anomaly detection	Reporting efficiency	Algorithmic transparency

Source: Developed by the authors based on sustainability accounting and ESG governance literature (2020–2025).

While ESG reporting enhances transparency, sustainable development ultimately requires measurable societal outcomes. The next section therefore advances from disclosure to SDG impact measurement and performance integration.

4. MEASURING SDG IMPACTS THROUGH ENTREPRENEURIAL ACCOUNTING PRACTICES

The increasing worldwide focus on the Sustainable Development Goals (SDGs) has heightened the demand for more thorough methods of assessing organisational performance. Governments, investors, international institutions, and civil society increasingly anticipate that organisations will exhibit not only financial sustainability but also quantifiable benefits to environmental preservation, social inclusiveness, and enduring developmental resilience. As a result, accounting systems face mounting pressure to transition from traditional financial evaluation to more comprehensive sustainability-oriented impact assessment.

Conventional performance measurement techniques frequently encounter significant limitations in this scenario. Financial metrics alone are typically inadequate for assessing climate resilience, social welfare results, ecological restoration, or long-term community effects. Numerous sustainability projects, especially those related to circular economy programs, renewable energy transitions, or public-sector development interventions, produce value that is challenging to quantify using solely short-term accounting criteria. Consequently, organisations often find it challenging to illustrate how sustainability investments provide demonstrable and credible contributions to broader societal outcomes.

These constraints have led to the development of impact-oriented accounting methodologies that aim to amalgamate financial and non-financial aspects of organisational success. Sustainability accounting frameworks are progressively striving to integrate environmental indicators, social consequences, governance structures, and strategic decision-making into cohesive systems of responsibility. In this overarching transition, SDG assessment evolves from a routine reporting activity to a governance tool that shapes organisational priorities, investment distribution, and stakeholder confidence.

Recent advancements in sustainability disclosure standards and impact assessment methodology further bolster this transition. Frameworks like IFRS S1–S2, the GRI Universal Standards, Impact-Weighted Accounts (IWA), and Social Return on Investment (SROI) increasingly urge organisations to assess sustainability results using more systematic and evidence-based methodologies. Despite variations in scope, technique, and institutional focus, these frameworks collectively demonstrate a greater trend toward including societal impact into conventional organisational evaluation systems.

Simultaneously, assessing SDG-related outcomes continues to be methodologically intricate. Organisations persistently encounter difficulties concerning data quality, attribution methodologies, indicator comparability, and the verification of long-term impacts. Sustainability results are frequently multifaceted, context-dependent, and shaped by various actors functioning within interconnected institutional frameworks. Thus, dependable SDG measuring necessitates accounting systems that can incorporate quantitative indicators, governance controls, stakeholder involvement, and assurance procedures within a more flexible and transdisciplinary framework.

Digital technologies progressively facilitate this shift by enhancing data collection, traceability, and analytical capabilities. Artificial intelligence, blockchain technology, sophisticated analytics, and integrated ESG platforms facilitate organisations in efficiently processing substantial amounts of sustainability-related data. Nonetheless, these technologies do not resolve the governance difficulties related to SDG measurement. Instead, they raise further issues related to algorithmic transparency, interoperability, technical capability, and the reliability of non-financial verification methods, especially in developing nations and resource-limited organisations. In this context, the subsequent subsections analyse the primary frameworks, performance systems, and data-driven evaluation instruments presently employed to implement SDG impact measurement in entrepreneurial accounting practices.

4.1 Frameworks for SDG Impact Measurement

The measuring of SDG impact has solidified around the concepts of dual-materiality and methodological pluralism. Regarding standardization, IFRS S1–S2 delineate investor-relevant, decision-useful disclosure mandates encompassing governance, strategy, risk, metrics/targets, and climate-specific elements such as Scope 1–3. In contrast, GRI offers an impact-oriented framework aligned with due diligence and stakeholder implications (IFRS Foundation/ISSB, 2025; GRI, 2023). The interoperability agenda connects various frameworks through common indicators and controls (e.g., emissions intensity, worker safety, community results), facilitating both company value and social impact viewpoints.

Two predominant methodologies exist for impact quantification. IWA quantifies product, employment, and environmental impacts, facilitating direct comparisons of alternatives at the product or portfolio level (Serafeim & Trinh, 2020).

SROI develops a theory of change, involves stakeholders in outcome definition, and utilizes valuation proxies to articulate blended value; a thorough SLR delineates methodological strengths (stakeholder engagement, monetization) and persistent weaknesses (attribution, deadweight, valuation choices) (Corvo et al., 2022). A practical guideline is: employ IWA when product externalities are predominant and market comparability is essential; utilize SROI when programmatic or service outcomes with intricate stakeholder pathways are prevalent.

EMA and flow-based instruments (MFCA, LCA/CFP) support both methodologies by generating decision-grade quantitative data on materials, energy, and emissions (Swalih et al., 2024). These instruments detect hotspots, facilitate abatement cost curves, and reduce model risk in monetization. Ultimately, assurance completes the process: AI-driven analytics can evaluate internal consistency and identify outliers, whilst blockchain can safeguard chain-of-custody and recycled-content assertions (Mulligan et al., 2024).

Two design decisions are paramount. Initially, the establishment of boundaries (organizational, product, or jurisdictional) dictates the SDG methods that are encompassed. Secondly, counterfactuals: IWA's monetization can be associated with scenarios; SROI necessitates clear counterfactual assumptions. When frameworks converge on these characteristics and are integrated into planning and budgeting, SDG measurement transforms into an allocation mechanism rather than a mere reporting exercise.

Although these frameworks offer conceptual foundations for SDG-focused accountability, their efficacy ultimately hinges on the integration of sustainability indicators into routine organisational decision-making and performance monitoring systems. Therefore, the discourse must progress from disclosure frameworks to the operational incorporation of non-financial indicators inside management and governance procedures.

4.2 Integrating Non-Financial Indicators into Performance Systems

Incorporating non-financial variables into performance systems necessitates transforming these indications into incentives. Recent research in EMA indicates a transition from mere compliance to strategic application: metrics on resource intensity, waste, and emissions influence pricing, sourcing, and capital expenditure decisions, and are linked to internal carbon budgets and abatement strategies (Swalih et al., 2024). According to IFRS S1–S2, companies are progressively required to align measurements and targets with governance and strategy, such as linking board supervision and compensation to transition milestones (IFRS Foundation/ISSB, 2025).

Figure 3. Integrated SDG Impact Measurement Architecture

Source: *Developed by the authors based on IFRS Foundation/ISSB (2024; 2025), Global Reporting Initiative (GRI) Universal Standards (2023), OECD Green Budgeting Framework (2024), Serafeim and Trinh (2020), Corvo et al. (2022), and Mulligan et al. (2024).*

Figure illustrates an integrated architecture for SDG impact measurement within Entrepreneurial Accounting for Sustainable Development (EASD). The framework demonstrates how organizational inputs are transformed into measurable SDG outcomes through interconnected stages including green innovation activities, operational sustainability accounting systems, ESG reporting and disclosure frameworks, impact evaluation methodologies, and digital verification infrastructures. The figure highlights the role of accounting as a governance mechanism linking sustainability innovation, accountability, and public value creation.

An effective integration framework comprises: (1) Materiality mapping (linking GRI and IFRS topics to SDG targets); (2) KPI architecture that integrates process metrics (eco-efficiency, safety rates) with outcome metrics (absolute emissions reduction, avoided waste, equitable access); (3) decision rules (shadow pricing, hurdle-rate adjustments, supplier scorecards) that implement KPIs; and (4) review and assurance, featuring AI-driven anomaly detection and audit trails. Research on circular-economy accounting indicates that dialogic controls surpass merely diagnostic controls in innovation contexts, since they facilitate learning and coordinated efforts among life-cycle stakeholders (Aureli et al., 2023).

At the intersection of public finance, green budgeting formalizes non-financial metrics within budget classification, tagging, evaluation, and oversight establishing fiscal incentives that promote the achievement of outcomes (OECD, 2024). However, research warns against mere symbolic adoption: in the absence of methodological consistency and external oversight (e.g., Supreme Audit Institutions), designated budgets may fail to yield quantifiable advancements in Sustainable Development Goals. Recent evaluations of greenwashing for firms emphasize the necessity for a stronger connection between objectives, resource distribution, and validated results (Sundarasen et al., 2024).

Integration is effective when KPI ownership is cross-functional (including operations, finance, and sustainability), data lineage is transparent, and incentives ranging from executive compensation to supplier agreements are congruent with SDG outcomes. Where applicable, outcome-linked contracts (e.g., results-based procurement) associate payments with verifiable indicators, minimizing information asymmetry and accelerating the implementation of high-impact solutions.

As organisations progressively incorporate non-financial metrics into governance frameworks, the significance of dependable and prompt sustainability data escalates. This advancement elucidates the increasing significance of data-driven assessment technologies and digital frameworks in SDG-focused accounting systems.

4.3 Data-Driven Impact Evaluation Tools

Data-driven assessment provides specificity, immediacy, and reliability to assertions of SDG impact. In analytics, AI/ML can automate the classification of narratives (material topics, risk/opportunity tagging), identify anomalies in energy/emissions data, and predict KPI trajectories; preliminary evidence associates AI-driven workflows with enhanced disclosure quality and, in certain contexts, financial performancedependent on governance and data lineage (Alshareef, 2025). Flow-based measurement utilizes EMA/MFCA and LCA/CFP to generate granular signals that may be aggregated into organizational metrics and monetization frameworks (Swalih et al., 2024).

Blockchain provides tamper-proof provenance and chain-of-custody verification for recycled materials, deforestation-free products, and the final delivery of social services. A comprehensive analysis outlines policy-relevant use cases and warns about scalability and interoperability; hybrid modelsoff-chain analytics supported by on-chain proofsare emerging as practical frameworks (Mulligan et al., 2024). In the public sector, green-budget tagging systems and program dashboards are progressively integrating administrative records with geolocation and sensor data; yet, the OECD observes inconsistent methodological rigor and insufficient ex-post evaluation, suggesting a need for attribution-aware solutions (OECD, 2024).

Two methodological safeguards are required. Initially, counterfactual logic necessitates that evaluations distinguish between change and trend, regardless of whether quasi-experimental methods or scenario-based models are employed. Secondly, model governance: AI systems require specified data sources, drift monitoring, and explainability to prevent the automation of greenwashing or bias. Integrating machine learning with explicit theories of change (SROI) or parameterized externality models (IWA) harmonizes empirical strength with conceptual precision (Corvo et al., 2022; Serafeim & Trinh, 2020). When executed comprehensivelysensors/ERP→rules engines/ML→cryptographic anchoring→assurance data-driven assessment revolutionizes SDG reporting from static retrospectives into dynamic decision-making platforms for entrepreneurs, investors, and policymakers.

While several sustainability accounting frameworks derive from international standards and corporate reporting practices, their execution is significantly influenced by regional institutional capabilities and public-sector governance frameworks. Comparative regional experiences offer significant insights into the functioning of SDG-oriented accounting systems across varying developmental and regulatory contexts.

4.4 Comparative Insights: Southeast Asian Public Sector Practices

Southeast Asia offers a conducive environment for public entrepreneurship aligned with the Sustainable Development Goals, utilizing fiscal and regulatory mechanisms to encourage private sector involvement. Across the region, financial ministries are promoting green budgeting through budget tagging, climate expenditure assessments, and program classifications, while state-owned firms are becoming more subject to sustainable disclosure standards (OECD, 2024). The comparison lesson has two aspects. Initially, PFM-integrated variables (such as emissions, resilience, and inclusivity) can generate uniform demand signals via procurement and results-oriented instruments, hence expediting venture adoption. Secondly, capability deficiencies endure: disjointed data systems, restricted assurance capacity, and inconsistent methodological quality frequently result in symbolic rather than meaningful disclosurereflecting findings from public-sector sustainability-reporting evaluations (Manes Rossi et al., 2024).

At the meso level, circular-economy initiatives in municipal services (waste, water, transport) demonstrate how resource accounting and digital tracking can realign incentives within public-private networks, enhancing high-value recovery and guiding tariff and contracting reforms (Jorgensen et al., 2023). Countries implementing green public procurement delineate requirements for durability, recycled content, and repairability, fostering supplier innovation while presenting hurdles in verification and life-cycle costing (Andersson, 2024). Simultaneously, the swift expansion of sustainable finance (such as sovereign/SDG-themed bonds and sukuk) elevates the standards for impact reporting and post-issuance assessment, wherein IWA/SROI frameworks can enhance financial disclosures by linking proceeds to verified outcomes (Serafeim & Trinh, 2020; Corvo et al., 2022).

Cross-country analysis indicates that institutional readinesscomprising legal demands, standards acceptance, data governance, and assurance capacityaffects the efficacy of SDG measurement. In contexts of high readiness, budget allocations and procurement standards yield quantifiable outcomes; conversely, in poor readiness scenarios, reforms may result in mere documentation without tangible advancement. A regional roadmap would prioritize: (i) standardized indicators and data aligned with IFRS/GRI; (ii) centers of excellence for impact evaluation (methods, machine learning, and auditing); (iii) the expansion of results-based procurement with verifiable chains of custody (utilizing blockchain where applicable); and (iv) capacity-building for Supreme Audit Institutions and sub-national governments. These measures transform ESG/SDG disclosure from a mere compliance obligation into a governance technology that activates entrepreneurial solutions throughout Southeast Asia.

While Southeast Asia provides a dynamic laboratory for fiscal innovation, comparative insights from the European Union (CSRD implementation), Latin American green bond frameworks, and African Development Bank sustainable finance initiatives indicate varying institutional readiness levels. These comparisons reinforce that regulatory alignment must be accompanied by capacity development and assurance strengthening to avoid symbolic compliance.

Comparative experiences throughout Southeast Asia indicate that the efficacy of SDG-oriented entrepreneurial accounting relies more on institutional coordination capacity, data governance quality, and assurance readiness than merely on the formal presence of sustainability legislation. Countries exhibiting robust integration of public financial management systems, sustainability disclosure regulations, and procurement monitoring procedures typically achieve more quantifiable sustainability outcomes. In contrast, governments with disjointed reporting systems and inadequate verification infrastructure frequently find it challenging to convert sustainability pledges into practical responsibility. The regional disparities underscore the significance of enhancing institutional capacity as a fundamental element of sustainable entrepreneurial accounting execution.

5. POLICY AND INSTITUTIONAL PATHWAYS FOR SUSTAINABLE ENTREPRENEURIAL ACCOUNTING

The progress of Entrepreneurial Accounting for Sustainable Development (EASD) relies on both organisational innovation and the wider institutional contexts that govern and execute sustainability practices. Despite the rapid advancement of sustainability accounting frameworks, ESG reporting standards, and impact measurement methodologies, their efficacy ultimately depends on the presence of supportive policy systems, institutional capacities, and governance infrastructures that can convert sustainability commitments into operational accountability.

Sustainability governance is progressively transitioning from voluntary initiatives to more official legal and institutional frameworks across numerous jurisdictions. Governments, international organisations, financial regulators, and public-sector institutions are increasingly incorporating sustainability goals into budgeting systems, procurement processes, transparency mandates, and investment frameworks. This institutional change signifies an increasing acknowledgement that sustainable development issues cannot be resolved through separate organisational efforts alone, but necessitate integrated governance frameworks that integrate public policy, financial institutions, and entrepreneurial innovation.

Simultaneously, institutional preparedness is markedly inconsistent across many areas and industries. Although certain nations have established advanced sustainability disclosure frameworks, green budgeting mechanisms, and ESG assurance systems, numerous developing economies still encounter significant constraints concerning technical proficiency, regulatory alignment, data management, and execution capability. Thus, the efficacy of EASD relies not only on the presence of sustainability frameworks but also on institutions' capacity to operationalise, monitor, and consistently check sustainability-related information.

The institutional aspect is crucial as sustainable accounting increasingly serves as a governance tool rather than solely a reporting instrument. Accounting systems currently affect governmental resource allocation, investor assessments of organisational legitimacy, organisational management of transition risks, and public institution monitoring of SDG-related results. Sustainability accounting methods are being integrated into public financial management systems, policy coordination, and governance of sustainable development.

Recent advancements in green budgeting, ESG regulation, sustainable finance taxonomies, and digital assurance systems illustrate the increasing convergence of sustainability accounting and institutional governance mechanisms. Simultaneously, these advancements reveal significant obstacles, such as fragmented regulatory requirements, inconsistent reporting procedures, limitations in assurance, and unequal access to technology infrastructure, particularly among SMEs and emerging nations.

In this context, the subsequent subsections analyse the policy instruments, institutional capabilities, educational frameworks, and governance strategies necessary to enhance Entrepreneurial Accounting for Sustainable Development as a functional and globally applicable sustainability governance framework.

5.1 Policy Instruments Supporting Entrepreneurial Sustainability

Policy instruments are becoming increasingly vital in determining the financing, monitoring, and governance of sustainability-oriented entrepreneurial operations. In recent years, governments and international organisations have broadened the implementation of sustainability-oriented regulatory frameworks, fiscal incentives, green procurement systems, and ESG disclosure mandates to promote organisational conformity with climate and sustainable development goals. These policy tools affect organisational reporting behaviour, investment patterns, innovation priorities, and public accountability systems.

Figure 4. Policy and Institutional Pathway for Sustainable Entrepreneurial Accounting

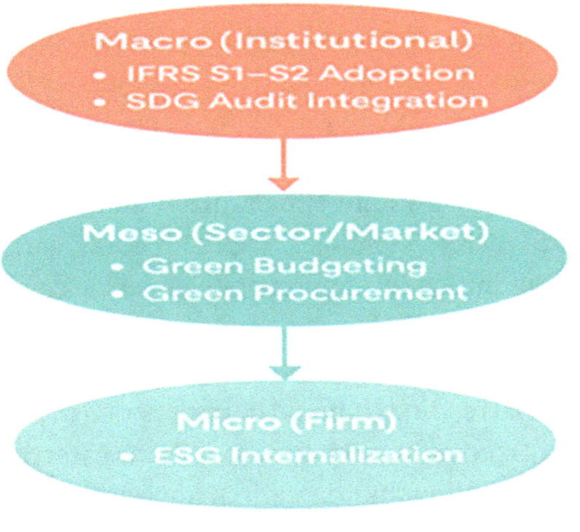

Source: *Author's adaptation based on IFRS Foundation (2025) and OECD (2024).*

This infographic illustrates a multi-level policy structure for sustainable entrepreneurial accounting. The Macro (Institutional) level includes IFRS S1–S2 adoption and SDG audit integration; the Meso (Sector/Market) level features green budgeting and procurement frameworks; and the Micro (Firm) level highlights ESG internalization within organizational practices.

Empirical research indicates that policy combinations-laws coupled with incentives yield enhanced results for innovation and accountability (Kivimaa et al., 2021). Green procurement norms that mandate lifecycle costing have stimulated eco-design innovation in municipal services (Andersson, 2024). In contrast, disjointed policies result in compliance fatigue and inconsistent measurements. Therefore, governments ought to implement policy coherence frameworks that synchronize national sustainability initiatives, corporate reporting standards, and entrepreneurial financing programs.

Developing jurisdictions within ASEAN provide valuable frameworks: Indonesia's SDG-aligned sovereign sukuk directs funds towards validated green initiatives, accompanied by comprehensive reporting and external verification; Malaysia and Singapore utilize ESG taxonomies to mitigate risks associated with green financing (ADB, 2023). A comprehensive policy instrument framework thereby integrates obligatory transparency, fiscal alignment, and market innovation. When combined with reliable indicators and audits, these tools transition incentives from mere compliance to ongoing enhancement, establishing accounting as a strategic catalyst for entrepreneurial sustainability.

5.2 Institutional Readiness and Capacity Building

Institutional readiness influences the implementation of policy into practice. Recent comparative research indicates that readiness is contingent upon (1) legal requirements for sustainability reporting, (2) inter-agency coordination frameworks, and (3) assurance and audit capabilities (Manes Rossi et al., 2024). In the presence of these requirements, data flows are standardized and subject to audit; in their absence, disclosures are merely symbolic. OECD nations with specialized green-budget units and training initiatives demonstrate superior consistency and quality in impact evaluation (OECD, 2024).

Capacity building include not just technical skills but also institutional culture.

Ultimately, institutional readiness should be understood as a dynamic governance capability rather than a fixed administrative condition. Effective sustainability accounting systems require continuous adaptation, inter-agency coordination, professional learning, and technological upgrading in response to evolving sustainability standards and policy expectations. Institutions that are capable of integrating these dimensions are generally better positioned to transform sustainability reporting from symbolic compliance into measurable public accountability.

5.3 Entrepreneurial Education and Research Integration

In addition to curriculum change, universities and research institutions increasingly serve as intermediary entities linking sustainability governance, entrepreneurial ecosystems, and professional accounting practices. Collaborative research projects, public-sector collaborations, and ESG-focused innovation laboratories can enhance the practical use of sustainability accounting frameworks by converting theoretical models into operational governance instruments. This intermediary position is especially crucial in developing countries, where institutional learning and the enhancement of professional ability are significant implementation obstacles.

The integration of research is equally essential. Sustainability accounting research should shift focus to policy-impact studies and digital approaches, such as AI-assisted assurance and blockchain transparency. Interdisciplinary initiatives connecting accounting, information systems, and public policy departments can produce scalable models for developing nations. Funding agencies and governments should endorse such consortia via competitive grants and open data platforms. Ultimately, the integration of education and research fosters a self-sustaining ecosystem in which academics provides expertise and empirical support for policy and entrepreneurial endeavors.

5.4 Toward a Global Framework for Sustainable Entrepreneurial Accounting

A worldwide framework for SEA would integrate current standards and innovative methodologies into a unified governance structure. The framework is based on three integration axes: (1) normative coherence the alignment of IFRS S1–S2 investor-material disclosures with GRI's impact-material approach; (2) methodological integration the harmonization of impact monetization methods (IWA, SROI) with EMA/MFCA/LCA for traceable and auditable measurement; and (3) digital interoperability the use of shared taxonomies and blockchain-enabled assurance (Mulligan et al., 2024; Serafeim & Trinh, 2020).

A global framework should delineate minimal capability standards: governance mechanisms for data integrity, independent assurance mandates, and visible capacity-building pathways for developing nations. The OECD and IFAC advocate for the integration of SDG tagging and sustainability audits into public financial management systems (OECD, 2024). Empirical research indicates that nations that attain standard alignment and capacity development concurrently exhibit superior SDG outcomes (Manes Rossi et al., 2024).

ASEAN and African Development Bank (ADB, 2023) projects illustrate that regional cooperation can expedite convergence via unified taxonomies and training. A global SEA framework may function similarly to the Basel Accords: principle-based norms enacted locally, however synchronized through peer review and capacity building. Digital infrastructure and open-data norms would support comparability and confidence.

Ultimately, a global SEA framework is not a novel standard but a meta-framework that integrates current standards and guarantees the integrity of their influence. By integrating policy, institutional capacity, education, and digital governance, this paradigm would position accounting at the center of global initiatives to finance and manage sustainable development.

Entrepreneurial Accounting for Sustainable Development signifies a comprehensive shift in the manner organisations conceptualise accountability, value generation, and enduring performance throughout sustainability transitions. Entrepreneurial accounting is evolving from a mere technical reporting tool to an integrated governance framework that links innovation, financial systems, institutional monitoring, and societal results. The unification of ESG reporting standards, impact assessment methodology, sustainability-focused management accounting, and digital verification systems signifies a broader institutional shift towards more quantifiable, transparent, and results-driven strategies for sustainable development.

The efficacy of these frameworks is significantly contingent upon the quality of governance, institutional preparedness, and implementation capability. Sustainability accounting systems are incapable of producing significant SDG impacts without credible assurance procedures, coordinated public policy frameworks, dependable data infrastructures, and a commitment to genuine organisational accountability. Thus, forthcoming advancements in Entrepreneurial Accounting for Sustainable Development will probably rely less on the expansion of new reporting frameworks and more on the capacity of organisations and institutions to assimilate existing sustainability standards into cohesive governance and decision-making systems.

The chapter emphasises the necessity for researchers to conduct more multidisciplinary and empirically based studies that investigate the functioning of sustainability accounting systems across various institutional and regional contexts. The discourse highlights the necessity for policymakers and practitioners to synchronise sustainability disclosure, public financial management, impact evaluation, and digital governance frameworks with overarching sustainable development strategies. Ultimately, Entrepreneurial Accounting for Sustainable Development should be perceived not merely as an extension of traditional accounting practices, but as a strategic tool for orchestrating innovation, accountability, and the creation of public value within an increasingly sustainability-focused global economy.

REFERENCES

Abhishek, N., Suraj, N., Muralidharan, M., Singh, A., & Chattopadhyay, A. (2024). Carbon management accounting: An evolving approach to enhance transparency and accountability in accounting and reporting practices. *Journal of Accounting & Organizational Change, 21*(3), 535–566. DOI: 10.1108/JAOC-05-2024-0156

Alshareef, M. N. (2025). Artificial intelligence-enhanced ESG disclosure quality and financial performance nexus in Saudi listed companies under Vision 2030. *Sustainability, 17*(16), 7421. DOI: 10.3390/su17167421

Andersson, I. (2024). Green innovative procurement in the municipality sectorPotential and challenges. *Geografisk Tidsskrift-Danish Journal of Geography, 124*(2), 141–155. DOI: 10.1080/00291951.2024.2395255

Asian Development Bank (ADB). (2023). *ASEAN Taxonomy for Sustainable Finance: Version 2*. ADB Publishing., DOI: 10.22617/TCS230092-2

Aureli, S., Foschi, E., & Paletta, A. (2023). Management accounting for a circular economy: Current limits and avenue for a dialogic approach. *Accounting, Auditing & Accountability Journal, 36*(9), 291–319. DOI: 10.1108/AAAJ-04-2022-5766

Bhandari, S., Liaqat, S., & Henao, D. (2025). Green public procurement as an effective way for sustainable development: A systematic literature review and bibliometric analysis. *Sustainable Development (Bradford), 33*(2), 2364–2391. Advance online publication. DOI: 10.1002/sd.3234

Blazey, A., & Lelong, M. (2022). Green budgeting: A way forward. *OECD Journal on Budgeting, 22*(2), 1–32. DOI: 10.1787/dc7ac5a7-en

Corvo, L., Pastore, L., Mastrodascio, M., & Cepiku, D. (2022). The social return on investment model: A systematic literature review. *Meditari Accountancy Research, 30*(7), 49–86. DOI: 10.1108/MEDAR-05-2021-1307

Dias, A. I., Rodrigues, L. L., & Branco, M. C. (2024). Gender diversity and climate disclosure: A TCFD perspective. *Environment, Development and Sustainability, 26*(3), 1–27. DOI: 10.1007/s10668-024-05203-2

Global Reporting Initiative. (2023). *Universal Standards* (GRI 1, 2, 3). https://www.globalreporting.org/standards/

Global Reporting Initiative (GRI). (2023). *Universal Standards* (GRI 1, 2, 3)effective 1 January 2023. https://www.globalreporting.org/standards/standards-development/universal-standards/

Henriques, C., Caldeirinha, V. R., & Ferreira Dias, J. (2025). Evaluating eco-innovation efficiency and club convergence in the EU: 2016–2023. *Journal of Cleaner Production, 463*, 143998. DOI: 10.1016/j.jclepro.2024.143998

IFRS Foundation. (2024). *Progress on corporate climate-related disclosures2024 report*. IFRS/ISSB.

IFRS Foundation / ISSB. (2025). *Introduction to the ISSB and IFRS sustainability disclosure standards (IFRS S1 and IFRS S2).* https://www.ifrs.org/sustainability/knowledge-hub/introduction-to-issb-and-ifrs-sustainability-disclosure-standards/

IFVI (Impact-Weighted Accounts Initiative). (2022). *Practitioner guide to calculating employment impact-weighted accounts.* https://ifvi.org/wp-content/uploads/2023/10/Practitioner-Guide-to-Calculating-Employment-Impact-Weighted-Accounts.pdf

International Financial Reporting Standards (IFRS) Foundation. (2023). General sustainability-related disclosures (IFRS S1) and climate-related disclosures (IFRS S2): Project summary and resources. https://www.ifrs.org/projects/completed-projects/2023/general-sustainability-related-disclosures/

Iqbal, M., Hati, H. P., & Irfan, A. (2024). Carbon management accounting considerations for MFCA and LCA integration. *International Journal of Sustainable Development and Planning*, *19*(5), 399–407. DOI: 10.18280/ijsdp.190536

Jorgensen, S., Pedersen, L. J. T., & Skard, S. (2023). Resource accounting for a circular economy: Evidence from a digitalised waste management system. *Accounting Forum*, *47*(4), 553–582. DOI: 10.1080/01559982.2023.2166001

Kivimaa, P., Hilden, M., & Kern, F. (2021). Policy mixes for sustainability transitions: New approaches and challenges. *Environmental Innovation and Societal Transitions*, *41*, 1–12. DOI: 10.1016/j.eist.2021.01.004

KPMG. (2025, October 10). Navigating the IFRS sustainability disclosure standards (IFRS S1 and IFRS S2). https://kpmg.com/ch/en/services/audit/esg-reporting-assurance/ifrs-s1-s2.html

Majid, S., Yasmeen, H., Rehman, A., & Saeed, I. (2023). Eco-efficiency, environmental and sustainable innovation in SMEs. *Sustainability*, *15*(12), 9465. DOI: 10.3390/su15129465

Manes Rossi, F., Brusca, I., Cohen, S., Caperchione, E., & Thomasson, A. (2024). Public financial management for Sustainable Development Goals: Challenges, experiences, and perspectives. *Financial Accountability & Management*, *40*(4), 1007–1016. DOI: 10.1111/faam.12424

Mulligan, C., Morsfield, S., & Cheikosman, E. (2024). Blockchain for sustainability: A systematic literature review for policy impact. *Telecommunications Policy*, *48*(2), 102676. DOI: 10.1016/j.telpol.2023.102676

OECD. (2024). *Green budgeting in OECD countries 2024*. OECD Publishing., DOI: 10.1787/9aea61f0-

Serafeim, G., & Trinh, K. (2020). A framework for product impact-weighted accounts (HBS Working Paper No. 20-076). SSRN. https://doi.org/DOI: 10.2139/ssrn.3532472

Sundarasen, S., Ooi, C. A., Heng, T. N., & Santoso, B. H. (2024). Sustainability reporting and greenwashing: A bibliometrics review and future research agenda. *Cogent Business & Management*, *11*(1), 2320812. DOI: 10.1080/23311975.2024.2320812

Sustainability Standards Board (GRI). (2023). GRI Standards: Universal Standards (2021) in effect from 1 January 2023. https://www.globalreporting.org/standards/

Swalih, M. M., Chithra, K. V., & Raj, R. G. (2024). Environmental management accounting for strategic decision-making: A systematic review. *Business Strategy and the Environment*, *33*(7), 6335–6367. Advance online publication. DOI: 10.1002/bse.3828

Chapter 9

Entrepreneurship and Marketing in Agri-Waste Valorization:

An Innovative and Sustainable Business Venture

Shormistha Majumdar
http://orcid.org/0009-0007-8855-8912
Woxsen University, Hyderabad, India

Preethi Venkannagari
Woxsen University, Hyderabad, India

Sai Sriya Tunuguntla
Woxsen University, Hyderabad, India

Subhranshu Biswas
Woxsen University, Hyderabad, India

Venkat Reddy Yasa
http://orcid.org/0009-0005-5775-2806
Woxsen University, Hyderabad, India

Pawan Prabhakar
http://orcid.org/0000-0002-3665-9486
Woxsen University, Hyderabad, India

ABSTRACT

Entrepreneurship in agri-waste valorization has arisen as a transformational strategy for tackling environmental issues while creating economic prospects. Entrepreneurs significantly contribute to sustainability and the circular economy by transforming agricultural wastes, food industry by-products, and other biomass waste into profitable products. The valorization of agricultural waste has several prospects in industries like bioenergy, biomaterials, biochemicals, and functional food components like phytocompounds. Entrepreneurs entering this sector enhance resource efficiency while generating employment opportunities, for rural and marginalized people. Nevertheless, obstacles such as insufficient funds, technical proficiency and legal impediments sometimes obstruct the growth of agri-waste valorization initiatives.

DOI: 10.4018/979-8-3373-7391-1.ch009

Therefore, in this chapter an extensive discussion has been done on entrepreneurial activity related to agri-waste valorization, problem and challenges and its significant potential to mitigate environmental and economic concerns.

1. INTRODUCTION

The increase in worldwide agricultural output has resulted in a significant rise in agricultural waste, encompassing various organic by-products such as crop residues, peels from fruits and vegetables, seed husks, nut shells, stems, stalks, leaves, bran, bagasse, and other processing remnants (Rao et al. 2024; Saxena et al., 2024). As food consumption increases owing to population expansion, urbanisation, and changes in dietary habits, agricultural output has risen significantly, resulting in greater waste production at every stage of the supply chain from farm to table (Singh et al., 2023). The increase of agricultural waste presents considerable environmental, economic, and logistical difficulties. A significant portion of this biomass is frequently left uncollected or incinerated in open areas, resulting in substantial air pollution, greenhouse gas emissions, and the loss of potentially valuable organic matter (Abubakar et al., 2022; Karungamye, 2024). In underdeveloped nations, insufficient waste management infrastructure and a lack of awareness intensify the issue, leading to soil and water resource degradation and public health hazards due to the proliferation of pests and illnesses. This extensive array of organic wastes is becoming acknowledged not just as a disposal challenge, but as a significant resource pool that may be converted into valuable goods through agri-waste valorization (Kibria et al., 2023; Raphela et al., 2024). The recent progress made in biotechnology, green chemistry, and cost-effective processing technologies has created novel avenues for transforming waste materials into bioenergy (including biogas and bioethanol), biofertilizers, compost, natural dyes, animal feed, packaging materials, biochar, and even nutraceuticals and cosmetic products (Mishra et al., 2023; Ezeorba et al., 2024). These improvements correspond with the tenets of the circular economy, in which waste is reintegrated into the production cycle, thereby diminishing dependence on non-renewable resources and lessening environmental impacts. The exponential increase in agricultural waste has prompted a transformation in viewpoint from waste management to resource exploitation-fostering opportunities for sustainable entrepreneurship, rural advancement, and industrial innovation (Tomić et al., 2020; Avilés-Palacios et al., 2021). The higher amount of agricultural waste necessitates immediate action to exploit its inherent potential by deliberate technological adoption, and value chain integration and governmental policy and guideline interventions. This necessitates cooperative endeavours among farmers, scientists, entrepreneurs, policymakers, and consumers to formulate and endorse systems that diminish waste while facilitating its transformation into environmentally sustainable and economically feasible products. Such activities can convert the difficulty of agricultural waste creation into a significant opportunity to promote green innovation, advance climate objectives, and promotesd a more sustainable and resilient agricultural economy (Kirchherr et al., 2023; Malau et al., 2024). As agriculture remains a major occupation for millions worldwide, specially in developing and agrarian economies, the challenge of managing the increasing volume of agricultural waste-comprising crop residues, fruit and vegetable peels, husks, shells, and various post-harvest by-products has acquired heightened urgency amid intensifying climate change, escalating environmental degradation, and increasing resource scarcity (Duque-Acevedo et al., 2020). The global agricultural system, essential for food security and livelihood sustainability, is fundamentally resource-intensive, utilising significant quantities of water, land, energy, and chemical inputs. Thus, the by-products produced throughout the production, harvesting, processing, and distribution phases have emerged as substantial sources of pollution if not properly controlled (Robinson, 2024). If mistreated or poorly disposed of through open-field burning or landfill dumping these organic residues contribute to air and water pollution, release strong greenhouse gases such as methane and nitrous oxide, and impair soil fertility over time (Koul et al., 2022). Furthermore, in areas where agricultural cycles are closely linked to local ecological systems and livelihoods, the improper management of agricultural waste intensifies susceptibility to climate variability, endangers biodiversity, and compromises the resilience of long-term food supply (Mihai et al., 2021). This paradigm shift is driving the development of innovative circular models that reconstitute waste as a resource, reintegrating it into the production cycle via valorization processes that yield bioenergy, compost, natural fibres, biodegradable packaging, organic soil amendments, and other environmentally advantageous products. Tackling the agricultural waste issue not only corresponds with sustainability objectives but also fosters inclusive prospects for rural entrepreneurship, job creation, and decentralised, community-oriented resource management systems (Pal et al., 2024). Therefore, the management of agricultural waste transcends mere technical or environmental issues; it has become a socioeconomic and developmental necessity that demands immediate, coordinated efforts from farmers, researchers, entrepreneurs, policymakers, and civil society to enhance the efficiency, circularity, and resilience of agricultural systems in response to a rapidly evolving planet (Duque-Acevedo et al., 2022). Agricultural wastes, once deemed low-value, burdensome, or nuisance materials that were frequently discarded, incinerated, or allowed to decompose, are now being redefined within the framework of the circular economy as valuable and versatile feedstocks to produce bio-based, value-added products. This change in perspective is propelled by an increasing global acknowledgement of the imperative to move from linear, wasteful production models to more regenerative, resource-efficient systems that reduce environmental impact while enhancing economic usefulness (Smith, 2025). In this context, agricultural waste including crop residues, husks, fruit peels, shells, bagasse, and other organic by-products is progressively utilised as a renewable resource for producing a diverse array of sustainable products such as compost and biofertilizers, which restore soil nutrients and diminish reliance on synthetic chemicals; bioplastics and biodegradable packaging materials, which provide environmentally friendly alternatives to petroleum-based plastics; and biochar, which improves soil fertility and sequesters carbon, thereby aiding in climate change mitigation (Ratu et al.,2023; Guo et al., 2024). Moreover, the conversion of agricultural waste into biogas via anaerobic digestion generates clean energy for rural households and decentralised power systems, while sophisticated biorefining technologies can isolate high-value compounds such as antioxidants, polyphenols, flavonoids, and essential oils for application in nutraceuticals, pharmaceuticals, and functional foods (Singh et al., 2023).

Agri-waste is being utilised in the formulation of animal feed, substituting costlier and less sustainable ingredients, as well as in the manufacture of construction materials such as agri-based composites, insulation boards and bricks, thereby diminishing the ecological impact of the building sector. These advances mitigate environmental impacts, including greenhouse gas emissions, water pollution, and land use pressures, while also generating economic opportunities throughout the value chain, encompassing farmers, processors, entrepreneurs, and academics (Kordi et al., 2024; Pamu and Alugubelli, 2025). The circular economy paradigm redefines trash as a resource, facilitating closed-loop systems that are fundamentally more sustainable and robust. This paradigm promotes a revaluation of agricultural production and post-harvest processes, compelling stakeholders to develop and invest in technology, laws, and business models that facilitate agri-waste valorization. This approach facilitates the emergence of a new generation of bioeconomy firms rooted in sustainability, inclusivity, and local empowerment, illustrating how materials formerly seen as garbage may, with appropriate interventions, serve as a foundation for green economic development (Maraveas, 2020; Khalife, 2024). This paradigm shift has unlocked a vast spectrum of entrepreneurial opportunities where small enterprises can thrive by combining innovation, sustainability, and locally available resources (Manzoor et al., 2024). Therefore, sustainable agribusiness aims to fulfil the increasing global demands for food, fibre, and fuel while safeguarding environmental integrity, maintaining economic viability, and promoting social fairness. In this setting, entrepreneurship and marketing are essential in connecting agricultural production with consumer demand, promoting innovation, minimising waste, and establishing inclusive rural economies (Gadanakis, 2024; Prabhakar et al., 2025). This paper also provides a conceptual framework that situates agricultural waste within the larger context of the circular economy and sustainable agriculture. The swift development of agriculture, propelled by population growth, urbanisation, and evolving consumption patterns, has markedly augmented the production of residues, including crop stalks, husks, fruit peels, shells, and other post-harvest by-products. Usually, these materials are discarded via open burning or landfilling, resulting in environmental deterioration, greenhouse gas emissions, and suboptimal resource utilisation. The framework designates agri-waste valorisation as the primary transformative process, facilitated by innovations in biotechnology, green chemistry, and bio-refining technologies. Agricultural leftovers can be transformed into value-added products such as bioenergy, compost, biofertilizers, biodegradable packaging, charcoal, and animal feed through these methods. The paradigm additionally integrates entrepreneurship, innovation, and market growth as intermediary elements linking technical potential to economic feasibility. Facilitated by robust policy, institutional cooperation, and stakeholder engagement, these processes jointly enhance environmental sustainability, rural economic advancement, and resilient agricultural systems as shown in Figure-1 given below.

Figure 1. Transforming agricultural waste within the circular economy: The conceptual framework that positions agricultural waste within the broader context of the circular economy and sustainable agribusiness

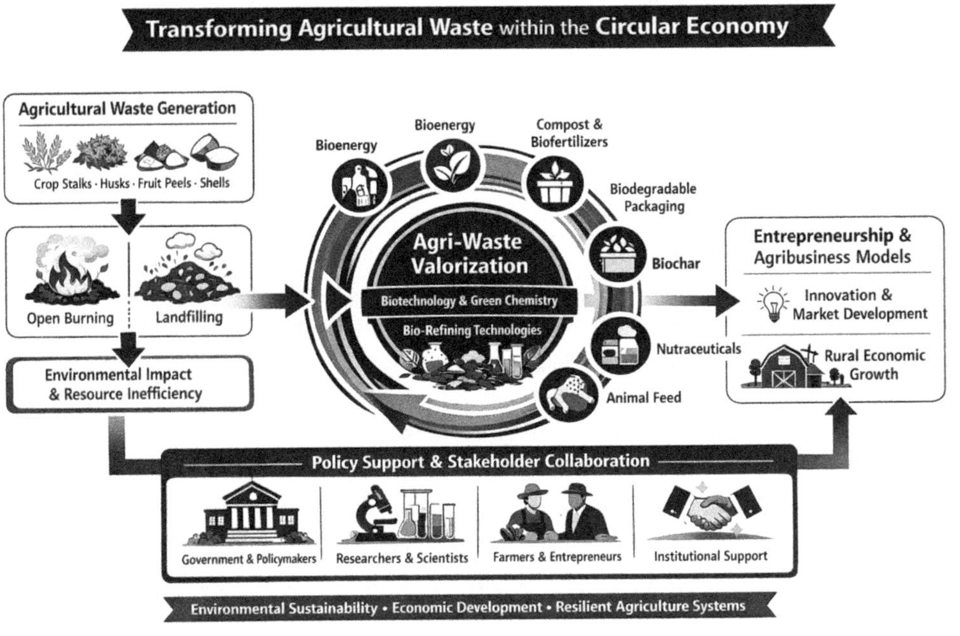

2. CONCEPT OF AGRI-WASTE VALORIZATION

Agri-waste valorization denotes the systematic conversion of agricultural waste into valuable goods, hence transitioning waste management from a disposal paradigm to a resource recovery framework. This is consistent with the tenets of the circular economy, enhancing sustainability, minimising carbon emissions, and cultivating new economic prospects (Sonam, 2018; Isah and Ozbay, 2020). The handling of agricultural waste presents significant challenges, impacting not just agriculture but also ecosystem conservation and sustainability (Ezeorba et al., 20204). Agricultural waste comprises the wastes produced as by-products during the harvesting and processing of agricultural products, particularly crops. Crop leftovers can be classified into two primary categories: field residues and agro-food processing residues, distinguished by their processing methods. These residues are inedible components of the crops; hence, they pose no risk or threat to the food supply competition or any disruption to current food security concerns or arable land. Agricultural and forestry residues are regarded as substantial sources of environmental trash. This trash serves as a potential resource for the development and manufacture of biofuels following the pretreatment of the available biomass in relevant places (Sadh et al., 2018; Bala et al., 2023).

Agricultural and forestry leftovers comprise rice husks, straws, timber, and other plant materials abundant in lignocellulosic content. Agricultural waste and crop leftovers consist of dry matter, with 35–50% cellulose, 20–35% hemicellulose, 15–20% lignin, and 15–20% extractive chemicals, including ash and protein. The ligament content in various crops ranges from 7% to 21%. The byproduct derived from processed agricultural products exhibits a substantial ratio of 21% to 45%, comprising 15% to 33% hemicellulose and 5% to 24% lignin The content ratio is significantly influenced by its source of origin. Waste rice bran is regarded as having a low lignin content of up to 5% and is viewed as a promising feedstock for bioethanol production (Devi et al., 2022). The waste material with elevated lignin concentration, such as sugarcane bagasse, necessitates pretreatment to eliminate excess lignin prior to ethanol production. The optimal raw material for biohydrogen, biogas, and alcohol production must possess specific qualities, including carbohydrates, which diminish due to their ease of breakdown. This waste can be classified based on various origins, including field waste, which comprises different crop components such as leaves, stems, stalks, husks, and roots; industrial waste, produced during the processing of agricultural or animal products, including byproducts from the food sector; livestock waste, which includes materials such as bedding, animal carcasses, and wastewater from animal hygiene; and food waste, consisting of edible food portions discarded at multiple stages of the food production (Jin et al., 2020; Beluhan et al., 2023). Various studies indicate that neglected and/or untreated agricultural waste is frequently disposed of by incineration, dumping, or landfilling. These practices substantially exacerbate greenhouse gas emissions (GHGs), generate harmful gaseous byproducts, contaminate soil and waterways, jeopardise wildlife through ingestion or entanglement, and facilitate the emergence of diseases, thereby threatening environmental integrity and the health of both animals and humans through multiple avenues (Siddiqua et al., 2022). The objective is to reduce waste production, lessen environmental repercussions, and generate economic prospects by converting agricultural waste into useful resources. By valorising agricultural waste, farmers and agricultural companies may enhance sustainable practices, optimise resource efficiency, and promote the circular economy. Diverse methodologies and technologies are currently implemented to extract useful resources from this waste, including organic matter, energy, significant bioactive chemicals, and nutrients, so mitigating its detrimental impacts on the entire ecosystem. Agricultural waste is rich in significant bioactive compounds, including proteins, lignin, polyphenols, fibres, and carbohydrates, which can serve as raw materials for diverse products such as soil nutrients, bio-pesticides, organic matter, energy, bio-based oil, plastics, leather, paper, board, and other agricultural products.

3. METHODS AND TECHNIQUES OF AGRI WASTE-VALORIZATION

The methodologies and techniques of agri-waste valorization entail transforming agricultural byproducts into valuable commodities using biological, chemical, thermochemical, and physical processes. Biological techniques such as composting, anaerobic digestion, fermentation, and vermicomposting utilise microorganisms to generate compost, biogas, bioethanol, and biofertilizers. Thermochemical methods, including pyrolysis, gasification, and combustion, convert biomass into charcoal, syngas, and renewable energy (Chojnacka, 2023; Ufitikirezi et al., 2024). Chemical processes such as hydrolysis and solvent extraction facilitate the production of biofuels, bioplastics, and bioactive substances. Physical and mechanical techniques, such as grinding, pelletization, and drying, condition biomass for energy production, animal feed, or subsequent processing (Ramo et al., 2022; Sharma et al., 2024). Innovative technologies such as microwave-assisted extraction, ultrasonication biorefineries, enzymatic valorization, and nanotechnology are improving the efficiency and sustainability of agricultural waste utilisation. The by-products produced from the processing of fruits and vegetables are predominantly underutilised and disposed of as organic waste. These organic wastes, comprising seeds, pulp, skin, rinds, etc., are potential sources of bioactive chemicals that confer health advantages. The extraction of bioactive chemicals from agricultural waste to produce functional food items is garnering heightened interest. The susceptibility of these chemicals to environmental influences limits their utility and bioavailability (Prabhakar and Banerjee, 2020; Usman et al., 2002; Gupta et al., 2024). Collectively, these strategies are essential for advancing a circular economy, minimising environmental damage, and generating new economic prospects within the agricultural sector. Here a detailed overview of these methods and techniques are given below:

3.1. Composting

Composting is a prevalent and eco-friendly technique for valorising agricultural waste, encompassing the aerobic microbial breakdown of organic leftovers, including crop stubble, fruit and vegetable peels, husks, manure, and other biodegradable materials (Azim et al., 2018; Ayilara et al., 2020). Organic debris is decomposed by the natural processes of bacteria, fungi, and other decomposers into a stable, nutrient-dense substance referred to as compost. This procedure aids in the management of substantial quantities of agricultural waste while generating a superior soil conditioner that improves soil structure, water retention, and microbial activity, thereby diminishing the necessity for chemical fertilizers (Meena et al., 2021; Zhao et al., 2024). Composting can be conducted at many scales, ranging from modest backyard systems to large-scale windrow or in-vessel composting operations, contingent upon the volume and nature of the waste. Furthermore, it aids in reducing greenhouse gas emissions by redirecting organic waste from landfills, where it would otherwise generate methane in anaerobic conditions. Composting serves as an economical, low-technology option that offers significant environmental and agronomic advantages, hence playing a crucial part in sustainable agriculture and circular bioeconomy frameworks (Ayilara et al., 2020; Nordah et al., 2023).

3.2. Bioenergy

Bioenergy production is a crucial method for valorising agricultural waste, converting residues into renewable energy sources such as biogas, bioethanol, biodiesel, and bioelectricity. Agricultural residues such as straw, husks, maize stover, sugarcane bagasse, and animal dung are abundant in organic matter, rendering them optimal feedstocks for bioenergy production (Shahzad et al., 2024). Methods like anaerobic digestion transform organic waste into biogas, comprising methane and carbon dioxide, which can be utilised for cooking, heating, or energy production. Biochemical processes such as fermentation transform carbohydrate-rich wastes into bioethanol, a clean-burning liquid fuel. Thermochemical processes, including pyrolysis and gasification, can convert dry biomass into bio-oil, syngas, and charcoal, yielding various energy products (Chen et al., 2021; Jameel et al., 2024). Bioenergy valorization of agricultural waste serves as a sustainable and scalable option, essential for enhancing energy security, mitigating greenhouse gas emissions, and furthering the objectives of a circular and low-carbon economy. The demand for alternative energy sources has led to the creation and implementation of sustainable fuels. These fuels are produced from waste biomass, rendering them a potentially reliable and sustainable answer to escalating energy demands and environmental issues (Islam et al., 2024; Ersoy and Ugurlu, 2024).

3.3. Bioplastics

The manufacturing of bioplastics from agricultural waste is an innovative and sustainable approach to valorising agri-waste, effectively tackling environmental pollution and resource efficiency issues. Agricultural leftovers, including corn stover, sugarcane bagasse, potato peels, and lignocellulosic biomass, are abundant in carbohydrates that can be hydrolysed into fermentable sugars and subsequently transformed into bioplastics via microbial fermentation and chemical synthesis. Widely used bioplastics, such as polylactic acid (PLA) and polyhydroxyalkanoates (PHA), originate from renewable feedstocks and are biodegradable or compostable under conditions (Zhao et al., 2023). Bioplastics provide an environmentally sustainable alternative to traditional petroleum-derived plastics, contributing to the reduction of carbon emissions, microplastic contamination, and dependence on limited fossil resources. Furthermore, employing inexpensive agricultural byproducts for bioplastic manufacturing improves the economic feasibility of this technology, rendering it an appealing choice for rural and industrial advancement (Rosenboom et al., 2022). With the increasing consumer and regulatory demand for sustainable packaging and materials, bioplastics derived from agricultural waste signify a vital innovation for advancing a circular economy, mitigating environmental impact, and enhancing the value of agricultural by-products that would otherwise be disposed of or incinerated (Ali et al., 2023).

3.4. Biofertilizers

Biofertilizers are essential for the valorization of agricultural waste, converting organic leftovers into valuable products that improve soil fertility and crop yield. Rather than allowing agricultural waste to degrade uncontrolled or incinerating it, which results in environmental damage, these residues can be composted, fermented, or treated to promote the proliferation of beneficial microbes (Du et al., 2018; Bhatia and Sindhu, 2024). This approach enables the development of biofertilizers containing nitrogen-fixing, phosphate-solubilizing, and potassium-mobilizing bacteria, providing a sustainable substitute for chemical fertilisers. Utilising agricultural waste as a substrate or carrier material fosters a circular economy and enhances soil health by augmenting microbial richness and organic matter content. This method aids in waste management, diminishes reliance on synthetic inputs, promotes organic farming techniques, and minimises greenhouse gas emissions (Samantaray et al., 2024).

3.5. Biochar

Biochar is a stable, carbon-rich solid material produced through the pyrolysis (thermal decomposition in the absence of oxygen) of biomass, including agricultural residues. Unlike ash or charcoal, biochar is specifically designed to be applied to soils to improve fertility, enhance microbial activity, and store carbon for long periods. Biochar is increasingly recognised as a significant result of agricultural waste valorization, providing a sustainable remedy for various agricultural and environmental issues (Gabhane et al., 2020). Biochar, a carbon-rich and porous substance, is generated via the pyrolysis of agricultural residues, including crop stalks, rice husks, coconut shells, and fruit peels, in an oxygen-limited environment. It possesses significant potential for enhancing soil health and sequestering carbon. Instead of permitting agricultural waste to accumulate, degrade, or be incinerated methods that emit greenhouse gases and contribute to pollution transforming this waste into biochar offers an environmentally sustainable approach to waste management (Amalina et al., 2022). The incorporation of biochar into soils promotes soil structure, improves nutrient and water retention, elevates microbial activity, and can substantially increase crop yields, particularly in degraded or nutrient-deficient soils. Furthermore, biochar's robust adsorptive characteristics render it effective for environmental remediation, particularly in the extraction of heavy metals and organic contaminants from water and soil. Its stability guarantees that the carbon it harbours is sequestered for hundreds to thousands of years, rendering it a promising instrument for climate change mitigation via long-term carbon sequestration (Kabir et al., 2023; Luo et al., 2023). In addition to agriculture, biochar is utilised in animal husbandry, construction materials, and energy generation, showcasing its versatility as a bioproduct. The prospects for biochar are quickly developing, fuelled by growing interest in circular economy activities, regenerative agriculture, and carbon trading mechanisms. Improvements in pyrolysis technology, optimisation of feedstock utilisation, and integration with decentralised rural industries are anticipated to enhance the economic viability and accessibility of biochar production for farmers globally (Afshar and Mofatteh, 2024).

3.6. Secondary Metabolites Extraction from Agri-Food By Products

The extraction of secondary metabolites and phytochemicals from agricultural food by-products constitutes a sustainable and economically feasible approach for waste valorisation in the food and agricultural sectors. Agri-food by-products, including fruit and vegetable peels, seeds, husks, pomace, cereal bran, and oilseed cakes, are frequently abundant in a diverse array of bioactive chemicals, such as phenolic acids, flavonoids, alkaloids, tannins, saponins, terpenoids, and carotenoids (Ribeiro et al., 2022). These compounds demonstrate considerable pharmacological and nutritional potential, showcasing antioxidant, antibacterial, anti-inflammatory, antidiabetic, and anticancer activities, so rendering them valuable for use in food, pharmaceutical, nutraceutical, and cosmetic compositions (Prabhakar and Banerjee, 2020, 2021; Verma and Thakur, 2021). The extraction of these phytochemicals necessitates meticulously engineered and optimized techniques to maintain their stability and high production (Kumar et al., 2023; Prabhakar et al, 2023a). Innovative green and non-thermal extraction technologies such as ultrasound-assisted extraction (UAE), microwave-assisted extraction (MAE), pressurised liquid extraction (PLE), enzymatic-assisted extraction (EAE), and supercritical fluid extraction (SFE) exhibit enhanced efficiency, diminished solvent consumption, and a reduced environmental footprint relative to traditional methods (Quitério et al., 2022; Prabhakar et al., 2024a; Cao et al., 2025). Key determinants affecting extraction efficiency comprise the selection of solvent, pH, temperature, duration, solid-to-solvent ratio, and the physical and chemical characteristics of the matrix (Zhang et al., 2018; Bitwell et al., 2023; Prabhakar et al., 2024b). Pretreatments such as drying, grinding, enzymatic hydrolysis, or fermentation might augment the accessibility and liberation of desired phytochemicals. The combination of extraction with purification processes (e.g., membrane filtration, chromatography) and analytical methodologies (e.g., HPLC, LC-MS/MS, FTIR) is crucial for the isolation, characterisation, and quantification of the target molecules. Notwithstanding technological advancements, obstacles remain in standardising extraction processes, mitigating batch-to-batch variability, assuring safety and regulatory compliance, and attaining cost-effective scalability for industrial applications (Prabhakar and Banerjee, 2021; Kumar et al., 2022; Altemimi et al, 2017). The application of interdisciplinary methods and bio-refinery principles can facilitate the conversion of agri-food leftovers into valuable resources, thereby aiding in waste reduction, environmental sustainability, and the development of high-value bioactive goods (Prabhakar, 2024; Carvalho et al., 2025).

4. ENTREPRENEURSHIP IN AGRI-WASTE VALORIZATION

Entrepreneurship in agri-waste valorization is rapidly emerging as a transformative force in the agricultural and environmental sectors, turning what was once considered waste into a wide range of high-value products. Driven by the growing need for sustainable practices, climate change mitigation, and rural economic development, innovative entrepreneurs are identifying opportunities to convert agricultural residues like crop stalks, husks, fruit peels, and animal waste into biofertilizers, biochar, biogas, bioplastics, organic chemicals, and even energy (Alli et al., 2024). By setting up enterprises that focus on collection, processing, and product development from agri-waste, entrepreneurs not only address critical issues of waste management and environmental pollution but also create new business models that are circular, resource-efficient, and community-driven. The potential market is vast, encompassing industries such as organic farming, renewable energy, sustainable packaging, and soil remediation. Entrepreneurial ventures in this sector often involve collaboration with farmers, research institutions, and government bodies to develop innovative technologies, establish supply chains, and ensure quality standards for the valorized products (Alan and Köker, 2023). Additionally, startups focusing on agri-waste valorization contribute significantly to rural employment, skill development, and women's empowerment, especially in regions where agriculture is the primary livelihood. With increasing availability of funding through green financing, impact investors, incubators, and government grants, the ecosystem for agri-waste entrepreneurship is becoming more supportive (Sonam et al., 2021a, b).

However, entrepreneurs must also navigate challenges such as seasonal availability of raw materials, lack of awareness among farmers, technology access barriers, and the need for scalable, cost-effective solutions. Looking ahead, the future of entrepreneurship in agri-waste valorization appears promising, especially with advancements in bioengineering, waste-to-energy technologies, and policy frameworks that encourage sustainable business practices. By innovatively linking agriculture, waste management, and circular economy principles, entrepreneurs in this field could build resilient businesses that not only generate profit but also deliver Agri-waste valorization enterprises represent a dynamic and growing sector that harnesses the untapped potential of agricultural residues to create economically valuable, environmentally sustainable products (Elroi et al., 2023; Gadanakis, 2024). These enterprises specialize in converting waste materials such as crop stalks, husks, fruit and vegetable peels, seeds, shells, and livestock residues into a wide array of products including biofertilizers, biochar, biogas, compost, bioplastics, natural fibers, and renewable energy. By doing so, they not only provide innovative solutions to the persistent problems of agricultural waste management and environmental degradation but also contribute significantly to rural economic development and sustainable agriculture. Enterprises in this sector often employ a combination of technologies such as pyrolysis, anaerobic digestion, fermentation, and composting to extract maximum value from waste streams. Many of them adopt circular economy models, ensuring that every output, including by-products, is repurposed, thereby minimizing waste generation entirely (Karim et al., 2025).

Agri-waste valorization enterprises frequently work in collaboration with local farmers, offering them additional income streams for supplying raw materials while also helping them adopt more sustainable farming practices. Moreover, these enterprises often create decentralized business models, setting up localized processing units close to farming communities to reduce logistics costs and environmental footprint. With growing awareness about climate change, soil health deterioration, and the need for renewable resources, the market for agri-waste derived products is expanding both domestically and globally. Governments, development agencies, and impact investors are increasingly supporting such ventures through grants, incentives, and capacity-building programs, recognizing their role in achieving sustainable development goals (SDGs) (Mishra et al., 2023; Prabhakar et al., 2023). However, agri-waste valorization enterprises also face challenges such as technology affordability, raw material variability, quality standardization, and market education. The future of these enterprises lies in innovation—developing new products, optimizing waste processing technologies, integrating digital tools for supply chain management, and building strong partnerships across sectors. As environmental regulations tighten and consumer demand shifts toward greener products, agri-waste valorization enterprises are poised to become key players in shaping a more sustainable and inclusive bioeconomy. significant environmental and social impact (Prabhakar and Nimesh, 2022; Sarker et al.,2024).

5. OPPORTUNITIES FOR SMALL AND MICRO ENTERPRISES (SMEs)

The valorization of agricultural waste presents numerous advantageous prospects for small and micro companies (SMEs), especially in rural and semi-urban regions where agricultural activities are prevalent. As the focus on sustainable development, circular economy, and rural entrepreneurship intensifies, SMEs can leverage the plentiful agricultural residues such as crop stalks, husks, fruit peels, and animal waste to produce value-added products including compost, biochar, organic fertilisers, biogas, natural fibres, bio-based packaging materials, and environmentally sustainable building materials (Ufitikirezi et al., 2024). Establishing small-scale composting units, biogas plants, decentralised biochar production facilities, or artisanal bioplastic enterprises can provide as economical and comparatively low-risk entry points for rural entrepreneurs. Small and medium-sized enterprises can investigate niche markets by manufacturing tailored products, such organic soil conditioners for organic agriculture, biofertilizer mixtures infused with beneficial bacteria, or artisanal items such as natural fibre handicrafts and biodegradable tableware. Moreover, there is an increasing demand for agri-waste collection, segregation, and processing services from larger corporations aiming to achieve their sustainability objectives (Baltrėnas et al., 2018). The government initiatives that advocate for waste management, rural industrialisation, and renewable energy offer financial incentives, technical assistance, and training programs, facilitating the entry of SMEs into the agri-waste valorization sector. Due to advancements in affordable, decentralised technologies and an increasing demand for sustainable products, small and micro firms are strategically positioned to develop lucrative business models that also promote environmental preservation, rural job creation, and local economic growth. To optimise success, SMEs must concentrate on establishing robust farmer connections, implementing suitable low-cost technologies, maintaining consistent product quality, and exploring burgeoning industries such as organic agriculture, carbon trading, and sustainable construction materials. With increasing awareness and assistance, agri-waste valorization emerges as a crucial domain for grassroots entrepreneurship and inclusive green growth (Doddapaneni and Kikas, 2021; Rossi and Srai, 2024).

Furthermore, innovations in affordable decentralised technology, availability of digital marketing platforms, and an increasing consumer inclination towards sustainable products create new opportunities for small businesses. Opportunities also exist in offering services such as garbage collection, processing, and supply chain management to larger corporations seeking to achieve sustainability objectives. Moreover, market development presents a considerable challenge; the markets for valorized agricultural waste products such as biochar, bioplastics, and organic fertilisers are still nascent and sometimes suffer from insufficient consumer awareness and acceptability, constraining the scalability of SME-led efforts. The establishment of robust farmer-producer cooperatives and public-private partnerships may enhance feedstock supply stability and improve market access (Costa et al., 2022; Koul et al., 2022). Capacity-building efforts emphasising technical training, company development, and financial literacy for rural entrepreneurs are crucial to promote sustained SME engagement. Although the prospects for SMEs in agri-waste valorization are significant and correspond with overarching objectives of sustainable development, rural empowerment, and climate resilience, actualising this potential necessitates coordinated efforts to tackle technological, financial, regulatory, and market-related obstacles. Despite facing challenges like limited financing options, technological barriers, and market access issues, their grassroots-level engagement, adaptability, and strong social networks make them critical catalysts for scaling agri-waste valorization initiatives. In the future, fostering partnerships between rural entrepreneurs, social enterprises, government bodies, NGOs, and impact investors will be key to maximizing the impact of agri-waste valorization, turning rural areas into hubs of innovation, sustainability, and inclusive green growth (Koiri et al., 2024; Sahu et al., 2025).

6. ORGANIZATIONS, COMPANIES, AND STARTUPS IN EMERGING AGRI WASTE VALORIZATION MARKET

Agri-waste valorization has gained significant momentum globally, with numerous companies and startups pioneering innovative ways to transform agricultural residues into high-value products. Companies like, *AgroSustain* (Switzerland) develops natural crop protection and preservation solutions derived from agri-waste, helping reduce post-harvest losses (Agrosustain, 2025). In India, *Krishi Jagran* and *Carbon Craft Design* utilize agricultural biomass to create sustainable construction materials and biochar, contributing to carbon sequestration and rural livelihoods (Economictimes, 2025). *Bio-bean* in the UK converts waste coffee grounds into advanced biofuels and biochemicals, showing how even niche agricultural waste streams can be commercially repurposed (Textile Word, 2025). *GreenPod Labs* (India) leverages plant-based biotechnology to develop active packaging solutions from agricultural residues, extending the shelf life of fruits and vegetables (Greenpod Labs, 2025). In Southeast Asia, *Entofood* uses food and agricultural waste to rear black soldier flies, producing protein-rich feed for aquaculture and poultry (Petfoodprocesing, 2025). Another notable player is *FullCycle Bioplastics* (USA), which transforms organic agri-waste into polyhydroxyalkanoates (PHAs), a compostable bioplastic (Fast Company, 2025). These companies illustrate the diverse technological pathways and business models from microbial fermentation and pyrolysis to enzymatic hydrolysis and circular bioeconomy strategies used to create sustainable value from agri-residues while addressing global challenges in waste management, climate change, and rural employment.

7. MARKETING STRATEGIES FOR AGRI-WASTE VALORIZATION

Marketing strategies for agri-waste-based products must be meticulously crafted to highlight their unique value propositions and to tackle the problems associated with market acceptability. The primary requisite is market education and awareness, as numerous consumers and companies may lack a comprehensive understanding of the potential advantages of products created from agricultural waste, including sustainability, reduced environmental impact, cost efficiency, and creativity (Donner et al., 2021). Formulating clear and persuasive narratives regarding the environmental, social, and economic benefits is essential, utilising storytelling to forge emotional connections with consumers and business associates. Brand positioning must highlight the circular economy dimension, presenting agri-waste goods as superior, environmentally responsible options that foster a sustainable future. Targeted segmentation is essential; strategies must distinguish between B2B (business to business) markets (e.g., businesses requiring raw materials such as bio-composites, bioplastics, bioenergy, and organic fertilisers) and B2C (business to consumer) markets e.g., sustainable home goods, fashion, and food products (Abdelmeguid et al., 2024).

7.1. Market segmentation and targeting strategies

Market segmentation and targeting strategies in agri-waste valorization involve identifying and categorizing potential customers based on their specific needs, industries, geographic locations, and sustainability preferences to effectively position and deliver products derived from agricultural residues. Segmentation can be done by industry, targeting sectors like bioenergy (biogas, biofuels), agriculture (organic fertilizers, soil conditioners), construction (bio-composites, insulation materials), textiles (fibres from plant waste), packaging (bioplastics, biodegradable materials), and food (upcycled ingredients, dietary fibres). Geographic segmentation distinguishes markets based on regional agricultural practices, waste generation volumes, infrastructure readiness, and environmental regulations such as focusing on developed economies with strong sustainability mandates or emerging economies with abundant agri-waste and resource needs (Donner et al., 2021; Onyeaka et al., 2023). Behavioural segmentation considers factors like environmental consciousness, readiness to adopt innovative materials, and price sensitivity, allowing companies to prioritize eco-conscious businesses and consumers willing to pay a premium for sustainable solutions. Demographic and firmographic segmentation classifying potential customers by size (small farms vs. agribusiness giants), market influence, or socio-economic status—can further refine marketing efforts. Once segments are identified, targeting strategies can be applied: companies may adopt a niche marketing approach for specialized products like high-end bioplastics for luxury brands or mass marketing for broader products like organic fertilizers suitable for large farming communities. Differentiated marketing can also be used, offering customized versions of products (e.g., premium-grade vs. standard-grade biofertilizers) for different customer groups. Ultimately, an effective segmentation and targeting strategy for agri-waste valorization ensures that marketing resources are focused on the most promising and profitable opportunities, aligning product offerings with specific market needs and sustainability-driven trends (Saleem et al., 2018).

7.2. Distribution channels (local markets, B2B, online platforms)

In agri-waste valorization marketing, distribution channels are essential for efficiently and effectively delivering products to the appropriate clients, while ensuring product quality, reducing costs, and expanding market reach. Considering the variety of goods generated from agricultural waste such as biofuels, bioplastics, organic fertilisers, biocomposites, textiles, and upcycled food ingredients—distribution methods must be customised to align with the product type, volume, client segment, and geographic scope. Direct distribution routes are prevalent when selling to substantial industrial purchasers, institutional clients, or governmental entities; for instance, firms may directly provide biomass briquettes to energy facilities or organic compost to extensive agricultural cooperatives. This paradigm facilitates enhanced client interactions, improved profit margins, and tailored services, however necessitates robust internal logistics capabilities (Ufitikirezi et al., 2024). Indirect distribution channels encompass intermediaries such as wholesalers, distributors, and retailers who facilitate access to broader markets, especially for consumer-oriented products like biodegradable packaging materials, eco-friendly home goods, or recycled food items. Organic fertilisers derived from agricultural waste may be disseminated via agricultural input suppliers, garden centres, or e-commerce platforms focused on eco-friendly items (Gerassimidou et al., 2021).

The online distribution has gained significant importance, as enterprises utilise their own websites, specialised e-marketplaces for sustainable products, and B2B platforms to efficiently reach remote or foreign customers. Partnership-oriented distribution approaches can be advantageous, particularly through collaboration with established agricultural supply chains, cooperatives, sustainability-driven companies, or governmental rural development programs to include agri-waste goods into wider efforts. Furthermore, third-party logistics (3PL) providers may be utilised to oversee intricate supply chains, particularly for the international export of processed agricultural waste products such as bioplastics or plant-based fibres (Gao et al., 2023). A nascent route is community-based distribution, wherein local entrepreneurs, farmer producer organisations (FPOs), or cooperatives are enabled to disseminate agri-waste products in rural or semi-urban regions, establishing a decentralised and inclusive distribution framework. The appropriate distribution mix is contingent upon the product's characteristics, target market inclinations, regulatory stipulations, cost frameworks, and the organization's operational competencies. A successful distribution strategy in agri-waste valorization guarantees that products are accessible, visible, and competitive in all target markets, while enhancing the sustainability and impact story integral to the brand (Morero et al., 2024).

7.3. Innovation and business model Development

Innovation and business model development for an agri-waste valorization enterprise require a multidisciplinary approach that combines sustainable technology, value chain integration, and market-driven strategies to transform agricultural residues into commercially viable products. The fundamental innovation involves employing sophisticated biotechnological, chemical, and mechanical processes such as anaerobic digestion, pyrolysis, supercritical fluid extraction, and bio-refinery systems to transform low-value agricultural residues, fruit and vegetable peels, husks, shells, and other by-products into high-value products including bioenergy, biofertilizers, biodegradable packaging, biochar, plant-based protein, dietary fibres, and natural colourants or preservatives. These solutions not only mitigate environmental degradation and greenhouse gas emissions but also foster a circular economy by enhancing resource efficiency and minimising waste (Somorin et al., 2023). An effective business strategy should be inclusive and decentralised, involving local farmers, self-help groups, and rural entrepreneurs as essential suppliers and stakeholders. It should include backward integration for procuring raw materials directly from agricultural communities and forward integration through processing, branding, and distribution networks. Revenue streams can be diversified by targeting several customer segments, including agribusinesses, the food and nutraceutical sectors, packaging firms, energy suppliers, and environmentally concerned consumers. Strategic alliances with research institutions, incubators, governmental programs, and environmental authorities can augment technological proficiency and facilitate access to subsidies or funding. From a marketing standpoint, the firm should highlight the sustainability narrative, the traceability of raw materials, and the multifunctionality of its goods. Narrative techniques, eco-labelling, certifications (such as organic or biodegradable labels), and the strategic deployment of digital platforms, including e-commerce, agri-tech applications, and social media, can substantially improve consumer involvement and market penetration. By integrating innovation into product development and business strategy, agri-waste valorization firms can create environmental, social, and economic benefits while establishing a resilient and future-oriented green enterprise (Donner et al., 2023; Sengupta et al., 2024).

7.4. Business model frameworks (e.g., Business Model Canvas)

The Business Model Canvas for agri-waste valorization highlights the conversion of agricultural leftovers into valuable goods, including biofertilizers, biogas, bio-based materials, and nutraceuticals. The primary value proposition is to enhance sustainability through waste reduction and the generation of new revenue sources. Target clientele comprises agribusinesses, energy corporations, and environmentally aware manufacturers. Essential activities encompass garbage collection, processing, and product development, bolstered by collaborations with farmers, research institutes, and governmental bodies. Revenue is derived from product sales and potential subsidies or carbon credits, whereas costs encompass shipping, processing, and research and development and this concept endorses both ecological and economic sustainability (Koul et al., 2022; Ufitikirezi et al., 2024).

7.5. Integration of digital technologies and industry 4.0

The use of digital technologies into the agri-waste valorization sector is revolutionising the management, processing, and commercialisation of agricultural wastes. Technologies include the Internet of Things (IoT), artificial intelligence (AI), and blockchain provide real-time monitoring, predictive analytics, and transparent traceability across the agricultural waste supply chain. IoT sensors enable effective collection and categorisation by monitoring the kind, volume, and quality of trash at the origin, while AI-driven models enhance conversion processes such as anaerobic digestion or pyrolysis for increased yields and less energy usage (Ahmed et al., 2022). Moreover, blockchain improves supply chain transparency, allowing stakeholders to authenticate the origin and sustainability qualifications of value-added products such as biofuels, bioplastics, and compost. These digital technologies enhance operational efficiency and facilitate the advancement of a circular bioeconomy by generating new revenue streams from agricultural by-products (Ahmed et al., 2022).

The combination of digitalisation and Industry 4.0 technologies has become progressively vital in augmenting the efficiency, transparency, and sustainability of contemporary business enterprises. The technologies such blockchain, artificial intelligence (AI), big data analytics, and the Internet of Things (IoT) are revolutionising conventional business paradigms by facilitating more astute decision-making and enhanced resource management. Blockchain technology has emerged as a potent instrument for enhancing supply chain transparency and traceability, enabling safe recording of all transactions and product movements in a decentralised and irreversible digital ledger. This fosters confidence among stakeholders, mitigates information asymmetry, and guarantees accountability throughout the supply chain (Kshetri, 2022). Similarly, artificial intelligence and machine learning algorithms play a crucial role in enhancing logistics and operational procedures. The AI-driven systems can evaluate extensive quantities of real-time data to forecast demand trends, enhance transportation routes, minimise operational expenses, and refine inventory management. These skills enhance logistical efficiency while diminishing energy consumption and environmental consequences, therefore promoting sustainable business practices (Bag et al., 2023).

Furthermore, digital technologies enable data-driven monitoring and performance evaluation, permitting businesses to measure sustainability metrics and operational efficacy more efficiently. Therefore, integrating these Industry 4.0 capabilities into entrepreneurial frameworks enhances organisations' capacity to create resilient and sustainable business models. Digital platforms facilitate enhanced coordination among producers, suppliers, and consumers, which is especially crucial in industries like agriculture and waste valorisation, where supply chains frequently exhibit fragmentation. Blockchain-based traceability systems can guarantee that agricultural waste or bio-based goods are sourced responsibly and processed sustainably, hence improving market credibility and consumer confidence (Saberi et al., 2023). Moreover, the use of digital technologies facilitates the shift towards circular economy practices, wherein resources are effectively reused, recycled, or valorised. Integrating blockchain transparency with AI-driven logistics optimisation enables firms to markedly enhance supply chain visibility, minimise waste production, and improve operational sustainability. Thus, incorporating digitalisation and Industry 4.0 innovations into the suggested framework would enhance the manuscript's contribution by establishing it as a contemporary, technology-oriented, and thorough guide for successful and sustainable entrepreneurship in the advancing digital economy.

7.7. Role of co-creation and participatory models with farmers and communities

Co-creation and participatory models play a pivotal role in the successful development and sustainability of agri-waste valorization small and medium enterprises (SMEs), especially in rural and agrarian settings. By actively involving farmers and local communities in the design, implementation, and scaling of valorization initiatives, these models foster a sense of ownership, build trust, and ensure that technologies and business practices are contextually relevant. Farmers contribute valuable indigenous knowledge about local waste streams, seasonal availability, and traditional uses, which can enhance the efficiency and cultural appropriateness of valorization processes (Worakittikul et al., 2025). The participatory approaches also enable capacity building through shared learning and training, helping communities to adopt new technologies and entrepreneurial practices. This inclusive engagement not only strengthens supply chain resilience but also creates equitable economic opportunities, encouraging the formation of decentralized, community-led bio economies rooted in circular principles (Prajapati et al., 2025). The combination of digitalisation and Industry 4.0 technologies has become progressively vital in augmenting the efficiency, transparency, and sustainability of contemporary business enterprises.

Technologies such blockchain, artificial intelligence (AI), big data analytics, and the Internet of Things (IoT) are revolutionising conventional business paradigms by facilitating more astute decision-making and enhanced resource management. Blockchain technology has emerged as a potent instrument for enhancing supply chain transparency and traceability, enabling safe recording of all transactions and product movements in a decentralised and irreversible digital ledger. This fosters confidence among stakeholders, mitigates information asymmetry, and guarantees accountability throughout the supply chain (Kshetri, 2022).

Likewise, artificial intelligence and machine learning algorithms play a crucial role in enhancing logistics and operational procedures. The AI-driven systems can evaluate extensive quantities of real-time data to forecast demand trends, enhance transportation routes, minimise operational expenses, and refine inventory management. These skills enhance logistical efficiency while diminishing energy consumption and environmental consequences, therefore promoting sustainable business practices (Bag et al., 2023). Furthermore, digital technologies enable data-driven monitoring and performance evaluation, permitting businesses to measure sustainability metrics and operational efficacy more efficiently. Thus, integrating these Industry 4.0 capabilities into entrepreneurial frameworks enhances organisations' capacity to create resilient and sustainable business models. Digital platforms facilitate enhanced coordination among producers, suppliers, and consumers, which is especially crucial in industries like agriculture and waste valorisation, where supply chains frequently exhibit fragmentation. Blockchain-based traceability systems can guarantee that agricultural waste or bio-based goods are sourced responsibly and processed sustainably, hence improving market credibility and consumer confidence (Saberi et al., 2023). Moreover, the use of digital technologies facilitates the shift towards circular economy practices, wherein resources are effectively reused, recycled, or valorised. Integrating blockchain transparency with AI-driven logistics optimisation enables firms to markedly enhance supply chain visibility, minimise waste production, and improve operational sustainability. Thus, incorporating digitalisation and Industry 4.0 innovations into the suggested framework would enhance the manuscript's contribution by establishing it as a contemporary, technology-oriented, and thorough guide for successful and sustainable entrepreneurship in the advancing digital economy.

8. SPECIFIC RISK MANAGEMENT STRATEGIES AND CONSUMER TRENDS TOWARD "CLEAN LABEL" PRODUCTS

Integrating targeted risk management measures and a comprehensive analysis of upcoming consumer trends, such as "clean label" items, can substantially augment the practical significance of a publication centred on agri-waste valorisation entrepreneurship. Theoretical discussions emphasise the environmental and economic potential of transforming agricultural waste into value-added products; however, entrepreneurs in this sector frequently encounter market volatility, supply chain disruptions, variable raw material availability, and evolving consumer preferences. Consequently, incorporating structured risk management frameworks inside the chapter would enhance its utility as a practical and strategic resource for practitioners. A primary technique for mitigating market volatility is the diversification of valorisation pathways. Entrepreneurs can mitigate reliance on a singular product or market by transforming agricultural leftovers into many outputs, like biofertilizers, bioenergy, charcoal, biodegradable packaging materials, or functional food ingredients. Diverse production systems enhance financial resilience and enable enterprises to adjust their focus in response to market demand and price fluctuations. Studies on bio-based circular economy models indicate that varied biomass utilisation enhances economic stability and mitigates operational risk in agricultural waste processing sectors (Dahiya et al., 2023). Another crucial technique entails establishing long-term partnerships with suppliers and buyers, which stabilise supply chains and guarantee regular availability of raw materials. Forming alliances with farmer cooperatives, food processing sectors, and agricultural markets helps ensure consistent waste sources while reducing procurement risks. Moreover, the data-driven forecasting and digital monitoring systems are integral to risk management. Utilising digital tools like predictive analytics, artificial intelligence, and real-time market data platforms enables entrepreneurs to foresee demand fluctuations, enhance production planning, and modify supply chain operations accordingly. This technological integration enhances decision-making abilities and enables organisations to adapt proactively to market fluctuations (Bag et al., 2023).

The financial risk can be alleviated by portfolio investment methods, governmental subsidies, and green finance channels, which are becoming accessible for circular economy and bio-based innovation initiatives. A comprehensive examination of consumer trends about “clean label” and sustainable products, in conjunction with risk management, would enhance the manuscript's pertinence. The clean label products prioritise natural ingredients, minimal processing, transparency in sourcing, and environmentally sustainable production practices. In recent years, customers have heightened their awareness of environmental concerns, food waste, and sustainable consumption practices, resulting in an increased demand for products sourced from natural or recycled materials. This transition generates new market prospects for entrepreneurs in agri-waste valorisation, especially within the domains of functional meals, nutraceuticals, cosmetics, and biodegradable packaging. Research demonstrates that customers are more receptive to products derived from recycled ingredients provided the environmental advantages and safety standards are effectively conveyed (Bhatt et al., 2023).

Furthermore, openness and traceability are essential in fostering consumer confidence in clean label products. Entrepreneurs can enhance their market positioning by using eco-labels, sustainability certifications, and transparent supply chain systems. Transparent communication regarding the ecological benefits of agri-waste-derived products such as diminished food waste, reduced carbon emissions, and circular resource utilization—can markedly improve consumer acceptance. Studies indicate that sustainability narratives and labelling methods enhance customer purchasing behaviour with upcycled food products (Aschemann-Witzel & Stangherlin, 2021).

9. SUSTAINABILITY, IMPACT ASSESSMENT CIRCULAR ECONOMY AND LIFE CYCLE ASSESSMENT

The evaluation of sustainability and impact within circular economy and closed-loop supply chain frameworks for agricultural waste valorization is essential for guaranteeing that the environmental, economic, and social advantages of these systems are quantifiable, scalable, and consistent with long-term development objectives. The fundamental concept of the circular economy is to separate economic growth from resource consumption and environmental harm by eliminating waste, maintaining material utility, and restoring natural systems (Cahyadi et al., 2024). In agri-waste valorization, this involves converting agricultural residues frequently neglected or underexploited into valuable products such as biofertilizers, bioplastics, bioenergy, animal feed, and soil amendments, thus completing the cycle within agricultural and food systems. Closed-loop supply chains (CLSCs) are essential to this transformation, since they enable the collection, reverse logistics, processing, and reintegration of agricultural waste products into the production cycle, enhancing resource efficiency and diminishing dependence on pure inputs (Rabbi & Amin, 2024). By methodically incorporating sustainability and impact evaluations into circular economy and closed-loop supply chain frameworks, stakeholders can discern optimal practices, alleviate risks, guide policy, attract green financing, and guarantee that agri-waste valorization fulfils its commitment to inclusive, low-carbon, and regenerative development (Osman et al., 2024).

Agri-waste valorization offers significant socio-economic benefits, particularly in terms of job creation and rural development, by fostering local entrepreneurship and creating new income-generating opportunities. As agri-waste is often abundant in rural areas, small and medium-scale agri-waste valorization enterprises can provide employment opportunities for local communities, especially for women, youth, and marginalized groups (Cahyadi et al., 2024). These enterprises can range from waste collection and processing to the production of value-added products such as biofuels, bioplastics, compost, and animal feed, creating diverse job roles across the value chain from raw material sourcing and logistics to manufacturing, sales, and distribution. In turn, this can lead to the development of local skills and the growth of a green economy, where workers gain expertise in sustainable technologies and practices, further contributing to human capital development (Ufitikirezi et al., 2024). Moreover, agri-waste valorization helps to reduce rural-urban migration by making rural areas more economically viable and attractive for young people looking for employment opportunities close to home. Beyond employment, these enterprises can stimulate local economies by creating new markets for agri-waste-derived products, boosting small-scale farming through organic waste recycling, and improving soil fertility. The positive ripple effects extend to infrastructure development, such as better waste management systems, improved road access for transportation, and enhanced public services, all of which contribute to the broader socio-economic upliftment of rural communities (Gamage et al., 2023). Thus, agri-waste valorization not only supports sustainable development but also plays a transformative role Gender and social inclusion are critical elements in the success and sustainability of agri-waste entrepreneurship, especially in rural areas where women and marginalized groups often face barriers to economic participation. Furthermore, inclusive business models that promote equal participation and fair wages can challenge gender norms, reduce inequalities, and improve the overall socio-economic outcomes for rural populations. Ultimately, gender and social inclusion in agri-waste entrepreneurship not only contribute to the empowerment of underrepresented groups but also strengthen the sustainability and scalability of these ventures, ensuring that the benefits of agri-waste valorization reach all sectors of society.in reducing poverty, improving livelihoods, and fostering economic resilience in rural areas.

One of the most accurate and thorough methods for assessing the environmental effects of business models, processes, and products across their whole life cycle is life cycle assessment, or LCA. The process evaluates the environmental costs associated with the extraction, processing, production, transportation, use, and disposal of raw materials at the end of their useful lives. LCA offers a methodical framework for assessing and contrasting the environmental performance of cutting-edge agri-waste valorisation techniques with conventional waste disposal techniques in the context of agricultural waste management. LCA aids in illustrating the environmental benefits of turning agricultural leftovers into useful resources by measuring effects including greenhouse gas emissions, energy use, resource depletion, and pollution potential (Molina et al., 2024). The latest research works highlighted the expanding relevance of life cycle assessment (LCA) in promoting circular bioeconomy and sustainable waste management. Crop stalks, husks, fruit peels, and processing by-products are among the agricultural leftovers that are rapidly being transformed into bioenergy, biofertilizers, biochar, and biodegradable materials. Researchers can assess the environmental benefits and trade-offs related to various valorisation processes using life cycle assessment (LCA) methodology. In a study on life cycle carbon accounting in agricultural supply chains, for example, Singh et al. (2026) discovered that including waste valorisation techniques greatly lowers lifecycle carbon emissions while improving the sustainability of food production systems. Their results demonstrate how circular strategies that recycle agricultural waste can support low-carbon agricultural development and climate mitigation. When compared to traditional petroleum-based products, research on the conversion of agricultural residues into bio-based materials shows significant environmental benefits. A life cycle assessment of agricultural waste conversion into biodegradable polymers and subsequent biochar production was carried out by Senga et al. in 2024. According to the study, these integrated valorisation systems increase overall resource efficiency, decrease landfill trash, and lessen reliance on fossil fuels. Additionally, the LCA results showed that using agricultural waste as a feedstock for bio-based goods resulted in much fewer environmental consequences related to the manufacturing and disposal stages. Furthermore, resource recovery systems outperform conventional disposal techniques in terms of environmental performance, according to life cycle assessment (LCA) studies that concentrate on waste management optimisation. In their analysis of several waste valorisation scenarios, Molina et al. (2024) discovered that systems that integrate recycling, energy recovery, and material reuse significantly lessen environmental consequences in a number of areas, such as ecosystem toxicity and the potential for climate change. These findings demonstrate that applying the concepts of the circular economy to the management of agricultural waste can have positive effects on the environment and the economy. Recently the studies also emphasise the significance of using life cycle frameworks to assess cutting-edge technologies employed in agri-waste valorisation. For instance, the environmental performance of removing bioactive chemicals from agri-food waste was evaluated by Martínez-Sánchez et al. (2025). According to their life cycle study, obtaining important phenolic compounds from agricultural leftovers might increase environmental efficiency and decrease waste production. The study also underlined how process optimisation and the integration of renewable energy sources might improve the sustainability of these systems. Considering all, the Life Cycle Assessment is an essential scientific instrument for confirming the advantageous environmental effects of agri-waste valorisation business models. LCA promotes the creation of sustainable agriculture systems and circular bioeconomy methods by offering quantitative proof of decreased emissions, enhanced resource efficiency, and reduced environmental impacts. Policymakers, researchers, and entrepreneurs can therefore create ecologically friendly solutions for managing agricultural wastes while advancing sustainable development by incorporating life cycle assessment (LCA) into agri-waste valorisation research.

10. REGULATORY FRAMEWORKS AND INTERNATIONAL STANDARDIZATION

Understanding the opportunities and structural limitations that affect sustainable and green entrepreneurship requires knowledge of the regulatory frameworks and international standardisation in the agri-waste valorisation sector. The legislative frameworks controlling the value-adding of agricultural waste are still dispersed between nations and regions, despite the fact that interest in circular bioeconomy initiatives has grown globally. Entrepreneurs looking to transform agricultural left-overs into value-added goods like biofertilizers, bioplastics, or renewable energy face regulatory obstacles because they are still categorised as waste in many countries rather than as potential industrial feedstock. Agri-waste processing operations are frequently subject to stringent waste management rules as a result of this classification, which raises compliance costs and stifles innovation. The commercialisation of waste-derived goods is thus still hampered by regulatory ambiguity, even if governments are increasingly encouraging circular economy practices (Dahiya et al., 2023). The absence of uniform international standards for goods made from agricultural waste is another serious problem. Despite the helpful guidelines provided by international frameworks like environmental management and lifecycle assessment standards, many agri-waste-based products continue to encounter uneven certification and quality assurance requirements across international markets. For instance, depending on the nation, biofertilizers, compost products, and materials formed from biomass are frequently governed by various industrial, environmental, or agricultural regulations. Entrepreneurs hoping to expand sustainable inventions globally face uncertainty and difficulties in cross-border trading as a result of this fragmentation. Researchers contend that to guarantee product quality, environmental safety, and consumer trust in bio-based products, standardised certification processes and shared sustainability criteria are required (Rana et al., 2024). Additionally, legal frameworks occasionally fall behind the quick technical developments in waste valorisation, such as integrated biomass utilisation systems, microbial conversion processes, and advanced biorefineries. Approvals and market entry are delayed because many of these technologies create new materials or compounds that do not cleanly fit into preexisting regulatory categories. This legal lag could deter private investment and restrict the expansion of creative start-ups in the field of the circular bioeconomy. However, small and medium-sized businesses (SMEs), who frequently lack the administrative and financial resources to handle complicated regulatory systems, may be disproportionately impacted by too stringent compliance requirements (Bhatia et al., 2022). Notwithstanding these obstacles, regulatory frameworks have significant chances to support sustainable entrepreneurship. In order to encourage companies to implement ecologically friendly production methods, governments are progressively supporting agri-waste valorisation through regulatory incentives, green financing channels, and sustainability targets. Markets for bio-based products made from agricultural residues may be established, innovation can be encouraged, and technological adoption can be facilitated by well-crafted regulatory laws. Policymakers must prioritise regulatory harmonisation, open certification processes, and adaptable regulations that consider new technology, nevertheless, if they want such frameworks to be successful. To enable agri-waste valorisation to make a significant contribution to sustainable development and green entrepreneurship, it will be essential to fortify international collaboration in standard setting and connect regulatory frameworks with the goals of the circular economy.

11. CONCLUSION

Agri-waste valorization represents a powerful confluence of entrepreneurship, environmental stewardship, and inclusive development. For small enterprises, it opens sustainable business avenues that contribute to rural industrialization and ecological balance. The synergistic application of innovative technologies and strategic marketing can transform agri-waste into a resource that fuels green economies and uplifts communities. With supportive policies, ecosystem enablers, and robust market linkages, agri-waste entrepreneurship holds immense potential to shape a resilient and sustainable future. Agri-waste entrepreneurship within small and medium-scale enterprises (SMEs) holds immense potential for fostering sustainable development, addressing environmental challenges, and driving socio-economic growth, particularly in rural areas. By transforming agricultural residues into valuable products such as biofuels, bioplastics, compost, and animal feed, these enterprises contribute to a circular economy that reduces waste, minimizes pollution, and decreases carbon footprints. The technical, financial, and regulatory challenges faced by entrepreneurs can be overcome through supportive policies, access to tailored financing, and the integration of digital technologies that optimize production and logistics. Moreover, the socio-economic benefits of agri-waste valorization are profound, including job creation, rural development, and the empowerment of marginalized groups, particularly women and youth, who can actively participate in value chains and entrepreneurship. Gender and social inclusion, when prioritized, further enhance the impact and sustainability of these ventures. Ultimately, agri-waste entrepreneurship not only promotes environmental sustainability but also provides pathways for economic resilience, community development, and social equity. By fostering innovation, collaboration, and investment, small and medium-scale enterprises can play a critical role in transforming the agri-waste sector into a driver of sustainable rural economies and a vital contributor to global sustainability goals.

CONFLICT OF RESEARCH INTERESTS

Authors declare no conflict of research interests.

REFERENCES

Abdelmeguid, A., Tsironis, G., Afy-Shararah, M., Tsagarakis, K. P., & Salonitis, K. (2024). Insights into sustainability and circular economy trends in luxury fashion: A LinkedIn topic modelling study. *Cleaner and Responsible Consumption*, *15*, 100228. DOI: 10.1016/j.clrc.2024.100228

Abubakar, I. R., Maniruzzaman, K. M., Dano, U. L., AlShihri, F. S., AlShammari, M. S., Ahmed, S. M. S., Al-Gehlani, W. A. G., & Alrawaf, T. I. (2022). Environmental sustainability impacts of solid waste management practices in the global South. *International Journal of Environmental Research and Public Health*, *19*(19), 12717. DOI: 10.3390/ijerph191912717

Afshar, M., & Mofatteh, S. (2024). Biochar for a sustainable future: Environmentally friendly production and diverse applications. *Results in Engineering*, *23*, 102433. DOI: 10.1016/j.rineng.2024.102433

Agrosustain. (2025). Agro sustain. Available on https://www.agrosustain.ch/ (Accessed on 7th March 2025).

Ahmed, R. A., Hemdan, E. E. D., El-Shafai, W., Ahmed, Z. A., El-Rabaie, E. S. M., & Abd El-Samie, F. E. (2022). Climate-smart agriculture using intelligent techniques, blockchain and Internet of Things: Concepts, challenges, and opportunities. *Transactions on Emerging Telecommunications Technologies*, *33*(11), e4607. DOI: 10.1002/ett.4607

Alan, H., & Köker, A. R. (2023). Analyzing and mapping agricultural waste recycling research: An integrative review for conceptual framework and future directions. *Resources Policy*, *85*, 103987. DOI: 10.1016/j.resourpol.2023.103987

Ali, S. S., Abdelkarim, E. A., Elsamahy, T., Al-Tohamy, R., Li, F., Kornaros, M., Zuorro, A., Zhu, D., & Sun, J. (2023). Bioplastic production in terms of life cycle assessment: A state-of-the-art review. *Environmental Science and Ecotechnology*, *15*, 100254. DOI: 10.1016/j.ese.2023.100254

. Alli, Y. A., Bamisaye, A., Bamidele, M. O., Etafo, N. O., CHKIRIDA, S., Lawal, A., ... & Al Nageim, H. (2024). Transforming waste to wealth: Harnessing carbon dioxide for sustainable solutions. *Results in Surfaces and Interfaces*, 100321.

Altemimi, A., Lakhssassi, N., Baharlouei, A., Watson, D. G., & Lightfoot, D. A. (2017). Phytochemicals: Extraction, isolation, and identification of bioactive compounds from plant extracts. *Plants, 6*(4), 42. DOI: 10.3390/plants6040042

Amalina, F., Abd Razak, A. S., Krishnan, S., Sulaiman, H., Zularisam, A. W., & Nasrullah, M. (2022). Biochar production techniques utilizing biomass waste-derived materials and environmental applications–A review. *Journal of Hazardous Materials Advances, 7*, 100134. DOI: 10.1016/j.hazadv.2022.100134

Aschemann-Witzel, J., & Stangherlin, I. (2021). Upcycled by-product use in food: Consumer perceptions and acceptance of food waste valorization. *Journal of Cleaner Production, 290*, 125815.

Avilés-Palacios, C., & Rodríguez-Olalla, A. (2021). The sustainability of waste management models in circular economies. *Sustainability (Basel), 13*(13), 7105. DOI: 10.3390/su13137105

Ayilara, M. S., Olanrewaju, O. S., Babalola, O. O., & Odeyemi, O. (2020). Waste management through composting: Challenges and potentials. *Sustainability (Basel), 12*(11), 4456. DOI: 10.3390/su12114456

Azim, K., Soudi, B., Boukhari, S., Perissol, C., Roussos, S., & Thami Alami, I. (2018). Composting parameters and compost quality: A literature review. *Organic Agriculture, 8*(2), 141–158. DOI: 10.1007/s13165-017-0180-z

Bag, S., Gupta, S., Kumar, A., & Sivarajah, U. (2023). Role of artificial intelligence in sustainable supply chain management and logistics efficiency. *Technological Forecasting and Social Change, 187*, 122195.

Bala, S., Garg, D., Sridhar, K., Inbaraj, B. S., Singh, R., Kamma, S., Tripathi, M., & Sharma, M. (2023). Transformation of agro-waste into value-added bioproducts and bioactive compounds: Micro/nano formulations and application in the agri-food-pharma sector. *Bioengineering (Basel, Switzerland), 10*(2), 152. DOI: 10.3390/bioengineering10020152

. Baltrėnas, P., Baltrėnaitė, E., Baltrėnas, P., & Baltrėnaitė, E. (2018). Small-Scale Composting Bioreactors as a Part of Biogas Plants. *Small Bioreactors for Management of Biodegradable Waste*, 263-300.

Beluhan, S., Mihajlovski, K., Šantek, B., & Ivančić Šantek, M. (2023). The production of bioethanol from lignocellulosic biomass: Pretreatment methods, fermentation, and downstream processing. *Energies, 16*(19), 7003. DOI: 10.3390/en16197003

Bhatia, S. K., Kumar, S., Kim, S. H., Yang, Y. H., & Kumar, V. (2022). Advances in biomass valorization for sustainable bio-based economy. *Bioresource Technology, 344*, 126181.

Bhatia, T., & Sindhu, S. S. (2024). Sustainable management of organic agricultural wastes: Contributions in nutrients availability, pollution mitigation and crop production. *Discover Agriculture, 2*(1), 1–42. DOI: 10.1007/s44279-024-00147-7

Bhatt, S., Lee, J., Deutsch, J., Ayaz, H., Fulton, B., & Suri, R. (2023). From food waste to value: Consumer acceptance of upcycled ingredients and clean-label products. *Sustainable Production and Consumption, 35*, 189–200.

Bitwell, C., Indra, S. S., Luke, C., & Kakoma, M. K. (2023). A review of modern and conventional extraction techniques and their applications for extracting phytochemicals from plants. *Scientific African, 19*, e01585. DOI: 10.1016/j.sciaf.2023.e01585

Cahyadi, E. R., Hidayati, N., Zahra, N., & Arif, C. (2024). Integrating Circular Economy Principles into Agri-Food Supply Chain Management: A Systematic Literature Review. *Sustainability (Basel), 16*(16), 7165. DOI: 10.3390/su16167165

Cao, S., Liang, J., Chen, M., Xu, C., Wang, X., Qiu, L., Zhao, X., & Hu, W. (2025). Comparative analysis of extraction technologies for plant extracts and absolutes. *Frontiers in Chemistry, 13*, 1536590. DOI: 10.3389/fchem.2025.1536590

Carvalho, A. C. F., Ghosh, S., Hoffmann, T. G., Prudêncio, E. S., de Souza, C. K., & Roy, S. (2025). Valuing agro-industrial waste in the development of sustainable food packaging based on the system of a circular bioeconomy: A review. *Cleaner Waste Systems, 11*, 100275. DOI: 10.1016/j.clwas.2025.100275

Chen, J., Zhang, B., Luo, L., Zhang, F., Yi, Y., Shan, Y., Liu, B., Zhou, Y., Wang, X., & Lü, X. (2021). A review on recycling techniques for bioethanol production from lignocellulosic biomass. *Renewable & Sustainable Energy Reviews, 149*, 111370. DOI: 10.1016/j.rser.2021.111370

Chojnacka, K. (2023). Valorization of biorefinery residues for sustainable fertilizer production: A comprehensive review. *Biomass Conversion and Biorefinery, 13*(16), 14359–14388. DOI: 10.1007/s13399-023-04639-2

Costa, I., Riccotta, R., Montini, P., Stefani, E., de Souza Goes, R., Gaspar, M. A., Martins, F. S., Fernandes, A. A., Machado, C., Loçano, R., & Larieira, C. L. C. (2022). The degree of contribution of digital transformation technology on company sustainability areas. *Sustainability (Basel), 14*(1), 462. DOI: 10.3390/su14010462

Dahiya, S., Kumar, A. N., Sravan, J. S., Chatterjee, S., Sarkar, O., & Mohan, S. V. (2023). Food waste biorefinery: Sustainable valorization of agricultural residues into value-added products. *Bioresource Technology, 369*, 128364.

Devi, A., Bajar, S., Kour, H., Kothari, R., Pant, D., & Singh, A. (2022). Lignocellulosic biomass valorization for bioethanol production: A circular bioeconomy approach. *BioEnergy Research, 15*(4), 1820–1841. DOI: 10.1007/s12155-022-10401-9

Doddapaneni, T. R. K. C., & Kikas, T. (2021). Thermochemical and biochemical treatment strategies for resource recovery from agri-food industry wastes. In *Valorization of Agri-food wastes and by-products* (pp. 787–807). Academic Press. DOI: 10.1016/B978-0-12-824044-1.00007-6

Donner, M., Verniquet, A., Broeze, J., Kayser, K., & De Vries, H. (2021). Critical success and risk factors for circular business models valorising agricultural waste and by-products. *Resources, Conservation and Recycling, 165*, 105236. DOI: 10.1016/j.resconrec.2020.105236

Du, C., Abdullah, J. J., Greetham, D., Fu, D., Yu, M., Ren, L., Li, S., & Lu, D. (2018). Valorization of food waste into biofertiliser and its field application. *Journal of Cleaner Production, 187*, 273–284. DOI: 10.1016/j.jclepro.2018.03.211

Duque-Acevedo, M., Belmonte-Ureña, L. J., Cortés-García, F. J., & Camacho-Ferre, F. (2020). Agricultural waste: Review of the evolution, approaches and perspectives on alternative uses. *Global Ecology and Conservation, 22*, e00902. DOI: 10.1016/j.gecco.2020.e00902

Duque-Acevedo, M., Lancellotti, I., Andreola, F., Barbieri, L., Belmonte-Ureña, L. J., & Camacho-Ferre, F. (2022). Management of agricultural waste biomass as raw material for the construction sector: An analysis of sustainable and circular alternatives. *Environmental Sciences Europe, 34*(1), 70. DOI: 10.1186/s12302-022-00655-7

Economictimes. (2025). Navigating the Agricultural Biomass Supply Chain in India. Available at https://energy.economictimes.indiatimes.com/news/oil-and-gas/navigating-the-agricultural-biomass-supply-chain-in-india/108812275 (Accessed on 7th March 2025).

Elroi, H., Zbigniew, G., Agnieszka, W. C., & Piotr, S. (2023). Enhancing waste resource efficiency: Circular economy for sustainability and energy conversion. *Frontiers in Environmental Science, 11*, 1303792. DOI: 10.3389/fenvs.2023.1303792

Ersoy, A. E., & Ugurlu, A. (2024). Bioenergy's role in achieving a low-carbon electricity future: A case of Türkiye. *Applied Energy, 372*, 123799. DOI: 10.1016/j.apenergy.2024.123799

Ezeorba, T. P. C., Okeke, E. S., Mayel, M. H., Nwuche, C. O., & Ezike, T. C. (2024). Recent advances in biotechnological valorization of agro-food wastes (AFW): Optimizing integrated approaches for sustainable biorefinery and circular bioeconomy. *Bioresource Technology Reports*, *26*, 101823. DOI: 10.1016/j.biteb.2024.101823

Fast Company. (2025). This startup turns food waste into bioplastic that can break down in the ocean. Available on https://www.fastcompany.com/90687372/this-startup-turns-food-waste-into-bioplastic-that-can-break-down-in-the-ocean. (Access on 18th March 2025)

Gabhane, J. W., Bhange, V. P., Patil, P. D., Bankar, S. T., & Kumar, S. (2020). Recent trends in biochar production methods and its application as a soil health conditioner: A review. *SN Applied Sciences*, *2*(7), 1–21. DOI: 10.1007/s42452-020-3121-5

Gadanakis, Y. (2024). Advancing farm entrepreneurship and agribusiness management for sustainable agriculture. *Agriculture*, *14*(8), 1288. DOI: 10.3390/agriculture14081288

Gamage, A., Gangahagedara, R., Gamage, J., Jayasinghe, N., Kodikara, N., Suraweera, P., & Merah, O. (2023). Role of organic farming for achieving sustainability in agriculture. *Farming System*, *1*(1), 100005. DOI: 10.1016/j.farsys.2023.100005

Gao, J., Siddik, A. B., Khawar Abbas, S., Hamayun, M., Masukujjaman, M., & Alam, S. S. (2023). Impact of E-commerce and digital marketing adoption on the financial and sustainability performance of MSMEs during the COVID-19 pandemic: An empirical study. *Sustainability (Basel)*, *15*(2), 1594. DOI: 10.3390/su15021594

Gerassimidou, S., Martin, O. V., Chapman, S. P., Hahladakis, J. N., & Iacovidou, E. (2021). Development of an integrated sustainability matrix to depict challenges and trade-offs of introducing bio-based plastics in the food packaging value chain. *Journal of Cleaner Production*, *286*, 125378. DOI: 10.1016/j.jclepro.2020.125378

Greenpod labs. (2025). Nature Inspired Solutions to Minimize Food Waste. Available on https://greenpodlabs.com/ (Accessed on 16th March 2025).

Guo, J., Zhang, Y., Fang, J., Ma, Z., Li, C., Yan, M., Qiao, N., Liu, Y., & Bian, M. (2024). Reduction and reuse of forestry and agricultural bio-waste through innovative green utilization approaches: A review. *Forests*, *15*(8), 1372. DOI: 10.3390/f15081372

Gupta, R. K., Ali, E. A., Abd El Gawad, F., Daood, V. M., Sabry, H., Karunanithi, S., & Srivastav, P. P. (2024). Valorization of fruits and vegetables waste byproducts for development of sustainable food packaging application. *Waste Management Bulletin*, *2*(4), 21–40. DOI: 10.1016/j.wmb.2024.08.005

Isah, S., & Ozbay, G. (2020). Valorization of food loss and wastes: Feedstocks for biofuels and valuable chemicals. *Frontiers in Sustainable Food Systems*, *4*, 82. DOI: 10.3389/fsufs.2020.00082

Islam, N. F., Gogoi, B., Saikia, R., Yousaf, B., Narayan, M., & Sarma, H. (2024). Encouraging circular economy and sustainable environmental practices by addressing waste management and biomass energy production. *Regional Sustainability*, *5*(4), 100174. DOI: 10.1016/j.regsus.2024.100174

Jameel, M. K., Mustafa, M. A., Ahmed, H. S., Mohammed, A., Ghazy, H., Shakir, M. N., Lawas, A. M., Mohammed, S., Idan, A. H., Mahmoud, Z. H., Sayadi, H., & Kianfar, E. (2024). Biogas: Production, properties, applications, economic and challenges: A review. *Results in Chemistry*, *7*, 101549. DOI: 10.1016/j.rechem.2024.101549

Jin, X., Song, J., & Liu, G. Q. (2020). Bioethanol production from rice straw through an enzymatic route mediated by enzymes developed in-house from Aspergillus fumigatus. *Energy*, *190*, 116395. DOI: 10.1016/j.energy.2019.116395

Kabir, E., Kim, K. H., & Kwon, E. E. (2023). Biochar as a tool for the improvement of soil and environment. *Frontiers in Environmental Science*, *11*, 1324533. DOI: 10.3389/fenvs.2023.1324533

Karim, R., Waaje, A., Roshid, M. M., & Yeamin, M. B. (2025). Turning the Waste Into Wealth: Progressing Toward Global Sustainability Through the Circular Economy in Waste Management. In *Sustainable Waste Management in the Tourism and Hospitality Sectors* (pp. 507-552). IGI Global Scientific Publishing.

Karungamye, P. (2024). Energy recovery from solid waste valorisation: Environmental and economic potential for developing countries. *Scientific African*, *26*, 02402. DOI: 10.1016/j.sciaf.2024.e02402

Khalife, E., Sabouri, M., Kaveh, M., & Szymanek, M. (2024). Recent advances in the application of agricultural waste in construction. *Applied Sciences (Basel, Switzerland)*, *14*(6), 2355. DOI: 10.3390/app14062355

Kibria, M. G., Masuk, N. I., Safayet, R., Nguyen, H. Q., & Mourshed, M. (2023). Plastic waste: Challenges and opportunities to mitigate pollution and effective management. *International Journal of Environmental Research*, *17*(1), 20. DOI: 10.1007/s41742-023-00507-z

Kirchherr, J., Yang, N. H. N., Schulze-Spüntrup, F., Heerink, M. J., & Hartley, K. (2023). Conceptualizing the circular economy (revisited): An analysis of 221 definitions. *Resources, Conservation and Recycling*, *194*, 107001. DOI: 10.1016/j.resconrec.2023.107001

Koiri, P., & Das, S. (2024). Agri-Food Waste Management and Treatment Approaches for Environmental Sustainability. In *Environmental Engineering and Waste Management: Recent Trends and Perspectives* (pp. 343–373). Springer Nature Switzerland. DOI: 10.1007/978-3-031-58441-1_12

Kordi, M., Farrokhi, N., Pech-Canul, M. I., & Ahmadikhah, A. (2024). Rice husk at a glance: From agro-industrial to modern applications. *Rice Science*, *31*(1), 14–32. DOI: 10.1016/j.rsci.2023.08.005

Koul, B., Yakoob, M., & Shah, M. P. (2022). Agricultural waste management strategies for environmental sustainability. *Environmental Research*, *206*, 112285. DOI: 10.1016/j.envres.2021.112285

Kshetri, N. (2022). Blockchain and supply chain transparency: A review of adoption and impacts. *International Journal of Information Management*, *65*, 102517.

Kumar, A., Rout, R. K., Rao, P. S., & Prabhakar, P. (2023). Optimization of pulsed mode sonication and in silico molecular docking study for antioxidant properties of mandarin (Citrus reticulata Blanco) peels. *Journal of Food Process Engineering*, *46*(6), e14111. DOI: 10.1111/jfpe.14111

Luo, L., Wang, J., Lv, J., Liu, Z., Sun, T., Yang, Y., & Zhu, Y. G. (2023). Carbon sequestration strategies in soil using biochar: Advances, challenges, and opportunities. *Environmental Science & Technology*, *57*(31), 11357–11372. DOI: 10.1021/acs.est.3c02620

Malau, A. G., Malau, A. G., & Simanjuntak, M. B. (2024). Innovating Sustainable Agriculture: Perspectives from Economy and Biology Professionals. [Jurnal Pendidikan Biologi Indonesia]. *Journal of Biological Education Indonesia*, *10*(1), 320–328. DOI: 10.22219/jpbi.v10i1.32587

Manzoor, S., Fayaz, U., Dar, A. H., Dash, K. K., Shams, R., Bashir, I., Pandey, V. K., & Abdi, G. (2024). Sustainable development goals through reducing food loss and food waste: A comprehensive review. *Future Foods : a Dedicated Journal for Sustainability in Food Science*, *9*, 100362. DOI: 10.1016/j.fufo.2024.100362

Maraveas, C. (2020). Production of sustainable construction materials using agro-wastes. *Materials (Basel)*, *13*(2), 262. DOI: 10.3390/ma13020262

Martínez-Sánchez, V.. (2025). Agri-food waste to phenolic compounds: Life cycle and eco-efficiency assessments. *Journal of Environmental Management*, *380*, 124935. DOI: 10.1016/j.jenvman.2025.124935

. Meena, A. L., Karwal, M., Dutta, D., & Mishra, R. P. (2021). Composting: phases and factors responsible for efficient and improved composting. *Agriculture and Food: e-Newsletter, 1*, 85-90.

Mihai, F. C., Gündoğdu, S., Markley, L. A., Olivelli, A., Khan, F. R., Gwinnett, C., Gutberlet, J., Reyna-Bensusan, N., Llanquileo-Melgarejo, P., Meidiana, C., Elagroudy, S., Ishchenko, V., Penney, S., Lenkiewicz, Z., & Molinos-Senante, M. (2021). Plastic pollution, waste management issues, and circular economy opportunities in rural communities. *Sustainability (Basel), 14*(1), 20. DOI: 10.3390/su14010020

Mishra, K., Siwal, S. S., Nayaka, S. C., Guan, Z., & Thakur, V. K. (2023). Waste-to-chemicals: Green solutions for bioeconomy markets. *The Science of the Total Environment, 887*, 164006. DOI: 10.1016/j.scitotenv.2023.164006

Molina, A.. (2024). Minimizing the environmental impacts of waste valorization systems using multi-criteria life cycle optimization. *Journal of Cleaner Production, 449*, 141619. DOI: 10.1016/j.jclepro.2024.141619

Morero, B., Lorenzon, A. B., & Cafaro, D. C. (2024). Integrated management of urban and rural wastes with energy recovery and low carbon emissions. *Journal of Cleaner Production, 434*, 139729. DOI: 10.1016/j.jclepro.2023.139729

Onyeaka, H., Tamasiga, P., Nwauzoma, U. M., Miri, T., Juliet, U. C., Nwaiwu, O., & Akinsemolu, A. A. (2023). Using artificial intelligence to tackle food waste and enhance the circular economy: Maximising resource efficiency and minimising environmental impact: A review. *Sustainability (Basel), 15*(13), 10482. DOI: 10.3390/su151310482

Osman, A. I., Fang, B., Zhang, Y., Liu, Y., Yu, J., Farghali, M., Rashwan, A. K., Chen, Z., Chen, L., Ihara, I., Rooney, D. W., & Yap, P. S. (2024). Life cycle assessment and techno-economic analysis of sustainable bioenergy production: A review. *Environmental Chemistry Letters, 22*(3), 1115–1154. DOI: 10.1007/s10311-023-01694-z

Pal, P., Singh, A. K., Srivastava, R. K., Rathore, S. S., Sahoo, U. K., Subudhi, S., Sarangi, P. K., & Prus, P. (2024). Circular bioeconomy in action: Transforming food wastes into renewable food resources. *Foods, 13*(18), 3007. DOI: 10.3390/foods13183007

Pamu, Y., & Alugubelli, S. (2025). Waste to Wealth: A Comprehensive Review of Agricultural Waste in Sustainable Building Materials. In *E3S Web of Conferences* (Vol. 616, p. 03002). EDP Sciences. DOI: 10.1051/e3sconf/202561603002

Petfoodprocesing. (2025). Insect protein producer receives $5.3 million in investments. Available on https://www.petfoodprocessing.net/articles/15754-insect-protein-producer-receives-53-million-in-investments. (Accessed on 17th March 2025).

Prabhakar, P. (2024). *Optimized Extraction and Characterization of Phytochemicals from Selected Ethnomedicinal Plants for Antidiabetic Phytopharmaceuticals* (Doctoral dissertation, IIT Kharagpur).

Prabhakar, P., & Banerjee, M. (2020). Antidiabetic phytochemicals: A comprehensive review on opportunities and challenges in targeted therapy for herbal drug development. *International Journal of Pharmaceutical Research, 12*(1), 1673–1696.

Prabhakar, P., Mukherjee, S., Kumar, A., Kumar, S., Verma, D. K., Dhara, S., Maiti, M. K., & Banerjee, M. (2023). Optimization of MAE for Carica papaya phytochemicals, and its in silico, in vitro, and ex vivo evaluation: For functional food and drug applications. *Food Bioscience, 54*, 102861. DOI: 10.1016/j.fbio.2023.102861

Prabhakar, P., Mukherjee, S., Kumar, A., Rout, R. K., Kumar, S., Verma, D. K., & Banerjee, M. (2024). In Silico, In Vitro and Ex Vivo Evaluation of the Antihyperglycaemic, Antioxidant and Cytotoxic Properties of Coccinia grandis L. Leaf Extract. *Food Technology and Biotechnology, 62*(2), 188–204. DOI: 10.17113/ftb.62.02.24.8162

Prabhakar, P., Verma, D. K., & Banerjee, M. (2024). Advances in enzyme-assisted extraction technique for antidiabetic phytochemicals: an emerging approach for green and economical technologies. In *Enzymatic Processes for Food Valorization* (pp. 191–216). Academic Press. DOI: 10.1016/B978-0-323-95996-4.00013-7

Prabhakar, S., & Nimesh, A. (2022). Skill development programmes for women in India: Current status and future perspectives. *World Journal of Advanced Engineering Technology and Sciences, 7*(1), 128–136. DOI: 10.30574/wjaets.2022.7.1.0105

Prabhakar, S., Nimesh, A., & Prabhakar, P. (2023). Startup ecosystem for rural development in India. In *Socio-Economic Disparities, Vulnerable Communities, and the Future of Work and Entrepreneurship* (pp. 26-50). IGI Global. DOI: 10.4018/978-1-6684-6990-3.ch003

Prabhakar, S., Prabhakar, P., Nimesh, A., & Banerjee, M. (2025). Production and Development of Nutraceuticals Using Sustainable Food System. In *Food Bioactives and Nutraceuticals: Dietary Medicine for Human Health and Well-Beings* (pp. 59–86). Springer Nature Singapore. DOI: 10.1007/978-981-97-9723-3_3

Prajapati, C. S., Priya, N. K., Bishnoi, S., Vishwakarma, S. K., Buvaneswari, K., Shastri, S., Tripathi, S., & Jadhav, A. (2025). The Role of Participatory Approaches in Modern Agricultural Extension: Bridging Knowledge Gaps for Sustainable Farming Practices. *Journal of Experimental Agriculture International*, *47*(2), 204–222. DOI: 10.9734/jeai/2025/v47i23281

Quitério, E., Grosso, C., Ferraz, R., Delerue-Matos, C., & Soares, C. (2022). A critical comparison of the advanced extraction techniques applied to obtain health-promoting compounds from seaweeds. *Marine Drugs*, *20*(11), 677. DOI: 10.3390/md20110677

. Rabbi, M. F., & Amin, M. B. (2024). Circular economy and sustainable practices in the food industry: A comprehensive bibliometric analysis. *Cleaner and Responsible Consumption*, 100206.

Rana, R. L., Lombardi, M., & Giungato, P. (2024). Circular economy and waste valorization: Policy frameworks and sustainability implications. *Journal of Cleaner Production*, *433*, 140195.

Rao, M. M., Botsa, S. M., Rao, T. P., Goddu, S. R., & Vijayasanthi, C. (2024). A comprehensive review on agricultural waste production and onsite management with circular economy opportunities. *Discover Sustainability*, *5*(1), 288. DOI: 10.1007/s43621-024-00492-z

Raphela, T., Manqele, N., & Erasmus, M. (2024). The impact of improper waste disposal on human health and the environment: A case of Umgungundlovu District in KwaZulu Natal Province, South Africa. *Frontiers in Sustainability*, *5*, 1386047. DOI: 10.3389/frsus.2024.1386047

Ribeiro, T. B., Voss, G. B., Coelho, M. C., & Pintado, M. E. (2022). Food waste and by-product valorization as an integrated approach with zero waste: Future challenges. In *Future foods* (pp. 569–596). Academic Press. DOI: 10.1016/B978-0-323-91001-9.00017-7

Robinson, G. M. (2024). Global sustainable agriculture and land management systems. *Geography and Sustainability*, *5*(4), 637–646. DOI: 10.1016/j.geosus.2024.09.001

Rosenboom, J. G., Langer, R., & Traverso, G. (2022). Bioplastics for a circular economy. *Nature Reviews. Materials*, *7*(2), 117–137. DOI: 10.1038/s41578-021-00407-8

Rossi, L. A., & Srai, J. S. (2024). Configuring circular by-product supply networks through public-private partnerships–A case study of rice straw stubble agri-waste in Punjab. *Journal of Cleaner Production*, *468*, 143093. DOI: 10.1016/j.jclepro.2024.143093

Saberi, S., Kouhizadeh, M., Sarkis, J., & Shen, L. (2023). Blockchain technology and its relationships to sustainable supply chain management. *International Journal of Production Research, 61*(6), 1791–1810.

Sadh, P. K., Duhan, S., & Duhan, J. S. (2018). Agro-industrial wastes and their utilization using solid state fermentation: A review. *Bioresources and Bioprocessing, 5*(1), 1–15. DOI: 10.1186/s40643-017-0187-z

Sahu, D. K., & Choudhary, D. (2025). An investigation of circular economy from sustainability perspective in agricultural sector of Indian markets: An extended PEST-O framework. *Journal of Foodservice Business Research*, •••, 1–44.

Samantaray, A., Chattaraj, S., Mitra, D., Ganguly, A., Kumar, R., Gaur, A., Mohapatra, P. K. D., Santos-Villalobos, S., Rani, A., & Thatoi, H. (2024). Advances in microbial based bio-inoculum for amelioration of soil health and sustainable crop production. *Current Research in Microbial Sciences, 7*, 100251. DOI: 10.1016/j.crmicr.2024.100251

Sarker, A., Ahmmed, R., Ahsan, S. M., Rana, J., Ghosh, M. K., & Nandi, R. (2024). A comprehensive review of food waste valorization for the sustainable management of global food waste. *Sustainable Food Technology, 2*(1), 48–69. DOI: 10.1039/D3FB00156C

Saxena, S., Moharil, M. P., Jadhav, P. V., Ghodake, B., Deshmukh, R., & Ingle, A. P. (2024). Transforming waste into wealth: Leveraging nanotechnology for recycling agricultural byproducts into value-added products. *Plant Nano Biology*, •••, 100127.

Senga, R., Nasr, M., Fujii, M., & Abdelhaleem, A. (2024). Sustainable valorization of agricultural waste into bioplastic and its end-of-life recyclability for biochar production: Economic profitability and life cycle assessment. *Chemosphere, 369*, 143847. DOI: 10.1016/j.chemosphere.2024.143847

Sengupta, S., Choudhary, S., Obayi, R., & Nayak, R. (2024). Reducing food loss through sustainable business models and agricultural innovation systems. *Supply Chain Management, 29*(3), 540–572. DOI: 10.1108/SCM-01-2023-0059

Shahzad, H. M. A., Asim, Z., Khan, S. J., Almomani, F., Mahmoud, K. A., Mustafa, M. R. U., & Rasool, K. (2024). Thermochemical and biochemical conversion of agricultural waste for bioenergy production: An updated review. *Discover Environment, 2*(1), 134. DOI: 10.1007/s44274-024-00171-w

Sharma, C., Pathak, P., & Gautam, S. (2024). Transforming agri-crop residue biomass for value addition: an innovative strategy toward resilient circular economy. In *Handbook of biomass* (pp. 1517–1542). Springer Nature Singapore. DOI: 10.1007/978-981-99-6727-8_66

Siddiqua, A., Hahladakis, J. N., & Al-Attiya, W. A. K. (2022). An overview of the environmental pollution and health effects associated with waste landfilling and open dumping. *Environmental Science and Pollution Research International, 29*(39), 58514–58536. DOI: 10.1007/s11356-022-21578-z

Singh, A. K., Pal, P., Rathore, S. S., Sahoo, U. K., Sarangi, P. K., Prus, P., & Dziekański, P. (2023). Sustainable utilization of biowaste resources for biogas production to meet rural bioenergy requirements. *Energies, 16*(14), 5409. DOI: 10.3390/en16145409

Singh, N., Biswas, R., & Banerjee, M. (2026). Life cycle carbon accounting and waste valorisation in litchi supply chains for climate-resilient food systems. *Sustainable Food Technology, 4*(2), 1577–1595. DOI: 10.1039/D5FB00519A

Smith, A. (2025). Systemic Analysis of Circular Economy Principles in Agricultural Waste Management and Their Synergy with National Sustainable Development Objectives. *Transdisciplinary Advances in Social Computing, Complex Dynamics, and Computational Creativity, 15*(2), 10–21.

Somorin, T., Campos, L. C., Kinobe, J. R., Kulabako, R. N., & Afolabi, O. O. D. (2023). Sustainable valorisation of agri-food waste from open-air markets in Kampala, Uganda via standalone and integrated waste conversion technologies. *Biomass and Bioenergy, 172*, 106752. DOI: 10.1016/j.biombioe.2023.106752

. Sonam, Kala, S., Prabhakar, P., & Banerjee, M. (2021). Post-training Knowledge and Attitude Assessment of the Women Entrepreneurs towards Mushroom Cultivation.

Sonam, Shishir, K., & Prabhakar, P. (2021). Constraint Analysis in Mushroom Cultivation among Women Mushroom Cultivators in the State of Bihar, India. *Advances in Management, 14*(2), 7–11.

. Sonam (2018). Sustainability of women mushroom growers and its impact on their livelihood, Msc. Thesis, *Dr. Rajendra Prasad Central Agricultural University, Pusa, India.*

Tomić, T., & Schneider, D. R. (2020). Circular economy in waste management–Socio-economic effect of changes in waste management system structure. *Journal of Environmental Management, 267*, 110564. DOI: 10.1016/j.jenvman.2020.110564

Ufitikirezi, J. D. D. M., Filip, M., Ghorbani, M., Zoubek, T., Olšan, P., Bumbálek, R., Strob, M., Bartoš, P., Umurungi, S. N., Murindangabo, Y. T., Heřmánek, A., Tupý, O., Havelka, Z., Stehlík, R., Černý, P., & Smutný, L. (2024). Agricultural waste valorization: Exploring environmentally friendly approaches to bioenergy conversion. *Sustainability (Basel)*, *16*(9), 3617. DOI: 10.3390/su16093617

Usman, I., Hussain, M., Imran, A., Afzaal, M., Saeed, F., & Javed, M. & A. Saewan, S. (. (2022). Traditional and innovative approaches for the extraction of bioactive compounds. *International Journal of Food Properties*, *25*(1), 1215–1233. DOI: 10.1080/10942912.2022.2074030

Usman, I., Sana, S., Afzaal, M., Imran, A., Jaffar, H. M., Sukhera, S., Munir, M., Asghar, A., & Urugo, M. M. (2025). Phytochemicals in plant food waste: Innovative insight and implications. *Journal of Agriculture and Food Research*, *20*, 101779. DOI: 10.1016/j.jafr.2025.101779

Verma, D. K., & Thakur, M. (Eds.). (2021). *Phytochemicals in food and health: Perspectives for research and technological development*. CRC Press. DOI: 10.1201/9781003082125

Worakittikul, W., Srisathan, W. A., Rattanpon, K., Kulkaew, A., Groves, J., Pontun, P., & Naruetharadhol, P. (2025). Cultivating Sustainability: Harnessing Open Innovation and Circular Economy Practices for Eco-Innovation in Agricultural SMEs. *Journal of Open Innovation*, *11*(1), 100494. DOI: 10.1016/j.joitmc.2025.100494

World, T. (2025). Coffee Recycling Company Bio-Bean Launches Inficaf-Using Upcycled, Spent Coffee Grounds For Sustainable Product Innovations. Available on https://www.textileworld.com/textile-world/fiber-world/2021/07/coffee-recycling-company-bio-bean-launches-inficaf-using-upcycled-spent-coffee-grounds-for-sustainable-product-innovations/ (Accessed on 16th March 2025).

Zhang, Q. W., Lin, L. G., & Ye, W. C. (2018). Techniques for extraction and isolation of natural products: A comprehensive review. *Chinese Medicine*, *13*(1), 1–26. DOI: 10.1186/s13020-018-0177-x

Zhao, X., Wang, Y., Cai, D., & Xi, B. (2024). Tailored composting and fertilization strategies can inspire the transformation of agriculture for sustainable development. *Journal of Agricultural and Food Chemistry*, *72*(16), 8874–8875. DOI: 10.1021/acs.jafc.4c02708

Chapter 10
Transitioning to a Circular Economy:
The Role of Electric Vehicles in India's Sustainable Future

Kathirvel Ayyaswamy
http://orcid.org/0000-0002-5347-9110
Department of Computer Science and Engineering, Saveetha Engineering College, Chennai, India

Naren Kathirvel
http://orcid.org/0009-0003-7581-5482
Anand Institute of Higher Technology, India

ABSTRACT

Central to this transition is the adoption of electric vehicles (EVs), which present a unique opportunity to address environmental concerns and reduce dependence on fossil fuels. This paper examines the role of EVs in fostering a circular economy in India, focusing on key aspects such as battery recycling, the life cycle of EV components, and the reduction of fossil fuel dependence. We analyze the Indian government's approach to promote EVs through policy initiatives, subsidies, and infrastructure development, and we highlight the nation's commitment to sustainable transportation. Furthermore, the paper delves into the challenge that hinder EV adoption, which include high upfront costs, few charging stations, and consumer anxiety about the range of EVs. By exploring the opportunities and challenges of EV integration, this research provides valuable insights into India's transition towards a circular economy, with implications for policymakers, industry stakeholders, and the global community who invest in sustainable development.

DOI: 10.4018/979-8-3373-7391-1.ch010

1. INTRODUCTION

1.1 Why Wind-Centric Circular E-Mobility Now?

India's push toward clean mobility is colliding—productively—with the rapid rise of wind and solar power. Electric vehicles (EVs) promise lower local air pollution and, when charged with low-carbon electricity, deep climate benefits. Yet those benefits depend on *how* and *when* we charge, *which* resources supply the grid, and *how* we manage materials across the EV lifecycle. A **circular economy** lens helps India do more with less: use fewer virgin materials, extend component life, and recover value at end-of-life. A **wind-centred** system adds another lever—leveraging India's growing wind fleet to cut EV charging emissions and absorb variable renewable power. Artificial intelligence (AI) is the glue: it predicts wind and load, schedules charging, manages battery health, and orchestrates vehicle-to-grid (V2G) services at scale (IEA, 2023; IEA, 2025).

Two system facts anchor this chapter. First, India's grid is decarbonizing but remains emissions-intensive by OECD standards. The Central Electricity Authority's latest *CO_2 Baseline Database* shows a **Combined Margin** near **0.757 kg CO_2/kWh** for 2023–24—down as renewables grow, but still significant (CEA, v19/v20).

Second, India is adding renewables at record rates; MNRE reports RE capacity crossed **220 GW** by March 31, 2025, with **wind additions rebounding** in FY2025 (adding ~4.2 GW) (MNRE, 2025; JMK Research, 2025; PIB, 2025). These trends make EV–wind integration not just plausible but timely.

This chapter advances three contributions.

1. **Framework.** We propose an **AI-enabled EV–wind integration model** and explicitly map the **9Rs** (Refuse, Rethink, Reduce, Reuse, Repair, Refurbish, Remanufacture, Repurpose, Recycle) across the EV value chain—batteries *and* non-battery components—to restore the circular-economy depth missing from many EV policy discussions.
2. **Original, transparent calculation.** We present a **simple India-specific emissions scenario** comparing EV and ICE gCO_2/km now (using CEA grid factors) and under wind-rich charging, across **2-wheeler, 3-wheeler, and compact car** segments. Results show immediate benefits for two- and three-wheelers, and a clear break-even grid-intensity threshold for cars. (Section 4).
3. **Practice-ready patterns and cases.** Drawing on current initiatives—smart charging guidance from IEA (2023), India's **TPDDL–ISGF** V2G demonstration in Delhi, and state-level wind expansion—**we turn the EV narrative into wind-system practice** (Sections 6–7).

Crucially, a circular framing must include **policy updates**: India's **Battery Waste Management Rules, 2022** (which supersede the 2001 rules) embed **Extended Producer Responsibility** (EPR) for batteries, raising the floor for safe collection and high-value recycling/repurposing—policy levers your original manuscript referenced only partially (MoEFCC/CPCB, 2022–2025).

With wind-aligned charging (e.g., night-wind or day-time if co-located with wind-solar hybrids), AI-orchestrated demand shifting, and stronger EPR, India can **reduce EV charging emissions today** while building a **materials-circular** EV sector for tomorrow.

Learning objectives. After this chapter, readers will be able to:

- Explain **how EV charging strategy and resource mix** (especially wind) shape real-world EV emissions in India;
- Apply the **9Rs** across EV components (batteries, motors, power electronics, body) to design circular interventions;
- Describe **AI use-cases** (forecasting, smart charging, battery health, V2G scheduling) that integrate EVs with wind power;
- Use a **simple break-even formula** to compare EV vs ICE emissions under different grid intensities and consumption values;
- Identify **policy instruments** (EPR, FAME, CAFE, state EV/wind policies) that enable circular EV–wind systems.

2. CONCEPTUAL FRAMEWORK: AI-ENABLED EV–WIND INTEGRATION FOR A CIRCULAR ECONOMY

India's EV transition delivers the largest carbon and air-quality benefits when charging is aligned with wind-rich hours and when materials are managed across the full 9Rs hierarchy. In this framework, AI links the power system and mobility system—forecasting wind, scheduling smart charging and V2G, and protecting battery health—so both electrons and materials circulate efficiently. We first map the 9Rs to EVs, charging assets, and the grid (Section 3.1). We then show, with a transparent India-specific calculation, when EVs beat ICE on today's grid and under wind-aligned charging (Section 4). Finally, Sections 5–9 turn the framework into practice with India-focused design patterns, policies, and cases.

Table 1. The 9Rs applied to India's EV–Wind system (battery and non-battery components)

R-strategy	EV batteries	Motors & power electronics	Body/Interior	Charging & grid	What AI adds
Refuse	Avoid oversizing packs for use-case; spec LFP where appropriate	Avoid rare-earth magnets via magnet-free designs where feasible	Avoid exotic composites unless recyclability is proven	Avoid overspec chargers that sit idle	Right-sizing via data-driven duty-cycle analysis
Rethink	Shift from ownership to BaaS/swapping for fleets	Shift to modular motor/inverter kits	Design modular interiors for fleet refurb	Co-locate wind–solar–storage–EV hubs	Reinforcement learning for optimal siting/ sizing
Reduce	Improve pack energy density; lightweight enclosures	High-efficiency inverters; lower copper	Lightweighting with high-strength steels	Smart charging to reduce peak capacity	Forecast-based charge scheduling (IEA, 2023) IEA
Reuse	2nd-life stationary storage (wind balancing)	Reuse motors/ inverters after testing	Reuse seats/ panels in fleet refresh	Reuse AC chargers in new sites	Prognostics to screen reusable parts
Repair	Module-level repair, BMS updates	Board/component-level repair guidance	Replace trim/ hardware over full replacements	Repairable connectors, replaceable cables	AI diagnostics and guided repair
Refurbish	Pack remanufacture (cells/modules)	Motor rewinding; inverter refurbishment	Refurbish interiors for new service life	Refurbish chargers, swap power modules	Predictive maintenance windows
Remanufacture	Cell sorting + reman lines	Remanufactured inverter/motor programs	Structural reman (fleet vehicles)	Factory reman of DC fast chargers	Digital twins to qualify reman parts
Repurpose	Non-automotive storage; microgrids	Motors in stationary drives	Panels to non-critical uses	Retire DC stacks to community storage	Optimal asset allocation
Recycle	Hydromet/direct recycling for Li, Ni, Co, graphite	Copper/aluminium recycling	High-yield steel recycling	Metals/cables recovery	Traceability + scrap quality control

A circular economy replaces 'take-make-dispose' with design strategies that keep products and materials in use (9Rs); in EV systems this applies to batteries, power electronics, vehicle bodies, and even the charging network.

3. METHODS & SIMPLE EMISSIONS SCENARIO

3.1 Methods: Policy–Technology–Economy lens + calculation

We combine (i) a policy scan (EPR, FAME/CAFE/state EV & wind), (ii) a technology mapping (Section 3), and (iii) a simple transparent emissions calculation for three Indian segments.

Assumptions

- Grid emission factor (Combined Margin): 0.757 kg CO_2/kWh (2023–24) (CEA v19/v20).
- Wind life-cycle emissions ~ 11 g CO_2/kWh (onshore median; NREL/IPCC compilations).
- Vehicle energy use: E2W 0.017 kWh/km (NITI Aayog); E4W compact 0.15 kWh/km (real-world average); E3W 0.08 kWh/km (assumption consistent with India studies/specs).
- ICE petrol CO_2: 2.31 kg CO_2/litre; representative fuel economy: E2W 45 km/l, E3W 25 km/l, E4W 18 km/l; CAFE targets ~130 g/km (Phase I) and 113 g/km (Phase II) for cars (context).

Formulas

1. EV gCO_2/km = (kWh/km) × (grid kg/kWh) × 1,000
2. EV gCO_2/km with wind = (kWh/km) × (wind kg/kWh) × 1,000
3. ICE gCO_2/km = (2.31 kg/L ÷ km/L) × 1,000
4. Break-even grid factor (kg/kWh) = ICE gCO_2/km ÷ [1,000 × (kWh/km)]

Table 2. EV vs. ICE emissions—India scenario

Segment	EV on today's grid (gCO_2/km)	EV on wind LCA (gCO_2/km)	ICE petrol (gCO_2/km)	Grid break-even for EV (kg CO_2/kWh)
2-wheeler (E2W) 0.017 kWh/km	12.9	0.19	51.3	3.02
3-wheeler (E3W) 0.08 kWh/km	60.6	0.88	92.4	1.16
4-wheeler (E4W) 0.15 kWh/km	113.6	1.65	128.3	0.856

Grid factor: CEA Combined Margin 2023–24 ≈ 0.757 kg CO_2/kWh.
Wind LCA: onshore median ≈ 11 g CO_2/kWh.
Energy use: E2W 0.017 kWh/km; E3W 0.08 kWh/km; compact E4W 0.15 kWh/km.
CE emissions: 2.31 kg CO_2/L; sample FE—E2W 45 km/L; E3W 25 km/L; E4W 18 km/L.

Results rounded to one decimal.

Interpretation.

E2W/E3W already win by a wide margin even on today's grid; wind-aligned charging is "gravy."

For compact E4Ws, the break-even grid intensity ≈ 0.856 kg/kWh—i.e., India's current Combined Margin (~0.757) already puts many EVs at or below typical ICE g/km; charging aligned to wind improves the margin further. (CEA; NREL/IPCC.)

4. BATTERY TECHNOLOGY AND RECYCLING

4.1. Advances in Battery Technology

4.1.1. Overview of Battery Types Used in EVs

Lithium-ion Batteries: Dominate the current EV market owing to their high energy density, long lifespan relative to other batteries, and decreasing production costs (Miao et al., 2019; Zeng et al., 2019; Srinivasan et al., 2008).

Solid-State Batteries: Emerging as a promising alternative to Li-ion. Solid state batteries have higher potential energy density, recharge faster, and are safer because the contents are solid electrolytes instead of flammable liquid ones (Nicola, 2024).

Other Battery Chemistries: Research continues in other battery chemistries, such as lithium-sulfur and lithium-air, which hold the potential for even higher energy densities, but these technologies require more research to improve lifespan and price (Zeng et al., 2019).

4.1.2. Innovations in Battery Design and Performance

Cathode and Anode Materials: Research continues into new materials and modifications to improve energy density, charging speed, and stability. This includes advancements in high-voltage cathodes and high-capacity anodes (Argonne National Laboratory, 2012).

Electrolytes: Developing safer and more efficient electrolytes is crucial, particularly for solid-state batteries. Research focuses on solid electrolytes that conduct ions more efficiently and have wide electrochemical windows (Argonne National Laboratory, 2012).

Battery Management Systems (BMS): Sophisticated BMS are essential to monitor battery health, optimize performance, and ensure safety. Advancements in BMS algorithms and sensor technology contribute to longer battery life and improved reliability (Brown et al., 1988; Srinivasan et al., 2008).

4.2. Challenges and Opportunities in Battery Recycling

4.2.1. Current State of Battery Recycling in India

Emerging Industry: Battery recycling in India is still in its nascent stage but presents significant potential for growth. While projections vary, millions of EV batteries are likely to expire in India by 2030, creating both an environmental challenge and a substantial economic opportunity (ATTERO, 2021).

Policy and Regulatory Framework: The Indian government is actively developing policies and regulations to promote battery recycling and manage battery waste. This includes policies for Extended Producer Responsibility, which hold manufacturers accountable for the safe disposal and recycling of their products, including EV batteries (BATX Energies, 2022).

Key Players: Several companies are beginning to recycle batteries in India, including Attero and BATX Energies, which focus on recovering valuable materials from spent batteries (ATTERO, 2021; BATX Energies, 2022).

4.2.2. Technologies and Processes for Battery Recycling

Hydrometallurgy: A common method that involves dissolving battery components in acids to extract valuable metals like lithium, cobalt, and nickel (Arambarri et al., 2019).

Pyrometallurgy: This process utilizes high temperature to melt down battery materials and recover metals such as cobalt and nickel (Arambarri et al., 2019).

Direct Recycling: A newer approach that recovers and reuses entire battery components, which reduces environmental impact and improves resource utilization (Ali et al., 2021).

4.2.3. Economic and Environmental Benefits of Battery Recycling

Resource Recovery: Recycling significantly reduces the need to mine critical minerals such as lithium, cobalt, and nickel: all of which are essential for battery production but often derive from regions with fragile environments (Arambarri et al., 2019; Volan et al., 2021)

Economic Opportunities: Establishing a robust battery recycling industry in India can create new jobs, attract investment, and foster a domestic supply chain for battery materials, which will make the country more competitive economically (Volan et al., 2021).

Environmental Protection: Proper battery recycling prevents hazardous materials from entering landfills, where these materials can leach into the environment and pose risks to human health. Recycling also contributes to a circular economy by reducing the overall environmental footprint of EV batteries (Arambarri et al., 2019; Mertens et al., 2024).

4.2.4. Challenges Specific to India

Informal Recycling Sector: A large portion of battery recycling in India currently takes place informally, by businesses or individuals who lack the technology and safety standards to protect the environment properly (E-Vehicleinfo, 2021).

Logistics and Collection Networks: Establishing efficient and comprehensive logistic networks for collecting spent batteries from across the country is crucial for scaling up recycling efforts (Bonu & Panigrahi, 2019).

4.2.5. Government Incentives and Schemes

The Indian government is exploring various incentives and schemes to encourage investment in battery recycling technologies and infrastructure. These may include tax breaks, subsidies, and grants to support the development of a sustainable and competitive battery recycling industry in India (Battery Recycling Companies India, 2019).

4.3 Battery policy in India: Battery Waste Management Rules, 2022 (EPR focus)

India's **Battery Waste Management Rules, 2022** (MoEFCC/CPCB) supersede the 2001 Batteries Rules and establish **Extended Producer Responsibility (EPR)** across portable, automotive, and industrial traction batteries. Producers must ensure collection, transportation, recycling or refurbishment to prescribed recovery rates;

maintain digital records/QR-enabled traceability; and meet material recovery targets through authorized recyclers. For EV traction batteries this makes the CE loop (repair, remanufacture, repurpose, recycle) an enforceable compliance pathway rather than a voluntary option. These provisions align your chapter's 9Rs with current Indian law and remove the need to rely on EU regulations in this core Indian policy paragraph.

5. SUSTAINABLE SOURCING OF EV COMPONENTS

5.1. Ethical and Sustainable Sourcing of Raw Materials

5.1.1. Critical Materials in EVs

Battery Materials: Lithium, cobalt, nickel, manganese, and graphite are essential for EV battery performance. While each plays a crucial role, certain materials have tenuous supply chains. For instance, many allege that the cobaltmines in the Democratic Republic of Congo exploit workers. (Lipman & Maier, 2021; Miao et al., 2019).

Motor Materials: High-performance EV motors often rely on permanent magnets, which require rare earth elements such as neodymium, dysprosium, and praseodymium. These elements are critical for motor efficiency, but these elements only exist in a few regions of the world, which creates a tenuous supply chain. (Lipman & Maier, 2021)

5.1.2. Issues Related to Mining and Sourcing

Environmental Impact: Mining for battery materials can have detrimental environmental consequences, including deforestation, habitat loss, water pollution from chemical leaching, and greenhouse gas emissions. For example, lithium extraction, particularly in the 'Lithium Triangle' of South America, can use an excess of water in arid regions (Agusdinata et al., 2018; Climate Nexus, 2021).

Labor Practices: Allegations abound of human rights abuses in cobalt mines, primarily in artisanal mines., These allegations include the exploitation of child labor and unsafe working conditions, Ethics throughout the supply chain are important (Agusdinata et al., 2018; Climate Nexus, 2021).

Geopolitical Concerns: The global distribution of critical material reserves is highly concentrated, raising geopolitical concerns. For example, China controls a sizeable portion of global rare earth elements, which creates a vulnerable supply chain (Cheng et al., 2024; Zeng et al., 2022).

Lithium: Over 50% of global lithium reserves are in the "Lithium Triangle" of Chile, Argentina, and Bolivia (Jones et al., 2020).

Cobalt: The Democratic Republic of Congo holds over 70% of global cobalt reserves (Jones et al., 2020).

Rare Earth Elements: China accounts for over 60% of global rare earth element extraction (Jones et al., 2020).

5.1.3. Challenges and Opportunities for India

Import Dependence: Currently, India relies on many imports for EV battery materials, which leaves India vulnerable to global supply chain disruptions and price fluctuations (Elshkaki, 2020).

Ethical Sourcing: To scale up its EV industry, India must ensure that the suppliers of raw materials conduct business ethically. India should promote responsible mining practices, monitor partners to ensure they conduct their affairs ethically,, and favor partnerships with countries that adhere to high environmental and labor standards (Material Insights, 2023).

Domestic Resource Development: While India possesses few reserves of some critical materials, there are opportunities to explore for more domestic supply and reduce import dependence. Geological surveys, research and development of new extraction technologies, and promoting circular economy principles to recover valuable materials from spent products all can reduce India's dependence upon foreign supply sources (Elshkaki, 2020).

5.2. Strategies for Reducing Material Dependency

5.2.1. Alternative Materials and Resource Substitution

Battery Chemistries: Discovering alternative battery chemistries that rely less on critical materials is crucial.

Lithium Iron Phosphate: LFP batteries have a lower energy density than some alternatives, but these are becoming increasingly popular, especially in China, because these batteries use less cobalt and nickel (Miao et al., 2019).

Sodium-ion Batteries: Research into sodium-ion batteries, which utilize abundant sodium, holds promise as a potential long-term alternative to lithium-ion. However, these batteries have a lower energy density than lithium-ion batteries (Miao et al., 2019).

Material Substitution:

Manganese-rich Cathodes: The use of manganese-rich cathodes in batteries can reduce reliance on nickel and cobalt. However, research must improve the lifespan and performance of manganese cathodes to match those of nickel-rich cathodes. (Miao et al., 2019)

Magnet-free Motors: Developing magnet-free motors, such as synchronous reluctance motors, eliminates the need for rare earth elements. However, these motors often cannot achieve the same power as their permanent magnet counterparts. Larger and heavier motors may be necessary to achieve comparable performance. (Lipman & Maier, 2021)

5.2.2. Reducing Material Consumption through Design Innovation

Lightweighting: Lightweighting techniques that use materials such as high-strength steel and aluminum alloys can reduce the material requirements for EVs. However, use of these advanced materials can increase manufacturing costs.

Design for Disassembly and Recycling: Designing EVs for easy disassembly and material recovery at the end of their life cycle is essential for a circular economy. However, implementing these design principles may require changes in manufacturing processes and may increase production costs (Dumée, 2021).

Component Standardization: Standardizing EV components, particularly batteries, can simplify recycling processes and improve material recovery rates. However, achieving industry-wide standardization can be challenging owing to rapid technological advancements and diverse company priorities (Dumée, 2021).

Extending Vehicle Lifespan: Designing EVs for durability that extends their lifespan can reduce the need for frequent vehicle replacements and lower total material consumption. However, durable EVs may require more robust components, which could increase the price of EVs (Rissman et al., 2020).

6. INFRASTRUCTURE AND RENEWABLE ENERGY INTEGRATION

6.1. Development of Charging Infrastructure

6.1.1. Current State of EV Charging in India

Limited but Growing Network: While still small compared to developed countries, India's EV charging network is expanding. Government initiatives such as the FAME-II scheme incentivize the development of charging infrastructure (Datta, 2018).

Urban Concentration: Charging stations concentrate in major cities with fewer in smaller towns and rural areas.

Charging Standards: The adoption of standard charging protocols (e.g., Bharat DC-001 and AC charging standards) will ensure compatability between EVs and charging stations (Kumar et al., 2021).

6.1.2. Challenges and Opportunities in Expansion

Investment: Attracting sizeable investments to build a widespread charging network is crucial. Both public and private sector funds are necessary (Datta, 2018).

Grid Capacity: Rapid EV adoption will strain existing power grids. There is a need to upgrade the grid and install smart charging solutions to manage peak demand (Energy Agency, 2023).

Land Availability: Securing land for charging stations, especially in densely populated urban areas, poses a challenge. Solutions include placing charging infrastructure in existing parking lots or commercial buildings.

Rural Electrification: Extending charging infrastructure to rural areas is essential for equitable EV adoption. A prerequisite for this expansion is a reliable electric grid that consumers can afford (Datta, 2018).

Renewable Energy Integration: Using renewable energy sources, such as solar and wind power, to supply the charging infrastructure will reduce the carbon footprint of EVs. Charging stations can be solar powered, and EVs can disperse energy storage and resupply the grid through vehicle-to-grid (V2G) technology (Large, 2021; Energy Agency, 2023).

6.2. Integrating Renewable Energy with EV Charging

6.2.1. Powering EVs with Renewables

Reducing Carbon Footprint: Using renewable energy sources such as solar, wind, and hydro power to charge electric vehicles (EVs) can reduce greenhouse gas emissions significantly. Conventional power generation from fossil fuels produces high carbon emissions, which counteracts the environmental benefits of EVs. By using renewable energy to supply the EV charging infrastructure, we can ensure that the entire lifecycle of EVs, from production to disposal, is as eco-friendly as possible. This approach not only mitigates climate change by lowering carbon emissions but also enhances the sustainability of the transportation sector. Studies have shown that the carbon emissions from EVs charged with renewable energy are lower than those charged with electricity that the burning of coal and natural gas produces (Large, 2021).

Energy Independence Another advantage of using renewable energy to charge EVs is thatIndia will be more independent of foreign energy sources. India imports a large portion of its fossil fuels, which makes it vulnerable to global market fluctuations and geopolitical tensions. By relying more on domestic renewable energy resources, India can reduce its reliance on imported fuels and ensure greater energy security. Domestic supply stabilizes the economy by reducing the trade deficit and fosters a more resilient energy system that is capable of withstanding global supply disruptions (Joseph & Elangovan, 2018).

Solar-Powered Charging Stations

Solar-powered charging stations are increasingly popular in India, particularly in sunny regions. These stations use rooftop solar panels to generate electricity on-site and provide a clean and sustainable source of energy for EVs. This dispersion of power generation reduces the burden on the national grid and reduces transmission losses. Solar-powered stations are particularly advantageous in remote and rural areas where connections to the grid may be unreliable or unavailable. Additionally, these solar-powered stations can integrate renewable energy with smart grid technologies, which optimizes energy use and storage (Large, 2021).

Wind Energy Integration

Wind energy also can power EV charging infrastructure, especially in windy coastal and high-altitude regions. Wind energy can complement solar power and provide a more consistent and reliable energy supply. For instance, wind farms can be near major highways and transport hubs where the farms can supply power to fast-charging stations directly. Batteries and hydro station storage tanks with pumps can supplement wind and solar resources when these are unavailable as part of an energy management system. By using these renewable resources, India can create a diversified and resilient EV charging network that supports a large fleet of EVs (Joseph & Elangovan, 2018).

6.2.2. Smart Grids and V2G Technology

Managing Peak Demand

Smart grid technologies help to optimize the charging process for electric vehicles (EVs) by coordinating energy demand and supply. One difficulty with widespread adoption of EVs is the potential strain on the electrical grid, especially during peak demand periods. Smart grids, equipped with modern meters that communicate through the grid, can alleviate the strain by varying charging times based on grid load conditions. By creating incentives for EV owners to charge their vehicles during off-peak hours or when renewable energy generation is at its peak, such as during sunny or windy conditions, smart grids can help balance the load. This prevents grid congestion and improves the use of clean energy sources, which reduces the overall carbon footprint of EVs. Moreover, pricing that varies based upon supply generation can encourage consumers to charge their EVs during periods of low demand and contribute to a more efficient and resilient energy system (Energy Agency, 2023).

Vehicle-to-Grid (V2G)

Vehicle-to-Grid (V2G) technology transforms how EVs integrate into the energy ecosystem. V2G enables two-way energy flow between EVs and the grid, which allows vehicles to draw power or discharge electricity back to the grid. This capability transforms EVs into energy storage systems that can support the grid during peak demand periods. For example, during times of high electricity demand, such as in the evening when household consumption peaks, EVs connected to the grid can supply stored energy andreduce the demand on power plants, thereby mitigating blackouts. This process stabilizes the grid and offers financial incentives to EV owners who can sell surplus energy back to the grid. V2G technology enables a more flexible and decentralized energy system and better integration of intermittent renewable energy sources such as solar and wind (Energy Agency, 2023).

Grid Stability and Ancillary Services

In addition to augmenting the grid during periods of peak demand, V2G technology and smart grids can enhance grid stability and reliability through ancillary services. EVs equipped with V2G capabilities can assist in voltage regulation, frequency control, and other activities necessary for stable electricity supply. For instance, by discharging energy in response to deviations in electrical frequency, EVs can help maintain the grid's frequency within safe operational limits. This is particularly valuable in grids that rely on renewable energy, because changes in the quantity of power generation can lead to frequency instability. Additionally, V2G-enabled EVs can react when power wanes by keeping the voltage stable and reducing transmission losses. These ancillary services enhance the resilience and efficiency of the grid and create new revenue opportunities for EV owners and aggregators. By participating in these grid services, EVs contribute to a more robust and adaptable energy infrastructure that is capable of supporting the transition to a future in which renewable energy is ubiquitous (Large, 2021).

6.3. Case Studies of Successful Implementations

While few comprehensive case studies with detailed data on EV charging infrastructure integrated with renewable energy exist in the research that is now available, a few examples illustrate the progress thus far:

Case Box A — Gujarat: wind corridors + expressway fast-charging hubs (2024–2025).

Wind-rich Kutch–Saurashtra corridors can anchor co-located wind-solar-storage charging hubs on national highways. Fleet charging windows can be aligned to night-wind hours, with day-time top-ups coming from hybrid sites

Case Box B — Delhi: V2G + BESS for urban reliability (2024–2025).

Pilot V2G with government and delivery fleets in depots; pair with DISCOM-scale BESS so EVs absorb surplus wind at night and support the evening peak.

7. POLICY INITIATIVES AND INCENTIVES

7.1.1. National and State-Level Policies

FAME-II Scheme

The Faster Adoption and Manufacturing of Electric Vehicles (FAME) scheme, particularly its second phase (FAME-II), is a cornerstone of India's efforts to accelerate the use of electric vehicles (EVs). Launched in 2019, FAME-II aims to promote EVs through a comprehensive set of measures that include financial incentives for EV buyers, subsidies for electric buses, and the development of charging infrastructure. The scheme provides direct incentives for the purchase of electric two-wheelers, three-wheelers, four-wheelers, and buses, which lowers the initial cost for consumers. Additionally, FAME-II supports the establishment of a robust charging network by providing capital for the construction of charging stations, particularly in metropolitan areas, highways, and key urban centers. The scheme's objectives align with India's broader goals of reducing vehicular emissions, curbing air pollution, and decreasing dependency on fossil fuels (Bassi, 2024).

National Electric Mobility Mission Plan (NEMMP)

The National Electric Mobility Mission Plan (NEMMP) 2020 outlines India's strategic vision for transitioning to electric mobility. Launched in 2013, NEMMP sets a long-term framework for the promotion and adoption of EVs, focusing on creating conditions conducive to EV manufacturing and adoption. The plan envisions widespread deployment of EVs, from two-wheelers to commercial vehicles. The goal was significant fuel savings and emissions reductions by 2020. NEMMP emphasizes research and development (R&D) in battery technology, power electronics, and vehicle design, in order to build a strong domestic EV manufacturing base. It also highlighted the need for incentives to foster market growth that include subsidies, tax exemptions, and public awareness campaigns (Maheshwari et al., 2021).

State-Level EV Policies

In addition to national policies, several Indian states have introduced their own electric vehicle policies, which provide additional incentives to accelerate EV adoption. These state policies often complement the national initiatives by offering local benefits: such as tax rebates, registration fee waivers, and subsidies for setting up EV charging infrastructure. For example, Delhi's EV policy aims to achieve 25% EV market share in new vehicle registrations by 2024 by offering incentives for the purchase of electric two-wheelers, autos, and goods carriers. The policy also includes provisions for establishing public charging and battery swapping stations, as well as creating green jobs through the promotion of EV-related industries. States such as Maharashtra, Karnataka, and Tamil Nadu have deployed similar EV policies specific to their regional needs, which further bolsters the national push for electric mobility (Zhang et al., 2014).

Battery Swapping Policy

In response to the growing demand for EVs and the need to overcome consumer anxiety about the range of EVs, the Indian government has introduced initiatives to promote battery swapping recently. The battery swapping policy aims to separate the ownership of the vehicle and the battery and allows consumers to swap discharged batteries with fully charged ones at swapping stations. This approach reduces the initial cost of EVs by excluding the battery from the price and minimizes charging time, which makes EVs more convenient for consumers. Battery swapping can be very beneficial for commercial fleets, such as taxis and delivery vehicles, where uptime and operational efficiency are critical. The policy encourages the standardization of battery specifications and connectors to facilitate compatibility among the products of different manufacturers. Additionally, it supports the establishment of a comprehensive network of swapping stations across urban and rural areas, which makes EVs more convenient for consumers. This initiative is likely to play a major role in accelerating EV adoption in India by alleviating concerns about the range of EVs.

Demand-Side Incentives

The Indian government has implemented a range of incentives to increase consumer demand for electric vehicles . These incentives aim to lower the purchase price of EVs to make them more competitive with internal combustion engine vehicles. Key incentives include:

- **Subsidies on Vehicle Purchase**: Under schemes like FAME-II, buyers of electric two-wheelers, three-wheelers, four-wheelers, and buses receive subsidies. These subsidies reduce the purchase price of EVs, so that these vehicles are more affordable. For example, those who purchase an electric two-wheelers can receive a subsidy of up to INR 20,000, while electric cars may receive higher amounts, depending on the battery capacity (Bassi, 2024).
- **Tax Rebates**: To further encourage EV purchases, the government offers tax rebates under Section 80EEB of the Income Tax Act. This allows individual taxpayers to claim a deduction of up to INR 1.5 lakh on the interest for loans to purchase electric vehicles. This rebate improves financing the purchase of an EV and encourages high-income consumers to switch to cleaner transportation.
- **Exemptions from Road Tax and Registration Fees**: Many states have introduced exemptions from road tax and registration fees for EVs also. These exemptions reduce the total cost to own an EV, improving the appeal of EVs

compared to conventional vehicles. Such measures are very effective in urban areas where road taxes can be high.

Supply-Side Incentives

In addition to incentives for consumers, the Indian government provides various incentives to promote domestic EV manufacturing and related industries. These incentives encourage manufacturing and reduce the country's dependence on imported components. Key incentives for producers include:

- **Tax Breaks**: Manufacturers of EVs and related components, such as batteries and power electronics, are eligible for various tax benefits. These include reduced corporate tax rates, exemptions on import duties for raw materials, and tax holidays in special economic zones (SEZs). These measures lower the production costs for manufacturers and encourage them to invest in EV economy (Zhang et al., 2014).
- **Subsidies on Manufacturing Investments**: The government offers capital subsidies and other financial incentives for constructing EV manufacturing plants and research facilities. This includes grants manufacturing plants and testing facilities as well as subsidies for acquiring advanced machinery and technology. Such support is crucial for fostering innovation and scaling up production capacity.
- **Support for Research and Development (R&D)**: To promote innovation and technological advancements in the EV sector, the government provides grants and funding for R&D. This support is aimed at innovations such as advanced battery chemistries and efficient powertrains that will improve the performance and price of EVs. By investing in R&D, the government seeks to position India as a global hub for EV technology.

Subsidy Trends

Providing substantial subsidies for EVs has become a trend in India. According to a report by the International Institute for Sustainable Development (IISD), subsidies for EVs in India increased by 160%, reaching a record high of INR 2,358 crore in the fiscal year 2021-22. This surge is the result of the government's commitment to accelerating the adoption of EVs and transitioning to cleaner transportation (International Institute for Sustainable Development, 2022).

However, there is now a debate about whether India can sustain high subsidies indefinitely. While these financial incentives have spurred market growth, there are concerns about the fiscal burden on the government and the potential distortion of market dynamics. Critics argue that continued reliance on subsidies may not be possible in the long run, and that the government should phase out subsidies gradually as the market matures. This transition would require a comprehensive strategy that includes enhancing infrastructure, reducing battery costs, and promoting public awareness to create a permanent EV market (Jain, 2019).

By implementing a comprehensive set of policies and incentives, the Indian government aims to create favorable conditions for EV adoption and promote a transition towards a more circular economy in transportation.

7.2. Role of Public-Private Partnerships

7.2.1. Successful Collaborations

Charging Infrastructure Development

Public-private partnerships (PPPs) are important to develop the infrastructure that a large number of EVs in India will require. One area of collaboration is the establishment of EV charging networks. Partnerships between government entities and private companies are crucial to expand access to charging stations across the country. For instance, companies such as Tata Power and Fortum have been constructing charging infrastructure in collaboration with various state governments and local authorities. These partnerships make use of the strengths of both sectors—helpful government policy and private sector expertise in technology and operations—to create a robust and reliable charging network. Such initiatives are instrumental in alleviating anxiety about the range of EVs and foster adoption of electric mobility.

Technology Development and Deployment

The development and deployment of novel technologies in the EV industry often result from collaboration between research institutions, government agencies, and private companies. These collaborations contribute to the development of new battery technology, charging solutions, and new forms of smart grid integration. For example, the Asia LEDS Partnership, a collaborative initiative that includes various public and private stakeholders, facilitates dialogue on sustainable transportation, including EVs. This partnership has addressed key topics related to EV batteries, such as enhancing energy density, improving safety, and reducing costs. By bringing together experts from different fields, such initiatives accelerate the innovation and deployment of novel technologies that make EVs more efficient and accessible. Additionally, collaborations in smart grid technologies enable the integration of

EVs into the broader energy system, which improves energy use and enhances grid stability (ICLEI South Asia, 2024).

Skill Development and Training

The rapid growth of the EV industry requires a skilled workforce capable of supporting the sector's various needs, from manufacturing to maintenance and construction. Public-private partnerships are necessary to create training programs and educational initiatives that provide workers the appropriate skills. Government training institutes, in collaboration with private sector companies, offer special courses and certifications in EV technologies. These programs cover a wide range of topics, including EV design and assembly, battery management systems, charging infrastructure installation, and maintenance services. By aligning the curriculum with industry standards and novel technologies, these partnerships equip the workforce with the latest skills and knowledge. Furthermore, these initiatives often include firsthand training and apprenticeships that provide practical experience in the burgeoning EV sector.

By fostering strong public-private partnerships, India can use the strengths of both sectors to accelerate the adoption of EVs, promote a circular economy, and achieve its sustainable development goals.

The adoption of electric vehicles in India faces several challenges, including high upfront costs, limited charging infrastructure, and lack of consumer awareness (Kumar et al., 2020; Kresnawan et al., 2022). The Government of India has taken various measures to promote EVs, such as the FAME-II scheme and the National Electric Mobility Mission Plan (Maheshwari et al., 2021).

However, mass adoption of EVs remains a challenge owing to the higher price of EVs compared to internal combustion engine vehicles, as well as the lack of charging infrastructure and consumer fear of battery range limits (Maheshwari et al., 2021).

To address these challenges, the government has implemented policies and incentives to stimulate both the demand for and supply of EVs (Kumar et al., 2020).

To stimulate demand, the government provides subsidies, tax rebates, and exemptions for EV buyers (Maheshwari et al., 2021). To improve supply, the government offers incentives to manufacturers and component suppliers, such as tax breaks and support for research and development (Maheshwari et al., 2021).

While these policies have had some success, there is debate about whether or not the government can continue such subsidies indefinitely. Some argue that a more moderate approach is needed (Kumar et al., 2020).

8. CONSUMER BEHAVIOR AND MARKET DYNAMICS

8.1. Understanding Consumer Perceptions and Preferences

8.1.1. Factors Influencing EV Adoption

Economic Considerations

One hindrance to the adoption of electric vehicles (EVs) in India is economic. In general, the purchase price of EVs is higher than that of comparable internal combustion engine vehicles. This price difference results primarily from the high cost of batteries, which constitute a substantial portion of an EV's cost. While government incentives and subsidies, such as those offered under the FAME-II scheme, help mitigate this price disparity, the upfront cost remains a barrier for many consumers (Tu & Yang, 2019; Zhang et al., 2014). However, the total cost of ownership over the life of the vehicle, which includes running costs, maintenance, and fuel savings, often favors EVs. EVs typically have lower maintenance costs owing to fewer moving parts and lower energy costs, because electricity is often cheaper than gasoline. These long-term economic benefits can make EVs a better option for frugal consumers, especially when one considers rising fuel prices and the possibility that future regulations will favor low-emission vehicles.

Range Anxiety and Charging Infrastructure

Another hindance to EV adoption is range anxiety, which is the fear that an EV will run out of battery power before reaching a charging station. This concern is particularly relevant in India, where the charging infrastructure is still in its nascent stages. The limited driving range of many EVs, combined with the scarcity of charging stations, especially in rural areas and along highways, exacerbates this anxiety. Long-distance travel poses an extra challenge, because consumers are unsure if there will be reliable charging facilities en route (Xu et al., 2020). The development of a robust and widespread charging network will alleviate these concerns. Government and private sector initiatives to expand charging infrastructure, including fast-charging stations and battery swapping facilities, can reduce range anxiety and encourage more consumers to consider EVs as a viable alternative to traditional vehicles (Tu & Yang, 2019).

Environmental Concerns

Environmental awareness now plays a larger role in the choices of consumers. The growing recognition of climate change and the detrimental effects of air pollution have made many consumers more conscious of their environmental impact. Many consumers now perceive EVs as a cleaner and more sustainable alternative to gasoline vehicles, because EVs produce no tailpipe emissions and can be powered by renewable energy sources. The societal push towards sustainability and the increasing availability of information about the environmental benefits of EVs reinforce this perception (Xu et al., 2020). For environmentally conscious consumers, the potential to reduce their carbon footprint and contribute to a cleaner environment can be a strong motivator to switch to electric mobility.

Performance and Technology

The technological advances in EVs have enhanced their performance and make them competitive with traditional vehicles. Modern EVs offer impressive acceleration, smooth driving, and advanced features such as regenerative braking and smart connectivity. These attributes appeal to savvy consumers who value innovation. Additionally, the continuous improvement in battery technology that has led to longer ranges and shorter charging times further enhances the appeal of EVs. Increasingly, consumers recognize that EVs are not only environmentally friendly alternatives but also high-performance vehicles that offer a unique driving experience (Tu & Yang, 2019).

Social Status and Brand Image

The perception of EVs as status symbols and the influence of brand image also persuade consumers to make purchases. In many urban areas, people associate ownership of an EV with environmental responsibility, modernity, and prescience. These perceptions can enhance the social status of EV owners, making EVs an attractive option for consumers who seek prestige. Moreover, the brand image of EV manufacturers shapes consumer preferences. Brands that consumers perceive as innovative and committed to sustainability often have a competitive advantage in the EV market. The presence of luxury EV brands and the entry of established automotive companies into the electric mobility market further reinforce the perception of EVs as desirable and prestigious (Asadi et al., 2021).

8.1.2. Awareness and Nescience

Despite growing interest in electric vehicles (EVs), nescience on the part of some hinder widespread adoption in India. Information campaigns and educational initiatives can promote EVs and facilitate the transition to a circular economy.

Technical Aspects

A significant barrier to EV adoption is the lack of consumer knowledge about the technical details of these vehicles. Many potential buyers are unfamiliar with how EVs function, the types of charging infrastructure available, and the range of batteries. For instance, misconceptions about battery life, charging times, and the overall reliability of EVs can deter consumers. Some may not understand the differences between various charging levels (such as Level 1, Level 2, and DC fast charging) and how these affect charging times. Moreover, there is often confusion about the maintenance requirements of EVs compared to traditional internal combustion engine vehicles. Some consumers believe erroneously that EVs require more frequent service (Bridi & Hosani, 2021). Providing clear information to the public on these technical details will dispel myths and build consumer confidence in EV technology.

Government Incentives

While the Indian government offers a range of incentives and subsidies to encourage EV adoption, some Indians are unaware of these benefits. Potential buyers may not be cognizant of available financial incentives, such as subsidies under the FAME-II scheme, tax rebates, and exemptions from road tax and registration fees. This nescience can prevent consumers from realizing the potential savings that an EV purchase can provide. Additionally, some people may be confused about how to apply for these incentives and the eligibility criteria, which impairs their ability to make good decisions. Increasing public awareness of government programs and simplifying the process for accessing these benefits will boost EV adoption rates (Tu & Yang, 2019).

Environmental Benefits

While general awareness of environmental issues is on the rise, many consumers lack a deeper understanding of the environmental benefits of EVs. For example, although many people may be aware that EVs produce no tailpipe emissions, they may not fully understand the broader implications for air quality and public health.

Furthermore, there may be incomplete knowledge about how EVs can reduce greenhouse gas emissions, especially when powered by renewable energy sources. This nescience can diminish how people perceive EVs as a sustainable alternative to traditional vehicles. Educating consumers about the environmental advantages of EVs, including their role in reducing dependence on fossil fuels and mitigating climate change, will foster positive perceptions and encourage adoption (Xu et al., 2020).

Addressing nescience requires a comprehensive approach that includes:

1. **Targeted Information Campaigns**: These campaigns should provide clear and accurate information about the technical aspects of EVs, the availability of charging infrastructure, and the benefits of government incentives. Various channels are available to disseminate information including social media, traditional media, and public events.
2. **Educational Initiatives**: Collaborations with educational institutions and community organizations can help create programs that educate the public about EV technology and its environmental benefits. Workshops, seminars, and online courses can offer insight and answer common questions.
3. **Partnerships with Industry**: Auto manufacturers, dealerships, and other stakeholders can educate consumers as well. By offering test drives, informational brochures, and customer support, they can help demystify EV ownership and build consumer confidence.

By removing nescience, stakeholders can better inform the public about the advantages of EVs and support India's transition to a more sustainable and circular economy.

8.2. Market Trends and Future Projections

8.2.1. Analysis of Market Growth and Potential

The Indian electric vehicle (EV) market is ready for substantial growth, driven by a combination of government initiatives, technological advancements, and shifting consumer preferences. This section delves into the market's rapid growth trajectory, the government's ambitious targets, analysis of the various segments of the EV market, and regional variations.

Rapid Growth Trajectory

The Indian EV market is on a trajectory for rapid growth, with industry reports projecting significant expansion in the coming years. **Global EV Outlook 2020** expects the Indian EV market to grow at a compound annual growth rate (CAGR) of approximately 36% from 2020 to 2030. Increasing consumer awareness of the environmental benefits of EVs, government incentives, and the rising cost of conventional fuels will cause this growth. The **Electric Powertrain Market Size, Share & Growth** report highlights similar trends, indicating strong demand for electric powertrains as the industry shifts towards more sustainable transportation. Advancements in battery technology, which are likely to lower costs and improve vehicle performance will make EVs more accessible and appealing to a broader consumer base and bolster the market's potential for growth.

Government Targets

The Indian government has set an ambitious target of achieving 100% EV sales by 2030. This target, part of the National Electric Mobility Mission Plan (NEMMP), aims to promote sustainable transportation and reduce the country's dependence on fossil fuels. The government's commitment to this goal is evident through various policy measures, such as the Faster Adoption and Manufacturing of Electric Vehicles (FAME-II) scheme, which provides financial incentives for EV buyers and manufacturers. Achieving this target would transform the market for automobiles and position the country as a global leader in electric mobility. However, the realization of this goal depends on overcoming several obstacles, including the development of a robust charging infrastructure, enhancing battery manufacturing capabilities, and fostering consumer acceptance (Maheshwari et al., 2021).

Segment Analysis

The growth potential of the Indian EV market varies across different vehicle segments, based upon unique factors and consumer demands.

- **Two-Wheelers**: This segment has seen the most significant growth and accounts for the majority of EV sales in India. Electric two-wheelers are affordable, convenient, and practical, which make them an attractive option for urban commuters. Government incentives and the increasing availability of low-cost models have accelerated their adoption.
- **Three-Wheelers**: Electric three-wheelers, often used as auto-rickshaws, are becoming popular owing to their lower operational costs and reduced emis-

sions. This segment is particularly important in urban areas, where they serve as a primary mode of transport for short distances.

- **Passenger Cars**: While the market for electric passenger cars is growing more slowly than that for two-wheelers, the market is expanding. High initial costs and range anxiety remain significant barriers, but analysts expect advancements in battery technology and the availability of more affordable models to boost growth in this segment.
- **Commercial Vehicles**: The commercial vehicle segment, including electric buses and trucks, is still nascent. However, there is growing interest from fleet operators and government agencies to electrify public transport and logistics, because of the potential for cost savings and environmental benefits. (MarketsandMarkets, 2010)

Regional Variations

The adoption rates of EVs vary significantly across different regions in India, owing to differences such as local government policies, availability of charging infrastructure, and consumer preferences.

- **Urban Areas**: Major cities like Delhi, Mumbai, Bangalore, and Hyderabad have higher EV adoption rates owing to better infrastructure, higher environmental awareness, and local government initiatives that promote electric mobility.
- **Rural Areas**: In contrast, rural areas have lower adoption rates, mostly because of a paucity of charging infrastructure and EV models suitable for rural use. However, with government efforts to expand charging networks and introduce affordable electric models, these rates may increase in the coming years.
- **State-Level Policies**: States like Delhi, Maharashtra, and Tamil Nadu have introduced regional EV policies that offer additional incentives and support for EV adoption. These policies include subsidies for EV purchases, reduced road taxes, and incentives for constructing charging infrastructure. The regional variations in policy frameworks affect market dynamics and adoption rates across different states (MarketsandMarkets, 2010).

In summary, the Indian EV market is at the point of a significant transformation and has the potential for robust growth across various segments. The combination of supportive government policies, technological advancements, and increasing consumer interest in sustainable transportation can drive the market forward. However, realizing this potential will require addressing key challenges, such as infrastructure development, cost reduction, and public awareness.

8.2.2. Impact of Technological Advancements

Battery Technology

Advancements in battery technology are paramount for the widespread adoption of electric vehicles. Key developments include an increase in energy density, which will allow EVs to travel longer distances on a single charge, and faster charging times, which will reduce the inconvenience of long recharging periods. Additionally, reduction in battery costs is making EVs more affordable for more consumers. These improvements are essential for making EVs a viable alternative to traditional internal combustion engine vehicles. According to a report on current Li-Ion battery technologies in electric vehicles, ongoing advancements present opportunities to further enhance EV performance and increase adoption (Miao et al., 2019).

Charging Infrastructure

The development and expansion of charging infrastructure will support the growth of the EV market. Innovations in this area include faster charging technologies, which can significantly reduce the time needed to recharge EV batteries, and smart charging solutions that improve charging efficiency and cost. Moreover, battery swapping systems are emerging as a promising way to quickly replenish EV energy stores, particularly for commercial fleets and high-usage vehicles. A forecast on the electric vehicle charging station market highlights the importance of these innovations in ensuring a robust and accessible charging network (Strategic Market Research, 2022).

Connectivity and Autonomous Driving

"Connected cars" and advancements in autonomous driving could revolutionize the EV market. These technologies enhance the driving experience by providing real-time data, improving navigation, and increasing vehicle safety. Furthermore, autonomous driving capabilities can lead to new business models and uses for EVs, such as autonomous fleets and automated ride-hailing services. Research by Campatelli et al. explores these new business models and highlights the transformative potential of connectivity and autonomous technologies in the EV sector (Campatelli et al., 2014).

By analyzing market trends and considering the impact of these technological advancements, stakeholders can make informed decisions to profit on the growth opportunities in the evolving EV market in India.

9. CHALLENGES AND OPPORTUNITIES

9.1. Key Challenges in the Transition to EVs and Circular Economy

9.1.1. Technological, Economic, and Social Barriers

High Upfront Costs: The higher purchase price of electric vehicles (EVs) compared to conventional vehicles remains an obstacle, particularly for frugal consumers in markets such as India. This economic hurdle can deter widespread adoption, as highlighted in a study that discusses the challenges to EV adoption from an Indian perspective (Kumar et al., 2020).

Limited Charging Infrastructure: The paucity of charging stations, especially for long-distance travel, poses another obstacle to EV adoption. This lack of infrastructure can lead to inconvenience and uncertainty for potential EV owners, as the same study emphasizes (Kumar et al., 2020).

Range Anxiety: The current state of charging infrastructure exacerbates consumer concerns about the limited range of EVs on a single charge. This issue, or range anxiety, deters many potential buyers (Kumar et al., 2020).

Battery Performance and Lifespan: There are concerns about battery degradation and the convenience of reliable and affordable battery replacement options. Relieving these concerns is crucial for the long-term sustainability and practicality of EVs. A report on India's looming electric vehicle challenges highlights battery performance and lifespan (Ghanekar, 2021).

Raw Material Supply Chains: The need for secure and sustainable supply chains for critical raw materials used in EV batteries, such as lithium, cobalt, and nickel, is another difficulty. Ensuring a stable supply of these materials is essential for the growth of the EV market. This issue is central in discussions about creating an ecosystem for EV batteries in India (Ghanekar, 2021).

9.1.2. Infrastructure and Regulatory Challenges

Grid Capacity and Stability: The transition to widespread electric vehicle (EV) use requires substantial upgrades to grid infrastructure to manage the increased electricity demand. Presently, infrastructure inadequacies are a significant hurdle for India's EV ambitions, as discussed by Govindarasu and Venkatesh (2019).

Standardization of Charging Infrastructure: It is vital to develop common standards for charging infrastructure to ensure compatibility and prevent system fragmentation. The EVConnect Journey report emphasized the need for collaborative efforts in establishing charging infrastructure(Yadav, 2019).

Policy Consistency and Long-Term Vision: To attract investment and support the sustainable growth of EVs, consistent policies and a clear long-term vision are essential. The EVConnect Journey report also highlights the lack of coordinated policy efforts as an impediment to progress (Yadav, 2019).

Recycling and End-of-Life Management: Managing the safe and sustainable disposal and recycling of EV batteries is a significant challenge. Resolutions to these problems are necessary for the long-term viability of the EV industry, as detailed in a report on India's electric vehicle challenges (Ghanekar, 2021).

9.2. Opportunities for Innovation and Growth

The shift towards electric vehicles and a circular economy presents opportunities for innovation and growth in India. By combining emerging business models, new technologies, and the potential for economic development, India can accelerate its transition to a sustainable future. This section explores these opportunities in detail, focusing on how India can overcome the challenges and promote widespread EV adoption.

9.2.1. Emerging Business Models and Technologies

Battery Swapping Stations:

Battery swapping stations offer a solution to one of the major challenges to EV adoption: long charging times. Unlike traditional charging stations, battery swapping allows EV owners to exchange depleted batteries for fully charged ones within minutes. This model is particularly advantageous for commercial vehicles, such as taxis and delivery trucksthat require constant use. Additionally, battery swapping can be an effective in areas with little grid capacity, because batteries can be charged elsewhere and transported to swapping stations. This approach can also reduce the upfront cost of EVs by separating the cost of the battery from the vehicle, which would make EVs more affordable .

Vehicle-to-Grid (V2G) Technology:

V2G technology enables EVs to function as mobile energy storage units that can supply electricity back to the grid during peak demand periods. This two-way flow of electricity can enhance grid stability, provide backup power during outages, and create new revenue streams for EV owners through energy trading. V2G technology also supports the integration of renewable energy sources by storing excess power generated during periods of high renewable output and supplying it back to the grid when needed. As India continues to expand its renewable energy capacity, V2G technology could play a crucial role in balancing supply and demand, reducing grid congestion, and enhancing energy efficiency.

Shared Mobility and Ride-Hailing Services:

The growing popularity of new forms of public transportation and ride-hailing services presents a significant opportunity for deploying EV fleets. Companies such as Ola and Uber are exploring the use of electric vehicles in their fleets to reduce operating costs and meet sustainability targets. The "shared mobility model" offers a unique advantage for EV adoption, as it can use vehicles more efficiently and reduce the total number of vehicles on the road. This more efficient use of vehicles can lead to lower emissions, reduced congestion, and better air quality in urban areas. Moreover, ride-hailing companies can invest in centralized charging stations and battery management systems, which improve fleet operations and reduce the overall cost of ownership.

9.2.2. Potential for Job Creation and Economic Development

Manufacturing and Assembly:

The growth of the EV industry in India promotes job creation, particularly in the manufacturing and assembly of electric vehicles, batteries, and components. As the demand for EVs increases, the need for skilled labor in manufacturing, quality control, and logistics will also rise. Additionally, the establishment of EV manufacturing facilities can stimulate local economies, attract foreign investment, and foster the development of ancillary industries, such as battery recycling and component supply chains. India's emphasis on self-reliance (Atmanirbhar Bharat) and the Make in India initiative further support the development of a robust domestic EV manufacturing sector.

Charging Infrastructure Development and Maintenance:

The expansion of EV charging infrastructure is another area that promotes job creation. The installation, operation, and maintenance of charging stations require a wide range of skills, from electrical engineering to customer service. As the charging network grows, there will be a demand for technicians, electricians, and engineers to operate and maintain these facilities. Moreover, the development of smart charging solutions and energy management systems will create additional opportunities for software development, data analytics, and cybersecurity. These roles are necessary for charging operations, managing grid interactions, and enhancing customer satisfaction.

Software Development and Data Analytics:

The use of microchips in the automotive industry and the invention of EVs with internet connections have led to a growing demand for software developers, data analysts, and other skilled professionals. Software is essential in various aspects of the EV ecosystem, from vehicle management systems and charging infrastructure to fleet management and customer interfaces. Data analytics allows for the analysis of driving patterns, optimal battery performance, predicting maintenance needs, and improving overall efficiency. The development of AI and machine learning algorithms can further enhance the capabilities of EV systems by enabling smarter energy management, predictive maintenance, and a more personal user experience.

India's transition to electric vehicles and a circular economy presents both challenges and opportunities. While problems persist in the technology, economy, and infrastructure, the potential for innovation and growth is immense. By embracing emerging business models and technologies, promoting public-private partnerships, and creating supportive regulations, India can overcome these challenges and position itself as a global leader in sustainable transportation. The opportunities for job creation and economic development are vast and offer a pathway for India to achieve its sustainability goals while fostering economic growth and improving quality of life.

10. CONCLUSION AND RECOMMENDATIONS

India can capture near-term climate and air-quality gains by (i) aligning EV charging with wind-rich hours and (ii) enforcing a circular, EPR-driven battery pathway. Your simple India scenario shows that two- and three-wheelers already beat ICE on today's grid, and compact cars clear the breakeven when charging is wind-aligned. AI ties the system together—forecasting wind and loads, scheduling charging and V2G, and protecting battery health across a 9Rs lifecycle.

10.1 Recommendations:

1. Charge with the wind. Publish DISCOM wind-hour tariffs; enable day-ahead signals in public/ fleet chargers; prefer co-located wind-solar-storage hubs on highways.
2. Make 9Rs the default. Require design-for-disassembly, repairability scoring, and standardized pack interfaces; certify refurbish/repurpose routes for traction batteries.
3. Enforce EPR with data. Implement QR/ledger-based battery tracking to verify collection and high-value recycling; set minimum recycled content targets in new packs.
4. Scale V2G where it pencils out. Start with depots/campuses; compensate flexibility via time-of-use and ancillary-services products; protect battery warranty via AI-managed cycling.
5. De-risk costs for 2W/3W fleets. Expand battery-swapping as a service; offer concessional finance tied to wind-aligned charging contracts.

6. Close data gaps. Require standardized reporting: charger utilization, energy mix during sessions, and end-of-life battery pathways.

10.2 Future Research Directions

Future research could delve deeper into the lifecycle analysis of EV batteries in Indiaby evaluating sustainable sources of raw materials, documenting recycling infrastructure, and explaining how the Indian economy can make use of spent batteries. Additional research could investigate the social equity of EV adoption to ensure equitable access to charging infrastructure and affordable EV options across different socioeconomic groups.

10.3. Final Thoughts

The transition to a circular economy through EV adoption is not merely an environmental imperative but also a strategic opportunity for India. By embracing this transformation, India can position itself as a global leader in sustainable transportation, reduce its dependence on fossil fuels, create new economic opportunities, and pave the way for a cleaner, greener, and more prosperous future.

REFERENCES

Agusdinata, D. B., Liu, W., Eakin, H., & Romero, H. (2018). Socio-environmental impacts of lithium mineral extraction: Towards a research agenda. *Environmental Research Letters*, *13*(12), 123001. DOI: 10.1088/1748-9326/aae9b1

Ali, H., Khan, H. A., & Pecht, M. (2021). Circular economy of Li batteries: Technologies and trends. *Journal of Energy Storage*, *40*, 102690. Advance online publication. DOI: 10.1016/j.est.2021.102690

Arambarri, J., Hayden, J. S., Elkurdy, M., Meyers, B., Hamatteh, Z. S. A., Abbassi, B., & Omar, W. (2019). Lithium-ion car batteries: Present analysis and future predictions. *Environmental Engineering Research*, *24*(4), 699–710. DOI: 10.4491/eer.2018.383

Argonne National Laboratory. (2012, July 18). The long, winding road to advanced batteries for electric cars. https://www.anl.gov/article/the-long-winding-road-to-advanced-batteries-for-electric-cars

Asadi, S., Nilashi, M., Samad, S., Abdullah, R., Mahmoud, M., Alkinani, M. H., & Yadegaridehkordi, E. (2021). Factors impacting consumers' intention toward adoption of electric vehicles in Malaysia. *Journal of Cleaner Production*, *282*, 124474. Advance online publication. DOI: 10.1016/j.jclepro.2020.124474

Attero. (2021, July 8). Electronic waste recycling company in India | Li-ion battery recycling. https://attero.in

Attero. (2021, June 22). Lithium-ion battery recycling companies in India. https://attero.in

Bassi, M. K. A. (2024, February 20). A sustainable asset valuation of the FAME II policy in India. International Institute for Sustainable Development. https://www.iisd.org/publications/report/savi-electric-vehicles-india-fame-policy

Bonu, S. R., & Panigrahi, D. S. (2019, December). Recollection and recycling of automotive Lithium Ion batteries in India. In 2019 IEEE Transportation Electrification Conference (ITEC-India) (pp. 1-5). IEEE. DOI: 10.1109/ITEC-India48457.2019.ITECINDIA2019-47

Bridi, R. M., & Al Hosani, N. A. (2021). Theoretical reflections on consumer behavior: The adoption and non-adoption of electric vehicles. In *Proceedings of the 2021 International Conference on Renewable Energy: Generation and Applications (ICREGA)*. IEEE. DOI: 10.1109/ICREGA50506.2021.9388315

Brown, P., Barber, K., & Kirk, R. S. (1988). Potential of electric vehicles in present and future transportation systems. SAE Technical Paper 885179. DOI: 10.4271/885179

Campatelli, G., Benesperi, F., Barbieri, R., & Meneghin, A. (2014). New business models for electric mobility. In *Proceedings of the IEEE International Electric Vehicle Conference (IEVC)*. IEEE. DOI: 10.1109/IEVC.2014.7056136

Cheng, A., Fuchs, E. R., Karplus, V. J., & Michalek, J. J. (2024). Electric vehicle battery chemistry affects supply chain disruption vulnerabilities. *Nature Sustainability*, *15*(1). PMID: 38459029

Climate Nexus. (2021, November 29). Impacts from mining lithium, cobalt, and other materials for electric car batteries. https://climatenexus.org

Council on Energy, Environment and Water. (2023, January 29). India's electric vehicle transition. https://www.ceew.in/publications/indias-electric-vehicle-transition-electric-mobility-support-sustainable-economic-recovery

Datta, M. A. (2018, July 25). Creating the charging infrastructure to power EVs in India. The Energy and Resources Institute. https://www.teriin.org/article/creating-charging-infrastructure-power-evs-india

Dumée, L. F. (2021). Circular materials and circular design: Review on challenges towards sustainable manufacturing and recycling. *Circular Economy and Sustainability*, *2*(1), 9–23. DOI: 10.1007/s43615-021-00085-2 PMID: 34888565

E-VehicleInfo. (2021, June 15). Battery recycling business for small-scale industries in India. https://e-vehicleinfo.com/battery-recycling-business-for-ssi/

Elshkaki, A. (2020). Long-term analysis of critical materials in future vehicles electrification in China and their national and global implications. *Energy*, *202*, 117697. DOI: 10.1016/j.energy.2020.117697

Energies, B. A. T. X. (2022, May 21). Lithium (Li)-ion battery recycling company in India. https://batxenergies.com

European Commission. (2022, December 9). Batteries. https://environment.ec.europa.eu/topics/waste-and-recycling/batteries_en

European Commission. (2023, August 17). New law on more sustainable, circular and safe batteries enters into force. https://environment.ec.europa.eu/news/new-law-more-sustainable-circular-and-safe-batteries-enters-force-2023-08-17_en

European Union. (2023, July 28). Regulation (EU) 2023/1542 of the European Parliament and of the Council concerning batteries and waste batteries. Official Journal of the European Union. https://eur-lex.europa.eu/legal-content/EN/TXT/?uri=CELEX%3A32023R1542

Ghanekar, N. (2021, April 19). India's looming electric vehicle challenge: Spent batteries. IndiaSpend. https://www.indiaspend.com/earthcheck/indias-looming-electric-vehicle-challenge-spent-batteries-742352

Govindarasu, A., & Venkatesh, A. S. (2019). Electric vehicle vision 2030: Challenges and solutions. In Proceedings of the IEEE Transportation Electrification Conference (ITEC India). IEEE. DOI: 10.1109/ITEC-India48457.2019.ITECINDIA2019-35

ICLEI South Asia. (2024, January 25). Asia LEDS Partnership study tour addresses key topics related to EV batteries. https://southasia.iclei.org/news/asia-leds-partnership-study-tour-addresses-key-topics-related-to-ev-batteries/

India Brand Equity Foundation. (2022, May 5). Electric vehicles market in India. https://www.ibef.org

International Energy Agency. (2023, May 12). How can smart charging steer electric vehicle uptake in India? https://www.iea.org/commentaries/how-can-smart-charging-steer-electric-vehicle-uptake-in-india

International Institute for Sustainable Development. (2022, December 20). Subsidies for EVs in India increased 160%, reached record high of Rs 2,358 crore in FY22: IISD report. https://www.iisd.org/articles/iisd-news/subsidies-evs-india-increased-160-reached-record-high-rs-2358-crore-fy22-iisd

Jain, T. L. P. (2019, July 24). India's energy transition: Subsidies for gasoline, diesel and electric vehicles. International Institute for Sustainable Development. https://www.iisd.org/publications/brief/indias-energy-transition-subsidies-gasoline-diesel-and-electric-vehicles

Jones, B., Elliott, R. J., & Nguyen-Tien, V. (2020). The EV revolution: The road ahead for critical raw materials demand. *Applied Energy*, *280*, 115072. DOI: 10.1016/j.apenergy.2020.115072 PMID: 33052165

Joseph, P. K., & Elangovan, D. (2018). All-vehicle electrification by 2030 project in India: Impacts and solutions. Journal of Advanced Research in Dynamical and Control Systems, 9(4). (Publication details should be verified.)

Kresnawan, M. R., Yurnaidi, Z., Bilqis, A., Wijaya, T. N., & Suryadi, B. (2022). Electric vehicle readiness in Southeast Asia: A PEST policy review. *IOP Conference Series. Earth and Environmental Science*, *997*(1), 012001. Advance online publication. DOI: 10.1088/1755-1315/997/1/012001

Kumar, K. J., & Kumar, S., & V. S., N. (2021). Standards for electric vehicle charging stations in India: A review. *Energy Science & Engineering*, *4*(1). Advance online publication. DOI: 10.1002/est2.261

Kumar, R., Jha, A., Damodaran, A., Bangwal, D., & Dwivedi, A. (2021). Addressing the challenges to electric vehicle adoption via sharing economy: An Indian perspective. *Management of Environmental Quality*, *32*(1), 82–99. DOI: 10.1108/MEQ-03-2020-0058

Large, K. (2021, March 22). Use renewable energy to charge electric vehicles in India. The Third Pole. https://www.thethirdpole.net/en/climate/use-renewable-energy-to-charge-electric-vehicles-in-india/

Lipman, T., & Maier, P. (2021). Advanced materials supply considerations for electric vehicle applications. *MRS Bulletin*, *46*(12), 1164–1175. DOI: 10.1557/s43577-022-00263-z

Maheshwari, N., Dua, R., & Kumar, A. (2021). *Electric mobility in India: A dawn of new era*. SAGE Publications., DOI: 10.4135/9781529759754

MarketsandMarkets. (2010, January 13). Electric powertrain market size, share & growth. https://www.marketsandmarkets.com/Market-Reports/electric-powertrain-market-97605711.html

Material Insights. (2023). Material profile features. https://www.material-insights.org/

Mertens, J., Dewulf, J., Breyer, C., Belmans, R., Gendron, C., Geoffron, P., Goossens, L., Fischer, C., Du Fornel, E., Hayhoe, K., Hirose, K., Le Cadre-Loret, E., Lester, R., Maigné, F., Maitournam, H., de Miranda, P. E. V., Verwee, P., Sala, O., Webber, M., & Debackere, K. (2024). From emissions to resources: Mitigating the critical raw material supply chain vulnerability of renewable energy technologies. *Mineral Economics*, *37*(3), 669–676. DOI: 10.1007/s13563-024-00425-2

Miao, Y., Hynan, P., Von Jouanne, A., & Yokochi, A. (2019). Current Li-ion battery technologies in electric vehicles and opportunities for advancements. *Energies*, *12*(6), 1074. DOI: 10.3390/en12061074

Nicola, J. (2024, February 7). The new car batteries that could power the electric vehicle revolution. *Nature*, *626*(7998), 248–251. Advance online publication. DOI: 10.1038/d41586-024-00325-z PMID: 38326600

Organisation for Economic Co-operation and Development. (2020). Global EV outlook 2020. DOI: 10.1787/d394399e-en

Press Information Bureau, Government of India. (2021, March 18). Govt driving transition from linear to circular economy. https://pib.gov.in

Priyanka. (2021, December 14). Have you heard about environmental impact assessment? ABC Techno Lab. https://abctechnolab.com/have-you-heard-about-environmental-impact-assessment/

Research, J. M. K. (2019, September 24). Lithium-ion battery manufacturers | Battery recycling companies India. https://jmkresearch.com/electric-vehicles-published-reports/recycling-of-lithium-ion-batteries-in-india-1000-million-opportunity/

Rissman, J., Bataille, C., Masanet, E., Aden, N., Morrow, W. R.III, Zhou, N., Elliott, N., Dell, R., Heeren, N., Huckestein, B., Cresko, J., Miller, S. A., Roy, J., Fennell, P., Cremmins, B., Koch Blank, T., Hone, D., Williams, E. D., de la Rue du Can, S., & Helseth, J. (2020). Technologies and policies to decarbonize global industry: Review and assessment of mitigation drivers through 2070. *Applied Energy*, *266*, 114848. DOI: 10.1016/j.apenergy.2020.114848

Srinivasan, V., Hafemeister, D., Levi, B. G., Levine, M., & Schwartz, P. D. (2008). Batteries for vehicular applications. *Physics Today*, *61*(12), 34–39. DOI: 10.1063/1.2993726

Strategic Market Research. (2022). Electric vehicle charging station market size, forecast | 2030. https://www.strategicmarketresearch.com/market-report/electric-vehicle-charging-station-market

Tu, J. C., & Yang, C. (2019). Key factors influencing consumers' purchase of electric vehicles. *Sustainability (Basel)*, *11*(14), 3863. Advance online publication. DOI: 10.3390/su11143863

Turner, J. M., & Nugent, L. M. (2015). Charging up battery recycling policies: Extended producer responsibility for single-use batteries in the European Union, Canada, and the United States. *Journal of Industrial Ecology*, *20*(5), 1148–1158. DOI: 10.1111/jiec.12351

Volan, T., Vaz, C. R., & Maldonado, M. U. (2021). Scenarios for end-of-life (EOL) electric vehicle batteries in China. *International Journal of Energy Sector Management*, *28*(4), 335–357.

Xu, G., Wang, S., Li, J., & Zhao, D. (2020). Moving towards sustainable purchase behavior: Examining the determinants of consumers' intentions to adopt electric vehicles. *Environmental Science and Pollution Research International*, *27*(18), 22535–22546. DOI: 10.1007/s11356-020-08835-9 PMID: 32319053

Yadav, N. (2019, November 22). EVconnect journey: Five insights on e-vehicle adoption in India. World Resources Institute India. https://wri-india.org/blog/evconnect-journey-five-insights-e-vehicle-adoption-india

Zeng, A., Chen, W., Rasmussen, K. D., Zhu, X., Lundhaug, M. C., Müller, D. B., Tan, J., Keiding, J. K., Liu, L., Dai, T., Wang, A., & Liu, G. (2022). Battery technology and recycling alone will not save the electric mobility transition from future cobalt shortages. *Nature Communications*, *13*(1), 1341. Advance online publication. DOI: 10.1038/s41467-022-29022-z PMID: 35292628

Zeng, X., Li, M., El-Hady, D. A., Alshitari, W., Al-Bogami, A. S., Lü, J., & Amine, K. (2019). Commercialization of lithium battery technologies for electric vehicles. *Advanced Energy Materials*, *9*(27), 1900161. Advance online publication. DOI: 10.1002/aenm.201900161

Zhang, X., Xie, J., Rao, R., & Liang, Y. (2014). Policy incentives for the adoption of electric vehicles across countries. *Sustainability (Basel)*, *6*(11), 8056–8078. DOI: 10.3390/su6118056

Chapter 11

Jute Bags as a Catalyst for Green Solutions: A Comparative Study of Environmental Benefits

Suhashini Awadhesh Chaurasia
http://orcid.org/0000-0002-7443-0105
Ramdeobaba University, Nagpur

Bharti Ingle
Symbiosis International (Deemed to be) University, India

Ekta Narkhede
Symbiosis International (Deemed to be) University, India

Poorva Agrawal
Mukesh Patel School of Technology, Management, and Engineering, India

Gagandeep Kaur
http://orcid.org/0009-0004-2834-9850
Mukesh Patel School of Technology Management and Engineering, Shirpur, India

Purva Pandey
Symbiosis International (Deemed to be) University, India

ABSTRACT

Plastic bag waste is rapidly becoming a global concern these days. Plastic shopping bags have an extended environmental impact and consume a lot of resources. Jute bags provide an eco-friendly alternative since they are biodegradable, eco-friendly, and plant-based. Jute is an eco-friendly as it is a natural, biodegradable, and plant-based fiber. Among its ecological benefits, jute reduces carbon emissions while improving conditions for efficient waste management, just like the virtuous circle of a circular economy-that supports resource reutilization with minimal waste generation. It contributes to economic growth because it avails jobs to rural farmers. Even though jute bags have these advantages, they are not as strong as plastic, and

DOI: 10.4018/979-8-3373-7391-1.ch011

farm labor-based practices can easily give way to exploitations. Innovations, in farming and production, made jute more viable, with more efficient and automated manufactures making jute products more available and competitive.

I. INTRODUCTION

Plastic bag waste is rapidly becoming a global concern these days, as plastic shopping bags account for much of this. Plastic shopping bags have an extended environmental impact and consume a lot of resources. Jute bags provide an eco-friendly alternative since they are biodegradable, eco-friendly, and plant-based; they are primarily cultivated in India and Bangladesh. Jute is an eco-friendly alternative to plastics, as it is a natural, biodegradable, and plant-based fiber. While jute decomposes in months under specific conditions like composting, its degradation in less favorable environments, such as a landfill, can take over two years. This is in stark contrast to plastics, which take hundreds of years to decompose and contribute to pollution and fossil fuel consumption. It also uses much less energy and water compared to plastics.

Among its ecological benefits, jute reduces carbon emissions while improving conditions for efficient waste management, just like the virtuous circle of a circular economy-that supports resource reutilization with minimal waste generation and efficient consumption (Florencia et al., 2024). Again, such an industry supports economic growth because it avails jobs to rural farmers in developing countries.

Even though jute bags have these advantages, they are not as strong as plastic, and farm labour-based practices can easily give way to exploitations. Innovations, especially in farming and production, made jute more viable, with more efficient and automated manufactures making jute products more available and competitive.

All of this can be achieved through government policies, bans on plastic bags, incentives for ecofriendly products. The shifts in consumer behaviour towards sustainable consumption are also partly a result of consumer awareness and education and incentives (Alimuzzaman et al., 2024). There is hope in the future of jute bags as public and corporate attitudes transform to more environmentally friendly products; they support a global movement against single-use plastics and foster a more sustainable economy.

The chapter "Jute Bags as a Driver for Green Solutions: A Comparative Analysis of Environmental Prospects" offers an essential examination of how an age-old agricultural commodity might serve as the foundation of the current bio-economy. Although previous literature has demonstrated the basic biodegradability and carbon-neutral cultivation of jute, this detailed study examines the technologies, economics, and institutions that make jute a better global option than artificial materials by 2026.

II. LITERATURE REVIEW

Thes below mentioned studies together demonstrate that jute may be a viable eco-friendly substitute material for plastic, holding big potential both environmentally and economically. Authors demonstrate how canvas and cotton bags may reduce the waste of plastics while creating belief in local entrepreneurs of Indonesia. The recycling process of plastic is not easy; therefore, it is a menace to the environment. Authors wants to ensure the creation of a green environment with less pollution caused by plastic waste, especially plastic bags that are very resistant to degradation. Furthermore, author hopes to create job vacancies to boost the creativity of youths and pride themselves in such innovations. Using this innovation, it will be believed that using tote bags will be a good initiative for both males and females. Looking at the numerous benefits of using tote bags, tote bags can be used as shopping bags that can be used instead of plastic bags. Using this innovation, author hopes to eliminate plastic bags in Indonesia (Florencia et al., 2024). Researchers discuss jute bags as durable alternatives to synthetic products, emphasizing their eco-friendliness and sustainability (Alimuzzaman et al., 2024).

The central objective of this study is to explore the variables which impact the consumers' purchase intentions concerning eco-friendly bags. The purpose of this study includes providing valuable information to the stakeholders such as companies, government representatives, and non-profit organizations. The research will explore the variables that affect customer purchase intentions in relation to environmentally friendly products, their role in achieving sustainability objectives, such as reduction of resources consumption, limitation of waste generation, and lowering carbon emissions. The core objective of the research is the promotion of the environmentally responsible and socially accountable behaviour of the consumers who develop sustainable relationships with the environment. Design/Methodology/Approach: This research is based on secondary data gathered from scholarly articles found on such databases as Google scholar, ResearchGate, Web of Science, SSRN, and many others. Focus group discussion is also used in order to come up with hypotheses and determine the variables that affect the consumer intentions to purchase environmentally friendly bags. Findings/Results: This research makes use of empirical data and conceptual models to examine the drivers of customer purchase intentions in terms of eco-friendly bags. Variables considered include consumers' awareness, social aspects, product characteristics, willingness to invest and the perception of environmental benefits. Authors explore the positive influence of eco-friendly shopping bags, like jute, on business reputation and consumer demand (Ashwini et al., 2023).

"Golden Fiber" in the 2026 Bio-Economy: The traditional "rural packing fibre" is now categorized as a high-performance technical bio-fibre. Jute falls in the middle ground of the sustainability discussion today, with regards to both SDG 12 and SDG 13. Carbon Sequestration Efficiency: Not only does jute absorb CO2; recent statistics show that one hectare of jute plants can fix as much as 15 tons of CO2 and giving off 11 tons of O2 in just a 100-day span of growing cycle. Such an ability has made jute one of the most effective "carbon sinkers" in the plant kingdom, with efficiency far better than that of timber forests. The Methane Reduction Ability: While synthetic fibres release greenhouse gases due to their thermal production process, the methane gas produced because of water retting of the jute plant fibre has now been addressed. With enzyme-based retting technology, by 2025, the microbial inoculant has already shortened the retting period from 21 to 7 days, resulting in 60% less water pollution and export-quality fibre.

The sheets made of synthetic plastic are primarily made of derivatives of long chains of petrochemicals. Plastic pollution has been recognized as a significant environmental threat not only in marine but also terrestrial ecosystems, in which these plastic products take more time to degrade biophysically, negatively affect human beings' well-being, and have limited disposal opportunities. The present study focuses on characterizing and analysing the efficiency of biodegradable sheets produced with natural materials to minimize the reliance on synthetic plastic products, thereby reducing plastic pollution. The multifunctional features of the biodegradable sheet prepared from raw jute materials were relatively impressive; the tensile strength of the biodegradable sheet rose to nearly 22 MPa, while that of the synthetic plastic sheet is approximately 15 MPa. Besides, the elongation rate fell to about 53%. The degradation test confirmed the degradation potential of the biodegradable sheet; the rate of biodegradation of the prepared sheet was higher than the synthetic plastic sheet, and its appearance was appealing because of its colorization with a natural pigment (turmeric). The remarkable physic-mechanical characteristics, excellent colour resistance, and biodegradability of the coloured sheet developed from raw jute may make it highly suitable as an alternative to synthetic plastic sheets and investigate biodegradable coloured jute sheets made with turmeric, which could replace synthetic plastics in various applications (Nayab-Ul-Hossain et al., 2023).

Jute is an eco-friendly, cheap and excellent fiber, traditionally used for sacking and hessian. India produces 80% of jute of total global demand. Owing to environmentally friendly properties, this 'golden fiber' has been used as a safe material for packing and transport. However, dilution of JPM act coupled with competition from synthetic/ man-made fibers, demand of jute for traditional usages i.e. sacking and hessian has decreased over past five years. Under such circumstances, application of jute for diversified products has become necessary for survival of around 44 lakhs direct and indirectly related workers (covering farmers and mill workers) associated with the jute industry. Jute diversified products like shopping bags, wall hangings, floor covering, non-ovens, geo-textiles, composites etc. has opened a new realm beyond traditional application of jute. Export of jute diversified products has increased from INR 363.593 to 590.215 corers during 2012-13 to 2016-17. Present status paper reports various types of jute diversified products along with their market scope, performance and opportunity across the world. Authors explore new uses for jute in textiles and composites, expanding its role in sustainable industries (Ray & Ghosh, 2018).

The awareness about the environment in the global scenario has brought forth the opportunities for Jute because of its environment-friendly properties. The purpose of this analysis is to assess the impact of Jute production on the environment in Bangladesh. For this purpose, data about the area under cultivation of Jute in Bangladesh has been considered over a period of 19 years. Jute improves soil fertility, helps in protecting the ozone layer by absorbing carbon dioxide and contributes to improving air quality by releasing oxygen into the atmosphere. The use of Jute as vegetables, geotextiles, biogas, and biodegradable items affects the environment. Some of the suggested measures include scientific methods of cultivation of Jute, legislation to use Jute instead of synthetic materials, formulating a Jute policy, expanding the applications of Jute, and increasing awareness about Jute as an environmentally friendly fibre. Authors examine the environmental benefits of jute in Bangladesh, particularly in soil conservation, biodiversity promotion, and pollution reduction (Islam & Ahmed, 2012).

The plastic bag is a source of pollution that poses a significant environmental threat. This paper composite made from jute fibre and laminated paper and also this paper laminate without reinforcement fibre can serve as a solution in combating this environmental menace. The results revealed that paper laminate without reinforcement fibre has several folds higher tensile strength compared to paper strip. Also, an improvement in the tensile property can be attained when continuous jute fibre is added into paper laminate. The study jute-reinforced paper composites, showing their high strength and eco-friendliness (Verma, 2009).

Concerning solid waste recycling, this study focuses on creating a composite biodegradable kraft paper using buffing dust (BD) and post-consumed jute fibre (JF). In this case, simple solution casting technique was used with polyurethane as a binder to produce the kraft paper. To characterize the product, several analytical techniques such as UV-Vis, FTIR, XRD, SEM, TGA, OTR, biodegradability, and tensile testing methods were utilized. It was discovered that there was an existence of covalent and hydrogen bonds between the two components to form a uniform surface. Interestingly, the composite exhibited better thermal stability, better gas barrier performance, and biodegradability when compared with individual components. The composite also outperformed other components concerning mechanical characteristics; the paper had 57% more tensile strength, 38% greater elongation, 20% higher hardness, and 9% higher density when compared with buffing dust.

In comparison with jute fibre, the improvements are 125%, 91%, 30%, and 19% respectively. Additionally, the composite demonstrated superior gas barrier properties, improving by 61% and 73% when compared with buffing dust and jute fibre respectively. Therefore, the study shows immense potential that the composite material can be used widely for many purposes, such as manufacturing of packaging and interior furnishing industries and as reinforcing. The focus on the use of jute and industrial waste to create biodegradable kraft paper for sustainable packaging (Noyon et al., 2023).

ESG sustainability of green materials is defined as the evaluation of the environment, social, and governance-related aspects of the production, utilization, and waste treatment of the material that claims environmental friendliness or sustainability. The driving force for the current study is aimed at offering a review of the standard literature about the topics of environment, social and governance (ESG) sustainability of green materials in circular economies for 2015-2023 via bibliometric approach. Bibliometric approach was chosen to help to illustrate the newest trends as well as the most interesting fields in ESG sustainability of green materials. The VOS viewer software will be used to perform bibliometric analysis to reveal the sustainability of green materials in circular economies. A total of 306 research papers will be reviewed to analyze the research structure of ESG sustainability of green materials in circular economies during 2015-2023 (Singh et al., 2026).

The worldwide concern about the environment is what has made the opportunity for Jute possible, owing to its environmentally friendly nature. This study is aimed at examining the environmental impact of Jute production in Bangladesh. In this study, data concerning the Production Area of Jute for 19 years has been considered for the purpose. Jute helps increase soil fertility, protects the ozone layer by absorbing carbon dioxide, and helps cleanse the atmosphere by releasing oxygen into it. These are some of the many benefits that Jute brings to the environment. Some of the recommendations include the adoption of a scientific approach to cultivation, implementation of laws to encourage the use of jute rather than synthetic materials, formulating a jute policy, expanding applications for jute, increasing public awareness of jute as an environmentally friendly material, and so on. The advocate for jute fiber composites as alternatives to non-renewable polymers to reduce environmental pollution and conserve resources (Sayeed et al., 2019). While initiatives like Bangladesh's 'Sonali Bag' highlight the potential of jute-based biopolymers to replace single-use plastic bags and contribute to economic growth, they also face challenges such as high production costs, limited scalability, and a need for independent, third-party validation. While jute bags may have higher upfront costs than plastic, their durability and reusability offer a stronger long-term value proposition, breaking even after multiple uses.

Technology Adoption: In recent studies, there is a shift from mere jute weaving to composite and biopolymer forms of jute material, solving past challenges such as high moisture content and low tensile strength.

Circular Economy Approach: The literature shows that research focuses on jute as a means of recycling industrial waste products such as buffing dust and adopting zero-waste manufacturing. Table 1 shows Analysis of Recent Trends from 2022–2026. Regulatory Compliance: The literature shows that as of early 2026, more than 127 nations had banned single-use plastics, creating a need for scaling up jute production.

Table 1. Analysis of Recent Trends from 2022–2026

Authors & Year	Title / Topic	Primary Focus	Key Findings & Environmental Benefit
Chen et al. (2026)	Mechanical and morphological evaluation of jute fibre reinforced epoxy composites	Sustainable structural and automotive engineering applications.	Jute fibres require significantly lower energy for manufacturing and disposal compared to synthetic fibres, reducing the overall carbon footprint
Islam et al. (2024)	Full article: Jute Fiber and Its Composites: Processing, Properties, and Applications	Review of natural fibre-reinforced composites (NFRC) in aerospace and automotive sectors.	Jute fibres are nontoxic and biodegradable; deployment of NFRCs can reduce synthetic material reliance and decrease vehicle weight by 30–40%
Sakib (2025)	Eco-Friendly Innovation in Packaging: Sustainable Business Strategies for Sonali Bag	Viability and strategy for jute-based biopolymers (Sonali Bag).	Sonali Bags offer a 100% plastic-free, biodegradable alternative. By-product lignin sales can offset production costs by nearly 16%
Yewle et al. (2023)	Improved food storage in jute packaging: Functional enhancements	Comparative study of food grain preservation in jute vs. synthetic bags.	Functional treatments (chitosan/neem) on jute fabric enhance pest resistance; multi-layer jute-poly systems provide eco-friendly, insect-free storage
Zhou et al. (2025)	Fabrication of solid-state substrates made from jute fibres	Industrial fabrication of biodegradable substrates.	Demonstrated high rigidity in jute composites comparable to glass fibre, suitable for rigid agricultural packaging
Dharmawan (2026)	Jute Bags Market Outlook 2025-2034	Market analysis of structural demand transformation in retail.	Jute has emerged as the most commercially viable replacement for plastic in grocery retail, projected to reach a $5.1 billion market value by 2034
Nani et al. (2025)	pH measurement and colour variations of cotton, flax, and jute fibres	Morphological properties of natural fibres in industrial use.	Jute's natural cellulose content provides superior stiffness for heavy-duty packaging (up to 30 kg) without the chemical load of synthetic polymers

continued on following page

Table 1. Continued

Authors & Year	Title / Topic	Primary Focus	Key Findings & Environmental Benefit
Patel (2025)	Eco-Friendly Jute Bags Wholesale: Sustainable Business in 2025-2026	Life-cycle assessment of widespread jute bag adoption.	Widespread jute bag use is estimated to save approximately 1.5 million tons of CO2 annually; bags degrade naturally within 3–6 months
Coherent Market Insights (2026)	Jute Packaging Market Size, Share & Trends Forecast 2026-2033	Global regulatory and technological trend impact assessment.	Transformation of the market is driven by evolving ESG (Environmental, Social, and Governance) trends and digital integration for traceability
Kovacevic et al. (2024)	Fabrication of recycled jute/TiO2/Polyaniline for metal ion adsorption	Environmental remediation using recycled jute fibre.	Recycled jute fibres can be functionalized to adsorb heavy metals, extending their life cycle beyond simple packaging into pollution control

III. OBJECTIVES

- Technical Skill Enhancement: Develop skills in using state-of-the-art technology to minimize mistakes and enhance operational efficiency by improving productivity by 20% during the following fiscal year.
- Process Optimization: Analyze current work procedures and remove inefficiencies in order to achieve improved project completion speed without sacrificing quality.
- Collaboration Skills Improvement: Ensure effective collaboration within the team by hosting bi-weekly meetings and ensuring everyone is aligned regarding performance metrics and goals.
- Data-Driven Decisions: Employ data analysis skills to support better decision making, striving to raise the ROI of the entire department by 15% through proper management.
- Leadership Abilities: Mentoring junior employees and taking on larger responsibilities is crucial in preparation for future growth within the company.
- Client Satisfaction Maintenance: Achieve a customer retention rate above 95% by providing excellent service that surpasses client expectations.

IV. THE ROLE OF JUTE IN REDUCING PLASTIC WASTE AND PROMOTING SUSTAINABLE DEVELOPMENT

Jute bags have proven to be good and environment-friendly alternatives to plastic packing as they are bio-degradable and carbon negative in nature. Jute does not degrade the environment as it decomposes naturally, while its counterpart's polyethylene and polypropylene take centuries for decomposition and form microplastics. Cultivation of jute increases the quality of the soil and the storage of carbon. Besides this, jute is a sustainable product, whereas jute bags have a lower carbon footprint and prevent less waste, hence governed by the rule of the circular economy. The overall impacts of their findings are promoting environmental health and economic growth in the jute-producing communities.

However, academic literature on jute packaging has progressed beyond environmentalist rhetoric towards an all-encompassing analysis of its significance in circular economies. Contemporary scientific discussions stress the unique ability of jute materials to decompose fully and return to nature within months; still, such "green" characteristics are highly conditional and depend on specific life cycle stages. Researchers point out the capacity of the Corchorus plant to sequester atmospheric CO_2, but they simultaneously underscore the excessive use of H2O and methane emissions during retting.

From a technological standpoint, the sector has reached a critical crossroads. The introduction of cutting-edge technologies in "Jute 4.0" encompasses the utilization of advanced digital systems like Jute Smart 2.0 and AI-enhanced weaving. These innovations seek to address previous shortcomings in jute logistics that had been identified by environmentalists as wasteful due to labour-intensive production. In addition to decreasing the "green premium" associated with jute products, researchers are exploring the application of blockchain technology in establishing QR codes that verify social gains of the material, such as creating millions of job opportunities in South Asian rural regions.

A. Sustainable Alternatives to Plastic Packaging

Some substitutes for plastic packaging include jute bags, which are biodegradable and compostable and carbon negative as they break down within a few months and even promote a sustainable agriculture alternative to plastic. Paper packaging can be sourced from recycled paper or from sustainably sourced and harvested forests and generates the huge resource that becomes available in the form of a biodegradable and recyclable product.

Biodegradable plastic from renewable resources such as cornstarch or cellulose degrades faster than the old plastic, but only under certain conditions. Bamboo is another sustainable option because it grows very quickly and requires few resources; thus, it is quite durable and also biodegradable for most packaging applications. Glass and metal are long-term alternatives because they can be recycled and reused, and glass is non-toxic and metal is lightweight, with a strong recyclability factor.

Probably, their strategy could be the production of edible or biodegradable plant-based films, using seaweed, starch, or proteins, as an alternative to plastic wraps. Last but not least, reusable fabric bags made from cotton, hemp, and recycled materials encourage users to repetitively use the bags in the name of environmental protection - a fact that saves them from the degradation caused by the so-called single-use waste. The goal is to reduce the devastating environmental damage presently caused by traditional plastic packaging materials in order to implement a more circular economy.

B. Life Cycle of jute bags

The lifecycle of a jute bag goes through a circular cradle-to-grave lifecycle, starting from the planting of Corchorus plants. In the growing stage, the jute is a carbon sink since it absorbs more CO_2 than it releases. Then comes extraction (retting) when stems are put in the water to separate fibers which are subsequently stripped, dried, and spun into threads.

In the production stage, threads are woven into "Hessian" cloth and stitched together to make a bag. Contrary to plastic that has single use only, the lifecycle of a jute bag is characterized by reusability because the durability of the material lets it be used repeatedly. In the end, in the end-of-life stage, a jute bag can be recycled completely since it is made of natural cellulose and thus is completely biodegradable and compostable taking several months to decompose and releasing nutrients back into the soil. Figure 1shows conceptual illustration of jutes biodegradation profile.

Figure 1. Conceptual illustration of jutes biodegradation profile

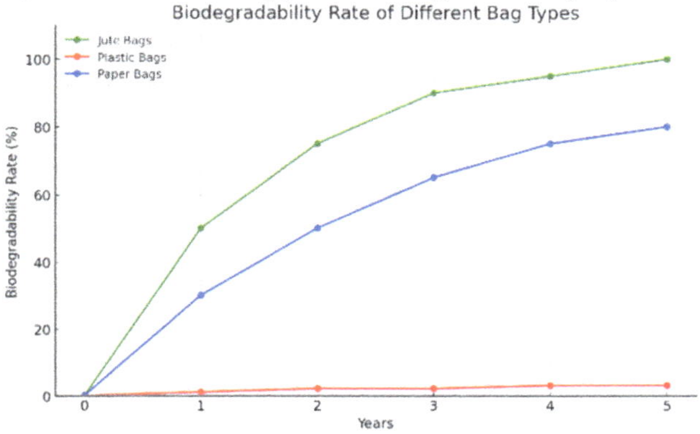

While the physical cycle of jute provides a clear starting point for understanding its lifecycle, the ability of jute to scale as a viable solution globally must consider more difficult issues of economics and technology trade-offs. Academic discussions often gravitate toward the "cotton-jute-plastic paradox," wherein jute uses much less energy than cotton; however, jute's high-water consumption ($96,750$ liters per ton) in retting processes can lead to local environmental degradation. In recent years, academics have identified the need to implement "Jute 4.0" technology to address this issue. By AI-powered water recycling systems and enzyme retting, methane emissions and water usage have been dramatically cut down, enhancing the environmental benefits.

Moreover, the transition to a circular economy has been made possible with the implementation of blockchain-powered traceability. The introduction of digital passports enables retailers to monitor carbon sequestration data and ensure fair labor practices in real-time. While concerns remain about geographical concentration and price volatility, the prospects of jute have been positively impacted by developments in jute biopolymer technology, which allows jute to be utilized for purposes beyond the production of textiles. Through this technological advancement, jute can serve as an advanced engineered material

Comparative Life Cycle Assessment (LCA): Jute vs. Modern Synthetics is being implemented as per table 2. According to a 2026 "Cradle-to-Gate" study, the ecological footprint of 1kg of jute is 23 times smaller than 1kg of virgin plastic (HDPE).

Table 2. Comparative life cycle assessment

Impact Category	Jute (per kg)	Plastic (per kg)	Environmental Benefit
Global Warming Potential (GWP)	0.0267 kg CO_2	0.634 kg CO_2	96% Lower Carbon Impact
Freshwater Ecotoxicity	3.95×10−5	2.97×10−3	98% Lower Water Toxicity
Microplastic Leakage	Zero	High (Primary Source)	Total Marine Safety
Decomposition Rate	2–3 Months	500+ Years	Immediate Soil Enrichment

When plastics form "dead zones" in the terrestrial and aquatic ecosystems, jute bags serve as soil conditioners. In the end stages of their lifecycle, they replenish the soil with nutrients (NPK), while plastics break down to become microplastics and enter the human food chain.

C. Environmental Impact of Jute Packaging

This jute packaging has an extremely positive impact on the environment compared to other conventional plastic packaging. Jute is a natural, renewable fibre that is biodegradable and can decompose in a period of months, returning to the earth without harm; hence, the cultivation of jute is environmentally friendly because jute absorbs big amounts of CO_2 and releases oxygen for the decrease of greenhouses and quality air in the environment.

Jute farming also uses little or no pest and fertilizer since it helps sustain the freshness of soil and minimizes water pollution. Besides, jute prevents soil erosion and increases the fertility of the soil, thus making it a crop that farmers can bank on its sustainability. The production process of jute products is less harmful to the environment than producing synthetic plastics based on petrochemicals with high CO_2 emission.

This means that industries can curb the spread of microplastics, which degrade not just wildlife but also contaminate the environment, by replacing plastic packaging with jute. Hence, it provides an opportunity for fostering circular economy engagements through reusable and recyclable packaging solutions by making use of the durability and versatility of jute for different packaging needs. Generally, jute packaging matches up with the goals of sustainable development since it involves reducing plastic waste, supporting eco-friendly production systems, and encouraging stewardship of the environment.

D. Sustainable Goal Development

As of 2026, the global sustainability landscape is defined by a "stark contradiction." While significant breakthroughs have been made in infrastructure and health, the world faces a $4 trillion annual financing gap and accelerating environmental regressions.

By 2026, specific targets within the following Sustainable Development Goals (SDGs) have shown the most resilient progress:

- SDG 7: Affordable and Clean Energy: This remains the fastest-moving goal. Access to electricity has reached near-universal levels in major emerging regions, and renewables are now the dominant source of new power generation globally.
- SDG 9: Industry, Innovation, and Infrastructure: Driven by the "Digital Decade," mobile network coverage is nearly 100% worldwide, fostering unprecedented levels of inclusive digital infrastructure.
- SDG 3: Good Health and Well-being: Sustained global efforts have successfully achieved long-term reductions in maternal, neonatal, and under-five mortality rates.
- SDG 1: No Poverty: While extreme poverty persists in conflict zones, broad income poverty has fallen significantly over the last decade, particularly across Asia and parts of Africa.

The primary sustainability debate in 2026 centres on Biodiversity Finance. The 2026 UNEP "State of Finance for Nature" report highlights that for every dollar spent on protection, $30 is still spent on nature-negative activities like fossil fuel subsidies. Key debates also focus on SDG 13 (Climate Action), SDG 14 (Life Below Water), and SDG 15 (Life on Land), where progress is not just stalling but actively deteriorating due to record-high emissions and "marine ecosystem collapse." The 2026 High-Level Political Forum (HLPF) is currently debating the Sevilla Commitment, a renewed framework to triple the lending capacity of multilateral banks to save the 2030 Agenda.

E. Economic Feasibility and Corporate Branding

The economic feasibility of jute packaging seems promising, especially in the light of the environment, as pollution through plastic is an issue of major concern for many businesses across the world. Jute is an easily available crop in Bangladesh and India, which have mass cultivated this crop. Given that the raw material source is not very costly, that jute bags have a higher upfront cost compared to plastic bags. For producing jute packaging, its strength and reusability will cancel out initial investments. Moreover, generating employment opportunities through jute industries shall contribute to stimulating local economies with higher agricultural growth.

Corporate branding would consider changing to jute packaging because of the reputation that comes with such change. Increasingly, more people prefer companies that adopt green values. They see those who are committed to the environment as morality conscious and thus align with such brands. This enables the company to be in a position of leadership in the market space for green products. One possible CSR initiative that the company could engage in is the utilization of eco-friendly material, such as jute since it contributes to building their trust, creates competition in the market due to doing something different, or obeys more rigid environmental regulations.

F. Social and Corporate Responsibility (CSR)

Jute packaging plays a vital role in incorporating social and corporate responsibility (CSR) into a firm's strategy, addressing issues on both environmental and community development fronts. Companies that focus on the integration of sustainability into their operations have taken a strong stand on reducing their ecological footprint, which corresponds to efforts by organizations in other parts of the world in fighting against pollution and climate change. From such an angle, business organizations would contribute to reducing plastic waste and encouraging a circular economy, which would explain their responsibility as caretakers of the environment.

On the social side, jute has provided many individuals with a source of employment across different economies, particularly in countries like Bangladesh and India, among other jute-producing countries. The industry provides employment opportunities mainly to rural communities and the poor, hence enabling them toward a higher quality life economically. The firms further support traditionally managed industries by funding jute, in addition to promoting fair labor practices.

Jute packaging can be added value for CSR strategies since corporate reputation benefits from it. Not only have consumers become more cognizant of the ethical practice of their favorite brands but also more demanding of product lines from companies that make efforts for social and environmental good. The adoption of a sustainability policy, say, biodegradable packaging, by a company will give a firm hold of customers and strengthen brand loyalty and create differences in the marketplace. The CSR practices about jute have, therefore resulted in social welfare and good environmental stewardship besides providing long-term sustainability and resiliency.

G. Jute Economics, Technology, and Logistics

The incorporation of jute within the packaging industry worldwide is a dynamic process that balances between short-term problems and future prospects. In order to comprehend how it serves as an environmental-friendly material, one needs to separate existing logistics from future possibilities within technology and production.

The incorporation of jute within the packaging industry worldwide is a dynamic process that balances short-term problems and prospects. To comprehend how it serves as an environmental-friendly material, one needs to separate existing logistics from future possibilities within technology and production.

Economic and Technological Factors

Jute's present economic sustainability is based on its competitive advantage relative to synthetic polymers. Despite low prices for raw jute, its finished form tends to come with an extra "green premium" owing to its current production technology.

Technological Changes: By 2026, the entire process will have transitioned from hand-made to automated weaving using artificial intelligence. The development of hydrophobic surface chemistry has resolved jute's tendency to attract moisture and opened new markets such as refrigerated transportation, automotive, and geotextile applications.

Market Growth: The overall size of the jute bag market is anticipated to grow by a compound annual rate of about 9.8%, resulting in revenues of just under $2.95 billion by the end of 2026. This is driven by legislative requirements along with a 62% rise in consumer preference for green products since 2021.

Supply Chain and Structure Reconfiguration

The jute supply chain is currently undergoing a digital revolution to comply with international transparency standards.

Traceability: Industry leaders are implementing blockchain technology using QR codes, providing each bag with a "digital passport," which helps in validating the carbon-negative status and guarantees ethical labor practices.

Geographical Clustering: As 90 percent of the world's raw fibers come from India and Bangladesh, the supply chain is still susceptible to local disruptions. The trend for 2026 reveals an increase in nearshoring, where converters within Europe and North America collaborate with jute mills in South Asia. Table 3 shows comparative study for 10 years

Table 3. Timeline and key constraints along with opportunities

Timeline	Key Constraints & Opportunities
Short-Term (1–3 Years)	High upfront costs, seasonal supply volatility, and land-use competition with food crops. Market entry is primarily driven by plastic bags and mandatory packaging acts.
Long-Term (5–10 Years)	Scalability through "Jute 4.0" (smart factories). Jute is expected to move beyond bags into biodegradable biopolymers, replacing heavy industrial plastics and contributing to a $5.1 billion market by 2034.

In conclusion, although immediate adoption may be motivated by regulatory compliance, the future of jute depends on its transition from being merely a material for textiles to becoming an advanced biomaterial that enables a circular economy.

H. Challenges and Future Prospects

While on the positive aspect, jute packaging is both eco-friendly as well as economically efficient, its growth is hindered by limitations such as scalability issues, shortage that typically occurs during peak seasons, and higher initial costs, making it not competitive with some businesses. Other factors are consumer awareness and cost-prioritization, and future potential includes technological improvements that may alter jute properties, government incentives to increase its market. Creating more awareness, and collaborations between businesses, NGOs, and governments can create higher production, affordability, and broader usage, eventually making jute a big player in combating plastic pollution and sustainability. Table 4 depicts challenges, prospects and solutions for jute packages. Whereas table 5 show the future prospects and their solutions.

Table 4. Challenges, Prospects, and Solutions for Jute Packaging

Challenge	Prospect	Solution
Scalability of jute production	Increased demand for eco-friendly packaging	Significant investment in cultivation, processing infrastructure, and technological advancements
Limited availability and seasonal dependence	Consistent supply	Improved cultivation techniques and storage facilities
Higher initial costs	Long-term benefits	Government subsidies, incentives, and partnerships to reduce upfront costs
Consumer awareness and behavior	Growing preference for sustainable products	QR code traceability shows carbon savings per use.

Table 5: Prospects and Solutions

Prospect	Solutions
Innovation in jute processing technology	Enhanced properties and versatility
Blending jute with other biodegradable materials	Expanded utility and appeal
Government policies and international trade incentives	Boosted jute market
Increased consumer awareness and education	Shift towards sustainable products
Public-private partnerships	Improved practices and research

In the graph "Biodegradability Rate of Different Bag Types," decomposition rates of jute and plastic and paper bags are compared over 5 years. Percentages of biodegradation are shown on the y-axis, and the x-axis is in terms of years. Biodegradability rate is highest in jute bags at nearly 100% after 5 years. Plastic bags demonstrate little or no degradation. Paper bags are moderate in their decomposition rate between that of jute and plastic. Therefore, this graphical model illustrates the environmental advantage of jute over their plastic and paper counterparts.

The bar graph titled "Carbon Footprint Comparison of Different Bag Types" illustrates various kinds of bags in comparison with their carbon footprint. Here, the y-axis represents the carbon footprint measured in kilograms of CO2 equivalent and the x-axis shows the type of bags. Figure 2 presents a conceptual comparison of the relative carbon footprints of different bags, based on general industry data. While jute is a renewable resource with a low carbon footprint, it is important to note that many peer-reviewed life-cycle assessments (LCAs) have shown that the energy-intensive production of paper bags often gives them a higher carbon footprint than single-use plastic bags. Jute's environmental impact is generally lower than both, but this can vary based on specific manufacturing processes and supply chains.

Figure 2. Conceptual comparison of carbon footprints for various bags

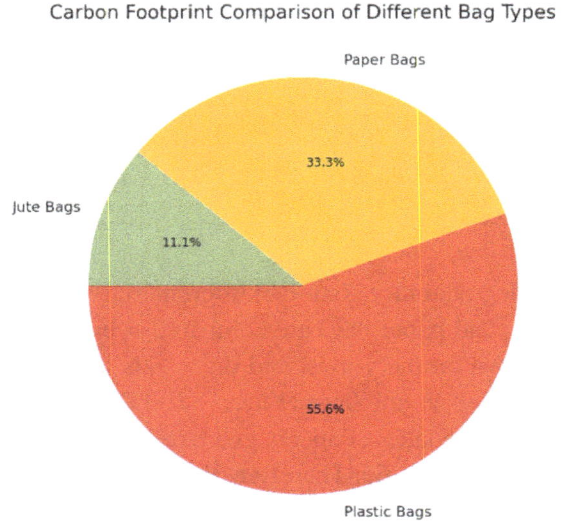

However, from an academic perspective, debates have highlighted that despite its high capacity for decomposition (100%) and carbon sink (15 tons CO_2), LCAs show that it has very highwater footprints ($96,750$ L/ton), besides being vulnerable to methane emissions when retted. From an economic standpoint, the problem of labor cost and price competition still prevails.

I. Technological Modernization: "Jute 4.0"

The most important trend from 2024 to 2026 is the industrialization of jute manufacturing. Jute has now entered an age of Smart Manufacturing:

Weaving through AI: With the use of new automated looms that come with AI-vision systems, fiber defects can now be detected on the spot, resulting in a reduction of waste by 18%. This ensures that jute shopping bags meet the high aesthetic requirements of luxury retail companies.

Hydrophobic Nanocoating's: In a bid to remedy the problem of moisture absorption that had characterized jute in the past, 2025 saw a breakthrough in research where bio-based hydrophobic nanocoating's were produced from natural waxes of plants. This made it possible to use jute for chilled food logistics, a field monopolized by plastics.

Juco – Hybrid Textiles: Juco refers to textiles made up of 75% jute mixed with 25% cotton. They have brought an innovation to the world of promotional bags.

J. Economic Viability & Market Dynamics

The global jute bag market will touch $4.5 billion by 2026, expanding at a CAGR of 12%. However, the exponential growth of industry is not based on environmental altruism; rather, it is due to Regulatory Necessity:

Global Plastic Bans: To date, more than 130 nations have passed stringent restrictions or placed taxes on single-use plastics. In India, the Jute Packaging Materials (JPM) Act requires that 100% of food grains and 20% of sugar products must be packaged in jute, establishing an institutional foundation for the industry.

Green Premium & Long-Term ROI: Yes, while jute bags cost $1.50 compared to plastic bags that retail at just $0.10 per piece. However, a single jute bag can sustain 50+ usages while plastic bags are thrown away after one use. The average number of usages required to bring down costs to below plastic bag prices is around 10.

Rural Socioeconomics: Over 4 million farmers and 400,000 workers in the mills in South Asia support jute production. Hence, the choice of jute over other materials by global brands aligns perfectly with SDG #8, Decent Work and Economic Growth

K. Strategic Recommendations for Stakeholders

To make jute the "Green Solution" that everyone uses, the following three-step strategy is recommended:

For Governments: Adopt "Green Procurement Policy," whereby any government-sponsored distribution system must use only natural fibers. Offer subsidies for adopting "Ribbon Retting" technology, which increases water efficiency in rural agriculture.

For Corporates (CSR): Move from "Green Washing" to Blockchain-Verified Packaging. Using QR codes on the jute bag packaging will show the consumer exactly which village has provided the raw materials for the product and the carbon savings from using jute products.

For Research: Use the by-products. Lignin and hurd are currently being studied to produce biodegradable filament for 3D printing and biofuels, making the jute mill a multi-purpose Bio-Refinery.

L. Trade-offs

While the environmental impacts of jute have been mostly favorable, there are major constraints associated with it. First of all, the "retting" technique, whereby the stems are submerged to separate the fibers, demands huge amounts of water. As a result, jute cultivation may contribute to pollution of local bodies of water if the biological waste is not properly handled. Another important constraint relates to land consumption. Being a very intensive crop, jute sometimes competes for arable lands with food crops, such as rice.

Speaking about the global logistical factors affecting the industry, one can point out emissions related to transportation, which are an issue for a commodity that must be transported across continents. Since the major sources of jute are concentrated in India and Bangladesh, shipping jute across the ocean to Europe or North America produces a considerable amount of CO_2. Lastly, it is necessary to address the labor-intensive processes and usage of chemical additives that are common in inferior quality products.

M. Geopolitical and International Policy Context of Jute

By 2026, the role of jute as a regional agricultural crop will transform into that of a global trade diplomacy issue. With the "Green Trade" initiative, spearheaded by the European Union and North America, beginning to incorporate natural fiber requirements into their bilateral trade deals, the emphasis will shift towards the international policy framework of jute. This is mainly due to the signing of the UN Global Treaty for Plastic Pollution in 2025.

N. Consumer Psychology and Tactile Trust

There is a deep-rooted psychological angle to the embracing of jute. Research in consumer psychology suggests that consumers have "tactile trust" towards jute bags, which cannot be achieved by plastic or paper. There is something about the feel of an organic jute bag, including its density and quality, that makes consumers think of environmental friendliness. As such, the market of 2026 has seen the emergence of the "Luxury Jute" trend, whereby top-notch brands integrate high-quality, high-density jute material as a permanent packaging option. This strategy transforms the consumers' view of a disposable bag into a durable product. Consumers no longer fear the initial expenses for the purchase since they perceive jute as a luxury product that can be used both as fashion and as an ordinary household item.

V. LIMITATIONS OF JUTE BAGS AS A SUSTAINABLE ALTERNATIVE

- Despite their ecological benefits compared to plastic, the use of jute bags faces several obstacles that prevent their full potential from being realized:
- Increased Manufacturing Expenses: The upfront cost of producing jute bags is significantly greater than the one-time use of plastic bags. This economic

barrier discourages many companies and individuals who prioritize immediate savings over sustainability.

- Supply and Scalability Problems: Jute crops are primarily grown in India and Bangladesh. This geographic dependency, combined with the seasonal nature of agriculture, may result in limited availability and difficulties in meeting worldwide demands.
- Strength and Performance Weaknesses: While resistant to wear and tear, jute fibers lack the elasticity present in plastic. They are vulnerable to moisture damage, causing decay or mold formation if not adequately preserved. Furthermore, they cannot provide an airtight seal essential for some industrial packaging applications.
- Manual Labor Dependence: Traditional cultivation and retting techniques continue to rely on manual labor. If not addressed, this may pose efficiency issues and potential labor abuse in less developed countries.
- Jute Decomposition at Landfills: Even though jute is biodegradable, it needs certain conditions for it to decompose faster. Since landfills lack oxygen, the process may take up to two years.

VI. CONCLUSION

Jute can now be seen as one of the foremost sustainability-centered substitutes for conventional synthetic packaging owing to its fast renewability and biodegradability characteristics. Also considered a "golden fiber", jute provides a natural solution to the plastic problem that exists globally, as it is biodegradable in comparison to plastics, which have been known to take hundreds of years to decompose. Besides being a sustainable substitute to plastic, the use of jute also helps spur economic growth in countries that heavily utilize jute, such as India and Bangladesh, by providing employment opportunities and boosting the economies of small-scale farms. From a technical perspective, jute's ability to withstand reuse as well as its tensile strength makes it an ideal choice of packaging. It even proves advantageous from a climate standpoint, as jute absorbs more carbon dioxide (CO_2) than its manufacture releases, which matches up with the goals of a carbon-negative economy. Jute farming increases biodiversity and improves soil fertility rather than relying on non-renewable fossil fuels used in producing plastic. Thus, jute can help address the problem of microplastics in the environment as well as provide social resilience.

Overcoming barriers in integrating jute packaging and its prospects is elaborated further. Although jute presents a strong environmental argument, the broad adoption of the material faces numerous barriers at present. The major impediments to wider usage include increased expenses of its production compared to artificial substitutes, its inability to scale beyond local markets due to limited cultivation area and pressing demands for innovative processing technologies that would replace traditional methods. Currently, jute cannot compete with the economy and cost-effectiveness of plastic products on a large scale.

Yet, these obstacles create a special chance for visionary businesses. Utilization of jute packaging enables companies to boost their branding efforts and pursue objectives set forth under Corporate Social Responsibility (CSR). Amid an environmentally sensitive consumer base, implementation of "golden fiber" demonstrates true dedication to ecological values, contributing greatly to the reputation of the firm.

The effective adoption of jute-based packaging necessitates a multisectoral collaboration strategy that would facilitate close cooperation among all key players including governmental bodies, commercial businesses, and scientific organizations. The transformation on the international scale towards sustainable materials presupposes well-coordinated actions that would allow introducing new technologies, subsidies for costly initial production and advanced methods of farming capable of increasing crop yields.

Thus, one of the major priorities should be the implementation of efficient infrastructure and modern technologies instead of archaic production methods. The establishment of a sophisticated production chain would enable providing high-quality products on an industrial level, which means that such solutions would be able to compete effectively against synthetics in terms of costs. Moreover, the application of government measures that would promote eco-friendly materials and ban the use of non-degradable polymers would contribute considerably.

Therefore, with the development of proper infrastructure and reduced prices, the future of jute seems very promising. Far from being just an additional alternative, jute can become a central element of the circular economy system, thus contributing significantly to environmental conservation and the establishment of long-term economic sustainability in developing countries.

The jute bag is not just a replacement to plastic bags but an emblem for Environmental Restoration. As the world moves towards achieving the goals of sustainability by 2030, jute can be described as a rare commodity that has properties such as being Renewable, Recyclable and Restorative.

The shift from Petro-economy to bioeconomy is no longer an option; it is a matter of survival. In this process of shifting from one form of economy to another, the jute bag becomes the "catalyst," showing that it is possible for mankind to fulfill their industrial and commercial requirements while remaining in tune with the carbon cycle of nature.

REFERENCES

Alimuzzaman, S., Arin, M. R. A., Mamun, M. A. A., Rahman, A. M., & Islam, M. R. (2024). A novel approach to manufacturing sustainable seamless jute bags and evaluation of their properties: A comparative study with commercial bags. *Journal of Natural Fibers*, *21*(1), 2299548. DOI: 10.1080/15440478.2023.2299548

Ashwini, V., & Aithal, P. S. (2023). Development of a new conceptual model: Consumers' purchase intention towards eco-friendly bags. [IJMTS]. *International Journal of Management, Technology, and Social Sciences*, *8*(4), 154–195.

Chen, H., ... (2026). Mechanical and morphological evaluation of jute fiber reinforced epoxy composites for sustainable structural and automotive applications. ResearchGate. https://www.researchgate.net/publication/399338858

Coherent Market Insights. (2026). Jute packaging market size, share & trends forecast 2026–2033. openPR.

Dharmawan, V. (2026). *Jute bags market research report 2034*. Dataintelo.

Florencia, L. E., Princella, A., Anjelina, M., Barus, R. M., Darmawan, V., & Rembulan, G. D. (2024). Pengembangan bisnis totebag sebagai alternatif usaha untuk mengurangi limbah plastik. Jurnal Pengabdian dan Kewirausahaan, 8(1).

Islam, M. S., & Ahmed, S. K. (2012). The impacts of jute on environment: An analytical review of Bangladesh. *Journal of Environment and Earth Science*, *2*(5), 24–31.

Islam, S., Karim, M. R., & Islam, M. R. (2024). Jute fiber and its composites: Processing, properties, and applications. *Journal of Natural Fibers*. Advance online publication. DOI: 10.1080/15440478.2026.2635010

Nani, G.. (2025). pH measurement and color variations of cotton, flax, and jute fibers. *Textile Research Journal*.

Nayab-Ul-Hossain, A. K. M., Sela, S. K., Alam, S. M. M., Hassan, M. N., Sarkar, J., Ahmed, C. M., Sadman, S., Hridoy, R. M., Mohsin, N., Hossain, M. B., & Mia, S. (2023). Substitution of synthetic plastic sheet by naturally colored (Turmeric) biodegradable sheet prepared from nanocellulose of raw jute, and evaluation of its quality performance (Multifunctional properties). *Current Research in Green and Sustainable Chemistry*, *6*, 100351. DOI: 10.1016/j.crgsc.2022.100351

Noyon, A. R., Karim, S., Rouf, A., Jamal, M., Layek, R. K., Sivanantham, G., & Uddin, E. (2023). Fabrication of biodegradable kraft paper from buffing dust and jute fiber: Green solutions for packaging. *Polymer Engineering and Science*, *63*(12), 4032–4042. DOI: 10.1002/pen.26503

Patel, R. (2025). *Eco-friendly jute bags wholesale India: Top picks for sustainable business in 2025–2026*. Techno Aid.

Ray, D. P., & Ghosh, R. K. (2018). Perspective of jute in a new realm beyond sacking. *Economic Affairs*, *63*(4), 981–986. DOI: 10.30954/0424-2513.4.2018.22

Sakib, N. (2025). Eco-friendly innovation in packaging: Sustainable business strategies for Sonali Bag. *Journal of Sustainable Marketing*, *15*(2).

Sayeed, M. A., Muhammad Sayem, A., & Haider, J. (2019). Opportunities with renewable jute fiber composites to reduce eco-impact of non-renewable polymers.

Singh, P., Kushwaha, J., Kushwaha, R., Rajput, S., & Jain, P. (2026). Sustainability of green materials in circular economies: A bibliometric analysis on ESG. In Futureproofed sustainability amidst climate change polycrisis: Advancing SDGs and ESG for the cities of tomorrow (pp. 97–136). IGI Global Scientific Publishing.

Verma, B. B. (2009). Continuous jute fiber reinforced laminated paper composite and reinforcement-fiber free paper laminate. *Bulletin of Materials Science*, *32*(6), 589–595. DOI: 10.1007/s12034-009-0090-0

Yewle, A., ... (2023). Improved food storage in jute packaging: An assessment of the current uses, constraints, and functional enhancements of jute bags. ResearchGate. https://www.researchgate.net/publication/391639141

Zhou, X., ... (2025). Fabrication of solid-state substrates made from jute fibers. Composite Structures.

Compilation of References

Abdelmeguid, A., Tsironis, G., Afy-Shararah, M., Tsagarakis, K. P., & Salonitis, K. (2024). Insights into sustainability and circular economy trends in luxury fashion: A LinkedIn topic modelling study. *Cleaner and Responsible Consumption*, *15*, 100228. DOI: 10.1016/j.clrc.2024.100228

Abdul Basit, S., Gharleghi, B., Batool, K., Hassan, S. S., Jahanshahi, A. A., & Kliem, M. E. (2024). Review of enablers and barriers of sustainable business practices in SMEs. *Journal of Economy and Technology*, *2*, 79–94. DOI: 10.1016/j.ject.2024.03.005

Abhishek, N., Suraj, N., Muralidharan, M., Singh, A., & Chattopadhyay, A. (2024). Carbon management accounting: An evolving approach to enhance transparency and accountability in accounting and reporting practices. *Journal of Accounting & Organizational Change*, *21*(3), 535–566. DOI: 10.1108/JAOC-05-2024-0156

Aboflan, Y. E., Kpotchou, K., Kabo, K., & Ionut-Petrisor, A. (2025). Territorial entrepreneurship: A driving force for sustainable innovation. *Journal of Ecohumanism*, *4*(4). Advance online publication. DOI: 10.62754/joe.v4i4.7020

Aboramadan, M., & Karatepe, O. M. (2021). Green human resource management, perceived green organizational support and their effects on hotel employees' behavioral outcomes. *International Journal of Contemporary Hospitality Management*, *33*(10), 3199–3222. DOI: 10.1108/IJCHM-12-2020-1440

Abubakar, I. R., Maniruzzaman, K. M., Dano, U. L., AlShihri, F. S., AlShammari, M. S., Ahmed, S. M. S., Al-Gehlani, W. A. G., & Alrawaf, T. I. (2022). Environmental sustainability impacts of solid waste management practices in the global South. *International Journal of Environmental Research and Public Health*, *19*(19), 12717. DOI: 10.3390/ijerph191912717

Adebayo, A. A. (2025). Efficacy of digital green supply chain management technologies on triple bottom line performance: Moderating role of mandatory external regulatory pressure. *International Journal of Marketing and Management Sciences*, *6*(1).

Afshar, M., & Mofatteh, S. (2024). Biochar for a sustainable future: Environmentally friendly production and diverse applications. *Results in Engineering*, *23*, 102433. DOI: 10.1016/j.rineng.2024.102433

Agbedahin, A. V. (2019). Sustainable development, Education for Sustainable Development, and the 2030 Agenda for Sustainable Development: Emergence, efficacy, eminence, and future. *Sustainable Development (Bradford)*, *27*(4), 669–680. DOI: 10.1002/sd.1931

Agrawal, R., Agrawal, S., Samadhiya, A., Kumar, A., Luthra, S., & Jain, V. (2024). Adoption of green finance and green innovation for achieving circularity: An exploratory review and future directions. *Geoscience Frontiers*, *15*(4), 101669. DOI: 10.1016/j.gsf.2023.101669

Agrosustain. (2025). Agro sustain. Available on https://www.agrosustain.ch/ (Accessed on 7th March 2025).

Agusdinata, D. B., Liu, W., Eakin, H., & Romero, H. (2018). Socio-environmental impacts of lithium mineral extraction: Towards a research agenda. *Environmental Research Letters*, *13*(12), 123001. DOI: 10.1088/1748-9326/aae9b1

Aguzman, G., Pratiwi, C. P., Eni, Y., & Sasongko, A. H. (2024). *The influence of social entrepreneurship orientation on the sustainability of tourism villages through community empowerment*. Indonesian Journal of Business and Entrepreneurship., DOI: 10.17358/ijbe.10.3.488

Ahluwalia, I. J. (2019). Urban governance in India. *Journal of Urban Affairs*, *41*(1), 83–102. DOI: 10.1080/07352166.2016.1271614

Ahmad, F., Boumaiza, A., Sanfilippo, A., & Al-Fagih, L. (2025). A Detailed Comprehensive Role of Digital Technologies in Green Finance Initiative for Net-Zero Energy Transition. *Advanced Energy and Sustainability Research*, *6*(10), 2500066. DOI: 10.1002/aesr.202500066

Ahmed, M., & Ahmed, M. J. (2026). Sustainable Industrial Operations Through IoT-Generated Big Data Insights. In *Sustainable Operations in the Age of AI and Big Data* (pp. 37–82). DOI: 10.4018/979-8-2600-0216-2.ch002

Ahmed, M., Al Amareen, O. S., & Arafat, Y. (2026). Harnessing Big Data for Reverse Logistics and Waste Management: Pathways to Sustainable Supply Chains. In *Enhancing Sustainability in Global Supply Chains With Big Data Analytics* (pp. 175–210). IGI Global Scientific Publishing. DOI: 10.4018/979-8-3373-6896-2.ch006

Ahmed, I., Zhang, Y., Jeon, G., Lin, W., Khosravi, M. R., & Qi, L. (2022). A blockchain-and artificial intelligence-enabled smart IoT framework for sustainable city. *International Journal of Intelligent Systems*, *37*(9), 6493–6507. DOI: 10.1002/int.22852

Ahmed, M., Mubarik, M. S., & Shahbaz, M. (2021). Factors affecting the outcome of corporate sustainability policy: A review paper. *Environmental Science and Pollution Research International*, *28*(9), 10335–10356. DOI: 10.1007/s11356-020-12143-7 PMID: 33403636

Ahmed, R. A., Hemdan, E. E. D., El-Shafai, W., Ahmed, Z. A., El-Rabaie, E. S. M., & Abd El-Samie, F. E. (2022). Climate-smart agriculture using intelligent techniques, blockchain and Internet of Things: Concepts, challenges, and opportunities. *Transactions on Emerging Telecommunications Technologies*, *33*(11), e4607. DOI: 10.1002/ett.4607

Al Halbusi, H., Popa, S., Alshibani, S. M., & Soto-Acosta, P. (2024). Greening the future: Analyzing green entrepreneurial orientation, green knowledge management and digital transformation for sustainable innovation and circular economy. *European Journal of Innovation Management*. Advance online publication. DOI: 10.1108/EJIM-02-2024-0169

Alamandi, M. (2025). Sustainable Innovation Management: Balancing Economic Growth and Environmental Responsibility. *Sustainability (Basel)*, *17*(10), 4362. DOI: 10.3390/su17104362

Alan, H., & Köker, A. R. (2023). Analyzing and mapping agricultural waste recycling research: An integrative review for conceptual framework and future directions. *Resources Policy*, *85*, 103987. DOI: 10.1016/j.resourpol.2023.103987

Alao, O. E., Alao, P. O., & Elijah, T. M. (2023). Developing the entrepreneurial skills of Nigerian business education students for sustainability: Policy and practice imperatives. *Contemporary Educational Researches Journal*, *13*(4), 251–263. DOI: 10.18844/cerj.v14i4.8965

Alayed, S., Alateeg, S., & Albaz, M. M. (2025). Integrating economic and social sustainability with technological competence: The mediating effect of organizational values on economic performance. *Sustainability (Basel)*, *17*(22), 10404. Advance online publication. DOI: 10.3390/su172210404

Ali, H., Khan, H. A., & Pecht, M. (2021). Circular economy of Li batteries: Technologies and trends. *Journal of Energy Storage*, *40*, 102690. Advance online publication. DOI: 10.1016/j.est.2021.102690

Alimuzzaman, S., Arin, M. R. A., Mamun, M. A. A., Rahman, A. M., & Islam, M. R. (2024). A novel approach to manufacturing sustainable seamless jute bags and evaluation of their properties: A comparative study with commercial bags. *Journal of Natural Fibers*, *21*(1), 2299548. DOI: 10.1080/15440478.2023.2299548

Ali, S. S., Abdelkarim, E. A., Elsamahy, T., Al-Tohamy, R., Li, F., Kornaros, M., Zuorro, A., Zhu, D., & Sun, J. (2023). Bioplastic production in terms of life cycle assessment: A state-of-the-art review. *Environmental Science and Ecotechnology*, *15*, 100254. DOI: 10.1016/j.ese.2023.100254

Al-Mamary, Y. H. (2025). Factors shaping green entrepreneurial intentions towards green innovation: An integrated model. *Future Business Journal*, *11*(1), 21. DOI: 10.1186/s43093-025-00443-8

Alshaflut, A. (2024). Enhancing smart city infrastructure: An iot-integrated system approach for real-time urban management. *Indian Journal of Science and Technology*, *17*(29), 3012–3017. DOI: 10.17485/IJST/v17i29.1070

Alshareef, M. N. (2025). Artificial intelligence-enhanced ESG disclosure quality and financial performance nexus in Saudi listed companies under Vision 2030. *Sustainability*, *17*(16), 7421. DOI: 10.3390/su17167421

Alshibani, S. M., Shabir, S., & Albishri, N. (2024). Women entrepreneur's perspective towards sustainable entrepreneurship in the apparel sector of Saudi Arabia. *Sustainability (Basel)*, *16*(19), 8636. Advance online publication. DOI: 10.3390/su16198636

Altemimi, A., Lakhssassi, N., Baharlouei, A., Watson, D. G., & Lightfoot, D. A. (2017). Phytochemicals: Extraction, isolation, and identification of bioactive compounds from plant extracts. *Plants*, *6*(4), 42. DOI: 10.3390/plants6040042

Alwakid, W., Aparicio, S., & Urbano, D. (2021). The Influence of Green Entrepreneurship on Sustainable Development in Saudi Arabia: The Role of Formal Institutions. *International Journal of Environmental Research and Public Health*, *18*(10), 5433. DOI: 10.3390/ijerph18105433 PMID: 34069588

Amalina, F., Abd Razak, A. S., Krishnan, S., Sulaiman, H., Zularisam, A. W., & Nasrullah, M. (2022). Biochar production techniques utilizing biomass waste-derived materials and environmental applications–A review. *Journal of Hazardous Materials Advances*, *7*, 100134. DOI: 10.1016/j.hazadv.2022.100134

Ammar, M., Bangsawan, G., & Asriani, A. (2024). Designing the concept of regional innovation sustainability: The triple bottom line concept approach and sustainable evaluation. *Jurnal Bina Praja, 16*(3), 523–539. DOI: 10.21787/jbp.16.2024.523-539

Amutha, T., Vimala, V., Hemavathy, R., Sathiya, R. D., & Professor, A. (n.d.). The role of women in sustainable entrepreneurship: Addressing challenges and identifying prospects. Library Progress International, 44(3). Retrieved from www .bpasjournals.com

Anant, B. C. (2025). Factors affecting growth and success of green and sustainable entrepreneurship: An empirical study of Indian startups. Journal of Informatics Education and Research, 5. http://jier.org

Andersson, I. (2024). Green innovative procurement in the municipality sectorPotential and challenges. *Geografisk Tidsskrift-Danish Journal of Geography, 124*(2), 141–155. DOI: 10.1080/00291951.2024.2395255

Andjelković, A., Janković Milić, V., Radosavljević, M., Petković, S., Kule, D., & Debarliev, S. (2025). Sustainable entrepreneurship in the Western Balkan countries: Key constraints. *Sustainability (Basel), 17*(21), 9406. Advance online publication. DOI: 10.3390/su17219406

ANGED. (2022). Rapport sur la gestion des déchets en Tunisie.

Anggraini, G., & Hermawan, A. (2025). Sustainability awareness in Indonesia's oil and gas sector. *JRAK, 17*(2), 332–347. DOI: 10.23969/jrak.v17i2.26356

Anjanappa, J. (2023). Assessing Barriers to Scale-up Adaptation Finance for India. SSRN *Electronic Journal*. DOI: 10.2139/ssrn.4489053

Arambarri, J., Hayden, J. S., Elkurdy, M., Meyers, B., Hamatteh, Z. S. A., Abbassi, B., & Omar, W. (2019). Lithium-ion car batteries: Present analysis and future predictions. *Environmental Engineering Research, 24*(4), 699–710. DOI: 10.4491/eer.2018.383

Argonne National Laboratory. (2012, July 18). The long, winding road to advanced batteries for electric cars. https://www.anl.gov/article/the-long-winding-road-to-advanced-batteries-for-electric-cars

Arici, H. E., & Uysal, M. (2022). Leadership, green innovation, and green creativity: A systematic review. *Service Industries Journal, 42*(5–6), 280–320. DOI: 10.1080/02642069.2021.1964482

Arshad, Q. U. A., Khan, W. Z., Azam, F., Khan, M. K., Yu, H., & Zikria, Y. B. (2023). Blockchain-based decentralized trust management in IoT: Systems, requirements and challenges. *Complex & Intelligent Systems*, *9*(6), 6155–6176. DOI: 10.1007/s40747-023-01058-8

Asadi, S., Nilashi, M., Samad, S., Abdullah, R., Mahmoud, M., Alkinani, M. H., & Yadegaridehkordi, E. (2021). Factors impacting consumers' intention toward adoption of electric vehicles in Malaysia. *Journal of Cleaner Production*, *282*, 124474. Advance online publication. DOI: 10.1016/j.jclepro.2020.124474

Aschemann-Witzel, J., & Stangherlin, I. (2021). Upcycled by-product use in food: Consumer perceptions and acceptance of food waste valorization. *Journal of Cleaner Production*, *290*, 125815.

Ashwini, V., & Aithal, P. S. (2023). Development of a new conceptual model: Consumers' purchase intention towards eco-friendly bags. [IJMTS]. *International Journal of Management, Technology, and Social Sciences*, *8*(4), 154–195.

Asian Development Bank (ADB). (2023). *ASEAN Taxonomy for Sustainable Finance: Version 2*. ADB Publishing., DOI: 10.22617/TCS230092-2

Assembly, U. G. (2015). Transforming our world: the 2030 Agenda for Sustainable Development.

Atsukwei, M. E., Ande, J., & Jim-Suleiman, S. (2025). Effect of Corporate Sustainability Reporting on Economic Value Added of Oil and Gas Companies in Nigeria. Journal of Human Resources and Management Science.

Atta, A., & Ali, L. (2024). Linking social entrepreneurship with sustainability: Mediating role of social business operations. 3, 32–55. https://doi.org/DOI: 10.33282/rr.vx9i4.3

Attah, E., & Yonkor, E. D. (2025). Social Entrepreneurship and Sustainable Development Goals. SSRN *Electronic Journal*. DOI: 10.2139/ssrn.5550899

Attero. (2021, July 8). Electronic waste recycling company in India | Li-ion battery recycling. https://attero.in

Attero. (2021, June 22). Lithium-ion battery recycling companies in India. https://attero.in

Audretsch, D. B., Lehmann, E. E., & Paleari, S. (2015). Academic policy and entrepreneurship: A European perspective. *The Journal of Technology Transfer*, *40*(3), 363–368. DOI: 10.1007/s10961-014-9359-6

Aureli, S., Foschi, E., & Paletta, A. (2023). Management accounting for a circular economy: Current limits and avenue for a dialogic approach. *Accounting, Auditing & Accountability Journal*, *36*(9), 291–319. DOI: 10.1108/AAAJ-04-2022-5766

Avilés-Palacios, C., & Rodríguez-Olalla, A. (2021). The sustainability of waste management models in circular economies. *Sustainability (Basel)*, *13*(13), 7105. DOI: 10.3390/su13137105

Ayilara, M. S., Olanrewaju, O. S., Babalola, O. O., & Odeyemi, O. (2020). Waste management through composting: Challenges and potentials. *Sustainability (Basel)*, *12*(11), 4456. DOI: 10.3390/su12114456

Azim, K., Soudi, B., Boukhari, S., Perissol, C., Roussos, S., & Thami Alami, I. (2018). Composting parameters and compost quality: A literature review. *Organic Agriculture*, *8*(2), 141–158. DOI: 10.1007/s13165-017-0180-z

Badjeena, B. P., Ali, E., Wonyra, K. O., & Tamou, K. (2024). Green entrepreneurship: Opportunities and challenges for the transition to a circular economy in Togo, West Africa. *World Development Sustainability*, *5*, 100181. DOI: 10.1016/j.wds.2024.100181

Bag, S., Gupta, S., Kumar, A., & Sivarajah, U. (2023). Role of artificial intelligence in sustainable supply chain management and logistics efficiency. *Technological Forecasting and Social Change*, *187*, 122195.

Bahuriddin, N. S., Saman, M. Z. M., Mohamad-Ali, N., Ngadiman, N. H. A., & Maulana, M. I. I. M. (2025). State of sustainability assessments of metal additive manufacturing: Literature review and triple-bottom-line perspectives. *Environmental Science and Pollution Research International*, *32*(35), 20825–20843. DOI: 10.1007/s11356-025-36889-0 PMID: 40866783

Bala, S., Garg, D., Sridhar, K., Inbaraj, B. S., Singh, R., Kamma, S., Tripathi, M., & Sharma, M. (2023). Transformation of agro-waste into value-added bioproducts and bioactive compounds: Micro/nano formulations and application in the agri-food-pharma sector. *Bioengineering (Basel, Switzerland)*, *10*(2), 152. DOI: 10.3390/bioengineering10020152

Bandna, P. K. (2025). *Hussain, I., Shah, M. A., & Bhalla, M.* Principles and Frameworks for Sustainable Finance., DOI: 10.1002/9781394311682.ch5

Banerjee, S. B. (2003). Who sustains whose development? Sustainable development and the reinvention of nature. *Organization Studies*, *24*(1), 143–180. DOI: 10.1177/0170840603024001341

Bankins, S., & Formosa, P. (2023). The ethical implications of artificial intelligence (AI) for meaningful work. *Journal of Business Ethics*, *185*(4), 725–740. DOI: 10.1007/s10551-023-05339-7

Basile, V., Capobianco, N., & Vona, R. (2025). Business model development in the circular bioeconomy: A focus on the fashion-textile industry. *Journal of Cleaner Production*, *494*, 144944. DOI: 10.1016/j.jclepro.2025.144944

Bassi, M. K. A. (2024, February 20). A sustainable asset valuation of the FAME II policy in India. International Institute for Sustainable Development. https://www.iisd.org/publications/report/savi-electric-vehicles-india-fame-policy

Battilana, J., Leca, B., & Boxenbaum, E. (2009). 2 how actors change institutions: Towards a theory of institutional entrepreneurship. *The Academy of Management Annals*, *3*(1), 65–107. DOI: 10.5465/19416520903053598

Battilana, J., Lee, M., Walker, J., & Dorsey, C. (2012). In search of the hybrid ideal. *The Academy of Management Annals*, *6*(1), 51–96.

Belgaroui, R. (2025). Advancing sustainable entrepreneurship through digital innovation: A systematic review. *Asian Journal of Education and Social Studies*, *51*(12), 229–246. DOI: 10.9734/ajess/2025/v51i122689

Beluhan, S., Mihajlovski, K., Šantek, B., & Ivančić Šantek, M. (2023). The production of bioethanol from lignocellulosic biomass: Pretreatment methods, fermentation, and downstream processing. *Energies*, *16*(19), 7003. DOI: 10.3390/en16197003

Benavides-Sánchez, E. P., Moya-Clemente, I., & Pérez-Sánchez, M. (2025). Bibliometric analysis and systematic literature review of the relationship between sustainable development goals and sustainable entrepreneurship over time. *Discover Sustainability*, *6*(1), 1–18. DOI: 10.1007/s43621-024-00572-0

Berniak-Woźny, J., Sliż, P., & Siciński, J. (2025). Empowering Smart Cities Through Start-Ups: A Sustainability Framework for Incubator-City Collaboration. *Systems*, *13*(4), 219. DOI: 10.3390/systems13040219

Berrone, P., Rousseau, H. E., Ricart, J. E., Brito, E., & Giuliodori, A. (2023). How can research contribute to the implementation of sustainable development goals? An interpretive review of SDG literature in management. *International Journal of Management Reviews*, *25*(2), 318–339. DOI: 10.1111/ijmr.12331

Bhandari, S., Liaqat, S., & Henao, D. (2025). Green public procurement as an effective way for sustainable development: A systematic literature review and bibliometric analysis. *Sustainable Development (Bradford)*, *33*(2), 2364–2391. Advance online publication. DOI: 10.1002/sd.3234

Bhatia, S. K., Kumar, S., Kim, S. H., Yang, Y. H., & Kumar, V. (2022). Advances in biomass valorization for sustainable bio-based economy. *Bioresource Technology*, *344*, 126181.

Bhatia, T., & Sindhu, S. S. (2024). Sustainable management of organic agricultural wastes: Contributions in nutrients availability, pollution mitigation and crop production. *Discover Agriculture*, *2*(1), 1–42. DOI: 10.1007/s44279-024-00147-7

Bhatnagar, M., Taneja, S., & Özen, E. (2022). A wave of green start-ups in India—The study of green finance as a support system for sustainable entrepreneurship. *Green Finance*, *4*(2), 253–273. DOI: 10.3934/GF.2022012

Bhatt, S., Lee, J., Deutsch, J., Ayaz, H., Fulton, B., & Suri, R. (2023). From food waste to value: Consumer acceptance of upcycled ingredients and clean-label products. *Sustainable Production and Consumption*, *35*, 189–200.

Biermann, F., Kanie, N., & Kim, R. E. (2017). Global governance by goal-setting: The novel approach of the UN Sustainable Development Goals. *Current Opinion in Environmental Sustainability*, *26*, 26–31. DOI: 10.1016/j.cosust.2017.01.010

Bitwell, C., Indra, S. S., Luke, C., & Kakoma, M. K. (2023). A review of modern and conventional extraction techniques and their applications for extracting phytochemicals from plants. *Scientific African*, *19*, e01585. DOI: 10.1016/j.sciaf.2023.e01585

Blazey, A., & Lelong, M. (2022). Green budgeting: A way forward. *OECD Journal on Budgeting*, *22*(2), 1–32. DOI: 10.1787/dc7ac5a7-en

Bocken, N. M. P., Short, S. W., Rana, P., & Evans, S. (2014). A literature and practice review to develop sustainable business model archetypes. *Journal of Cleaner Production*, *65*, 42–56. DOI: 10.1016/j.jclepro.2013.11.039

Bonu, S. R., & Panigrahi, D. S. (2019, December). Recollection and recycling of automotive Lithium Ion batteries in India. In 2019 IEEE Transportation Electrification Conference (ITEC-India) (pp. 1-5). IEEE. DOI: 10.1109/ITEC-India48457.2019.ITECINDIA2019-47

Bowen, G. A. (2009). Document analysis as a qualitative research method. *Qualitative Research Journal*, *9*(2), 27–40. DOI: 10.3316/QRJ0902027

Braun, V., & Clarke, V. (2006). Using thematic analysis in psychology. *Qualitative Research in Psychology*, *3*(2), 77–101. DOI: 10.1191/1478088706qp063oa

Bridi, R. M., & Al Hosani, N. A. (2021). Theoretical reflections on consumer behavior: The adoption and non-adoption of electric vehicles. In *Proceedings of the 2021 International Conference on Renewable Energy: Generation and Applications (ICREGA)*. IEEE. DOI: 10.1109/ICREGA50506.2021.9388315

Brown, P., Barber, K., & Kirk, R. S. (1988). Potential of electric vehicles in present and future transportation systems. SAE Technical Paper 885179. DOI: 10.4271/885179

Budaya, P., Dan, O., Stakeholder, T., Kemampuan, T., Artisan, B., Madura, E., Ma'arif, T., Hasanah, U., Putu, N., Arnani, R., & Madura, U. T. (2024). The influence of organizational culture and stakeholder pressure on the ability to innovate artisan entrepreneurship Madura. Management Studies and Entrepreneurship Journal, 5(2). https://journal.yrpipku.com/index.php/msej

Budumuru, U. R., & Paruchuru, M. (2025). Tracing the evolution of ecosystems in social entrepreneurship: Perspectives on innovation and sustainability. *Sustainable Futures : An Applied Journal of Technology, Environment and Society*, *9*, 100645. DOI: 10.1016/j.sftr.2025.100645

Cahyadi, E. R., Hidayati, N., Zahra, N., & Arif, C. (2024). Integrating Circular Economy Principles into Agri-Food Supply Chain Management: A Systematic Literature Review. *Sustainability (Basel)*, *16*(16), 7165. DOI: 10.3390/su16167165

Campatelli, G., Benesperi, F., Barbieri, R., & Meneghin, A. (2014). New business models for electric mobility. In *Proceedings of the IEEE International Electric Vehicle Conference (IEVC)*. IEEE. DOI: 10.1109/IEVC.2014.7056136

Cao, S., Liang, J., Chen, M., Xu, C., Wang, X., Qiu, L., Zhao, X., & Hu, W. (2025). Comparative analysis of extraction technologies for plant extracts and absolutes. *Frontiers in Chemistry*, *13*, 1536590. DOI: 10.3389/fchem.2025.1536590

Caro-Gonzalez, A. (2024). *Transformative Governance for the Future: Navigating Profound Transitions*. Springer Nature Switzerland., DOI: 10.1007/978-3-031-43132-6

Carvalho, A. C. F., Ghosh, S., Hoffmann, T. G., Prudêncio, E. S., de Souza, C. K., & Roy, S. (2025). Valuing agro-industrial waste in the development of sustainable food packaging based on the system of a circular bioeconomy: A review. *Cleaner Waste Systems*, *11*, 100275. DOI: 10.1016/j.clwas.2025.100275

CDC. (2024). Global Startup Ecosystem Report – Tunisia insights.

Central Pollution Control Board. (2021). *Management of municipal solid waste in India*. Ministry of Environment, Forest and Climate Change.

CGDR. (2013).La Dynamisation de l'Entrepreneuriat Social en Tunisie.

Chakraborty, S., & Karandikar, A. (2025). Policies driving India's innovation-driven growth in science and technology: Pathway to progressive excellence over the past decade and roadmap to Viksit Bharat-2047. *Proceedings of the Indian National Science Academy. Part A, Physical Sciences*, *91*(1), 1–8. DOI: 10.1007/s43538-025-00436-9

Chandran, R., Chandran, M. C. S., Achuthan, K., & Sahib, P. R. (2025). Theoretical perspectives on green banking adoption in India: Regulatory uncertainty, institutional barriers, and policy solutions. *Discover Sustainability*, *6*(1), 581. DOI: 10.1007/s43621-025-01406-3

Charmaz, K. (2014). Constructing grounded theory.

Chen, H., ... (2026). Mechanical and morphological evaluation of jute fiber reinforced epoxy composites for sustainable structural and automotive applications. ResearchGate. https://www.researchgate.net/publication/399338858

Cheng, A., Fuchs, E. R., Karplus, V. J., & Michalek, J. J. (2024). Electric vehicle battery chemistry affects supply chain disruption vulnerabilities. *Nature Sustainability*, *15*(1). PMID: 38459029

Chen, J., Zhang, B., Luo, L., Zhang, F., Yi, Y., Shan, Y., Liu, B., Zhou, Y., Wang, X., & Lü, X. (2021). A review on recycling techniques for bioethanol production from lignocellulosic biomass. *Renewable & Sustainable Energy Reviews*, *149*, 111370. DOI: 10.1016/j.rser.2021.111370

Chipalkatti, N., Prasuna, A., Rishi, M., & Siva Kumar, S. N. V. (2025). ESG disclosure scores and Indian banks: A search for relevance. *Cogent Economics & Finance*, *13*(1), 2552874. DOI: 10.1080/23322039.2025.2552874

Chirambo, D. (2020). Principles for Enhancing Earth System Governance and Sustainable Development Through Informality. *International Journal of Entrepreneurship and Governance in Cognitive Cities*, *1*(1), 47–67. DOI: 10.4018/IJEGCC.20200101.oa1

Chojnacka, K. (2023). Valorization of biorefinery residues for sustainable fertilizer production: A comprehensive review. *Biomass Conversion and Biorefinery*, *13*(16), 14359–14388. DOI: 10.1007/s13399-023-04639-2

Choudhury, N. (2018). The influence of IoT and AI convergence on industrial automation ecosystems. https://doi.org/DOI: 10.1080/00207543.2020.1824085

Climate Nexus. (2021, November 29). Impacts from mining lithium, cobalt, and other materials for electric car batteries. https://climatenexus.org

Cohen, B., & Winn, M. I. (2007). Market imperfections, opportunity and sustainable entrepreneurship. *Journal of Business Venturing*, *22*(1), 29–49. DOI: 10.1016/j.jbusvent.2004.12.001

Coherent Market Insights. (2026). Jute packaging market size, share & trends forecast 2026–2033. openPR.

Corvo, L., Pastore, L., Mastrodascio, M., & Cepiku, D. (2022). The social return on investment model: A systematic literature review. *Meditari Accountancy Research*, *30*(7), 49–86. DOI: 10.1108/MEDAR-05-2021-1307

Costa, I., Riccotta, R., Montini, P., Stefani, E., de Souza Goes, R., Gaspar, M. A., Martins, F. S., Fernandes, A. A., Machado, C., Loçano, R., & Larieira, C. L. C. (2022). The degree of contribution of digital transformation technology on company sustainability areas. *Sustainability (Basel)*, *14*(1), 462. DOI: 10.3390/su14010462

Council on Energy, Environment and Water. (2023, January 29). India's electric vehicle transition. https://www.ceew.in/publications/indias-electric-vehicle-transition-electric-mobility-support-sustainable-economic-recovery

Creswell, J. W., & Clark, V. L. P. (2017). *Designing and conducting mixed methods research*. Sage publications.

Creswell, J. W., & Creswell, J. D. (2018). *Research design: Qualitative, quantitative, and mixed methods approaches* (5th ed.). Sage.

Dacin, M. T., Dacin, P. A., & Tracey, P. (2011). Social entrepreneurship: A critique and future directions. *Organization Science*, *22*(5), 1203–1213. DOI: 10.1287/orsc.1100.0620

Dahiya, S., Kumar, A. N., Sravan, J. S., Chatterjee, S., Sarkar, O., & Mohan, S. V. (2023). Food waste biorefinery: Sustainable valorization of agricultural residues into value-added products. *Bioresource Technology*, *369*, 128364.

Dale, A. (2007). *At the edge: Sustainable development in the 21st century* (Vol. 6). UBC press.

Datta, M. A. (2018, July 25). Creating the charging infrastructure to power EVs in India. The Energy and Resources Institute. https://www.teriin.org/article/creating-charging-infrastructure-power-evs-india

de Melo, F. L. N. B., & Soares, A. M. J. (2025). Ecofarming: A gamified simulation for teaching sustainable entrepreneurship in Brazilian biomes. Revista de Administração Contemporânea, 29(1). https://doi.org/DOI: 10.1590/1982-7849rac2025240218.en

Dean, T. J., & McMullen, J. S. (2007). Toward a theory of sustainable entrepreneurship: Reducing environmental degradation through entrepreneurial action. *Journal of Business Venturing*, *22*(1), 50–76. DOI: 10.1016/j.jbusvent.2005.09.003

Demirel, P., Li, Q. C., Rentocchini, F., & Tamvada, J. P. (2019). Born to be green: New insights into the economics and management of green entrepreneurship. *Small Business Economics*, *52*(4), 759–771. DOI: 10.1007/s11187-017-9933-z

Deng, W., Huang, T., & Wang, H. (2023). A Review of the Key Technology in a Blockchain Building Decentralized Trust Platform. *Mathematics*, *11*(1), 101. DOI: 10.3390/math11010101

Denzin, N. K. (1978). *The Research Act: A Theoretical Introduction to Sociological Methods* (2nd ed.). McGraw-Hill.

Derdabi, A., & Dvouletý, O. (2025). Funding sustainable entrepreneurship: A hybrid systematic literature review and bibliometric analysis. *Nankai Business Review International*, *16*(2), 359–380. DOI: 10.1108/NBRI-03-2024-0025

Devi, A., Bajar, S., Kour, H., Kothari, R., Pant, D., & Singh, A. (2022). Lignocellulosic biomass valorization for bioethanol production: A circular bioeconomy approach. *BioEnergy Research*, *15*(4), 1820–1841. DOI: 10.1007/s12155-022-10401-9

Dhar, B. K., Roshid, M., Dissanayake, S., Chawla, U., & Faheem, M. (2026). Leveraging FinTech and GreenTech for long-term sustainability in South Asia: Strategic pathways toward Agenda 2050. *Green Technologies and Sustainability*, *4*(1), 100263. DOI: 10.1016/j.grets.2025.100263

Dharmawan, V. (2026). *Jute bags market research report 2034*. Dataintelo.

Dhewa, C., Makurumidze, S., & Mukapiku, K. P. (2025). Spearheading sustainable youth entrepreneurship through financial literacy training - A case of one TVET institution in Zimbabwe. *African Journal of Pedagogy and Curriculum*, *7*(1), 95–110. DOI: 10.63569/ajopac/07/01/07

Dias, A. I., Rodrigues, L. L., & Branco, M. C. (2024). Gender diversity and climate disclosure: A TCFD perspective. *Environment, Development and Sustainability*, *26*(3), 1–27. DOI: 10.1007/s10668-024-05203-2

DiMaggio, P. J., & Powell, W. W. (1983). The iron cage revisited: Institutional isomorphism and collective rationality in organizational fields. *American Sociological Review*, *48*(2), 147–160. DOI: 10.2307/2095101

Doddapaneni, T. R. K. C., & Kikas, T. (2021). Thermochemical and biochemical treatment strategies for resource recovery from agri-food industry wastes. In *Valorization of Agri-food wastes and by-products* (pp. 787–807). Academic Press. DOI: 10.1016/B978-0-12-824044-1.00007-6

Donner, M., Verniquet, A., Broeze, J., Kayser, K., & De Vries, H. (2021). Critical success and risk factors for circular business models valorising agricultural waste and by-products. *Resources, Conservation and Recycling*, *165*, 105236. DOI: 10.1016/j.resconrec.2020.105236

DPIIT. (2025). *Startup India annual report 2024–25*. Government of India.

Du, C., Abdullah, J. J., Greetham, D., Fu, D., Yu, M., Ren, L., Li, S., & Lu, D. (2018). Valorization of food waste into biofertiliser and its field application. *Journal of Cleaner Production*, *187*, 273–284. DOI: 10.1016/j.jclepro.2018.03.211

Du, J. (2024). Ethical and legal challenges of AI in human resource management. *Journal of Computing and Electronic Information Management*, *13*(2), 71–77. DOI: 10.54097/83j64ub9

Dumée, L. F. (2021). Circular materials and circular design: Review on challenges towards sustainable manufacturing and recycling. *Circular Economy and Sustainability*, *2*(1), 9–23. DOI: 10.1007/s43615-021-00085-2 PMID: 34888565

Duque-Acevedo, M., Belmonte-Ureña, L. J., Cortés-García, F. J., & Camacho-Ferre, F. (2020). Agricultural waste: Review of the evolution, approaches and perspectives on alternative uses. *Global Ecology and Conservation*, *22*, e00902. DOI: 10.1016/j.gecco.2020.e00902

Duque-Acevedo, M., Lancellotti, I., Andreola, F., Barbieri, L., Belmonte-Ureña, L. J., & Camacho-Ferre, F. (2022). Management of agricultural waste biomass as raw material for the construction sector: An analysis of sustainable and circular alternatives. *Environmental Sciences Europe*, *34*(1), 70. DOI: 10.1186/s12302-022-00655-7

Durst, S., & Gerstlberger, W. (2020). Financing Responsible Small- and Medium-Sized Enterprises: An International Overview of Policies and Support Programmes. *Journal of Risk and Financial Management*, *14*(1), 10. DOI: 10.3390/jrfm14010010

Economictimes. (2025). Navigating the Agricultural Biomass Supply Chain in India. Available at https://energy.economictimes.indiatimes.com/news/oil-and-gas/navigating-the-agricultural-biomass-supply-chain-in-india/108812275 (Accessed on 7th March 2025).

Eisenhardt, K. M. (1989). Building theories from case study research. *Academy of Management Review*, *14*(4), 532–550. DOI: 10.2307/258557

Eisenhardt, K. M., & Graebner, M. E. (2007). Theory building from cases: Opportunities and challenges. *Academy of Management Journal*, *50*(1), 25–32. DOI: 10.5465/amj.2007.24160888

Elf, P., Owen, R., Lyon, F., & Da Gama Torres, H. (2025). Developing sustainable entrepreneurial finance ecosystems in an emerging market context: The role of keystone actors in managing competing institutional logics. *Venture Capital*, •••, 1–26. DOI: 10.1080/13691066.2025.2496192

Elkington, J. (1997). *Cannibals with forks: The triple bottom line of 21st century business*. Capstone.

Elkington, J., & Rowlands, I. H. (1999). Cannibals with forks: The triple bottom line of 21st century business. *Alternatives Journal*, *25*(4), 42.

Ellen MacArthur Foundation. (2015). Towards a circular economy: Business rationale for an accelerated transition.

Ellen MacArthur Foundation. (2023). Circular Economy Overview.

Elroi, H., Zbigniew, G., Agnieszka, W. C., & Piotr, S. (2023). Enhancing waste resource efficiency: Circular economy for sustainability and energy conversion. *Frontiers in Environmental Science*, *11*, 1303792. DOI: 10.3389/fenvs.2023.1303792

Elshkaki, A. (2020). Long-term analysis of critical materials in future vehicles electrification in China and their national and global implications. *Energy*, *202*, 117697. DOI: 10.1016/j.energy.2020.117697

Emon, M. M. H., & Mazid-Ul-Haque, M. (2025). Balancing Usability and Security: Enhancing User Experience Without Compromising Privacy. In *User-Centric Cybersecurity Implications for Sustainable Digital Transformation* (pp. 309–342). IGI Global Scientific Publishing. DOI: 10.4018/979-8-3373-3171-3.ch010

Energies, B. A. T. X. (2022, May 21). Lithium (Li)-ion battery recycling company in India. https://batxenergies.com

Ersoy, A. E., & Ugurlu, A. (2024). Bioenergy's role in achieving a low-carbon electricity future: A case of Türkiye. *Applied Energy*, *372*, 123799. DOI: 10.1016/j.apenergy.2024.123799

Ersoy, P., Börühan, G., Kumar Mangla, S., Hormazabal, J. H., Kazancoglu, Y., & Lafcı, Ç. (2022). Impact of information technology and knowledge sharing on circular food supply chains for green business growth. *Business Strategy and the Environment*, *31*(5), 1875–1904. DOI: 10.1002/bse.2988

European Commission. (2022, December 9). Batteries. https://environment.ec.europa.eu/topics/waste-and-recycling/batteries_en

European Commission. (2023, August 17). New law on more sustainable, circular and safe batteries enters into force. https://environment.ec.europa.eu/news/new-law-more-sustainable-circular-and-safe-batteries-enters-force-2023-08-17_en

European Union. (2023, July 28). Regulation (EU) 2023/1542 of the European Parliament and of the Council concerning batteries and waste batteries. Official Journal of the European Union. https://eur-lex.europa.eu/legal-content/EN/TXT/?uri=CELEX%3A32023R1542

E-VehicleInfo. (2021, June 15). Battery recycling business for small-scale industries in India. https://e-vehicleinfo.com/battery-recycling-business-for-ssi/

Ezeorba, T. P. C., Okeke, E. S., Mayel, M. H., Nwuche, C. O., & Ezike, T. C. (2024). Recent advances in biotechnological valorization of agro-food wastes (AFW): Optimizing integrated approaches for sustainable biorefinery and circular bioeconomy. *Bioresource Technology Reports*, *26*, 101823. DOI: 10.1016/j.biteb.2024.101823

Farhoud, M. (2025). Institutional voids and entrepreneurial generational dynamics in Tunisian corporate sustainability: Multi-method SEM test and comparative analysis (France-Germany-Morocco-UAE), MENA perspective. Arabian Journal of Business and Management Review, 14(4), 125–137. www.j.arabianjbmr.com

Farukh, M. U., Khan, A., & Kumar, A. (n.d.). Entrepreneurship and the environment: A critical examination of the sustainability of entrepreneurship activity. International Journal of Environmental Sciences, 11(24). Retrieved from https://www.theaspd.com/ijes.php

Fast Company. (2025). This startup turns food waste into bioplastic that can break down in the ocean. Available on https://www.fastcompany.com/90687372/this-startup-turns-food-waste-into-bioplastic-that-can-break-down-in-the-ocean. (Access on 18th March 2025)

Ferasso, M., Beliaeva, T., Kraus, S., Clauss, T., & Kailer, N. (2020). Circular economy business models: The state of research and avenues ahead. *Business Strategy and the Environment*, *29*(8), 3006–3021. DOI: 10.1002/bse.2554

Florencia, L. E., Princella, A., Anjelina, M., Barus, R. M., Darmawan, V., & Rembulan, G. D. (2024). Pengembangan bisnis totebag sebagai alternatif usaha untuk mengurangi limbah plastik. Jurnal Pengabdian dan Kewirausahaan, 8(1).

Forcadell, F. J., & Aracil, E. (2019). Can multinational companies foster institutional change and sustainable development in emerging countries? A case study. *Business Strategy & Development*, *2*(2), 91–105. DOI: 10.1002/bsd2.45

Freeman, R. E. (2010). *Strategic management: A stakeholder approach*. Cambridge university press. DOI: 10.1017/CBO9781139192675

Fu, C., Lu, L., & Pirabi, M. (2023). Advancing green finance: A review of sustainable development. *Digital Economy and Sustainable Development*, *1*(1), 20. DOI: 10.1007/s44265-023-00020-3

Fürst, T., & Akdağ, H. C. (2025). *Integrating Circular Economy Principles in the Fashion Industry: A Case Study of Patagonia*., DOI: 10.1007/978-3-031-83611-4_24

Gabhane, J. W., Bhange, V. P., Patil, P. D., Bankar, S. T., & Kumar, S. (2020). Recent trends in biochar production methods and its application as a soil health conditioner: A review. *SN Applied Sciences*, *2*(7), 1–21. DOI: 10.1007/s42452-020-3121-5

Gadanakis, Y. (2024). Advancing farm entrepreneurship and agribusiness management for sustainable agriculture. *Agriculture*, *14*(8), 1288. DOI: 10.3390/agriculture14081288

Gallardo-Vázquez, D. (2025). Defining the path to sustainability based on triple bottom line dimensions. *Corporate Social Responsibility and Environmental Management*, *32*(4), 4743–4768. DOI: 10.1002/csr.3216

Gamage, A., Gangahagedara, R., Gamage, J., Jayasinghe, N., Kodikara, N., Suraweera, P., & Merah, O. (2023). Role of organic farming for achieving sustainability in agriculture. *Farming System*, *1*(1), 100005. DOI: 10.1016/j.farsys.2023.100005

Gao, J., Siddik, A. B., Khawar Abbas, S., Hamayun, M., Masukujjaman, M., & Alam, S. S. (2023). Impact of E-commerce and digital marketing adoption on the financial and sustainability performance of MSMEs during the COVID-19 pandemic: An empirical study. *Sustainability (Basel)*, *15*(2), 1594. DOI: 10.3390/su15021594

García-Jurado, A., Pérez-Barea, J. J., & Nova, R. J. (2021). A New Approach to Social Entrepreneurship: A Systematic Review and Meta-Analysis. *Sustainability (Basel)*, *13*(5), 2754. DOI: 10.3390/su13052754

Geels, F. W. (2002). Technological transitions as evolutionary reconfiguration processes: A multi-level perspective and a case-study. *Research Policy*, *31*(8-9), 1257–1274. DOI: 10.1016/S0048-7333(02)00062-8

Geissdoerfer, M., Savaget, P., Bocken, N. M., & Hultink, E. J. (2017). The Circular Economy–A new sustainability paradigm? *Journal of Cleaner Production*, *143*, 757–768. DOI: 10.1016/j.jclepro.2016.12.048

George, G., Merrill, R., & Schillebeeckx, S. (2021). Digital sustainability and entrepreneurship. *Journal of Business Venturing*, *36*(1).

Gerassimidou, S., Martin, O. V., Chapman, S. P., Hahladakis, J. N., & Iacovidou, E. (2021). Development of an integrated sustainability matrix to depict challenges and trade-offs of introducing bio-based plastics in the food packaging value chain. *Journal of Cleaner Production*, *286*, 125378. DOI: 10.1016/j.jclepro.2020.125378

Ghanekar, N. (2021, April 19). India's looming electric vehicle challenge: Spent batteries. IndiaSpend. https://www.indiaspend.com/earthcheck/indias-looming-electric-vehicle-challenge-spent-batteries-742352

Ghimire, B., & Dhakal, S. C. Santosh, & Bastakoti, R. C. (2025). Assessing production risks and value chain sustainability in Nepal's lentil (Lens culinaris Medik.) sector: An evidence-based econometric analysis. DOI: 10.21203/rs.3.rs-7043104/v1

Ghisellini, P., Cialani, C., & Ulgiati, S. (2016). A review on circular economy: The expected transition to a balanced interplay of environmental and economic systems. *Journal of Cleaner Production*, *114*, 11–32. DOI: 10.1016/j.jclepro.2015.09.007

Ghosh, D., & Hamid, M. A. (2025). Environment-friendly practices in entrepreneurship for sustainable development: Insights from a qualitative study. *BJBE*, *6*(1), 259–274. DOI: 10.58481/BJBE/2515

GIZ. (2020).Améliorer la protection du climat à travers l'économie circulaire en Tunisie.

Glass, A. (2007). Understanding generational differences for competitive success. *Industrial and Commercial Training*, *39*(2), 98–103. DOI: 10.1108/00197850710732424

Global Reporting Initiative (GRI). (2023). *Universal Standards* (GRI 1, 2, 3)effective 1 January 2023. https://www.globalreporting.org/standards/standards-development/universal-standards/

Global Reporting Initiative. (2023). *Universal Standards* (GRI 1, 2, 3). https://www.globalreporting.org/standards/

Government of India. (2015). *National action plan on climate change*. Ministry of Environment, Forest and Climate Change.

Govindarasu, A., & Venkatesh, A. S. (2019). Electric vehicle vision 2030: Challenges and solutions. In Proceedings of the IEEE Transportation Electrification Conference (ITEC India). IEEE. DOI: 10.1109/ITEC-India48457.2019.ITECINDIA2019-35

Greenpod labs. (2025). Nature Inspired Solutions to Minimize Food Waste. Available on https://greenpodlabs.com/ (Accessed on 16th March 2025).

Griggs, D., Stafford-Smith, M., Gaffney, O., Rockström, J., Öhman, M. C., Shyamsundar, P., Steffen, W., Glaser, G., Kanie, N., & Noble, I. (2013). Sustainable development goals for people and planet. *Nature*, *495*(7441), 305–307. DOI: 10.1038/495305a PMID: 23518546

Grolleau, G., Mzoughi, N., & Pekovic, S. (2025). Entrepreneurship experience and environmental and social sustainability in new companies. *Business Strategy and the Environment*, *34*(8), 9863–9877. DOI: 10.1002/bse.70109

Guo, J., Zhang, Y., Fang, J., Ma, Z., Li, C., Yan, M., Qiao, N., Liu, Y., & Bian, M. (2024). Reduction and reuse of forestry and agricultural bio-waste through innovative green utilization approaches: A review. *Forests*, *15*(8), 1372. DOI: 10.3390/f15081372

Gupta, P., & Antony, A. (2026). Institutional voids and financial markets: an institutional theory perspective. *Qualitative Research in Financial Markets*, 1-31.

Gupta, R. (2025). Women-Led Green Entrepreneurship: Motivators and Challenges. SSRN *Electronic Journal*. DOI: 10.2139/ssrn.5517519

Gupta, R. K., Ali, E. A., Abd El Gawad, F., Daood, V. M., Sabry, H., Karunanithi, S., & Srivastav, P. P. (2024). Valorization of fruits and vegetables waste byproducts for development of sustainable food packaging application. *Waste Management Bulletin*, *2*(4), 21–40. DOI: 10.1016/j.wmb.2024.08.005

Gupta, V., & Sharma, A. (2023). Sustainable agriculture and green entrepreneurship in India. *Asian Journal of Sustainable Development*, *12*(2), 89–105.

Gu, W., Pan, H., Hu, Z., & Liu, Z. (2022). The Triple Bottom Line of Sustainable Entrepreneurship and Economic Policy Uncertainty: An Empirical Evidence from 22 Countries. *International Journal of Environmental Research and Public Health*, *19*(13), 7758. DOI: 10.3390/ijerph19137758 PMID: 35805416

Hair, J. F. (2014). *A primer on partial least squares structural equation modeling (PLS-SEM)*. sage.

Haldar, S. (2019). Green entrepreneurship in theory and practice: Insights from India. *International Journal of Green Economics, 13*(2), 99. DOI: 10.1504/IJGE.2019.103232

Hällerstrand, L., Reim, W., & Malmström, M. (2023). Dynamic capabilities in environmental entrepreneurship: A framework for commercializing green innovations. *Journal of Cleaner Production, 402*, 136692. DOI: 10.1016/j.jclepro.2023.136692

Hall, J. K., Daneke, G. A., & Lenox, M. J. (2010). Sustainable development and entrepreneurship: Past contributions and future directions. *Journal of Business Venturing, 25*(5), 439–444. DOI: 10.1016/j.jbusvent.2010.01.002

Hameed, I., Zaman, U., Waris, I., & Shafique, O. (2021). A Serial-Mediation Model to Link Entrepreneurship Education and Green Entrepreneurial Behavior: Application of Resource-Based View and Flow Theory. *International Journal of Environmental Research and Public Health, 18*(2), 550. DOI: 10.3390/ijerph18020550 PMID: 33440814

Hanaysha, J. R., Al-Shaikh, M. E., Joghee, S., & Alzoubi, H. M. (2022). Impact of Innovation Capabilities on Business Sustainability in Small and Medium Enterprises. *FIIB Business Review, 11*(1), 67–78. DOI: 10.1177/23197145211042232

Hart, S. L., & Milstein, M. B. (1999). Global sustainability and the creative destruction of industries. *Sloan Management Review, 41*(1), 23–33.

Hasan, M. M., Mustafizur Rahman, K., Nath, A., Fuad, M. N., Inthakab Kabir, S. M., & Emee, A. F. (2025). Understanding User Adoption of Cybersecurity Practices through Awareness and Perception for Enhancing Network Security in Bangladesh. *2025 IEEE 2nd International Conference on Computing, Applications and Systems (COMPAS)*, 1–6. DOI: 10.1109/COMPAS67506.2025.11381666

Hasan, M. K., Emon, M. M. H., Hlali, A., & Khan, T. (2026). *Sustainable Operations in the Age of AI and Big Data* (Hasan, M. K., Emon, M. M. H., Hlali, A., & Khan, T., Eds.). IGI Global Scientific Publishing., DOI: 10.4018/979-8-2600-0216-2

Hasan, M. K., Khan, T., Hlali, A., & Emon, M. M. H. (2025). Enhancing Sustainability in Global Supply Chains With Big Data Analytics. In *Enhancing Sustainability in Global Supply Chains With Big Data Analytics*. IGI Global., DOI: 10.4018/979-8-3373-6896-2

Henriques, C., Caldeirinha, V. R., & Ferreira Dias, J. (2025). Evaluating eco-innovation efficiency and club convergence in the EU: 2016–2023. *Journal of Cleaner Production*, *463*, 143998. DOI: 10.1016/j.jclepro.2024.143998

Hockerts, K. (2017). Sustainable entrepreneurship: Past contributions and future directions. *Journal of Small Business Management*, *55*(1), 1–24.

Hockerts, K., & Wüstenhagen, R. (2010). Greening Goliaths versus emerging Davids: The role of incumbents and new entrants in sustainable entrepreneurship. *Research Policy*, *39*(4), 481–492.

Hockerts, K., & Wüstenhagen, R. (2010). Greening Goliaths versus emerging Davids—Theorizing about the role of incumbents and new entrants in sustainable entrepreneurship. *Journal of Business Venturing*, *25*(5), 481–492. DOI: 10.1016/j.jbusvent.2009.07.005

Hossain, M. (2021). Frugal innovation: A review and research agenda. *Journal of Cleaner Production*, •••, 182.

Hummels, H., & Argyrou, A. (2021). Planetary demands: Redefining sustainable development and sustainable entrepreneurship. *Journal of Cleaner Production*, *278*, 123804. DOI: 10.1016/j.jclepro.2020.123804

ICLEI South Asia. (2024, January 25). Asia LEDS Partnership study tour addresses key topics related to EV batteries. https://southasia.iclei.org/news/asia-leds-partnership-study-tour-addresses-key-topics-related-to-ev-batteries/

ICU. (2025).GREENSTEP Project: Embracing the Green Transition for Small and Medium-sized Enterprises.

IFRS Foundation / ISSB. (2025). *Introduction to the ISSB and IFRS sustainability disclosure standards (IFRS S1 and IFRS S2).* https://www.ifrs.org/sustainability/knowledge-hub/introduction-to-issb-and-ifrs-sustainability-disclosure-standards/

IFRS Foundation. (2024). *Progress on corporate climate-related disclosures2024 report*. IFRS/ISSB.

IFVI (Impact-Weighted Accounts Initiative). (2022). *Practitioner guide to calculating employment impact-weighted accounts.* https://ifvi.org/wp-content/uploads/2023/10/Practitioner-Guide-to-Calculating-Employment-Impact-Weighted-Accounts.pdf

Ilesanmi, J. (2024). Importance of Eco-Entrepreneurship as a Tool for Climate Action and LowCarbon Transition in Developing Countries: A Case Study of Nigeria. *Journal of Sustainable Development Law and Policy (The)*, *15*(2), 298–327. DOI: 10.4314/jsdlp.v15i2.11

India Brand Equity Foundation. (2022, May 5). Electric vehicles market in India. https://www.ibef.org

International Energy Agency. (2023, May 12). How can smart charging steer electric vehicle uptake in India? https://www.iea.org/commentaries/how-can-smart-charging-steer-electric-vehicle-uptake-in-india

International Financial Reporting Standards (IFRS) Foundation. (2023). General sustainability-related disclosures (IFRS S1) and climate-related disclosures (IFRS S2): Project summary and resources. https://www.ifrs.org/projects/completed-projects/2023/general-sustainability-related-disclosures/

International Institute for Sustainable Development. (2022, December 20). Subsidies for EVs in India increased 160%, reached record high of Rs 2,358 crore in FY22: IISD report. https://www.iisd.org/articles/iisd-news/subsidies-evs-india-increased-160-reached-record-high-rs-2358-crore-fy22-iisd

Iqbal, M., Hati, H. P., & Irfan, A. (2024). Carbon management accounting considerations for MFCA and LCA integration. *International Journal of Sustainable Development and Planning*, *19*(5), 399–407. DOI: 10.18280/ijsdp.190536

IRENA. (2022). *Renewable energy market analysis*. International Renewable Energy Agency.

Isah, S., & Ozbay, G. (2020). Valorization of food loss and wastes: Feedstocks for biofuels and valuable chemicals. *Frontiers in Sustainable Food Systems*, *4*, 82. DOI: 10.3389/fsufs.2020.00082

Isenberg, D. J. (2011). *The Entrepreneurship Ecosystem Strategy as a New Paradigm for Economic Policy: Principles for Cultivating Entrepreneurship. Babson Entrepreneurship Ecosystem Project. Babson Park*. Babson College.

Islam, M. S., & Ahmed, S. K. (2012). The impacts of jute on environment: An analytical review of Bangladesh. *Journal of Environment and Earth Science*, *2*(5), 24–31.

Islam, N. F., Gogoi, B., Saikia, R., Yousaf, B., Narayan, M., & Sarma, H. (2024). Encouraging circular economy and sustainable environmental practices by addressing waste management and biomass energy production. *Regional Sustainability*, *5*(4), 100174. DOI: 10.1016/j.regsus.2024.100174

Islam, S., Karim, M. R., & Islam, M. R. (2024). Jute fiber and its composites: Processing, properties, and applications. *Journal of Natural Fibers*. Advance online publication. DOI: 10.1080/15440478.2026.2635010

Ismail, A., Mohd Nazari, N., & Mohamed Zakaria, H. (2025). Embedding sustainability in cultural events: Insights from the Penang George Town Festival. Journal of Event. *Tourism and Hospitality Studies*, *5*, 94–104. DOI: 10.32890/jeth2025.5.6

Jabbour, C. J. C., Seuring, S., de Sousa Jabbour, A. B. L., & Jugend, D. (2020). Stakeholders, innovative business models for the circular economy and sustainable performance of firms in an emerging economy facing institutional voids. *Journal of Environmental Management*, *273*, 111105.

Jain, T. L. P. (2019, July 24). India's energy transition: Subsidies for gasoline, diesel and electric vehicles. International Institute for Sustainable Development. https://www.iisd.org/publications/brief/indias-energy-transition-subsidies-gasoline-diesel-and-electric-vehicles

Jameel, M. K., Mustafa, M. A., Ahmed, H. S., Mohammed, A., Ghazy, H., Shakir, M. N., Lawas, A. M., Mohammed, S., Idan, A. H., Mahmoud, Z. H., Sayadi, H., & Kianfar, E. (2024). Biogas: Production, properties, applications, economic and challenges: A review. *Results in Chemistry*, *7*, 101549. DOI: 10.1016/j.rechem.2024.101549

Jeyarajasekar, D., Chandran, B. S., & Santhosh, D. S. (n.d.). Sustainability in hospitals: Identifying boosting elements through the triple bottom line framework. International Journal of Environmental Sciences, 11(23). Retrieved from https://theaspd.com/index.php

Jiang, Z., Xu, Y., Zhu, X., Liu, W., & Liu, Y. (2024). Intellectual capital and green entrepreneurship: A systematic literature review. *Journal of Intellectual Capital*, *25*(4), 801–821. DOI: 10.1108/JIC-12-2023-0287

Jin, X., Song, J., & Liu, G. Q. (2020). Bioethanol production from rice straw through an enzymatic route mediated by enzymes developed in-house from Aspergillus fumigatus. *Energy*, *190*, 116395. DOI: 10.1016/j.energy.2019.116395

Jones, B., Elliott, R. J., & Nguyen-Tien, V. (2020). The EV revolution: The road ahead for critical raw materials demand. *Applied Energy*, *280*, 115072. DOI: 10.1016/j.apenergy.2020.115072 PMID: 33052165

Jorgensen, S., Pedersen, L. J. T., & Skard, S. (2023). Resource accounting for a circular economy: Evidence from a digitalised waste management system. *Accounting Forum*, *47*(4), 553–582. DOI: 10.1080/01559982.2023.2166001

Joseph, P. K., & Elangovan, D. (2018). All-vehicle electrification by 2030 project in India: Impacts and solutions. Journal of Advanced Research in Dynamical and Control Systems, 9(4). (Publication details should be verified.)

Juliansyah, E., Agoes, S., & Ahmar, N. (2025, July 19). Development of the pentuple bottom line model in moderating the influence of financial literacy and financial inclusion on the sustainability of MSMEs in West Java. *Global Interdisciplinary Journal of Economics and Administrative Sciences*, *3*(2), 304–315. Advance online publication. DOI: 10.38035/gijea.v3i2.468

Kaakandikar, R. (2025). THE THREE PILLARS OF BUSINESS: A GUIDE TO INTEGRATED MARKETING, FINANCE & HR PRACTICES. SSRN *Electronic Journal*. DOI: 10.2139/ssrn.5161493

Kabir, E., Kim, K. H., & Kwon, E. E. (2023). Biochar as a tool for the improvement of soil and environment. *Frontiers in Environmental Science*, *11*, 1324533. DOI: 10.3389/fenvs.2023.1324533

Kademani, S., Nain, M. S., Singh, R., Kumar, S., Parsad, R., Sharma, D. K., Roy, S. K., Karjigi, K. D., Prabhakar, I., Mahapatra, A., & Patil, M. (2024). Unveiling challenges and strategizing solutions for sustainable agri-entrepreneurship development. *Frontiers in Sustainable Food Systems*, *8*, 1447371. Advance online publication. DOI: 10.3389/fsufs.2024.1447371

Kaetsu, P. T., Kumasaka, J. M., & Casado, T. (2024). Bioeconomy in Amazonia: Tensions and synergies of corporate sustainability. Revista de Administração Contemporânea, 28(5). https://doi.org/DOI: 10.1590/1982-7849rac2024240072.en

Kalra, D., Dadwal, S., & Arya, P. (2025). Exploring social entrepreneurship: Models, impact, and sustainability. *International Journal of Advanced Research*, *13*(7), 63–69. DOI: 10.21474/IJAR01/21309

Kar, B., Khandai, S., & Zupic, I. (2025). Resolving the "sustainability paradox": A bibliometric and topic modeling analysis of sustainable entrepreneurship and sustainable consumption. Journal of Enterprising Communities. DOI: 10.1108/JEC-11-2024-0235

Karim, R., Waaje, A., Roshid, M. M., & Yeamin, M. B. (2025). Turning the Waste Into Wealth: Progressing Toward Global Sustainability Through the Circular Economy in Waste Management. In *Sustainable Waste Management in the Tourism and Hospitality Sectors* (pp. 507-552). IGI Global Scientific Publishing.

Karungamye, P. (2024). Energy recovery from solid waste valorisation: Environmental and economic potential for developing countries. *Scientific African*, *26*, 02402. DOI: 10.1016/j.sciaf.2024.e02402

Kaur, G. P., & Shah, M. A. (2026). Artificial Intelligence in Circular Economy and Green Logistics. *Advances in Computational Intelligence and Robotics*, **•••**, 87–114. DOI: 10.4018/979-8-3373-5946-5.ch004

Kaur, P., & Kaur, D. S. (2019). Green entrepreneurship in India: A study of select green businesses. *International Journal of Applied Research*, *5*(3), 369–376. DOI: 10.22271/allresearch.2019.v5.i3d.10782

Kawimbe, S. (2025). Harnessing green entrepreneurship for sustainable growth in Zambia. *Journal of Environment*, *5*(4), 24–35. www.carijournals.org. DOI: 10.47941/je.3215

Khalife, E., Sabouri, M., Kaveh, M., & Szymanek, M. (2024). Recent advances in the application of agricultural waste in construction. *Applied Sciences (Basel, Switzerland)*, *14*(6), 2355. DOI: 10.3390/app14062355

Khanna, T., & Palepu, K. (2010). *Winning in emerging markets*. Harvard Business Press.

Khan, T., Emon, M. M. H., Rahman, K. M., Nipa, M. N., & Fuad, M. N. (2025). The Role of AI in Driving Customer Engagement Through Technological, Organizational and Environmental Enablers in E-Commerce. *2025 International Conference on Quantum Photonics, Artificial Intelligence, and Networking (QPAIN)*, 1–6. DOI: 10.1109/QPAIN66474.2025.11171949

Khymych, O. (2025). EU Insights on Innovative Entrepreneurship Ecosystems Following Sustainable Development Goals. In Steiner, B. E., & Makarenko, I. (Eds.), *Bridging Governance, Public Support, Innovation, and Transparency* (pp. 103–131). Springer Nature Switzerland., DOI: 10.1007/978-3-031-94082-8_5

Kibria, M. G., Masuk, N. I., Safayet, R., Nguyen, H. Q., & Mourshed, M. (2023). Plastic waste: Challenges and opportunities to mitigate pollution and effective management. *International Journal of Environmental Research*, *17*(1), 20. DOI: 10.1007/s41742-023-00507-z

Kim, J., & Song, H. G. (2024). Tracing the Convergence of Industrial Sectors: Has the 4th Revolution Arrived Already? Or Are We on the Track?. *Journal of the Korean Society of Industry Convergence, 27*(4_1), 781-795. https://doi.org/DOI: 10.21289/KSIC.2024.27.4.781

Kirchherr, J., Reike, D., & Hekkert, M. (2017). Conceptualizing the circular economy. *Resources, Conservation and Recycling*, *127*, 221–232. DOI: 10.1016/j.resconrec.2017.09.005

Kirchherr, J., Yang, N. H. N., Schulze-Spüntrup, F., Heerink, M. J., & Hartley, K. (2023). Conceptualizing the circular economy (revisited): An analysis of 221 definitions. *Resources, Conservation and Recycling*, *194*, 107001. DOI: 10.1016/j.resconrec.2023.107001

Kivimaa, P., Hilden, M., & Kern, F. (2021). Policy mixes for sustainability transitions: New approaches and challenges. *Environmental Innovation and Societal Transitions*, *41*, 1–12. DOI: 10.1016/j.eist.2021.01.004

Koe, W.-L., Nordin, N. M., & Othman, R. (2024). Fostering sustainable entrepreneurial intention: The role of institutional factors. *Management & Marketing*, *19*(1), 32–50. DOI: 10.2478/mmcks-2024-0003

Koiri, P., & Das, S. (2024). Agri-Food Waste Management and Treatment Approaches for Environmental Sustainability. In *Environmental Engineering and Waste Management: Recent Trends and Perspectives* (pp. 343–373). Springer Nature Switzerland. DOI: 10.1007/978-3-031-58441-1_12

Kordi, M., Farrokhi, N., Pech-Canul, M. I., & Ahmadikhah, A. (2024). Rice husk at a glance: From agro-industrial to modern applications. *Rice Science*, *31*(1), 14–32. DOI: 10.1016/j.rsci.2023.08.005

Korhonen, J., Honkasalo, A., & Seppälä, J. (2018). Circular economy: The concept and its limitations. *Ecological Economics*, *143*, 37–46. DOI: 10.1016/j.ecolecon.2017.06.041

Koul, B., Yakoob, M., & Shah, M. P. (2022). Agricultural waste management strategies for environmental sustainability. *Environmental Research*, *206*, 112285. DOI: 10.1016/j.envres.2021.112285

KPMG. (2025, October 10). Navigating the IFRS sustainability disclosure standards (IFRS S1 and IFRS S2). https://kpmg.com/ch/en/services/audit/esg-reporting-assurance/ifrs-s1-s2.html

Kresnawan, M. R., Yurnaidi, Z., Bilqis, A., Wijaya, T. N., & Suryadi, B. (2022). Electric vehicle readiness in Southeast Asia: A PEST policy review. *IOP Conference Series. Earth and Environmental Science*, *997*(1), 012001. Advance online publication. DOI: 10.1088/1755-1315/997/1/012001

Kshetri, N. (2022). Blockchain and supply chain transparency: A review of adoption and impacts. *International Journal of Information Management*, *65*, 102517.

Kumar, A., Rout, R. K., Rao, P. S., & Prabhakar, P. (2023). Optimization of pulsed mode sonication and in silico molecular docking study for antioxidant properties of mandarin (Citrus reticulata Blanco) peels. *Journal of Food Process Engineering*, *46*(6), e14111. DOI: 10.1111/jfpe.14111

Kumar, K. J., & Kumar, S., & V. S., N. (2021). Standards for electric vehicle charging stations in India: A review. *Energy Science & Engineering*, *4*(1). Advance online publication. DOI: 10.1002/est2.261

Kumar, R., Jha, A., Damodaran, A., Bangwal, D., & Dwivedi, A. (2021). Addressing the challenges to electric vehicle adoption via sharing economy: An Indian perspective. *Management of Environmental Quality*, *32*(1), 82–99. DOI: 10.1108/MEQ-03-2020-0058

Kumar, S., Roy, C., Sati, V. P., Pandey, K., Sarkar, T., & Singh, R. (2025). Out-migration from the Indian Himalayan Region (IHR) with drivers, patterns and policy implications for sustainable mountain development. *Discover Sustainability*, *6*(1), 1381. Advance online publication. DOI: 10.1007/s43621-025-02315-1

Kvale, S., & Brinkmann, S. (2009). Interviews: Learning the craft of qualitative research interviewing. sage.

Large, K. (2021, March 22). Use renewable energy to charge electric vehicles in India. The Third Pole. https://www.thethirdpole.net/en/climate/use-renewable-energy-to-charge-electric-vehicles-in-india/

Lazarte-Aguirre, A. (2024). Pathways to sustainable entrepreneurship: Analysing drivers of sustainable entrepreneurial orientation. *Sustainable Technology and Entrepreneurship*, *3*(3), 100081. DOI: 10.1016/j.stae.2024.100081

Lieder, M., & Rashid, A. (2016). Towards circular economy implementation: A comprehensive review in context of manufacturing industry. *Journal of Cleaner Production*, *115*, 36–51. DOI: 10.1016/j.jclepro.2015.12.042

Lipman, T., & Maier, P. (2021). Advanced materials supply considerations for electric vehicle applications. *MRS Bulletin*, *46*(12), 1164–1175. DOI: 10.1557/s43577-022-00263-z

Littlewood, D., Ciambotti, G., Holt, D., & Steinfield, L. (2022). Special issue editorial: Social innovation and entrepreneurship in Africa. *Africa Journal of Management*, *10*(2), 1–10. DOI: 10.1080/23322373.2022.2071579

Lundvall, B. A. (1992). *National systems of innovation: towards a theory of innovation and interactive learning* (Vol. 242). Pinter.

Luo, L., Wang, J., Lv, J., Liu, Z., Sun, T., Yang, Y., & Zhu, Y. G. (2023). Carbon sequestration strategies in soil using biochar: Advances, challenges, and opportunities. *Environmental Science & Technology*, *57*(31), 11357–11372. DOI: 10.1021/acs.est.3c02620

MacDonald, M. (2002). *Agendas for Sustainability: Environment and development into the 21st century*. Routledge.

Maheshwari, G., & Schrage, B. (2025). Emerging trends in social entrepreneurship and sustainability: A Southeast Asia analysis. *The Bottom Line (New York, N.Y.)*. Advance online publication. DOI: 10.1108/BL-06-2024-0064

Maheshwari, N., Dua, R., & Kumar, A. (2021). *Electric mobility in India: A dawn of new era*. SAGE Publications., DOI: 10.4135/9781529759754

Mair, J., & Marti, I. (2006). Social entrepreneurship research: A source of explanation, prediction, and delight. *Journal of World Business*, *41*(1), 36–44. DOI: 10.1016/j.jwb.2005.09.002

Mair, J., & Marti, I. (2009). Entrepreneurship in and around institutional voids. *Journal of Business Venturing*, *24*(5), 419–435. DOI: 10.1016/j.jbusvent.2008.04.006

Majid, S., Yasmeen, H., Rehman, A., & Saeed, I. (2023). Eco-efficiency, environmental and sustainable innovation in SMEs. *Sustainability*, *15*(12), 9465. DOI: 10.3390/su15129465

Majumdar, P. (2025). Illuminating the Path to Sustainability Analysing Global Electricity Access for Achieving SDG 7. *American Journal of Information Science and Technology*, *9*(1), 42–59. DOI: 10.11648/j.ajist.20250901.15

Malau, A. G., Malau, A. G., & Simanjuntak, M. B. (2024). Innovating Sustainable Agriculture: Perspectives from Economy and Biology Professionals. [Jurnal Pendidikan Biologi Indonesia]. *Journal of Biological Education Indonesia*, *10*(1), 320–328. DOI: 10.22219/jpbi.v10i1.32587

Mamash, A., Iyiola, K., & Aljuhmani, H. Y. (2025). The Role of Circular Economy Entrepreneurship, Cleaner Production, and Green Government Subsidy for Achieving Sustainability Goals in Business Performance. *Sustainability (Basel)*, *17*(9), 3990. DOI: 10.3390/su17093990

Managers. (2023). Écosystème entrepreneurial vert en Tunisie.

Manes Rossi, F., Brusca, I., Cohen, S., Caperchione, E., & Thomasson, A. (2024). Public financial management for Sustainable Development Goals: Challenges, experiences, and perspectives. *Financial Accountability & Management*, *40*(4), 1007–1016. DOI: 10.1111/faam.12424

Manzoor, S., Fayaz, U., Dar, A. H., Dash, K. K., Shams, R., Bashir, I., Pandey, V. K., & Abdi, G. (2024). Sustainable development goals through reducing food loss and food waste: A comprehensive review. *Future Foods : a Dedicated Journal for Sustainability in Food Science*, *9*, 100362. DOI: 10.1016/j.fufo.2024.100362

Maraveas, C. (2020). Production of sustainable construction materials using agro-wastes. *Materials (Basel)*, *13*(2), 262. DOI: 10.3390/ma13020262

Markard, J., Raven, R., & Truffer, B. (2012). Sustainability transitions: An emerging field of research and its prospects. *Research Policy*, *41*(6), 955–967. DOI: 10.1016/j.respol.2012.02.013

MarketsandMarkets. (2010, January 13). Electric powertrain market size, share & growth. https://www.marketsandmarkets.com/Market-Reports/electric-powertrain-market-97605711.html

Martínez-Sánchez, V.. (2025). Agri-food waste to phenolic compounds: Life cycle and eco-efficiency assessments. *Journal of Environmental Management*, *380*, 124935. DOI: 10.1016/j.jenvman.2025.124935

Mat, B., Çevrimli, M. B., Varalan, A., Barit, B., & Günlü, A. (2026). Determination of economic sustainability factors in sheep enterprises in Türkiye. *Veterinary Medicine and Science*, *12*(1), e70761. Advance online publication. DOI: 10.1002/vms3.70761 PMID: 41508816

Material Insights. (2023). Material profile features. https://www.material-insights.org/

Mauraise, J., Amokomoyen, C., Lamino, A., & Bakare, A. (2024). Green entrepreneurship: An empirical investigation of investment in environmental technologies and environmental reporting and disclosure on startup business sustainability in Nigeria. *Journal of Information Systems Engineering & Management*, *2025*(53s). https://www.jisem-journal.com/

Mazzucato, M. (2011). The entrepreneurial state. *Soundings*, *49*(49), 131–142. DOI: 10.3898/136266211798411183

Mendez, A., & Houghton, D. P. (2020). Sustainable Banking: The Role of Multilateral Development Banks as Norm Entrepreneurs. *Sustainability (Basel)*, *12*(3), 972. DOI: 10.3390/su12030972

Mertens, J., Dewulf, J., Breyer, C., Belmans, R., Gendron, C., Geoffron, P., Goossens, L., Fischer, C., Du Fornel, E., Hayhoe, K., Hirose, K., Le Cadre-Loret, E., Lester, R., Maigné, F., Maitournam, H., de Miranda, P. E. V., Verwee, P., Sala, O., Webber, M., & Debackere, K. (2024). From emissions to resources: Mitigating the critical raw material supply chain vulnerability of renewable energy technologies. *Mineral Economics*, *37*(3), 669–676. DOI: 10.1007/s13563-024-00425-2

Mia, M. A. (2022). Innovations in Non-Financial Products and Services of Microfinance Institutions: Bangladesh's Experience. In *Social Purpose, Commercialization, and Innovations in Microfinance* (pp. 69–86). Springer Singapore. DOI: 10.1007/978-981-19-0217-8_4

Mia, M. M., Rizwan, S., Zayed, N. M., Nitsenko, V., Miroshnyk, O., Kryshtal, H., & Ostapenko, R. (2022). The Impact of Green Entrepreneurship on Social Change and Factors Influencing AMO Theory. *Systems*, *10*(5), 132. DOI: 10.3390/systems10050132

Miao, Y., Hynan, P., Von Jouanne, A., & Yokochi, A. (2019). Current Li-ion battery technologies in electric vehicles and opportunities for advancements. *Energies*, *12*(6), 1074. DOI: 10.3390/en12061074

Mick, M. M. A. P., Kovaleski, J. L., Mick, R. L., & Chiroli, D. M. D. G. (2024). Developing a sustainable digital transformation roadmap for SMEs: Integrating digital maturity and strategic alignment. *Sustainability (Basel)*, *16*(20), 8745. DOI: 10.3390/su16208745

Mihai, F. C., Gündoğdu, S., Markley, L. A., Olivelli, A., Khan, F. R., Gwinnett, C., Gutberlet, J., Reyna-Bensusan, N., Llanquileo-Melgarejo, P., Meidiana, C., Elagroudy, S., Ishchenko, V., Penney, S., Lenkiewicz, Z., & Molinos-Senante, M. (2021). Plastic pollution, waste management issues, and circular economy opportunities in rural communities. *Sustainability (Basel)*, *14*(1), 20. DOI: 10.3390/su14010020

Miles, M. B., & Huberman, A. M. (2003). *Qualitative Data Analysis: A Sourcebook of New Methods* (2nd ed.). SAGE Publications.

Ministry of Micro, Small and Medium Enterprises. (2021). *MSME annual report 2020–21*. Government of India.

Mishra, K., Siwal, S. S., Nayaka, S. C., Guan, Z., & Thakur, V. K. (2023). Waste-to-chemicals: Green solutions for bioeconomy markets. *The Science of the Total Environment*, *887*, 164006. DOI: 10.1016/j.scitotenv.2023.164006

Mishra, P., & Singh, R. (2024). Green innovation strategies in Indian MSMEs. *Journal of Cleaner Production*, *379*, 135150.

Modaffari, G., & Beck, T. (2026). From Corporate Social Responsibility to Social Entrepreneurship: A Bibliometric Approach. *Corporate Social Responsibility and Environmental Management*, *33*(2), 2005–2017. DOI: 10.1002/csr.70259

Mol, A. P., & Spaargaren, G. (2000). Ecological modernisation theory in debate: A review. *Environmental Politics*, *9*(1), 17–49. DOI: 10.1080/09644010008414511

Molina, A.. (2024). Minimizing the environmental impacts of waste valorization systems using multi-criteria life cycle optimization. *Journal of Cleaner Production*, *449*, 141619. DOI: 10.1016/j.jclepro.2024.141619

Molina-Azorin, J. F. (2012). Mixed methods research in strategic management: Impact and applications. *Organizational Research Methods*, *15*(1), 33–56. DOI: 10.1177/1094428110393023

Mondal, S., Singh, S., & Gupta, H. (2025a). Analyzing the indicators of green entrepreneurship for the sustainable circular economy: A mixed-method approach. *Benchmarking*. Advance online publication. DOI: 10.1108/BIJ-04-2024-0356

Mondal, S., Singh, S., & Gupta, H. (2025b). Examining the impact of green entrepreneurship drivers on sustainable development in the context of emerging country. *Benchmarking*, *32*(9), 3584–3630. DOI: 10.1108/BIJ-11-2023-0835

Morero, B., Lorenzon, A. B., & Cafaro, D. C. (2024). Integrated management of urban and rural wastes with energy recovery and low carbon emissions. *Journal of Cleaner Production*, *434*, 139729. DOI: 10.1016/j.jclepro.2023.139729

Morton, S., Pencheon, D., & Squires, N. (2017). Sustainable Development Goals (SDGs), and their implementation: A national global framework for health, development and equity needs a systems approach at every level. *British Medical Bulletin*, *124*(1), 81–90. PMID: 29069332

Muhammad Rezky, D., Mulyadi, H., Utama, D. H., & Furqon, C. (2025). Fresh to cup coffee business planning and development in West Java using the triple layered business model canvas. Jurnal Riset Bisnis dan Manajemen, 18(2). https://journal.unpas.ac.id/index.php/jrbm/index

Mulligan, C., Morsfield, S., & Cheikosman, E. (2024). Blockchain for sustainability: A systematic literature review for policy impact. *Telecommunications Policy*, *48*(2), 102676. DOI: 10.1016/j.telpol.2023.102676

Muñoz, P., & Cohen, B. (2018). Sustainable entrepreneurship research: Taking stock and looking ahead. *Business Strategy and the Environment*, *27*(3), 300–322. DOI: 10.1002/bse.2000

Nani, G.. (2025). pH measurement and color variations of cotton, flax, and jute fibers. *Textile Research Journal*.

Nayab-Ul-Hossain, A. K. M., Sela, S. K., Alam, S. M. M., Hassan, M. N., Sarkar, J., Ahmed, C. M., Sadman, S., Hridoy, R. M., Mohsin, N., Hossain, M. B., & Mia, S. (2023). Substitution of synthetic plastic sheet by naturally colored (Turmeric) biodegradable sheet prepared from nanocellulose of raw jute, and evaluation of its quality performance (Multifunctional properties). *Current Research in Green and Sustainable Chemistry*, *6*, 100351. DOI: 10.1016/j.crgsc.2022.100351

Neumann, T. (2021). The impact of entrepreneurship on economic, social and environmental welfare and its determinants: A systematic review. *Management Review Quarterly*, *71*(3), 553–584. DOI: 10.1007/s11301-020-00193-7

Neumann, T. (2022). Impact of green entrepreneurship on sustainable development: An ex-post empirical analysis. *Journal of Cleaner Production*, *377*, 134317. DOI: 10.1016/j.jclepro.2022.134317

Nicola, J. (2024, February 7). The new car batteries that could power the electric vehicle revolution. *Nature*, *626*(7998), 248–251. Advance online publication. DOI: 10.1038/d41586-024-00325-z PMID: 38326600

Nidumolu, R., Prahalad, C. K., & Rangaswami, M. R. (2009). Why sustainability is now the key driver of innovation. *Harvard Business Review*, *87*(9), 56–64.

Nilsson, M., Griggs, D., & Visbeck, M. (2016). Policy: Map the interactions between sustainable development goals. *Nature*, *534*(7607), 320–322. DOI: 10.1038/534320a PMID: 27306173

Noyon, A. R., Karim, S., Rouf, A., Jamal, M., Layek, R. K., Sivanantham, G., & Uddin, E. (2023). Fabrication of biodegradable kraft paper from buffing dust and jute fiber: Green solutions for packaging. *Polymer Engineering and Science*, *63*(12), 4032–4042. DOI: 10.1002/pen.26503

Nuringsih, K. (2021). ROLE OF GREEN ENTREPRENEURSHIP IN RAISING THE EFFECT OF GREEN VALUE TOWARD SUSTAINABLE DEVELOPMENT. *International Journal of Economics, Business, and Entrepreneurship*, *3*(2), 29–46. DOI: 10.23960/ijebe.v3i2.69

Nuringsih, K., Mn, N., & Rosa, J. A. (2022). Mendorong Green Entrepreneurial Intention Melalui Green Economy dan Green Entrepreneurial Orientation. *Jurnal Ekonomi*, *27*(3), 417–438. DOI: 10.24912/je.v27i3.1203

Nussbaum, M. C. (2009). Creating capabilities: The human development approach and its implementation. *Hypatia, 24*(3), 211–215. DOI: 10.1111/j.1527-2001.2009.01053.x

Oduro, S., Maccario, G., & De Nisco, A. (2022). Green innovation: A multidomain systematic review. *European Journal of Innovation Management, 25*(2), 567–591. DOI: 10.1108/EJIM-10-2020-0425

OECD. (2018). *Business models for the circular economy: Opportunities and challenges for policy*. Organisation for Economic Co-operation and Development.

OECD. (2021). *Financing SMEs and entrepreneurs 2021: An OECD scoreboard*. OECD Publishing.

OECD. (2024). *Green budgeting in OECD countries 2024*. OECD Publishing., DOI: 10.1787/9aea61f0-

OECD. (2025). *Mind the SDG data gaps: Insights from the OECD SDGs Hub. OECD Policy Insights on Well-being, Inclusion and Equal Opportunity, No. 20*. OECD Publishing.

Onyeaka, H., Tamasiga, P., Nwauzoma, U. M., Miri, T., Juliet, U. C., Nwaiwu, O., & Akinsemolu, A. A. (2023). Using artificial intelligence to tackle food waste and enhance the circular economy: Maximising resource efficiency and minimising environmental impact: A review. *Sustainability (Basel), 15*(13), 10482. DOI: 10.3390/su151310482

Organisation for Economic Co-operation and Development. (2020). Global EV outlook 2020. DOI: 10.1787/d394399e-en

Osman, A. I., Fang, B., Zhang, Y., Liu, Y., Yu, J., Farghali, M., Rashwan, A. K., Chen, Z., Chen, L., Ihara, I., Rooney, D. W., & Yap, P. S. (2024). Life cycle assessment and techno-economic analysis of sustainable bioenergy production: A review. *Environmental Chemistry Letters, 22*(3), 1115–1154. DOI: 10.1007/s10311-023-01694-z

Palmié, M., Miehé, L., Mair, J., & Wincent, J. (2024). Valuation entrepreneurship through product-design and blame-avoidance strategies: How Tesla managed to change the public perception of sustainable innovations. *Journal of Product Innovation Management, 41*(3), 644–676. DOI: 10.1111/jpim.12732

Pal, P., Singh, A. K., Srivastava, R. K., Rathore, S. S., Sahoo, U. K., Subudhi, S., Sarangi, P. K., & Prus, P. (2024). Circular bioeconomy in action: Transforming food wastes into renewable food resources. *Foods, 13*(18), 3007. DOI: 10.3390/foods13183007

Pamu, Y., & Alugubelli, S. (2025). Waste to Wealth: A Comprehensive Review of Agricultural Waste in Sustainable Building Materials. In *E3S Web of Conferences* (Vol. 616, p. 03002). EDP Sciences. DOI: 10.1051/e3sconf/202561603002

Pandikar, E., Affandi, I., Disman, D., & Sundawa, D. (2024). Harmonizing Economic Principles, Islamic Values, and Entrepreneurial Attitudes for a Sustainable Environment. *Yupa: Historical Studies Journal*, *6*(2), 188–197. DOI: 10.30872/yupa.v6i2.3739

Pansera, M. (2018). Frugal or fair? The unfulfilled promises of frugal innovation. *Technology Innovation Management Review*, *8*(4), 6–13. DOI: 10.22215/timreview/1148

Pansera, M., & Sarkar, S. (2016). Crafting sustainable development solutions: Frugal innovations of grassroots entrepreneurs. *Sustainability (Basel)*, *8*(1), 51. DOI: 10.3390/su8010051

Parihar, J. S., Cichon, D., Kharbanda, A., Sala, D., & Sharma, G. D. (2025). Barriers and enablers: Review research on women entrepreneurship and its impact on sustainable tourism development. *Entrepreneurial Business and Economics Review*, *13*(4), 185–208. DOI: 10.15678/EBER.2025.130410

Parrales-Reyes, J., Cañarte-Quimis, L. Y., Salazar-Pionce, E., Saltos-Buri, V., Díaz-Romero, Y., Martínez-García, V., Espinoza-Vásquez, G., Rengifo-Lozano, R., Escobar-Molina, D., Delgado, D. R., & Rincón-Guio, C. (2025). Towards sustainability in organic coffee production: A holistic analysis of research trends, challenges, and future prospects. *Logforum*, *21*(3), 383–403. DOI: 10.17270/J.LOG.001233

Parvin Banu, I., Sivaramakrishnan, R., Kavithamani, R., & Nanee, M. D. (n.d.). Green entrepreneurship startups. Retrieved from www.ciitresearch.org

Patel, R. (2025). *Eco-friendly jute bags wholesale India: Top picks for sustainable business in 2025–2026*. Techno Aid.

Patrucco, A. S., Roath, A. S., Richey, R. G.Jr, Mathiyazhagan, K., & Shankar, R. (2026). From triple-A to AAA+: Recalibrating agility, adaptability, and alignment for digital, responsible, and resilient supply chains. *Journal of Business Logistics*, *47*(1), e70049. Advance online publication. DOI: 10.1111/jbl.70049

Patzelt, H., & Shepherd, D. A. (2011). Recognizing opportunities for sustainable development. In *Entrepreneurship & Sustainability – Business Solutions for the 21st Century*. DOI: 10.1111/j.1540-6520.2010.00386.x

Pauceanu, A. M., Rabie, N., Moustafa, A., & Jiroveanu, D. C. (2021). Entrepreneurial Leadership and Sustainable Development—A Systematic Literature Review. *Sustainability (Basel)*, *13*(21), 11695. DOI: 10.3390/su132111695

Peres, R. S., Jia, X., Lee, J., Sun, K., Colombo, A. W., & Barata, J. (2020). Industrial artificial intelligence in industry 4.0-systematic review, challenges and outlook. *IEEE Access : Practical Innovations, Open Solutions*, *8*, 220121–220139. DOI: 10.1109/ACCESS.2020.3042874

Peterson, M., Minton, E. A., Liu, R. L., & Bartholomew, D. E. (2021). Sustainable Marketing and Consumer Support for Sustainable Businsses. *Sustainable Production and Consumption*, *27*, 157–168. DOI: 10.1016/j.spc.2020.10.018

Petfoodprocesing. (2025). Insect protein producer receives $5.3 million in investments. Available on https://www.petfoodprocessing.net/articles/15754-insect-protein-producer-receives-53-million-in-investments. (Accessed on 17th March 2025).

Poderytė, I., Banaitienė, N., & Banaitis, A. (2025). Life cycle sustainability assessment of buildings: A scientometric analysis. *Buildings (Basel, Switzerland)*, *15*(3), 381. Advance online publication. DOI: 10.3390/buildings15030381

Polas, M. R. H., Afshar Jahanshahi, A., Islam, M. E., Kabir, A. I., Sohel-Uz-Zaman, A. S. M., & Al Fahad, A. (2025). A Journey From Traditional Supply Chain Processes to Sustainability-Oriented Blockchain Supply Chain: The Critical Role of Organizational Capabilities. *Business Strategy and the Environment*, *34*(3), 3522–3543. DOI: 10.1002/bse.4159

Polloni, E. (2026). Public, private and hybrid organizations collaborating for social sustainability.

Prabhakar, P. (2024). *Optimized Extraction and Characterization of Phytochemicals from Selected Ethnomedicinal Plants for Antidiabetic Phytopharmaceuticals* (Doctoral dissertation, IIT Kharagpur).

Prabhakar, S., Nimesh, A., & Prabhakar, P. (2023). Startup ecosystem for rural development in India. In *Socio-Economic Disparities, Vulnerable Communities, and the Future of Work and Entrepreneurship* (pp. 26-50). IGI Global. DOI: 10.4018/978-1-6684-6990-3.ch003

Prabhakar, P., & Banerjee, M. (2020). Antidiabetic phytochemicals: A comprehensive review on opportunities and challenges in targeted therapy for herbal drug development. *International Journal of Pharmaceutical Research*, *12*(1), 1673–1696.

Prabhakar, P., Mukherjee, S., Kumar, A., Kumar, S., Verma, D. K., Dhara, S., Maiti, M. K., & Banerjee, M. (2023). Optimization of MAE for Carica papaya phytochemicals, and its in silico, in vitro, and ex vivo evaluation: For functional food and drug applications. *Food Bioscience*, *54*, 102861. DOI: 10.1016/j.fbio.2023.102861

Prabhakar, P., Mukherjee, S., Kumar, A., Rout, R. K., Kumar, S., Verma, D. K., & Banerjee, M. (2024). In Silico, In Vitro and Ex Vivo Evaluation of the Antihyperglycaemic, Antioxidant and Cytotoxic Properties of Coccinia grandis L. Leaf Extract. *Food Technology and Biotechnology*, *62*(2), 188–204. DOI: 10.17113/ftb.62.02.24.8162

Prabhakar, P., Verma, D. K., & Banerjee, M. (2024). Advances in enzyme-assisted extraction technique for antidiabetic phytochemicals: an emerging approach for green and economical technologies. In *Enzymatic Processes for Food Valorization* (pp. 191–216). Academic Press. DOI: 10.1016/B978-0-323-95996-4.00013-7

Prabhakar, S., & Nimesh, A. (2022). Skill development programmes for women in India: Current status and future perspectives. *World Journal of Advanced Engineering Technology and Sciences*, *7*(1), 128–136. DOI: 10.30574/wjaets.2022.7.1.0105

Prabhakar, S., Prabhakar, P., Nimesh, A., & Banerjee, M. (2025). Production and Development of Nutraceuticals Using Sustainable Food System. In *Food Bioactives and Nutraceuticals: Dietary Medicine for Human Health and Well-Beings* (pp. 59–86). Springer Nature Singapore. DOI: 10.1007/978-981-97-9723-3_3

Prajapati, C. S., Priya, N. K., Bishnoi, S., Vishwakarma, S. K., Buvaneswari, K., Shastri, S., Tripathi, S., & Jadhav, A. (2025). The Role of Participatory Approaches in Modern Agricultural Extension: Bridging Knowledge Gaps for Sustainable Farming Practices. *Journal of Experimental Agriculture International*, *47*(2), 204–222. DOI: 10.9734/jeai/2025/v47i23281

Prakash, D., Bisla, M., & Arora, T. (2023). Role of environment dimensions to strive sustainable entrepreneurship: A triple bottom line approach. *International Journal of Professional Business Review*, *8*(3), e0698. Advance online publication. DOI: 10.26668/businessreview/2023.v8i3.698

Prasetyo, P. E., Azwardi, A., & Kistanti, N. R. (2023). Gender equality and social inclusion (GESI) and institutions as key drivers of green entrepreneurship. *International Journal of Data and Network Science*, *7*(1), 391–398. DOI: 10.5267/j.ijdns.2022.9.008

Prasnowo, M. A., Aziza, N., & Sulaiman, A. (2025). Entrepreneurship and sustainable development goals: An SCT model analysis. BIMA Journal (Business, Management, & Accounting Journal), 6(1), 11–18. DOI: 10.37638/bima.6.1.11-18

Press Information Bureau, Government of India. (2021, March 18). Govt driving transition from linear to circular economy. https://pib.gov.in

Priyanka. (2021, December 14). Have you heard about environmental impact assessment? ABC Techno Lab. https://abctechnolab.com/have-you-heard-about-environmental-impact-assessment/

Purwandani, J. A., & Michaud, G. (2021). What are the drivers and barriers for green business practice adoption for SMEs? *Environment Systems & Decisions, 41*(4), 577–593. DOI: 10.1007/s10669-021-09821-3 PMID: 34155474

Quitério, E., Grosso, C., Ferraz, R., Delerue-Matos, C., & Soares, C. (2022). A critical comparison of the advanced extraction techniques applied to obtain health-promoting compounds from seaweeds. *Marine Drugs, 20*(11), 677. DOI: 10.3390/md20110677

Radjou, N., & Prabhu, J. (2015). Frugal Innovation: How to Do More With Less.

Rahman, M. M. (2025). Data analytics for strategic business development: A systematic review analyzing its role in informing decisions, optimizing processes, and driving growth. *Journal of Sustainable Development and Policy, 1*(01), 285–314. DOI: 10.63125/he1tfg25

Raman, R., Ray, S., Das, D., & Nedungadi, P. (2025). Innovations and barriers in sustainable and green finance for advancing sustainable development goals. *Frontiers in Environmental Science, 12*, 1513204. DOI: 10.3389/fenvs.2024.1513204

Raman, R., Subramaniam, N., Nair, V. K., Shivdas, A., Achuthan, K., & Nedungadi, P. (2022). Women entrepreneurship and sustainable development: Bibliometric analysis and emerging research trends. *Sustainability (Basel), 14*(15), 9160. DOI: 10.3390/su14159160

Ramasamy, C., & Choudhury, A. (2023). Digital solutions and sustainability in Indian startups. *Technology in Society, 74*, 102241.

Ramos-Ruiz, J. E., Guzmán-Dorado, L., Ferreira-Gomes, P. C., & Algaba-Navarro, D. (2025). First time in the European Rally Championship: What's next for residents' perceptions of urban sustainability? *Urban Science (Basel, Switzerland), 9*(11), 441. Advance online publication. DOI: 10.3390/urbansci9110441

Rana, R. L., Lombardi, M., & Giungato, P. (2024). Circular economy and waste valorization: Policy frameworks and sustainability implications. *Journal of Cleaner Production, 433*, 140195.

Rao, M. M., Botsa, S. M., Rao, T. P., Goddu, S. R., & Vijayasanthi, C. (2024). A comprehensive review on agricultural waste production and onsite management with circular economy opportunities. *Discover Sustainability*, *5*(1), 288. DOI: 10.1007/s43621-024-00492-z

Raphela, T., Manqele, N., & Erasmus, M. (2024). The impact of improper waste disposal on human health and the environment: A case of Umgungundlovu District in KwaZulu Natal Province, South Africa. *Frontiers in Sustainability*, *5*, 1386047. DOI: 10.3389/frsus.2024.1386047

Rashid, M., Anser, M. K., Shah, S. T. H., Nabi, A. A., Ahmad, I., & Zaman, K. (2025). Fostering entrepreneurship: Analyzing the influence of access to finance, innovation investment, educational attainment, infrastructure development, and regulatory environment. *Future Business Journal*, *11*(1), 140. DOI: 10.1186/s43093-025-00557-z

Ray, D. P., & Ghosh, R. K. (2018). Perspective of jute in a new realm beyond sacking. *Economic Affairs*, *63*(4), 981–986. DOI: 10.30954/0424-2513.4.2018.22

Research, J. M. K. (2019, September 24). Lithium-ion battery manufacturers | Battery recycling companies India. https://jmkresearch.com/electric-vehicles-published-reports/recycling-of-lithium-ion-batteries-in-india-1000-million-opportunity/

Reuther, K., Dahle, Y., Schmidt, C., & Schösser, F. (2023). Motivational Facets of Sustainable Entrepreneurship: A Systematic Review and Future Research Agenda. *Sustainability (Basel)*, *15*(3), 2272. DOI: 10.3390/su15032272

Ribeiro, T. B., Voss, G. B., Coelho, M. C., & Pintado, M. E. (2022). Food waste and by-product valorization as an integrated approach with zero waste: Future challenges. In *Future foods* (pp. 569–596). Academic Press. DOI: 10.1016/B978-0-323-91001-9.00017-7

Rissman, J., Bataille, C., Masanet, E., Aden, N., Morrow, W. R.III, Zhou, N., Elliott, N., Dell, R., Heeren, N., Huckestein, B., Cresko, J., Miller, S. A., Roy, J., Fennell, P., Cremmins, B., Koch Blank, T., Hone, D., Williams, E. D., de la Rue du Can, S., & Helseth, J. (2020). Technologies and policies to decarbonize global industry: Review and assessment of mitigation drivers through 2070. *Applied Energy*, *266*, 114848. DOI: 10.1016/j.apenergy.2020.114848

Robinson, G. M. (2024). Global sustainable agriculture and land management systems. *Geography and Sustainability*, *5*(4), 637–646. DOI: 10.1016/j.geosus.2024.09.001

Rosenboom, J. G., Langer, R., & Traverso, G. (2022). Bioplastics for a circular economy. *Nature Reviews. Materials*, *7*(2), 117–137. DOI: 10.1038/s41578-021-00407-8

Rosliani, E., Muhafidin, D., Rusli, B., & Sumaryana, A. (2025). Contextualizing triple bottom line sustainability assessment in secondary education: A rapid appraisal from the Global South. *Sustainability (Basel)*, *17*(14), 6621. Advance online publication. DOI: 10.3390/su17146621

Rossi, L. A., & Srai, J. S. (2024). Configuring circular by-product supply networks through public-private partnerships–A case study of rice straw stubble agri-waste in Punjab. *Journal of Cleaner Production*, *468*, 143093. DOI: 10.1016/j.jclepro.2024.143093

Rumbayan, M., Kindangen, J., Sambul, A., Sompie, S., & Cross, J. (2025). Solar energy implementation in rural communities and its contributions to SDGs: A systematic literature review. *Unconventional Resources*, *6*, 100180. DOI: 10.1016/j.uncres.2025.100180

Saberi, S., Kouhizadeh, M., Sarkis, J., & Shen, L. (2023). Blockchain technology and its relationships to sustainable supply chain management. *International Journal of Production Research*, *61*(6), 1791–1810.

Sachs, J. D., Schmidt-Traub, G., Mazzucato, M., Messner, D., Nakicenovic, N., & Rockström, J. (2019). Six transformations to achieve the sustainable development goals. *Nature Sustainability*, *2*(9), 805–814. DOI: 10.1038/s41893-019-0352-9

Sadh, P. K., Duhan, S., & Duhan, J. S. (2018). Agro-industrial wastes and their utilization using solid state fermentation: A review. *Bioresources and Bioprocessing*, *5*(1), 1–15. DOI: 10.1186/s40643-017-0187-z

Saeedi, M., & Ashraf, B. N. (2024). The Role of Technology in Promoting Green Finance: A Systematic Literature Survey and the Development of a Framework. *Journal of Risk and Financial Management*, *17*(10), 472. DOI: 10.3390/jrfm17100472

Sahu, D. K., & Choudhary, D. (2025). An investigation of circular economy from sustainability perspective in agricultural sector of Indian markets: An extended PEST-O framework. *Journal of Foodservice Business Research*, •••, 1–44.

Said Al-Jahwari, N., Bathmanathan, V., & Ahmed, A. (n.d.). Doing good, doing well: The impact of green CSR on manufacturing SME sustainability in Oman. International Journal of Environmental Sciences, 11(8). Retrieved from https://www.theaspd.com/ijes.php

Sajib, T. R., Islam, M. J., & Gowindasamy, M. (2025). Sustainable of HRM system and strategies for corporate sustainability. *International Journal of Advanced Business Studies*, *2*(4), 57–79. DOI: 10.59857/ijabs.1470

Sakib, N. (2025). Eco-friendly innovation in packaging: Sustainable business strategies for Sonali Bag. *Journal of Sustainable Marketing*, *15*(2).

Salaheldeen, M., Ateeq, A., Al Ani, Z., Alzoraiki, M., Ali, S. A., & Milhem, M. (2024). *Green Entrepreneurship and Sustainability in Developing Countries: Opportunities*. Challenges, and Future Research Directions., DOI: 10.1007/978-3-031-54379-1_45

Samantaray, A., Chattaraj, S., Mitra, D., Ganguly, A., Kumar, R., Gaur, A., Mohapatra, P. K. D., Santos-Villalobos, S., Rani, A., & Thatoi, H. (2024). Advances in microbial based bio-inoculum for amelioration of soil health and sustainable crop production. *Current Research in Microbial Sciences*, *7*, 100251. DOI: 10.1016/j.crmicr.2024.100251

Sánchez-Hernández, M. I., Rabazo-Martín, A., Rodriguez-Rivero, E., & Guerrero-Cáceres, J. M. (2025). The Convergence of the Fourth Sector and Generation Z's Biospheric Values: A Regional Empirical Case Study in Spain. *WORLD (Oakland, Calif.)*, *6*(2), 83. DOI: 10.3390/world6020083

Sanchis, J. R., Campos, V., & Ejarque, A. T. (2025). A proposed typology for the validation of corporate sustainability. *Sustainability (Basel)*, *17*(16), 7358. Advance online publication. DOI: 10.3390/su17167358

Sarkar, A., Qian, L., Peau, A. K., & Shahriar, S. (2021). Modeling drivers for successful adoption of green business: An interpretive structural modeling approach. *Environmental Science and Pollution Research International*, *28*(1), 1077–1096. DOI: 10.1007/s11356-020-10490-z PMID: 32829426

Sarkar, S., & Ghosh, P. (2022). Renewable energy entrepreneurship and social impact in India. *Energy Policy*, *167*, 113024.

Sarker, A., Ahmmed, R., Ahsan, S. M., Rana, J., Ghosh, M. K., & Nandi, R. (2024). A comprehensive review of food waste valorization for the sustainable management of global food waste. *Sustainable Food Technology*, *2*(1), 48–69. DOI: 10.1039/D3FB00156C

Sarlin Venotha, A., & Alex, K. (n.d.). Sustainability of women entrepreneurship: Personal and social factors. International Journal of Commerce and Management Research. Retrieved from www.managejournal.com

Saxena, D. S. (2025). Corporate Social Responsibility as a Strategic Tool for Sustainable Growth: A Comparative Study of Startups in India and Southeast Asia. *Journal of Asia Entrepreneurship and Sustainability*, •••, 108–116. DOI: 10.53555/jaes.v21i2.35

Saxena, S., Moharil, M. P., Jadhav, P. V., Ghodake, B., Deshmukh, R., & Ingle, A. P. (2024). Transforming waste into wealth: Leveraging nanotechnology for recycling agricultural byproducts into value-added products. *Plant Nano Biology*, •••, 100127.

Sayeed, M. A., Muhammad Sayem, A., & Haider, J. (2019). Opportunities with renewable jute fiber composites to reduce eco-impact of non-renewable polymers.

Scartozzi, G., Delladio, S., Rosati, F., Nikiforou, A. I., & Caputo, A. (2025). The social and environmental impact of entrepreneurship: A review and future research agenda. *Review of Managerial Science*, *19*(4), 1041–1072. DOI: 10.1007/s11846-024-00783-9

Schaltegger, S. (2002). A framework for ecopreneurship. *Greener Management International*, *38*(38), 45–58. DOI: 10.9774/GLEAF.3062.2002.su.00006

Schaltegger, S., Hansen, E. G., & Lüdeke-Freund, F. (2016). Business models for sustainability: Origins, present research, and future avenues. *Organization & Environment*, *29*(1), 3–10. DOI: 10.1177/1086026615599806

Schaltegger, S., & Wagner, M. (2011). Sustainable entrepreneurship and sustainability innovation: Categories and interactions. *Business Strategy and the Environment*, *20*(4), 222–237. DOI: 10.1002/bse.682

Schaper, M. (2002). The essence of ecopreneurship. *Greener Management International*, *2002*(38), 26–30. DOI: 10.9774/GLEAF.3062.2002.su.00004

Schimperna, F., Schimperna, M., Gigli, S., & Manzari, A. (2025). Sustainability and higher education: Exploring ESG drivers of university performance through a multi-stakeholder lens. *International Journal of Information and Operations Management Education*, *8*(1), 74–96. DOI: 10.1504/IJIOME.2025.148369

Schumpeter, J. A. (1942). *Capitalism, socialism and democracy.* Harper & Brothers. https://scholar.google.com/scholar_lookup?title=Creative+destruction&publication_year=1942&pages=8285&journal=Capitalism,+Socialism+and+Democracy&author=J.+Schumpeter

Scott, W. R. (2013). *Institutions and organizations: Ideas, interests, and identities.* Sage publications.

Selvan, S., & Rajan, P. (2023). Sustainable packaging innovations in India. *Journal of Environmental Innovation and Societal Transitions*, *48*, 65–82.

Sen, A. (1999). *Freedom. Development.* Oxford University Press.

Senga, R., Nasr, M., Fujii, M., & Abdelhaleem, A. (2024). Sustainable valorization of agricultural waste into bioplastic and its end-of-life recyclability for biochar production: Economic profitability and life cycle assessment. *Chemosphere*, *369*, 143847. DOI: 10.1016/j.chemosphere.2024.143847

Sengupta, S., Choudhary, S., Obayi, R., & Nayak, R. (2024). Reducing food loss through sustainable business models and agricultural innovation systems. *Supply Chain Management*, *29*(3), 540–572. DOI: 10.1108/SCM-01-2023-0059

Serafeim, G., & Trinh, K. (2020). A framework for product impact-weighted accounts (HBS Working Paper No. 20-076). SSRN. https://doi.org/DOI: 10.2139/ssrn.3532472

Shah, M. A., & Ghayas, A. (2022). Impediments to Public-Private Partnership Projects In Aftermath of Covid-19 Pandemic. *Parikalpana: KIIT Journal of Management*, *18*(1), 85. DOI: 10.23862/kiit-parikalpana/2022/v18/i1/212347

Shah, M. A., & Singh, A. (2026). Examining the Impact of Circular Economy Practices and Brand Reputation on Financial Performance. *Circular Economy and Sustainability*, *6*(1), 2. Advance online publication. DOI: 10.1007/s43615-026-00751-3

Shah, M. A., & Uddin, F. (2023). Leveraging Blockchain Technology in the Construction Industry. *Advances in Business Information Systems and Analytics*, •••, 50–65. DOI: 10.4018/978-1-6684-7808-0.ch004

Shahzad, H. M. A., Asim, Z., Khan, S. J., Almomani, F., Mahmoud, K. A., Mustafa, M. R. U., & Rasool, K. (2024). Thermochemical and biochemical conversion of agricultural waste for bioenergy production: An updated review. *Discover Environment*, *2*(1), 134. DOI: 10.1007/s44274-024-00171-w

Sharma, C., Pathak, P., & Gautam, S. (2024). Transforming agri-crop residue biomass for value addition: an innovative strategy toward resilient circular economy. In *Handbook of biomass* (pp. 1517–1542). Springer Nature Singapore. DOI: 10.1007/978-981-99-6727-8_66

Sharma, G. D., Kraus, S., Chopra, R., Dev, D., & Ferraris, A. (2025). Strategic innovation for sustainability: A conceptual model linking digitalization, social dynamics, and climate change mitigation. *Business Strategy and the Environment*. Advance online publication. DOI: 10.1002/bse.70471

Sharma, N., Trivedi, M., & Choudhary, M. (2025). From tradition to transform: SDGs and the role of the Indian knowledge system in india's growth through ESE (Environment, Social, and Economic) factors. *Discover Sustainability*, *6*(1), 1110. DOI: 10.1007/s43621-025-01905-3

Sharma, S. N., & Subba, R. (2025). Entrepreneurship and Sustainability: Analyzing the impact of Green Startups on Economic Development. *Innovation and Green Development*, *4*(4), 100280. DOI: 10.1016/j.igd.2025.100280

Sharma, S., Nanda, M., Goel, R., Jain, A., Bhushan, M., & Kumar, A. (2019). Smart cities using internet of things: Recent trends and techniques. *International Journal of Innovative Technology and Exploring Engineering*, *8*(9S), 24–28. DOI: 10.35940/ijitee.I1004.0789S19

Shepherd, D. A., & Patzelt, H. (2011). The new field of sustainable entrepreneurship: Studying entrepreneurial action linking "what is to be sustained" with "what is to be developed". *Entrepreneurship Theory and Practice*, *35*(1), 137–163. DOI: 10.1111/j.1540-6520.2010.00426.x

Shourkaei, M. M., Taylor, K. M., & Dyck, B. (2024). Examining sustainable supply chain management via a social-symbolic work lens: Lessons from Patagonia. *Business Strategy and the Environment*, *33*(2), 1477–1496. DOI: 10.1002/bse.3552

Siddiqua, A., Hahladakis, J. N., & Al-Attiya, W. A. K. (2022). An overview of the environmental pollution and health effects associated with waste landfilling and open dumping. *Environmental Science and Pollution Research International*, *29*(39), 58514–58536. DOI: 10.1007/s11356-022-21578-z

Silvério, A., Fernandes, C. I., & Maran, T. K. (2025). Do green innovation strategies exist? Past, present and future trends in literature. *European Journal of Innovation Management*, *28*(11), 154–186. DOI: 10.1108/EJIM-12-2024-1427

Singh, P., Daga, S., Yadav, K., & Nguyen, P. M. (Eds.). (2025). *Advancing the SDGs in Developing and Emerging Economies: Volume II: Sustainable Development Challenges*. Springer Nature Switzerland. DOI: 10.1007/978-3-031-95103-9

Singh, P., Kushwaha, J., Kushwaha, R., Rajput, S., & Jain, P. (2026). Sustainability of green materials in circular economies: A bibliometric analysis on ESG. In Futureproofed sustainability amidst climate change polycrisis: Advancing SDGs and ESG for the cities of tomorrow (pp. 97–136). IGI Global Scientific Publishing.

Singh, A. K., Pal, P., Rathore, S. S., Sahoo, U. K., Sarangi, P. K., Prus, P., & Dziekański, P. (2023). Sustainable utilization of biowaste resources for biogas production to meet rural bioenergy requirements. *Energies*, *16*(14), 5409. DOI: 10.3390/en16145409

Singh, H., & Kumar, B. P. (2023). Organic agriculture and sustainable rural entrepreneurship in India. *International Journal of Agricultural Sustainability*, *21*(3), 201–219.

Singh, H., Kumar, P., & Dana, L. P. (2025). The green entrepreneurship landscape: Drivers, outcomes, and future directions. *The International Entrepreneurship and Management Journal*, *21*(1), 80. DOI: 10.1007/s11365-025-01079-4

Singh, N., Biswas, R., & Banerjee, M. (2026). Life cycle carbon accounting and waste valorisation in litchi supply chains for climate-resilient food systems. *Sustainable Food Technology*, *4*(2), 1577–1595. DOI: 10.1039/D5FB00519A

Singh, V. K., Keshari, A., Singh, D., Singh, P. C., & Gautam, A. (2024). Green export strategies and SMEs export performance: Mediating roles of innovation, readiness, and activities. *Journal of Innovation and Entrepreneurship*, *13*(1), 87. DOI: 10.1186/s13731-024-00451-y

Sizan, N. S., Dey, D., Layek, M. A., Uddin, M. A., & Huh, E. N. (2025). Evaluating blockchain platforms for iot applications in industry 5.0: A comprehensive review. *Blockchain: Research and Applications*, *100276*(3), 100276. Advance online publication. DOI: 10.1016/j.bcra.2025.100276

Smith, A. (2025). Systemic Analysis of Circular Economy Principles in Agricultural Waste Management and Their Synergy with National Sustainable Development Objectives. *Transdisciplinary Advances in Social Computing, Complex Dynamics, and Computational Creativity*, *15*(2), 10–21.

Soliman, S., Elkholy, S. M. A., & Elkharbotly, M. M. Y. (2023). EVALUATION OF ENVIRONMENTALLY-FRIENDLY ENTREPRENEURSHIP PROJECTS) FIELD STUDY. *Journal of Environmental Sciences (China)*, *52*(8), 29–55. DOI: 10.21608/jes.2023.213379.1532

Sołoducho-Pelc, L. (2020). Sustainable Entrepreneurship Utopian Idea or a New Business Model for the 21st Century? In Michałkiewicz, A., & Mierzejewska, W. (Eds.), *Contemporary organisation and management. Challenges and trends* (pp. 205–219). Wydawnictwo Uniwersytetu Łódzkiego., DOI: 10.18778/8220-333-2.12

Somorin, T., Campos, L. C., Kinobe, J. R., Kulabako, R. N., & Afolabi, O. O. D. (2023). Sustainable valorisation of agri-food waste from open-air markets in Kampala, Uganda via standalone and integrated waste conversion technologies. *Biomass and Bioenergy*, *172*, 106752. DOI: 10.1016/j.biombioe.2023.106752

Sonam, Shishir, K., & Prabhakar, P. (2021). Constraint Analysis in Mushroom Cultivation among Women Mushroom Cultivators in the State of Bihar, India. *Advances in Management*, *14*(2), 7–11.

Soomro, B. A., Moawad, N. F., Saraih, U. N., Abedelwahed, N. A. A., & Shah, N. (2024). Going green with the green market and green innovation: Building the connection between green entrepreneurship and sustainable development. *Kybernetes, 53*(4), 1484–1504. DOI: 10.1108/K-09-2022-1353

Sosa, M., & Ivanova, A. (2025). Innovation and Disruptive Technologies for Sustainable and Climate Finance. *Modern Economy, 16*(09), 1401–1419. DOI: 10.4236/me.2025.169065

Srinivasan, V., Hafemeister, D., Levi, B. G., Levine, M., & Schwartz, P. D. (2008). Batteries for vehicular applications. *Physics Today, 61*(12), 34–39. DOI: 10.1063/1.2993726

Srivani, M. G., & Prakash, C. (2024). Green entrepreneurship: A commitment to a sustainable and eco-friendly enterprise and products. International Journal of Multidisciplinary Research, Science. *Engineering and Technology, 7*(11), 16538. DOI: 10.15680/IJMRSET.2024.0711020

Stafford-Smith, M., Griggs, D., Gaffney, O., Ullah, F., Reyers, B., Kanie, N., Stigson, B., Shrivastava, P., Leach, M., & O'Connell, D. (2017). Integration: The key to implementing the Sustainable Development Goals. *Sustainability Science, 12*(6), 911–919. DOI: 10.1007/s11625-016-0383-3 PMID: 30147763

Stake, R. E. (1995). *The Art of Case Study Research*. SAGE Publications.

Stam, E. (2015). Entrepreneurial ecosystems and regional policy: A sympathetic critique. *European Planning Studies, 23*(9), 1759–1769. DOI: 10.1080/09654313.2015.1061484

Stam, E., & Van de Ven, A. (2021). Entrepreneurial ecosystem elements. *Small Business Economics, 56*(2), 809–832. DOI: 10.1007/s11187-019-00270-6

Stanković, S., Ilić, B., & Rabrenović, M. (2024). Using the Composite EEPSE Green Economy Index to Assess the Progress of Emerging Economies in Achieving the Sustainable Development Goals. *Problemy Ekorozwoju, 19*(1), 78–88. DOI: 10.35784/preko.5751

Startup Tunisia. (2022, 2024). Rapports annuels.

Steiner, B. E., & Makarenko, I. (Eds.). (2026). *Bridging Governance, Public Support, Innovation, and Transparency: A Combined Approach to Sustainable Development in Europe*. Springer Nature Switzerland., DOI: 10.1007/978-3-031-94082-8

Stephan, U., Uhlaner, L. M., & Stride, C. (2026). Institutions and social entrepreneurship: A hierarchy of institutions to revisit institutional voids, support, and configurations. *Journal of International Business Studies*, *57*(1), 4–25. DOI: 10.1057/s41267-025-00829-4

Strategic Market Research. (2022). Electric vehicle charging station market size, forecast | 2030. https://www.strategicmarketresearch.com/market-report/electric-vehicle-charging-station-market

Sudario, M. E. (n.d.). Sustainability struggles: Challenges encountered by small and micro-entrepreneurs in rural Philippines.

Sundarasen, S., Ooi, C. A., Heng, T. N., & Santoso, B. H. (2024). Sustainability reporting and greenwashing: A bibliometrics review and future research agenda. *Cogent Business & Management*, *11*(1), 2320812. DOI: 10.1080/23311975.2024.2320812

Supriaddin, N., & Ayu Ningtyas, S. (n.d.). The role of business performance in mediating relationship between triple bottom line and business survival.

Surana, K., Singh, A., & Sagar, A. D. (2020). Strengthening science, technology, and innovation-based incubators to help achieve Sustainable Development Goals: Lessons from India. *Technological Forecasting and Social Change*, *157*, 120057. DOI: 10.1016/j.techfore.2020.120057

Surbakti, L. P., Sari, R. P., Swatdikun, T., Nugraheni, R., & Wibawaningsih, E. J. (2025). Good corporate governance and corporate sustainability performance in Indonesia. Revista de Administração Mackenzie, 26(5). https://doi.org/DOI: 10.1590/1678-6971/eRAMF250129

Suryani, S., Umar Daihani, D., Gustina Amran, T. G. A., & Septiani, W. (2025). Systematic literature review of sustainable assessment model in vocational higher education. *Spektrum Industri*, *23*(2), 240–248. DOI: 10.12928/si.v23i2.459

Sustainability Standards Board (GRI). (2023). GRI Standards: Universal Standards (2021) in effect from 1 January 2023. https://www.globalreporting.org/standards/

Sutariya, J., & Arora, D. G. (2023). Empowering Rural Economies: The Role Of Microfinance Institutions In Transforming The Financial Landscape Of Rural Communities. *Educational Administration: Theory and Practice*, *29*(03). Advance online publication. DOI: 10.53555/kuey.v29i3.9991

Swalih, M. M., Chithra, K. V., & Raj, R. G. (2024). Environmental management accounting for strategic decision-making: A systematic review. *Business Strategy and the Environment*, *33*(7), 6335–6367. Advance online publication. DOI: 10.1002/bse.3828

Szopik-Depczyńska, K., Cheba, K., Vikhasta, M., & Depczyński, R. (2021). New form of innovations related to the environment—A systematic review. *Procedia Computer Science*, *192*, 5039–5049. DOI: 10.1016/j.procs.2021.09.282

Tahsina, K., Emon, M. M. H., Rahman, A., Abdul Hamid, A. B., Yaakub, N. I., Khan, T., Emon, M. M. H., Rahman, M. A., Hamid, A. B. A., Yaakub, N. I., Abdul Hamid, A. B., & Ya'akub, N. I. B. (2024). Bridging the Gap: Realizing GreenTech Potential. In *AI and Green Technology Applications in Society*. IGI Global., DOI: 10.4018/979-8-3693-9879-1.ch004

Tekala, K., Baradarani, S., Alzubi, A., & Berberoğlu, A. (2024). Green entrepreneurship for business sustainability: Do environmental dynamism and green structural capital matter? *Sustainability (Basel)*, *16*(13), 5291. Advance online publication. DOI: 10.3390/su16135291

Tenedero, E. Q., Sintos, J. R., & Araza, J. B. (2025). Working capital management practices of MSMEs in Samar, Philippines towards triple bottom line sustainability. *Environment and Social Psychology*, *10*(2). Advance online publication. DOI: 10.59429/esp.v10i2.3271

Thalut, N., & Ghani, G. M. (2025). Economic cooperation and environmental sustainability in the OIC region: A panel data analysis. Journal of Economic Cooperation and Development, 46.

Tien, N. H., Hiep, P. M., Dai, N. Q., Duc, N. M., & Hong, T. T. K. (2020). Green entrepreneurship understanding in Vietnam. *International Journal of Entrepreneurship*, *24*(2), 1–14.

Tiuncika, L., & Bormane, S. (2024). Sustainable Management of Manufacturing Processes: A Literature Review. *Processes (Basel, Switzerland)*, *12*(6), 1222. DOI: 10.3390/pr12061222

Tombak, M. L., Aiken, D. M., Toomeoja, E., & Tapaninen, U. P. (2025). Advancing port sustainability in the Baltic Sea region: A comparative analysis using the SMCC framework. *Sustainability (Basel)*, *17*(15), 6764. Advance online publication. DOI: 10.3390/su17156764

Tomić, T., & Schneider, D. R. (2020). Circular economy in waste management–Socio-economic effect of changes in waste management system structure. *Journal of Environmental Management*, *267*, 110564. DOI: 10.1016/j.jenvman.2020.110564

Trabelsi, E. (2024). Transition to sustainable environment and economic growth in Tunisia. *Journal of Environmental Management*, •••, 2772–655X.

Trivedi, A., Juyal, S. A., & Nautiyal, A. (2024). Ethical Implications And Workforce Adaptation In The Era Of Generative AI: A Deep Dive Into HRM Practices. *Migration Letters : An International Journal of Migration Studies, 21*(S3), 1754–1762. https://migrationletters.com/index.php/ml/article/view/9565

Tu, J. C., & Yang, C. (2019). Key factors influencing consumers' purchase of electric vehicles. *Sustainability (Basel), 11*(14), 3863. Advance online publication. DOI: 10.3390/su11143863

Turner, J. M., & Nugent, L. M. (2015). Charging up battery recycling policies: Extended producer responsibility for single-use batteries in the European Union, Canada, and the United States. *Journal of Industrial Ecology, 20*(5), 1148–1158. DOI: 10.1111/jiec.12351

Ufitikirezi, J. D. D. M., Filip, M., Ghorbani, M., Zoubek, T., Olšan, P., Bumbálek, R., Strob, M., Bartoš, P., Umurungi, S. N., Murindangabo, Y. T., Heřmánek, A., Tupý, O., Havelka, Z., Stehlík, R., Černý, P., & Smutný, L. (2024). Agricultural waste valorization: Exploring environmentally friendly approaches to bioenergy conversion. *Sustainability (Basel), 16*(9), 3617. DOI: 10.3390/su16093617

UNDP. (2019).Rapport National Volontaire sur la mise en œuvre des ODD en Tunisie.

UNEP. (2020). *Emissions gap report 2020*. United Nations Environment Programme.

UNEP. (2023). *SwitchMed in Tunisia*. Policy and Strategy.

Usman, I., Hussain, M., Imran, A., Afzaal, M., Saeed, F., & Javed, M. & A. Saewan, S. (. (2022). Traditional and innovative approaches for the extraction of bioactive compounds. *International Journal of Food Properties, 25*(1), 1215–1233. DOI: 10.1080/10942912.2022.2074030

Usman, I., Sana, S., Afzaal, M., Imran, A., Jaffar, H. M., Sukhera, S., Munir, M., Asghar, A., & Urugo, M. M. (2025). Phytochemicals in plant food waste: Innovative insight and implications. *Journal of Agriculture and Food Research, 20*, 101779. DOI: 10.1016/j.jafr.2025.101779

Van Zanten, J., & Van Tulder, R. (2018). Multinational enterprises and the Sustainable Development Goals: An institutional approach to corporate engagement. *Journal of International Business Policy, 1*(3-4), 208–233. DOI: 10.1057/s42214-018-0008-x

Veleva, V. (2021). The role of entrepreneurs in advancing sustainable lifestyles: Challenges, impacts, and future opportunities. *Journal of Cleaner Production, 283*, 124658. DOI: 10.1016/j.jclepro.2020.124658 PMID: 33078048

Velte, P. (2023). Which institutional investors drive corporate sustainability? A systematic literature review. *Business Strategy and the Environment, 32*(1), 42–71. DOI: 10.1002/bse.3117

Verma, B. B. (2009). Continuous jute fiber reinforced laminated paper composite and reinforcement-fiber free paper laminate. *Bulletin of Materials Science, 32*(6), 589–595. DOI: 10.1007/s12034-009-0090-0

Verma, D. K., & Thakur, M. (Eds.). (2021). *Phytochemicals in food and health: Perspectives for research and technological development*. CRC Press. DOI: 10.1201/9781003082125

Volan, T., Vaz, C. R., & Maldonado, M. U. (2021). Scenarios for end-of-life (EOL) electric vehicle batteries in China. *International Journal of Energy Sector Management, 28*(4), 335–357.

Wadghane, R. H., Madguni, O., & Baisakhi, B. (2025). Unlocking sustainability potential: A SAFA framework analysis of sugarcane agriculture in Marathwada, Maharashtra, India. *Sustainable Futures : An Applied Journal of Technology, Environment and Society, 10*, 101118. Advance online publication. DOI: 10.1016/j.sftr.2025.101118

Wang, C., Shan, W., Zhang, Q., & Tang, F. (2025). Driving sustainable business success: The interplay of corporate social responsibility, green innovation and institutional support. *Baltic Journal of Management, 20*(2), 210–229. DOI: 10.1108/BJM-10-2024-0607

Wang, J., Duan, Y., & Liu, G. (2021). A Study of Specific Open Innovation Issues from Perspectives of Open Source and Resources—The Series Cases of Tesla. *Sustainability (Basel), 14*(1), 142. DOI: 10.3390/su14010142

Watson, R., Nielsen, K. R., Wilson, H. N., Macdonald, E. K., Mera, C., & Reisch, L. (2023). Policy for sustainable entrepreneurship: A crowdsourced framework. *Journal of Cleaner Production, 383*, 135234. DOI: 10.1016/j.jclepro.2022.135234

Worakittikul, W., Srisathan, W. A., Rattanpon, K., Kulkaew, A., Groves, J., Pontun, P., & Naruetharadhol, P. (2025). Cultivating Sustainability: Harnessing Open Innovation and Circular Economy Practices for Eco-Innovation in Agricultural SMEs. *Journal of Open Innovation, 11*(1), 100494. DOI: 10.1016/j.joitmc.2025.100494

World Bank (2023). Tunisia Economic Monitor.

World Bank. (2022). *Sustainable entrepreneurship and innovation: Global trends and policy recommendations*. World Bank.

World, T. (2025). Coffee Recycling Company Bio-Bean Launches Inficaf-Using Upcycled, Spent Coffee Grounds For Sustainable Product Innovations. Available on https://www.textileworld.com/textile-world/fiber-world/2021/07/coffee-recycling-company-bio-bean-launches-inficaf-using-upcycled-spent-coffee-grounds-for-sustainable-product-innovations/ (Accessed on 16th March 2025).

Xu, G., Wang, S., Li, J., & Zhao, D. (2020). Moving towards sustainable purchase behavior: Examining the determinants of consumers' intentions to adopt electric vehicles. *Environmental Science and Pollution Research International*, *27*(18), 22535–22546. DOI: 10.1007/s11356-020-08835-9 PMID: 32319053

Yadav, N. (2019, November 22). EVconnect journey: Five insights on e-vehicle adoption in India. World Resources Institute India. https://wri-india.org/blog/evconnect-journey-five-insights-e-vehicle-adoption-india

Yang, T., Yi, X., Lu, S., Johansson, K. H., & Chai, T. (2021). Intelligent manufacturing for the process industry driven by industrial artificial intelligence. *Engineering (Beijing)*, *7*(9), 1224–1230. DOI: 10.1016/j.eng.2021.04.023

Yasir, N., Babar, M., Mehmood, H. S., Xie, R., & Guo, G. (2023). The Environmental Values Play a Role in the Development of Green Entrepreneurship to Achieve Sustainable Entrepreneurial Intention. *Sustainability (Basel)*, *15*(8), 6451. DOI: 10.3390/su15086451

Yewle, A., ... (2023). Improved food storage in jute packaging: An assessment of the current uses, constraints, and functional enhancements of jute bags. ResearchGate. https://www.researchgate.net/publication/391639141

Yi, G. (2021). From green entrepreneurial intentions to green entrepreneurial behaviors: The role of university entrepreneurial support and external institutional support. *The International Entrepreneurship and Management Journal*, *17*(2), 963–979. DOI: 10.1007/s11365-020-00649-y

Yin, C., Salmador, M. P., Li, D., & Lloria, M. B. (2022). Green entrepreneurship and SME performance: The moderating effect of firm age. *The International Entrepreneurship and Management Journal*, *18*(1), 255–275. DOI: 10.1007/s11365-021-00757-3

Yin, R. K. (2018). *Case Study Research and Applications: Design and Methods* (6th ed.). SAGE Publications.

York, J. G., & Venkataraman, S. (2010). The entrepreneur–environment nexus: Uncertainty, innovation, and allocation. *Journal of Business Venturing*, *25*(5), 449–463. DOI: 10.1016/j.jbusvent.2009.07.007

Yousaf, Z., Radulescu, M., Sinisi, C. I., Serbanescu, L., & Paunescu, L. M. (2021). Harmonization of Green Motives and Green Business Strategies towards Sustainable Development of Hospitality and Tourism Industry: Green Environmental Policies. *Sustainability (Basel), 13*(12), 6592. DOI: 10.3390/su13126592

Zaza Agustiana, U., & Pratama, G. (2025). Evidence from Indonesian cooperatives. 11(2).

Zeng, A., Chen, W., Rasmussen, K. D., Zhu, X., Lundhaug, M. C., Müller, D. B., Tan, J., Keiding, J. K., Liu, L., Dai, T., Wang, A., & Liu, G. (2022). Battery technology and recycling alone will not save the electric mobility transition from future cobalt shortages. *Nature Communications*, *13*(1), 1341. Advance online publication. DOI: 10.1038/s41467-022-29022-z PMID: 35292628

Zeng, X., Li, M., El-Hady, D. A., Alshitari, W., Al-Bogami, A. S., Lü, J., & Amine, K. (2019). Commercialization of lithium battery technologies for electric vehicles. *Advanced Energy Materials*, *9*(27), 1900161. Advance online publication. DOI: 10.1002/aenm.201900161

Zeqing, L., Alfansi, L., & Usman, B. (n.d.). Greening business for sustainability: The strategic role of green HRM, innovation and employee behavior in coal power plants in Sumatera, Indonesia. International Journal of Science. Retrieved from http://ijstm.inarah.co.id

Zhaksybayeva, N., Serikkyzy, A., Baktymbet, A., & Yousafzai, S. (2024). Circular shifts: Insights into kazakhstan's circular business ecosystem. *Cogent Business & Management*, *11*(1), 2431652. DOI: 10.1080/23311975.2024.2431652

Zhang, C., Zhou, B., & Tian, X. (2022). Political connections and green innovation: The role of a corporate entrepreneurship strategy in state-owned enterprises. *Journal of Business Research*, *146*, 375–384. DOI: 10.1016/j.jbusres.2022.03.084

Zhang, Q. W., Lin, L. G., & Ye, W. C. (2018). Techniques for extraction and isolation of natural products: A comprehensive review. *Chinese Medicine*, *13*(1), 1–26. DOI: 10.1186/s13020-018-0177-x

Zhang, X., Xie, J., Rao, R., & Liang, Y. (2014). Policy incentives for the adoption of electric vehicles across countries. *Sustainability (Basel)*, *6*(11), 8056–8078. DOI: 10.3390/su6118056

Zhao, X., Wang, Y., Cai, D., & Xi, B. (2024). Tailored composting and fertilization strategies can inspire the transformation of agriculture for sustainable development. *Journal of Agricultural and Food Chemistry*, *72*(16), 8874–8875. DOI: 10.1021/acs.jafc.4c02708

Zhao, X., Wang, Y., Chen, X., Yu, X., Li, W., Zhang, S., Meng, X., Zhao, Z.-M., Dong, T., Anderson, A., Aiyedun, A., Li, Y., Webb, E., Wu, Z., Kunc, V., Ragauskas, A., Ozcan, S., & Zhu, H. (2023). Sustainable bioplastics derived from renewable natural resources for food packaging. *Matter*, *6*(1), 97–127. DOI: 10.1016/j.matt.2022.11.006

Zhong, R. Y., Xu, X., Klotz, E., & Newman, S. T. (2017). Intelligent manufacturing in the context of industry 4.0: A review. *Engineering (Beijing)*, *3*(5), 616–630. DOI: 10.1016/J.ENG.2017.05.015

Zhou, X., ... (2025). Fabrication of solid-state substrates made from jute fibers. Composite Structures.

About the Contributors

Reshmy Krishnan, presently serving as the Head of the Research Centre and an Associate Professor in the Department of Computing at Muscat College, plays a pivotal role in higher education quality assurance. She is also the editor of conference proceedings published by Springer, including Lecture Notes in Educational Technology and Lecture Notes in Digital Transformation and AI in Practice. She serves as a program reviewer for Oman's Ministry of Higher Education, Research and Innovation (MoHERI) and is a Board Member of the Oman Association for Quality in Higher Education (QAQHE) under the Ministry of Social Affairs. From 2017 to 2021, she was a member of the IT Academic Council of the Indian Schools Board of Directors in Oman and continues to contribute on advisory boards of universities in both Oman and India. She supervises PhD candidates at government universities in India and evaluates doctoral theses across several institutions nationwide. An esteemed speaker, Dr. Reshmy has presented at numerous international conferences and professional forums and is widely acknowledged as a distinguished public speaker within academic and professional circles. Her notable recognitions include the Best National Research Award from the Research Council Oman (2014), the 'Woman Icon India Global Award' conferred by the Governor of Tamil Nadu (2019) for her contributions to education, the 'Distinguished Educator and Scholar Award' from the National Foundation for Entrepreneurship (2020), and the 'Distinguished Woman in Engineering Award' (2018) for her contributions to Computer Science and Engineering. Previously, she served as the Head of the Computing Department at Muscat College until September 2017 and chaired the Industry and Community Engagement Committee from 2017 to 2021. Currently, she leads the Research Centre at the institution. Her academic contributions include 21 book chapters published by Springer, 18 funded research projects, and over 643 research citations. She is the author of the book Computer Programming and has organized more than 50 national and international conferences, workshops, and symposiums. Furthermore, she has served as a keynote speaker and resource person at over 70 academic events worldwide. She is also a member of the editorial board of the International Journal of Business, Communication and Technology and actively contributes as a peer reviewer for several international journals, in addition to serving as a thesis evaluator for Indian universities.

Araby Madbouly Ahmed Hussain is the Assistant Dean for Academic Affairs at Muscat College. He is appointed as external reviewer in OAAAQA, Sultanate of Oman. Araby has over 40 published articles in international journals and papers presented in international conferences in international economics, finance, entrepreneurship, HR, marketing, knowledge management, and corporate governance. He has 3 published books Araby supervised many Ph.D. and MSc theses. Furthermore, he participated as an external examiner for many. HE participated as a keynote speaker and was assigned as a member of technical committees in many international conferences. He is an editorial board member of three international journals and a reviewer for other five international journals.

Buthaina Yahya Al Kharousi is an Assistant Professor and MBA Programme Coordinator at Muscat College, Oman. She is the director of the MBA Programme at Muscat College. She holds a PhD in Entrepreneurship from the University of Worcester, UK, and has over 18 years of experience in higher education, teaching, research, and academic leadership. Her research interests include entrepreneurship education, innovation, sustainability, artificial intelligence, digital transformation, and entrepreneurial ecosystems. She has published in internationally peer-reviewed journals and book chapters, serves as a reviewer for leading academic journals, and regularly presents her research at international conferences. Dr Al Kharousi actively contributes to research projects, curriculum development and international collaborations, with a strong commitment to advancing entrepreneurship education and sustainable development.

Nitha Mary possesses over nine years of extensive experience in research and teaching within the academic realm. Currently working as a Senior Lecturer in the Department of Business and Accounting at Muscat College, Sultanate of Oman. She has pursued a Bachelor of Engineering in Electronics and Communication from Anna University and received a Master of Business Administration from the Cochin University of Science and Technology. Her subject area includes Entrepreneurship, Project Management, Global Sustainability and Supply Chain Management. As a dedicated educator and mentor, she has provided guidance in both SPSS and NVivo to dissertation students and has hosted various Entrepreneurship competitions on campus. Additionally, she exhibits expertise in Microsoft Project Software and holds a CAPM certification, enabling her to impart knowledge in the project management discipline. With a Master's degree in Business Administration and an ongoing pursuit of a PhD, her research endeavors encompass diverse social science studies, focusing on Sustainability, Supply Chain Management, Human Resource Management, and Project Management disciplines.

***

Poorva Agrawal obtained her PhD degree in Computer Science and Engineering from Symbiosis International (Deemed University), Pune, India in 2020. She obtained her MTech degree in Computer Science and Engineering from SGSITS, Indore, India in 2012. She has been engaged in research and teaching for more than 14 years. At present she is working as Associate Professor in CE Dept, MPSTME, NMIMS University, Mumbai, MH, India. She has presented more than 70 papers in International/National Journals/ Conferences. Her research interests include Artificial Intelligence, Machine Learning, Data Science, Image Processing, and Computer Vision.

Mahdi Hasan Ahid is a research practitioner in the field of business and management, with a strong focus on key areas such as supply chain management, strategic innovation, marketing, enterprise efficiency, and management information systems. His research explores how emerging technologies and data-driven approaches can optimize organizational processes, enhance marketing effectiveness, and support sustainable growth across business ecosystems. By aligning innovation with practical business needs, he addresses real-world challenges through applied and impactful research. Ahid's work bridges academic theory and professional practice, making significant contributions to the evolving landscape of business, management, and digital transformation.

Kathirvel Ayyaswamy, acquired, B.E.(CSE), M.E. (CSE) from Crescent Engineering College affiliated to University of Madras and Ph. D (CSE.) from Anna University. He is currently working as Professor, Dept of Computer Science and Engineering, Saveetha Engineering College, Chennai. In-charge for CSE Cyber Forensics Research Group. He is a studious researcher by himself, completed 18 sponsored research projects worth of Rs 103 lakhs and published more than 110 articles in journals and conferences. 6 research scholars have completed Ph. D and 7 under progress under his guidance. He is working as scientific and editorial board member of many journals. He has reviewed dozens of papers in many journals. He has author of 13 books. His research interests are protocol development for wireless ad hoc networks, security in ad hoc network, data communication and networks, mobile computing, wireless networks, WSN and DTN. He is a Life member of the

ISTE (India), IACSIT (Singapore), Life Member IAENG (Hong Kong), Member ICST (Europe), IAES, etc. He has given a number of guest lecturers/expert talks and seminars, workshops and symposiums.

Suhashini Awadhesh Chaurasia has over twenty-seven years of teaching experience in Computer Science. She is currently serving as Assistant Professor at Department of Computer Science and Applications, Ramdeobaba University, Nagpur. Her primary research interests include Artificial Intelligence (AI) and Machine Learning (ML), with a focus on interdisciplinary applications of intelligent systems. Dr. Chaurasia has more than 70 research publications to her credit, including papers in reputed Scopus-indexed, IEEE, and Springer journals and conferences. She has authored two academic books — Linux Operating System and Software Engineering — and contributed multiple book chapters in international edited volumes. She has eight Indian patents published and one granted utility patent for 20 years, along with four copyrights. Her Scopus record includes 25 indexed documents, 53 citations and h index 4. She is also a Member of the Board of Studies at Rashtrasant Tukadoji Maharaj Nagpur University. In addition to her academic and research contributions, she has organized and participated in numerous Faculty Development Programs (FDPs), Orientation and Refresher courses, workshops, and symposia at both national and international levels.

D. Indhumathi has been a teaching professional in Collegiate Education since July 1, 2004, specializing in Accounts and Finance. She is deeply passionate about teaching and committed to nurturing students not only academically but also as ethical and responsible citizens. Upholding strong moral values and professional ethics, she integrates these principles into both her teaching and professional practice. Her dedication and integrity continue to contribute meaningfully to higher education.

Piali Haldar earned her MBA from the Institute of Rural Management Anand and completed her PhD at Birla Institute of Technology, Mesra. Her core areas of specialization include rural marketing, rural development, branding strategy, and consumer behaviour. With over 20 years of experience in academia and research, she has published extensively in renowned journals listed in ABDC and Scopus. She has authored one textbook on Marketing and edited three academic books. Dr. Haldar has presented her research at numerous national and international conferences and has contributed more than 50 papers to reputed journals, edited volumes, and conference proceedings.

Tahsin completed both her Bachelor's and Master's degrees in Statistics from the University of Dhaka. She subsequently earned her PhD in Management from Putra Business School, Universiti Putra Malaysia (UPM), a leading business school accredited by AACSB and known for its strong research culture. She is now working as an Assistant Professor in the Faculty of Business Adminstration at American International University-Bangladesh (AIUB). With over 12 years of combined teaching and research experience, she has developed strong expertise in quantitative methods, statistical modeling, and applied management research. She is proficient in a broad range of statistical software tools, including SPSS, STATA, NVivo, SmartPLS, and R programming, which she regularly uses for data analysis, structural equation modeling, mixed-methods research, and advanced statistical inference. Her research agenda focuses on intellectual capital, knowledge management practices, innovation, blockchain technology, and artificial intelligence, with a particular emphasis on the healthcare sector and the manufacturing industry. Her ongoing goal is to bridge theory and practice, empowering organizations through knowledge-based innovation and the adoption of technology.

Gagandeep Kaur obtained her PhD degree in Computer Science and Engineering from Lovely Professional University, Punjab, India in 2023. She has been engaged in research and teaching for more than 13 years. At present she is working as Assistant Professor in CSE Department at Symbiosis Institute of Technology Nagpur, Symbiosis International (Deemed University) Pune, India. She has presented more than 55 papers in International Journals/Conferences and written some book chapters. Her research interests include Artificial Intelligence, Machine Learning, Data Science, Image Processing, and Soft Computing.

Hariharan M is currently pursuing a Master of Business Administration (MBA) in Maritime Management. He earned his Bachelor of Business Administration (BBA) from SASTRA Deemed to be University, SRC Campus, Kumbakonam. His Academic Interests include Transportation, Shipping, Logistics, and Maritime Management.

Javed Mahmud is an Assistant Professor of Business Administration with a distinguished career in both academia and industry. He holds a Doctorate of Business Administration from the University of Dhaka and an MBA from Victoria University, Australia as well as an MBA from the most prestigious business school in Bangladesh, the IBA of the University of Dhaka. An expert in marketing and management, Dr. Mahmud has taught at numerous universities and has published research on consumer behavior and business management. He is also the Founder President of the Doctor of Business Administration Forum of Bangladesh.

Rimi Gusliana Mais is an academic specializing in Public Sector Accounting, CSR, and Sustainability Reporting. She currently serves as a lecturer and Head of the Institute for Research and Community Service at Sekolah Tinggi Ilmu

Ekonomi Indonesia Jakarta, where she plays a key role in the Tri Dharma of Higher Education. Her academic qualifications are extensive, including a Bachelor's degree in Accounting, a Master's degree in Accounting, and a Doctorate in Accounting from Brawijaya University, Malang. Rimi is also a certified specialist in sustainability reporting (Certified Sustainability Reporting Specialist (CSRS) and a Certified Sustainability Reporting Assuror (CSRA). In addition, she has authored numerous publications on Public Sector Accounting, Islamic Accounting, Sustainability Accounting, and CSR, making significant contributions to the academic community. Her passion for reading and writing reflects his commitment to lifelong learning and professional growth in her field

Kumar Mandal currently serves as an Assistant Professor in the Department of Management at Brainware University, Kolkata. Before this, he worked at ICRA Analytics Ltd and Shriram Finance Ltd. He holds an MBA in Finance and a Bachelor of Commerce degree from Vidyasagar University. Additionally, he has successfully cleared the UGC NET and WB SET examinations in Management.

Nizar Mtibaa earned his PhD in Entrepreneurship from the Faculty of Economics and Management Sciences (Faculté des Sciences Économiques et de Gestion), Sfax, Tunisia. Since 2015, he has been serving as a contractual lecturer and expert at the Higher Institute of Industrial Management of Sfax (ISGIS), Tunisia. His research interests focus primarily on three areas: entrepreneurial personalities and behaviors, sustainable entrepreneurship, and entrepreneurship education and training.

Munir is an academic specializing in Comparative Madhhab (Islamic legal schools of thought). His scholarly expertise centers on comparative fiqh, the methodology of legal reasoning (istinbā), and the analytical study of juristic diversity within the classical and contemporary traditions of Islamic law. His work emphasizes critical engagement with the rich intellectual heritage (turāth) of Islamic jurisprudence while addressing its relevance to modern legal and social contexts. As a lecturer in the undergraduate program at Sekolah Tinggi Ilmu Syariah Al-Manar, Munir is actively involved in teaching, academic mentoring, and curriculum development. He is committed to fostering analytical rigor, intellectual openness, and respect for juristic plurality among his students. His pedagogical approach integrates textual scholarship with contextual understanding, preparing students to navigate legal differences with scholarly integrity and professionalism. Through his academic contributions, Munir supports the institution's mission as a leading Sharia campus in Jakarta dedicated to nurturing a generation that is intellectually excellent, ethically grounded, and professionally competent.

Erita Oktasari is an Senior Lecturer (Lektor) at Universitas Bung Karno. She earned her Bachelor of Economics (S.E.), Master of Management (M.M.), and Master of Accounting (M.Ak.) degrees from Sriwijaya University. Currently, she serves as a full-time lecturer at the Faculty of Economics and Business, Universitas Bung Karno (UBK). In addition to her academic career, Erita is also recognized as an entrepreneur in the education sector, with a strong commitment to improving the quality of learning and promoting innovation in higher education. Her research interests focus on Accounting, Finance, and Entrepreneurship, and she has actively published several scientific articles in national accredited journals. Many of her works explore topics such as the application of Artificial Intelligence (AI) in accounting and corporate governance. Erita is also a registered member of the academic community through her profiles on SINTA (Science and Technology Index) under the Ministry of Education, Culture, Research, and Technology of Indonesia, as well as Google Scholar, which document her academic activities and publications.

Libeesh P C is a passionate professor of management and commerce subjects. He has cleared UGC-NET and Kerala SET. He holds a bachelor's degree in commerce and education. He has around Thirteen years of teaching experience, which includes 4.5 years of experience as a HOD of the Department of Commerce in TTGI Coimbatore. He is doing his Ph.D. in finance from Dr. NGP Arts and Science College Coimbatore. His teaching interests include Accounting, Taxation, Financial Management, and Business Economics. He has more than Eight years of experience in training and motivation, and he worked as a trainer and training coordinator of WWTA (World Wide Teacher Academy) for more than Three years and trained so many teachers.

Adnan Rahman is an Associate Professor of Digital Marketing and MIS at Uttara University, Dhaka, Bangladesh. Additionally, he is the Director of the Office of Brand & Communication and Public Relations of this university. Dr. Adnan is a postdoctoral researcher at Infrastructure University Kuala Lumpur (IUKL), Malaysia. Dr. Adnan holds a PhD in Marketing from Putra Business School (AACSB-Accredited), UPM, Malaysia; an MSc in MIS; and an MA in IHRM from the University of Bedfordshire, United Kingdom.

Santhiya Ramu is an MBA student with a Bachelor of Business Administration (BBA) background. Passionate about Finance and Marketing, she is keen on developing expertise in business strategy and financial management. She also has a strong interest in research writing, contributing to academic research articles, and continuously expanding her knowledge through learning and innovation.

Mushtaq Ahmad Shah is a finance expert with a PhD in Infrastructure Finance. He teaches banking, finance and economics at Lovely Professional University in India. Dr. Shah has over 8 years of experience teaching and researching at various institutions. He's written articles in academic journals and presented his work at conferences on banking, partnerships between public and private sectors, and behavioral finance.

Muh Ibnu Sholeh, M.Pd.I, born in Trenggalek on December 25, 1984, is an academic and researcher in Islamic Education Management and a lecturer in the Islamic Education Management Study Program at STAI KH. Muhammad Ali Shodiq, Tulungagung. He actively advances Islamic education scholarship and practice at the national level, focusing on curriculum development based on Islamic values and the Merdeka Belajar–Kampus Merdeka (MBKM) framework, leadership and organizational transformation in educational institutions, digital learning innovation and artificial intelligence (AI), as well as quality assurance through the Internal Quality Assurance System (SPMI) and accreditation. His research interests include educational leadership and management, curriculum development, teacher professional development, educational policy and governance, learning evaluation, educational technology, school quality improvement, organizational behavior in education, and educational reform. He serves as an editor and reviewer for various national and international journals indexed in SINTA and Scopus, and he has authored several books, including Manajemen Pendidikan Islam (2023), Manajemen SDM di Lembaga Pendidikan Islam (2023), Pengantar Manajemen Pendidikan Islam (2024), Manajemen Kurikulum (2024), and the international book Implementation of AI Tools in the Teaching and Learning Process (2025), with articles published in reputable international (Q2 and Q4) and nationally indexed journals, while actively engaging in international academic collaborations to strengthen adaptive and globally competitive Islamic education management.

Zerin Tasnim is an Assistant Professor of Supply Chain Management at North South University, Dhaka, Bangladesh, where she also serves as the Course Coordinator for the MBA program. She holds a PhD in Management from Putra Business School, Universiti Putra Malaysia (UPM), and a BSc in Mechanical Engineering from Bangladesh University of Engineering and Technology (BUET). Dr. Tasnim brings an interdisciplinary academic background and a global research perspective to her work, with research interests spanning digital supply chains, healthcare logistics, and sustainable and green operations.

Ririn Widyastuti Wulaningsih is an Assistant Lecturer (Asisten Ahli) at Universitas Bung Karno, specializing in Accounting and Financial Management.

She holds a bachelor's degree in Accounting and master's degrees in Management and Accounting. She is also certified specialist in sustainability reporting with Certified Sustainability Reporting Specialist (CSRS). She has demonstrated a strong dedication to teaching and research in the fields of cost accounting, finance, and sustainability. Her research interests include governance,sustainability, taxation and corporation. Through her academic and research activities, she aims to strengthen transparency, accountability, and sustainable development in Indonesian business practices.

Venkat Reddy Yasa is an Assistant professor, working at School of Business, Woxsen University. He holds a dual masters degree in mathematics and management. He is having 23 years of teaching experience and he has been teaching statistics, operations research and quantitative techniques subjects for management, engineering and under graduate students. He has published couple of research papers and articles in reputed International journals. Earlier he worked as a head of the department for management and got phenomenal appreciation from the peers for teaching abilities and bringing in constructive reforms within the department. He actively organized and flawlessly executed various management fests, inter college events and actively participated in various AICTE faculty development programs and couple of International conferences. He is an enthusiastic and hard working person with a passion towards nurturing education, delivering values and having strong social commitment. He is always willing to work for an organization, where he can hone his skills and contribute to the growth of the organization and as well as to the community. He is hard working, energetic and enthusiastic professional with excellent communication skills. And he always aligns his goals towards the goals of the organization.

Rahmat Yuliansyah is an academic specializing in Public Sector Accounting and Accounting Principle. He currently serves as a lecturer and Professional Certification Institute (LSP) at the Indonesian College of Economics Jakarta, serving as Administrative Manager, which is part of the National Professional Certification Agency (BNSP). Academically qualified with a Bachelor of Economics degree in Accounting with the title SE., Ak and a Master of Accounting with the title M.Ak, from the Indonesian College of Economics Jakarta, Rahmat Yuliansyah has also written numerous publications on Sector Public Accounting, and Accounting Principle, which have made significant contributions to the academic community. His passion for reading and writing reflects a commitment to lifelong learning and professional development in his field.

Index

F

G

H

I

J

M

P

R

S

www.ingramcontent.com/pod-product-compliance
Lightning Source LLC
LaVergne TN
LVHW062325300926
849161LV00007B/1581
* 9 7 9 8 3 3 7 3 7 3 9 1 1 *